Cassirer and Heidegger in Davos

The 1929 encounter between Ernst Cassirer and Martin Heidegger in Davos, Switzerland is considered one of the most important intellectual debates of the twentieth century and a founding moment of continental philosophy. At the same time, many commentators have questioned the philosophical profundity and coherence of the actual debate. In this book, the first comprehensive philosophical analysis of the Davos debate, Simon Truwant challenges these critiques. He argues that Cassirer and Heidegger's disagreement about the meaning of Kant's philosophy is motivated by their different views about the human condition, which in turn are motivated by their opposing conceptions of what the task of philosophy ultimately should be. Truwant shows that Cassirer and Heidegger share a grand philosophical concern: to comprehend and aid the human being's capacity to orient itself in and towards the world.

SIMON TRUWANT is FWO Postdoctoral Fellow at KU Leuven. He is the editor of *Interpreting Cassirer: Critical Essays* (Cambridge University Press, 2021) and has published articles in journals including *Epoché*, *Idealistic Studies*, and *International Journal of Philosophical Studies*.

T0371474

Cassirer and Heidegger in Davos

The Philosophical Arguments

Simon Truwant

KU Leuven

CAMBRIDGE
UNIVERSITY PRESS

Shaftesbury Road, Cambridge CB2 8EA, United Kingdom

One Liberty Plaza, 20th Floor, New York, NY 10006, USA

477 Williamstown Road, Port Melbourne, VIC 3207, Australia

314–321, 3rd Floor, Plot 3, Splendor Forum, Jasola District Centre, New Delhi – 110025, India

103 Penang Road, #05–06/07, Visioncrest Commercial, Singapore 238467

Cambridge University Press is part of Cambridge University Press & Assessment, a department of the University of Cambridge.

We share the University's mission to contribute to society through the pursuit of education, learning and research at the highest international levels of excellence.

www.cambridge.org
Information on this title: www.cambridge.org/9781009011440

DOI: 10.1017/9781009019569

First published 2022
First paperback edition 2024

A catalogue record for this publication is available from the British Library

ISBN   978-1-316-51988-2   Hardback
ISBN   978-1-009-01144-0   Paperback

Contents

Acknowledgements   *page* vii

Introduction: What Is at Stake in the Davos Debate?   1

1 Reconstructing the Davos Debate   15
   1.1 Preliminary Remarks   15
   1.2 The Davos Debate: Analysis of a Coherent Discussion   18
   1.3 The Cassirer–Heidegger Dispute: An Echo of the Davos Debate   36

Part I   The Lasting Meaning of Kant's Thought   45

2 Cassirer's Transformation of the Critique of Reason
   into a Critique of Culture   47
   2.1 Categories, Schemata, and Symbols   48
   2.2 The Diversity of the Cultural World   54
   2.3 The Two Kantian Conceptions of Objectivity in Cassirer's Philosophy
        of Culture   57

3 Heidegger's Reading of Transcendental Philosophy as
   Phenomenological Ontology   62
   3.1 On Kant's Concept of Philosophy: Transcendental Philosophy as Ontology   64
   3.2 On Kant's Philosophical Method: Critical Philosophy as Phenomenology   69
   3.3 On Kant's Hermeneutical Situation: The Problem of Metaphysics   78

4 Receptivity or Spontaneity: Two Readings of the *Critique
   of Pure Reason*   85
   4.1 Transcendental Philosophy as Ontology or Epistemology   85
   4.2 The Receptive and Spontaneous Nature of Transcendental Imagination   93
   4.3 Kant's Vacillating between Logic, Psychology, and Phenomenology   97
   4.4 The Finite or Spontaneous Nature of Human Reason   101

Part II   'What Is the Human Being?'   109

5 Cassirer's Functional Account of the Animal Symbolicum   111
   5.1 The Discrepancy between the Task and the Execution of the Philosophy
        of Symbolic Forms   111

5.2 The Primacy of the Relation and the Inaccessibility of
     Human Consciousness   113
5.3 Cassirer's Functional Conception of the Human Being   117
5.4 From 'Animal Rationale' to 'Animal Symbolicum'   121
5.5 Cassirer's Metaphysics of Human Subjectivity   124

6   Heidegger's Existential Analytic of Dasein   131
6.1 Dasein's Pre-ontological Understanding of Being   131
6.2 Dasein's 'Being-in-the-World'   137
6.3 Dasein as Care   143
6.4 Dasein's Ontological, Phenomenological, and Hermeneutic Being   148

7   Infinity or Finitude: The Quest for Existential Orientation   153
7.1 Cassirer's General Plan of Ideal Orientation   153
7.2 Heidegger on Orientation within and towards the World   158
7.3 Cassirer and Heidegger's Notions of Selfhood   167

Part III   The Task of Philosophy   177

8   Cassirer's Functional Conception of Philosophy   179
8.1 From Substance to Function   179
8.2 Cassirer's Historical Writings (1906–1919): A Functional Account
     of the History of Thought   181
8.3 Cassirer's Systematic Writings (1923–1942): A Functional Definition
     of Human Culture   186
8.4 Cassirer's Ethical Writings (1935–1946): The Normative Task
     of Philosophy   193

9   Heidegger's Hermeneutic Conception of Philosophy   196
9.1 The Three Interrelated Projects of Heidegger's Early Thought   196
9.2 Heidegger's Hermeneutic-Phenomenological Approach to Kant
     and Dasein   206
9.3 The 'Seinsfrage' as the Radicalization of Dasein's
     Hermeneutical Situation   215

10   Enlightenment or Therapy: The Cosmopolitan Task
     of Philosophy   220
10.1 Cassirer's Enlightened View of the Task of Philosophy   220
10.2 Heidegger's Therapeutic Conception of Philosophy   232

Conclusion: The *Terminus a Quo* and *Terminus ad Quem*
of the Davos Debate   245

Bibliography   249
Index   262

Acknowledgements

This monograph is the result of many years of wrestling with two profound thinkers who defended radically different worldviews by means of very distinct argumentation and writing styles. I have tried to do justice to both of these views without succumbing to the corresponding styles. As such, *Cassirer and Heidegger in Davos* is also the outcome of a long struggle to find my own philosophical perspective and voice. I am truly grateful to everyone who has guided me, in one way or another, during these struggles. They have been real.

First and foremost, my immeasurable thanks go out to Karin de Boer and Sebastian Luft for their wise guidance and honest feedback throughout the years. Without Karin, this research project would have been stranded somewhere halfway. She not only taught me a lot about how to combine philosophical clarity and depth, or to write in a more efficient manner, but also, most importantly, she helped me determine my own philosophical priorities. In retrospect, through her consistent support of my research, she may indirectly have a significant impact on the rehabilitation of Cassirer's philosophy, something she will not have anticipated. Sebastian has been an academic mentor in the richest possible sense of the word. He introduced me to the world of Cassirer scholarship and has continued to be an inspiring adviser, motivator, enabler, and collaborator to whom I could always turn. His own stellar research has also paved the way for many of my philosophical achievements, not in the least this monograph.

For shorter but no less fruitful periods of time, Rudolf Makkreel, who passed away in the fall of 2021, and Steven G. Crowell have also kindly taken up supervising roles that have immensely contributed to the research that led to this monograph. Their mentorship has been not just a pleasant experience but also a formative one. In addition, I am grateful to Smaranda Aldea, Fabien Capeillères, Paul Cortois, Diego d'Angelo, Nicolas de Warren, William Desmond, Sharin N. Elkholy, Erica Harris, Guido Kreis, Morganna Lambeth, Steve G. Lofts, John Lysaker, Christopher Merwin, David M. Peña-Guzmán, Martina Plümacher, Anne Pollok, Joel M. Reynolds, Tom Rockmore, Lanei Rodemeyer, Robert Scharff, Willem Styfhals, Stéphane Symons, Gerhard Thonhauser, Geert van

Eekert, Donald Verene, and Martin Weatherston for inspiring conversations and comments on earlier drafts of the following chapters. I further wish to thank Hilary Gaskin for the faith she has put in this project from the very beginning, and the editorial team at Cambridge University Press for bringing the project to a conclusion.

I have been immensely lucky to receive funding for my doctoral research from the Flemish Research Council (FWO), the Fulbright Commission, and the Belgian American Educational Foundation (BAEF). Their financial support allowed me to conduct parts of this research at the philosophy departments of KU Leuven, Duquesne University, Emory University, Rice University, and the Warburg Institute of the University of London. I am also grateful to the librarians of the Hoger Instituut voor Wijsbegeerte, the Simon Silverman Phenomenology Center, and the Beinecke Rare Book and Manuscript Library at Yale University for helping me find certain vital sources of documentation on the 'Davos debate'.

Ultimately, *Cassirer and Heidegger in Davos* would not have seen the light of day if it were not for the practical, moral, and existential support from my family and non-academic friends. Heartfelt thanks to my parents, Mieke and Jef, for the caring way in which they have thrown me into the world. Last but most, thank you Aïlien, my orientation point and my compass, 'de pool vanwaar ik dool'.

Some of the chapters of this monograph have previously been published elsewhere:

> Chapter 2 – 'From the Critique of Reason to a Critique of Culture: Cassirer's Transformation of Kant's Transcendental Philosophy', in: *Epoché: A Journal for the History of Philosophy*, 23/1, 2018, 85–104.
> Chapter 5 – 'Cassirer's Functional Conception of the Human Being', in: *Idealistic Studies*, 45/2, 2015, 169–189.
> Sections 7.1 and 10.1 – 'The Hierarchy among the Symbolic Forms: Cassirer's Enlightened View of Human Culture', in: *Cassirer Studies*, VII–VIII, 2014–2015, 119–139.
> Chapter 8 – 'The Concept of "Function" in Cassirer's Historical, Systematic, and Ethical Writings', in: Gerald Hartung and Sebastian Luft (eds.), *The Philosophy of Ernst Cassirer: A Novel Assessment*. Berlin: Walter de Gruyter, 2015, 289–312.

Introduction
What Is at Stake in the Davos Debate?

Five years after Thomas Mann situated *The Magic Mountain*, his famous novel about Hans Castorp's intellectual coming of age, in a sanatorium in the Swiss Alps town Davos, this place hosted a debate that would form the minds of multiple generations of philosophers. On 2 April 1929, two major figures of early twentieth-century philosophy, Ernst Cassirer and Martin Heidegger, faced each other during the second meeting of the *Internationale Davoser Hochschulkurse*. Taking place in a time of deep cultural and philosophical crisis, this annual conference had the explicit goal to reunite thinkers from a variety of nations and backgrounds. Yet, ideas like reconciliation or intellectual cross-pollination are entirely absent from the collective memory of the Davos debate between Cassirer and Heidegger. While the transcript of their discussion shows an animated debate between two thinkers who both alternated stronger with weaker moments, its eyewitnesses unanimously reported that the older Cassirer was in fact no match for Heidegger, who seemed to embody the sentiments of a new era.[1] Most famously, a young Emmanuel Levinas claimed that attending the Davos debate was 'like witnessing the end of the world and the creation of a new one'.[2]

One cannot deny that history proved Levinas right in this regard. Since the publication of *Being and Time* in 1927, Heidegger's philosophy has never ceased to be popular. Even though he soon abandoned the existentialist approach to the question of being that marks his *magnum opus*, and despite several scandals concerning his Nazism and anti-Semitism,[3] both Heidegger's early and later philosophy have continued to inspire philosophers until this

---

[1] Toni Cassirer, Ernst Cassirer's wife who attended the debate, later wrote that "the large majority of the students considered Heidegger as the victor, because he approached the *Zeitgeist* much better than Ernst" (*Mein Leben mit Ernst Cassirer*, Hamburg: Felix Meiner Verlag, 2003, 188 – my translation).

[2] François Poiré, *Emmanuel Levinas: Qui êtes-vous?*, Lyon: La Manufacture, 1987, 78. Other first-hand testimonies from Otto Friedrich Bollnow ('Gespräche in Davos', in: *Erinnerung an Martin Heidegger*, hrsg. von Günther Neske, Pfullingen, 1977, 25–29) and the *Frankfurter Zeitung* (Abendblatt 22 April 1929) offer almost identical assessments of the Davos debate.

[3] On the extent of Heidegger's Nazi sympathies and its influence on his accounts of Dasein, world, and history, see Victor Farias, *Heidegger and Nazism*, Philadelphia: Temple University Press,

day. In comparison, Cassirer's legacy endured a much harder fate. During the first decades of the twentieth century, Cassirer was a highly respected intellectual as both the spokesman of the then dominant philosophical movement of Neo-Kantianism and the author of an impressive series on the history of thought.[4] The events in Davos severely damaged this reputation: in the eyes of the next generation of European intelligentsia – Levinas, Eugen Fink, Leon Brunschvicg, Jean Cavaillès, Rudolf Carnap, Herbert Marcuse, among others – Heidegger outshone Cassirer in a philosophical, sociocultural, as well as a personal way. For one, Heidegger challenged Cassirer's allegiance to the system-oriented schools of Neo-Kantianism, whose dominant position in European philosophy would soon give way to more existentially motivated movements such as *Lebensphilosophie* and, of course, existentialism.[5] In this way, Heidegger also exposed Cassirer's untimely support of Enlightenment ideals that had lost all credibility after the First World War, such as the belief in the power of reason and the inevitability of progress.[6] Finally, the apparent difference between Heidegger's charismatic personality and Cassirer's erudite yet uninspiring appearance in Davos reportedly contributed to the popularity of the former and the rapidly declining interest in the latter's thought.[7]

1987; and Emmanuel Faye, *Heidegger: L'introduction du nazisme dans la philosophie. Autour des séminaires inédits de 1933–1935*, Paris: Albin Michel, 2005. On Heidegger's recently exposed conception of 'World-Judaism' and his firm ant-semitism in light of the 'tragedy of the history of being', consult Peter Trawny, *Heidegger und der Mythos der jüdischen Welverschwörung*, Frankfurt: Vittorio Klostermann, 2014.

[4] Long before developing his systematic 'philosophy of symbolic forms' and becoming known as a philosopher of culture, Cassirer had made name as a brilliant historian of philosophy thanks to his habilitation on Leibniz (1902) and the first three volumes of *The Problem of Knowledge* (1906, 1907, 1919).

[5] For an overview of the philosophical, historical, and political reasons for the decline of Neo-Kantianism after 1930, consult Rudolf A. Makkreel and Sebastian Luft (ed.), *Neo-Kantianism in Contemporary Philosophy*, Bloomington: Indiana University Press, 2010, 6–9; and Frederick Beiser, 'Weimar Philosophy and the Fate of Neo-Kantianism', in: Peter Eli Gordon and John P. McCormick (ed.), *Weimar Thought: A Contested Legacy*, Princeton/Oxford: Princeton University Press, 2013, 115–132. With regard to Cassirer's thought in particular, see also Enno Rudolph, *Ernst Cassirer im Kontext. Kulturphilosphie zwischen Metaphysik und Historismus*, Tübingen: Mohr Siebeck, 2003, 1–5.

[6] See Emmanuel Levinas, 'Entretien Avec Roger-Pol', in: *Les imprévus de l'histoire*, ed. Pierre Hayat, Montpellier: Fata Morgana, 1994, 203–210; Dominic Kaegi und Enno Rudolph (hrsg.), *Cassirer-Heidegger. 70 Jahre Davoser Disputation*, in: Cassirer-*Forschungen*, Band 9, Hamburg: Meiner Verlag, 2002, v–viii; and Sebastian Luft's review of the latter book in *Journal Phänomenologie*, 19, 2003, 91–94.

[7] The picture of Cassirer and Heidegger's radically different personalities, the former distinguished but almost boring, the latter unconventional but attractive, is confirmed by Pierre Aubenque ('Philosophie und Politik: Die Davoser Disputation zwischen Ernst Cassirer und Martin Heidegger in der Retrospektive', in: *Internationale Zeitschrift für Philosophie* 2, 1992, 290–312), Rudolf Carnap (Archives for Scientific Philosophy, University of Pittsburgh Libraries, ASP RC 025-73-03, 30 March 1929), Ludwig Englert ('Als Student bei den zweiten Davoser Hochschulkursen', in: *Nachlese zu Heidegger: Dokumente zu seinem Leben und Denken*, hrsg. von Guido Schneeberger, Bern: Private Edition, 1962, 4), Karl Jaspers ('Letter

Cassirer never got the chance to restore his image, as he emigrated – like most Jewish intellectuals – from Germany in 1933 and died in the United States, on the Columbia University campus, shortly before the Second World War ended. As a consequence, for many years Cassirer was mainly remembered – if at all – as an exceptional historian of philosophy who could, however, not match the profundity of Heidegger's thinking.[8]

Accordingly, the transcript of the Davos debate has long held the status of a mere historical document, recording a large shift in twentieth-century thinking rather than a profound philosophical *Auseinandersetzung*. Throughout the past century, commentators on the Davos debate have defended this view in mainly two manners.

The most radically dismissive position with regard to the Davos debate is found in the recurring suggestions that no real discussion took place between Cassirer and Heidegger in 1929 at all. Besides our protagonists, one other person took the word during the public debate: around halfway through the discussion, the Dutch linguist Henrik Pos remarked that "both men speak a completely different language", and doubted whether their most important concepts "would allow for translation into the other language".[9] Possibly inspired by this critical comment, the *Neue Zürcher Zeitung* on 10 April 1929, reported about the Davos debate in the following way: "Instead of being witness to the clash of two worlds, one at best enjoyed the scene of a very polite man [Cassirer] and a very intense man who also made an exceptional

[to Heidegger] 24, 21 July 1925', in: *Briefwechsel, 1920–1963*, hrsg. von Walter Biemel und Hans Saner, Frankfurt: Vittorio Klostermann, 1990, 51–52), Hendrik Pos ('Recollections of Ernst Cassirer', in: *The Philosophy of Ernst Cassirer*, ed. by Paul Arthur Schilpp, La Salle: Open Court, 1949, 67–69), Leo Strauss, 'Kurt Riezler (1882–1955)', in: *What Is Political Philosophy? and Other Studies*, Chicago: The University of Chicago Press, 1959, 246), and arguably even Cassirer's late colleague, publisher, and admirer Charles W. Hendel (*The Myth of the State*, New Haven: Yale University Press, 1979, viii).

[8] See Emmanuel Levinas et François Poiré, *Essai et entretiens*, Paris: Actes Sud, 1996, 80–81; Jürgen Habermas, 'Der Deutsche Idealismus der jüdischen Philosophie', in: *Philosophisch-politische Profile*, Frankfurt am Main: Suhrkamp, 1981, 52–54; and Hans Blumenberg, *Theorie der Lebenswelt*, Frankfurt am Main: Suhrkamp, 2010, 21. Edward Skidelsky recently held that, measured by today's standards, Cassirer's philosophy of symbolic forms is "no longer obviously philosophy at all". The only reason to still 'bother with Cassirer' is, then, "for the good reason that he was the twentieth century's most accomplished defender of the Humboldtian ideal". According to Skidelsky, Cassirer's thought thus remains historically relevant because of the view of culture that it represents, but should no longer be considered as philosophical (*Ernst Cassirer: The Last Philosopher of Culture*, Princeton/Oxford: Princeton University Press, 2008, 5–6, 209).

[9] The transcript of the Davos debate is included in the latest editions of Heidegger's *Kant and the Problem of Metaphysics*, which was written immediately following this debate: 'Davos Disputation between Ernst Cassirer and Martin Heidegger', in: Martin Heidegger, *Kant and the Problem of Metaphysics*, tr. by Richard Taft, Bloomington: Indiana University Press, 1997, 287 (193–207). Pos reiterates his assessment of the debate sixteen years later, at a memorial service for Cassirer's death ('Recollections of Ernst Cassirer', 67).

effort to be polite [Heidegger], holding monologues. Nevertheless, all listeners were moved and told each other how fortunate they were for having been there".[10] Much more recently, according to Dominic Kaegi and Enno Rudolph, the transcript of the Davos debate betrays that neither thinker really wanted to be there, that they only sought confirmation for their prejudices about the other, and that they thus left without gaining any new insight. Kaegi and Rudolph even add that it is only thanks to the mutual criticisms that Cassirer and Heidegger uttered elsewhere, that we now pay attention to this debate at all.[11]

Heidegger confirmed this view of the Davos debate as a missed opportunity for profound philosophical discussion, but put the blame on the format of the debate and on Cassirer's compliance therewith. In a letter to Elisabeth Blochmann (12 April 1929), he complains that he gained nothing in terms of philosophical content from the entire *Davoser Hochschulkurse*. On the one hand, Heidegger holds that the philosophical issues at hand were far too complex for a public debate, and that the entire seminar therefore gained an increasingly sensationalist focus on the personalities of its central participants. In light of this, he regrets that the lectures that Cassirer gave in Davos prior to their debate concentrated on *Being and Time*, thus manoeuvring Heidegger's position into the centre of their discussion. On the other hand, he reproaches Cassirer's reconciliatory attitude: "During the discussion, Cassirer was extremely gentlemanly and almost too obliging. I therefore met with too little opposition, which prevented the problems from gaining the necessary sharpness of formulation".[12]

Although Heidegger's aversion to philosophical conferences is generally known, it is especially Cassirer's reluctance or, worse, incapacity to challenge

---

[10] Ernst Howald, 'Betrachtungen zu den Davoser Hochschulkursen', *Neue Zürcher Zeitung*, 10 April 1929, Morgenausgabe, 1. We find the same assessment in the *Frankfurter Zeitung* two weeks later: "Unfortunately, one must say that a somewhat too far-reaching generosity of both opponents ultimately did not allow the oppositions between them to be seen in its full sharpness" (Hermann Herrigel, 'Denken dieser Zeit: Fakultäten und Nationen treffen sich in Davos', *Frankfurter Zeitung*, 22 April 1929, Hochschulblatt, 4); and in the report of Franz Josef Brecht, a student of Heidegger and attendee of the *Davoser Hochschulkurse*: "For here stood the greatest representatives of the two, last, fundamental positions in philosophy, for whom mutual discussion was logically no longer possible" ('Die Situation der gegenwärtigen Philosophie', *Neue Jahrbücher für Wissenschaft und Jugendbildung*, 6(1), 1930, 42). All three translations stem from Peter Gordon (cf. infra).

[11] Kaegi/Rudolph, *70 Jahre Davoser Disputation*, vi-vii. Luft counters this assessment: he admits that the transcript of the Davos debate does indeed not evince a sharp discussion, but also rejects the idea that Cassirer and Heidegger were just talking past one another (*Journal Phänomenologie* 19, 92). I share his conviction that, by acquainting ourselves with the philosophical context of the debate and Cassirer and Heidegger's presuppositions, we will find that a thorough philosophical debate *did* take place.

[12] Joachim W. Storck, *Martin Heidegger – Elisabeth Blochmann, Briefwechsel 1919–1969*, Marbarch am Neckar, 1989, 29–30.

him that was retained by the collective recollection of the Davos debate. The descriptions of Cassirer and Heidegger's contrasting personalities often lead to an assessment of their equally different philosophical profundity. The clearest example of this comes from Leo Strauss, who was not present at Davos, yet in 1956 he writes that "as soon as [Heidegger] appeared on the scene, he stood in its center and he began to dominate it. His domination grew almost continuously in extent and in intensity. He gave adequate expression to the prevailing unrest and dissatisfaction because he had clarity and certainty, if not about the whole way, at least about the first and decisive steps". Cassirer, Strauss continues, on the other hand "represented the established academic position. He was a distinguished professor of philosophy but he was no philosopher. He was erudite but had no passion. He was a clear writer but his clarity and placidity were not equaled by his sensitivity to problems".[13]

John Michael Krois, one of the pioneers of the renewed interest in Cassirer's thought beginning in the 1980s, also agrees about the absence of a real debate between Cassirer and Heidegger in Davos: "Whoever reads the protocol of the Davos debate today will get the impression that no debate took place, but that two ships rather passed each other in the night. Only declarations were made, whereby Cassirer seemed to evade everything".[14] However, Krois points to the political, anti-Jewish context in Germany at that time in order to explain this turn of events, thus countering the dismissive picture of Cassirer's performance in Davos. On his view, due to a series of anti-Semitic attacks on the Marburg Neo-Kantians, Hermann Cohen in particular, in the years and weeks prior to the Davos debate, Cassirer was more invested in defending his former teacher than in challenging Heidegger's philosophical critique of Neo-Kantianism on his own terms – even though, Krois adds, he had proven at other moments that he could easily do so. Cassirer indeed commences the Davos debate by calling Neo-Kantianism "the scapegoat of modern philosophy" and by asking Heidegger to explicate his view on this movement.[15]

---

[13] Strauss, *What Is Political Philosophy?*, 246.

[14] John Michael Krois, 'Warum fand keine Davoser Debatte zwischen Cassirer und Heidegger statt?', in: *70 Jahre Davoser Disputation*, 234; see also 'Why Did Cassirer and Heidegger Not Debate at Davos?', in: *Symbolic Forms and Cultural Studies. Ernst Cassirer's Theory of Culture*, ed. by Cyrus Hamlin and John Michael Krois, New Haven: Yale University Press, 2004, 244–262.

[15] *DD* 274. On the influence of the politically charged context of the Davos debate, in particular the anti-Semitic attacks on Neo-Kantianism and Heidegger's alleged sympathy therewith, consult Krois, 'Warum fand keine Davoser Debatte statt?', 238–244, and Toni Cassirer, *Mein Leben mit Ernst Cassirer*, 188. Michael Friedman, however, holds that "it would be a mistake to read back a dramatic political conflict into the encounter at Davos in 1929, or into the relationship between Heidegger and Cassirer more generally". He lends more weight to the immediate reports by Pierre Aubenque and Ludwig Englert than to the post-war recollections of Toni Cassirer and Hendrik Pos, thus emphasizing "an atmosphere of extraordinarily friendly

Krois' take on the Davos debate points us to the second trend in its general reception, which takes for granted the lack of philosophical depth to this debate but asserts its value in terms of political, cultural, religious, or sociological oppositions. Perhaps precisely because Cassirer and Heidegger's positions evinced little common ground, their dispute became paradigmatic for some of the ideological clashes that marked twentieth-century politics and sociology: between the Weimar Republic and *Third Reich*, Jewish cosmopolitanism and Catholic provincialism, pacifism and radicalism, optimism and pessimism, and between modern and postmodern thinking.[16] With each additional opposition, the disagreement became more and more unsurpassable.

Apart from these non-philosophical assessments – which I will not evaluate – recent scholarship has advocated the philosophical-historical importance of the encounter between Cassirer and Heidegger. The two most famous monographs on the Davos debate, Michael Friedman's *A Parting of the Ways* (2000) and Peter Gordon's *Continental Divide* (2010), follow this trend. Both works have been highly significant for the rekindled fame of this debate – and for the revived interest in Cassirer's thought as such – and Gordon's book is a magnificent reference work for the entire Cassirer–Heidegger dispute to which I am highly indebted. It is nevertheless worth noting that Friedman and Gordon are ultimately not concerned with the Davos debate *per se*, but rather

collegiality". To Friedman, then, "it is clear (at least before 1933) that no social or political differences interfered with the equally obvious admiration and respect with which they regarded one another" (*A Parting of the Ways. Cassirer, Heidegger, Carnap*, La Salle: Open Court, 2000, 5–7). The strongest indication of this respect is the reported fact that, when Cassirer fell ill during the first week of the convention, Heidegger visited his hotel room to inform him about his ongoing lectures at Davos (Karlfried Gründer's 'Cassirer und Heidegger in Davos 1929', in: *Über Ernst Cassirers Philosophie der symbolischen Formen*, hrsg. von Hans-Jürg Braun, Helmut Holzhey, und Ernst Wolfgang Orth, Frankfurt: Suhrkamp, 1988, 293; and Englert, *Nachlese zu Heidegger*, 3). Peter Gordon likewise finds it "important to note that [the Davos debate] was primarily a philosophical conversation and not a struggle between bitter adversaries" (*Continental Divide. Heidegger, Cassirer, Davos*, Cambridge: Harvard University Press, 2010, 37). He even dedicates an entire chapter of his monumental *Continental Divide* to the way in which the Davos debate became the subject of a plethora of *Hineininterpretierungen*: Gordon insists that there are absolutely no indications that anyone present in 1929 conceived of this debate in political terms, that the 'political dramatization' however originated in the very first recollections, and that it crystalized once Heidegger's Nazi sympathies became common knowledge and once again after Cassirer died in 1945 (135, 329–338). Friedman and Gordon thus contend that the Davos debate may have been a clash of personalities, but not a personal or political clash.

[16] See, for example, Daniel Maier-Katkin, *Stranger from Abroad: Hannah Arendt, Martin Heidegger, Friendship and, Forgiveness*, New York/London: W. W. Norton & Company, 2010, 75–76; Emily J. Levine, 'Cassirer's Cosmopolitan Nationalism', in: *Dreamland of Humanists. Warburg, Cassirer, Panofsky, and the Hamburg School*, Chicago/London: The University of Chicago Press, 2013, 213–217; and Sebastian Luft and Fabien Capeillères, 'Neo-Kantianism in Germany and France', in: *The History of Continental Philosophy*, volume 3: *The New Century: Bergsonism, Phenomenology, and Responses to Modern Science*, ed. by Keith-Ansell Pearson and Aland D. Schrift, London/New York: Routledge, 2010, 61.

with its *Wirkungsgeschichte*. Friedman revisits the events at Davos in order to reconsider the current gap between continental and analytic philosophy. He is concerned, thus, not so much with the structure or key issues of the Davos debate – of which he discusses only a few fragments – as with its symbolic meaning for the further course of twentieth- and twenty-first-century philosophy. His somewhat speculative thesis is that Cassirer's philosophy of culture offered the last attempt to prevent the impending 'parting of the ways' of continental and analytic philosophy – exemplified by Heidegger and Carnap, respectively – and that we must therefore revisit their trialogue if we wish to reconcile these traditions.[17]

Unlike Friedman, Gordon thoroughly analyses the transcript of the Davos debate in light of Cassirer and Heidegger's multiple other encounters, but he too does so in order to defend a broad thesis about the history of philosophy. By distinguishing between the historical facts and the different recollections of the Davos debate, Gordon tries to show that the nature of continental philosophy is such that "philosophical meaning cannot be easily disentangled from cultural and political memory. Philosophy partakes of common memory the moment it begins to ramify into the broader narrative of human affairs".[18] In this context, he retraces how a surprisingly broad range of first-class and second-class thinkers from the past century – Erich Przywara, Joachim Ritter, Paul Tillich, Strauss, Levinas, Hans Blumenberg, Pierre Bourdieu, and Jürgen Habermas – contributed to the rapidly developing idea that the events in Davos carry a symbolic meaning for the history and future of philosophy.[19]

I will not attempt to repeat Gordon's formidable research. Instead, this book aims *to narrow down the discussion about the Davos debate to its purely philosophical content*, and *to retrieve the coherence of Cassirer and Heidegger's interaction from that perspective*. This is not to deny that their public debate, as a non-scripted discussion, is much less coherent than some of their responses to each other's thought in other publications. There are indeed moments in Davos when Cassirer and Heidegger seem caught off guard by the claims that their discussion partner utters, and fail to properly address them. In spite of this, this book will consider the Davos debate as a fruitful departure point for investigating the overall philosophical relation between Cassirer and Heidegger, and this for three reasons.

---

[17] Friedman, *A Parting of the Ways*, 154–159. William Blattner likewise holds that Heidegger and Cassirer discussion about Kant's thought "was really a stalking horse for a larger debate, one that lies at the center of the contemporary division in philosophy between the so-called Continental and self-styled analytic philosophy" (*Heidegger's 'Being and Time'*, London/New York: Bloomsbury Publishing, 2006, 173).

[18] Gordon, *Continental Divide*, 324–325.

[19] See the final chapter of *Continental Divide*, titled 'Philosophy and Memory' (329–357).

First, I hold that the Davos debate hinges on the same philosophical issues that also structure Cassirer and Heidegger's entire conversation, which lasted from 1923 until 1946. Concretely, I identify three core topics in their dispute: the lasting meaning of Kant's thought, the human condition, and the task of philosophy – the other issues that were mentioned in 1929 either fall under one of these topics, or have little impact on Cassirer and Heidegger's mutual engagement. Their insights on these topics also constitute key motivations for their own philosophical projects, that is, Cassirer's lifelong attempt to develop a transcendental philosophy of culture and Heidegger's early attempt to revive ontology by means of an existential phenomenology.

Second, I maintain that the development of the Davos debate foreshadows – as well as contributes to – the evolution from agreement to disagreement that characterizes their overall dispute. This is the case, I will argue, because the three aforementioned topics stand in a 'hierarchical' relationship with regard to each other: Cassirer and Heidegger's disagreement about the meaning of Kant's philosophy is motivated by their different views on the human condition, which in turn are motivated by their opposing conceptions of the task of philosophy. Hence, these three issues cannot fully be understood apart from each other, and the true, philosophical stakes of Cassirer and Heidegger's conflict only comes to light as their conversation proceeds.

Third, despite their eventual animosity, it can be argued that Cassirer and the early Heidegger largely remained in agreement about philosophy's relevance for human life and how to thematize it. Both thinkers are fundamentally concerned with the human being's capacity to orient itself in and towards the world, and both believe that this capacity can only be properly addressed if one abandons the duality of subject and world. This shared concern may explain why they engaged with each other's thought for such an extended period of time.

On these grounds, I will consider the Davos debate as a thoughtful dialogue between two philosophical equals, giving as much consideration to Cassirer as to Heidegger.[20] In this way, I try to find a middle ground between the previous attempts to offer an exhaustive overview of the various topics that were brought up during the Davos debate, and the many recent articles that single out just one of them. In my view, the former investigations show too much respect for the chronology and variety of these topics to grasp the overall argumentative thread of the debate, and hence do not capture the mutual

---

[20] According to Hans-Georg Gadamer, Heidegger once referred to Cassirer as "the only thinker worth publicly responding to" (Dominic Kaegi, 'Davos und davor – Zur Auseinandersetzung zwischen Heidegger und Cassirer', in: Kaegi/Rudolph, *70 Jahre Davoser Disputation*, 72).

dependence between its *terminus a quo* and *terminus ad quem*.[21] The latter, although often highly illuminating, naturally also miss out on this internal coherence.[22] Hence, although recent scholarship has re-established the relevance of Cassirer's philosophy of symbolic forms, the Davos debate has become worth revisiting, and Heidegger's *philosophical* victory is no longer taken for granted, a thorough philosophical account of the stakes and the coherence of this memorable encounter is still lacking. This book aims to rectify this lack.

This attempt of course has its own limitations. First, as already mentioned, I will not engage with the broader historical and sociocultural context, presuppositions, and implications of the dispute between Cassirer and Heidegger. While this would add an interesting dimension to my undertaking, it falls

---

[21] Gordon aims at a complete overview of the topics treated in Davos and dissects the transcripts into ten rather artificial segments: 'Cohen's legacy', 'transcendental imagination', 'ethics and objectivity', *'terminus a quo, terminus ad quem'*, 'ontology and angels', 'God, finitude, truth', 'anxiety, culture, freedom', 'finitude and infinity', 'translation, aporia, difference', and 'the final exchange' (*Continental Divide*, 136–214). Gary Ronald Brown's dissertation, in turn, reads the Davos debate as a sequence of four relatively independent exchanges between Cassirer and Heidegger, concerning 'the question frame of each thinker', 'whether the being of human beings is infinite or finite', 'what each thinker's ontological commitments are', and 'how these commitments affect their relation to Kant's so-called Copernican revolution' (*The 1929 Davos Disputation Revisited*, Ann Arbor: UMI Dissertation Publishing, 2010, 5). In contrast to Gordon, my more selective approach aims to single out the few core themes that determine the philosophical stakes of both the Davos debate *and* the entire dispute between Cassirer and Heidegger. Since their public debate moves back and forth between these issues, I also find that Brown's linear reading of the transcript misses the mark. With regard to both, then, I deem my approach better suited for revealing the connection between the most fundamental disagreements between Cassirer and Heidegger, and for offering a coherent view of their famous encounter.

[22] A non-exhaustive list of contributions that have formed my understanding of the Davos debate should at least mention Jeffrey Andrew Barash's, 'Ernst Cassirer, Martin Heidegger, and the Legacy of Davos' (*History and Theory*, 51/3, 2012, 436–450); all essays in Kaegi/Rudolph's *70 Jahre Davoser Disputation*; Peter Eli Gordon's 'Myth and Modernity: Cassirer's Critique of Heidegger' (*New German Critique*, 94: *Secularization and Disenchantment*, 2005, 127–168) and 'Heidegger, Neo-Kantianism, and Cassirer', in: *The Bloomsbury Companion to Heidegger*, ed. by Francois Raffoul and Eric S. Nelson, London: Bloomsbury Publishing, 2013, 143–149; Dustin Peone's 'Ernst Cassirer's Essential Critique of Heidegger and *Verfallenheit*' (*Idealistic Studies*, 42(2/3), 2013, 119–130); Birgit Recki's *Cassirer*, in: *Grundwissen Philosophie*, Stuttgart: Reclam, 2013, 81–85; Michael Roubach's 'The Limits of Order. Cassirer and Heidegger on Finitude and Infinity', in: *The Symbolic Construction of Reality: The Legacy of Ernst Cassirer*, ed. by Jeffrey Andrew Barash, Chicago: The University of Chicago Press, 2008, 104–114; Frank Schalow's 'Thinking at Cross Purposes with Kant: Reason, Finitude, and Truth in the Cassirer-Heidegger debate' (*Kant Studien*, 87(2), 1996, 198–217); Skidelsky's *The Last Philosopher of Culture* (204–219); and Geert van Eekert's 'Synthesis speciosa' en de taak van de filosofie. Cassirer en Heidegger voor het tribunaal van de *Kritik der reinen Vernunft*' (*Gehelen en fragmenten: De vele gezichten van de filosofie*, red. door Bart Raymaekers, Leuven: Universitaire Pers, 1993, 230–234); and 'Freiheit und Endlichkeit: Cassirer, Heidegger und Kant' (*Life, Subjectivity & Art. Essays in Honor of Rudolf Bernet* ed. by Ulrich Melle and Roland Breeur, in: *Phaenomenologica* 201, Berlin: Springer, 2011, 195–216).

outside the scope of my investigations. Instead, I will approach the Davos debate from a purely philosophical angle.

Second, within these confines I also abstain from engaging with the immediate philosophical background of either Cassirer's philosophy of symbolic forms or Heidegger's fundamental ontology. I discuss some elements of Paul Natorp's thought in Chapter 5, but otherwise leave out how Hermann Cohen, Kurt Goldstein, Goethe, or Leibniz inspired Cassirer, and how Heidegger's thought relates to Edmund Husserl, Aristotle, or the Christian tradition. Since this book already deals with the view of two major thinkers on three hefty philosophical topics, I could not do justice to the originality of these other thinkers as well and, therefore, opted to leave them undiscussed altogether. The obvious exception to this approach is Kant, who one can consider a third, silent protagonist of the Davos debate. Since the meaning of Kant's thought is an explicit topic of contention between Cassirer and Heidegger, I cannot bypass his influence on their thinking in the same way. Yet, I cannot possibly engage with the complexity of Kant's philosophy on its own account either. I will thus either exclusively deal with the ways in which Cassirer and Heidegger interpreted, appropriated, or transformed the project of transcendental philosophy, or limit my discussions of Kant's own thought to those elements that were essential to both thinkers.

Finally, my focus on the interaction between Cassirer and Heidegger means that this book will only engage with a number of Heidegger's writings from before the so-called *Kehre* in his thinking. For one, Heidegger's interest in Cassirer quickly dematerialized after 1929. Cassirer, in turn, remained concerned about Heidegger's thought while living abroad, but seemed unaware of the significant changes that it underwent from the 1930s onwards. Hence, 'the late Heidegger' was in no way part of the dispute between Cassirer and Heidegger. Furthermore, Heidegger in this period also moved away from the first two topics of their dispute: his philosophical interests shifted from Kant to Nietzsche and from Dasein to art, poetry and the history of being. For these reasons, I will limit my scope to Heidegger's early view on the third topic, the task of philosophy, as well. Cassirer's thought, on the other hand, shows no comparable turn with regard to either these topics or his attitude towards Heidegger. Therefore, I will attempt to offer an encompassing, but obviously not exhaustive, view of his entire philosophy.

Chapter 1, Reconstructing the Davos Debate, offers a thorough reading of all texts in which Cassirer and Heidegger explicitly engaged with each other's thought. I first sketch the philosophical context of the Davos debate, which constitutes only one moment of a dispute that started in 1923 and continued until the publication of Cassirer's *The Myth of the State* in 1946 (1.1). Second, I argue that the public debate in Davos hinges on three interrelated topics: the proper interpretation of Kant's philosophy, the human condition, and the task of philosophy. Concretely, I show that Cassirer and Heidegger's diverging readings of Kant are motivated by their different views on the human condition, and that these views are in turn motivated by different conceptions of the task of philosophy, which I consider to be the fundamental breaking point between these two thinkers (1.2). Third, I explain that the same issues of contention also structure, in the same order and with the same increasing intensity, the entire, twenty-three-year-long Cassirer–Heidegger dispute (1.3). Taking these three issues as my lead, the remainder of this book is divided in three parts, each of which is in turn composed of three chapters.

Part I, The Lasting Meaning of Kant's Thought, addresses the first issue at stake in the Davos debate: the proper interpretation of Kant's philosophy. After separately considering Cassirer and Heidegger's transformations and appropriations of Kant's transcendental philosophy, I concentrate on the crucial aspects of their readings on which they explicitly or implicitly oppose each other.

Chapter 2, Cassirer's Transformation of the Critique of Reason into a Critique of Culture, retraces how Cassirer transforms Kant's transcendental philosophy into a philosophy of culture in *The Philosophy of Symbolic Forms*. First, Cassirer abandons Kant's notion of the category and instead models his conception of the symbol on the schema from *The Critique of Judgment* (2.1). Second, he understands such symbols as constituting not only the theoretical, practical, and aesthetic sphere, but all cultural domains, including myth, language, and the human sciences (2.2). This forces Cassirer to adopt two conceptions of objectivity: a constitutive conception that pertains to each cultural domain (or 'symbolic forms') and a regulative conception that befits human culture as a whole (2.3).

Chapter 3, Heidegger's Reading of Transcendental Philosophy as Phenomenological Ontology, argues that Heidegger considers all three elements of his own view of the 'concept and method' of philosophy – ontology, phenomenology, and hermeneutics – to be at work in Kant's *Critique of Pure Reason*. First, Heidegger's well-known 'ontological reading' of this work more specifically interprets it as a treatise on the possibility of general ontology (3.1). Further, he understands Kant's critical approach as an attempt at developing the phenomenological method that such an ontology requires (3.2). Ultimately, and most audaciously, Heidegger interprets the changes between the two editions of the first *Critique* as the result of Kant's hermeneutical reflection upon this attempt (3.3). This chapter puts forward a new reading of *Kant and the Problem of Metaphysics* (*GA* 3) and *Phenomenological Interpretation of Kant's 'Critique of Pure Reason'* (*GA* 25), but also draws from *What Is a Thing?* (*GA* 41), *Logic: The Question of Truth* (*GA* 21), and *Einleitung in die Philosophie* (*GA* 27).

Chapter 4, Spontaneity or Receptivity: Two Readings of the First
Critique, tackles the two main issues of contention between Cassirer's and
Heidegger's interpretation of Kant. I first examine why Heidegger opposes his
own 'ontological reading' of the first Critique to the 'epistemological reading'
that he attributes to the Neo-Kantians. I clarify what this opposition entails and
consider in what way it indeed applies to Cassirer (4.1). Next, I turn to Cassirer
and Heidegger's more specific disagreement regarding the relevance of Kant's
account of transcendental imagination. Remarkably, both thinkers not only
value how this account attempts to undercut the artificial opposition between
receptivity and spontaneity (4.2), but their agreement extends to the shared
thesis that Kant ultimately did not succeed because he lacked a truly phenomenological method (4.3). Yet, Cassirer and Heidegger still radically part ways
as soon as they evaluate why this (failed) attempt is so important: while
Heidegger takes transcendental imagination as the ground of human reason's
finite nature, Cassirer concludes from the primacy of this faculty to the
fundamentally spontaneous character of reason (4.4).

Part II, What Is the Human Being?, turns to the official topic of the
Davoser Hochschulkurse and the second key issue of the Davos debate: the
human condition. In analogy with Part One, I first elaborate on Cassirer and
Heidegger's respective views of the human being, and then examine the
similarities and differences between their philosophical approaches and claims.

Chapter 5, Cassirer's Functional Account of the 'Animal Symbolicum',
argues that Cassirer's philosophy of symbolic forms relies on an account of
human subjectivity that he deliberately keeps in the background of his
writings. Remarkably, even though Cassirer considers a systematic account
of human subjectivity to be an essential component of a philosophy of culture,
he never seems to develop one (5.1). This omission is the result of Cassirer's
belief that consciousness can only be approached through the mediation of
diverse cultural products (5.2). Cassirer solves this difficulty by developing a
'functional conception of human subjectivity' that forms the exact counterpart
of his account of objectivity and therefore needs no separate treatment (5.3).
This conception allows him to characterize the human being as an 'animal
symbolicum' in *An Essay on Man* (5.4). Cassirer's posthumous text *The
Metaphysics of Symbolic Forms* then merely translates this view of the human
being into the language of his contemporaries – rather than deviating from his
published writings, as is usually maintained (5.5). In sum, this chapter retrieves
the hidden, anthropological foundation of Cassirer's philosophy of culture.

Chapter 6, Heidegger's Existential Analytic of 'Dasein', reconstructs
Heidegger's well-known analysis of Dasein as analogous to his interpretation
of Kant: I argue that Heidegger also views Dasein as a (pre-)ontological,
phenomenological, and hermeneutic way of being. Demonstrating this requires
a circular reading of the first book of *Being and Time*. Following Heidegger's

own argumentation leads us from Dasein's usual and predominant understanding of being (6.1), through the structural moments of 'being-in-the-world' that constitute its possibility (6.2), to 'care' as the foundational unity of these conditions (6.3). Once this is established, reading Heidegger's magnum opus backwards shows that Dasein *is at its core* an ontological way of being due to its concern for the being of beings, *enacts* this concern in a phenomenological manner through its 'being-in', and is thereby both *enabled and hindered* by the hermeneutic situation of its everyday understanding (6.4). By distinguishing the argumentative procedure of *Being in Time* from the resulting picture of our human condition, this chapter provides a more systematic picture of Dasein's existential constitution than Heidegger managed to display.

Chapter 7, Infinite or Finite: The Quest for Existential Orientation, compares Cassirer's and Heidegger's take on the human being's capacity to orient itself in the world in a meaningful way. Cassirer's theory of the functions of consciousness, the only meat to his functional conception of human subjectivity, is used to describe the diverse, cultural compasses by means of which the 'symbolic animal' navigates the human world (7.1). Heidegger's accounts of 'the they' and of owned ('authentic') existence in turn provide a theory of Dasein's capacity to orient itself within and towards its world (7.2). In view of their shared interest in orientation, I discern an important distinction for both Cassirer and Heidegger between an orienting and an oriented self. With regard to both, they ultimately disagree about the infinite (cultural) or finite (temporal) nature of the human being (7.3).

Part III, The Task of Philosophy, addresses the third issue at stake in the Davos debate: the task of philosophy. In line with my previous procedure, I first consider Cassirer and Heidegger's respective conceptions of philosophy, and then spell out their diverging views on its existential and ethical task.

Chapter 8, Cassirer's Functional Conception of Philosophy returns to Cassirer's notion of function to argue that it continuously informs his conception of philosophy. Cassirer first develops this notion in his 1910 work *Substance and Function*: the mathematical idea of a function connects disparate elements under a variable rule, establishing a unity *through* diversity (8.1). Subsequently, his early historical writings (1906–1919) invoke the idea of a functional unity in order to explain the continuity and progress in the history of thought while simultaneously acknowledging the legitimacy of each historical epoch (8.2). Cassirer's mature, systematic writings (1923–1942) reconcile the unity of human culture and the synchronic diversity of our cultural domains by means of the same idea (8.3). Finally, the ethical reflections that we find in Cassirer's latest writings (1935–1946) are also rooted in this 'functional conception of philosophy' (8.4).

Chapter 9, Heidegger's Hermeneutic Conception of Philosophy, explains how Heidegger's interpretation of Kant and his analysis of Dasein relate to the primary interest of his philosophical enterprise: the retrieval of the question of being. The introduction to *Being and Time* indicates that these three projects formally presuppose one another because Heidegger weds the ontological task of philosophy to its phenomenological and hermeneutical method (9.1). At the same time, this threefold conception of philosophy – ontology, phenomenology, hermeneutics – establishes a hermeneutic situation that informed Heidegger's interpretations of Kant and Dasein (9.2). Heidegger admits to the circularity of this philosophical procedure, but defends it by distinguishing between a formal, a philosophical, and a factual 'starting point' of the 'hermeneutical circle' (9.3). At stake here is the relation between Dasein and philosophy, as well as Heidegger's contested choice to approach the meaning of being via our own existence.

Chapter 10, Enlightenment or Therapy: The Cosmopolitan Task of Philosophy, considers the implications of Cassirer and Heidegger's respective conceptions of philosophy for their views on its existential task. Cassirer asserts a hierarchy among the cultural domains based on the self-understanding of symbolic consciousness (10.1). Heidegger navigates the dialectics between disowned, average, and owned selfhood. On this basis, I address the ultimate breaking point between Cassirer and Heidegger: their respective Enlightened and 'therapeutic' conception of the task of philosophy. While for Cassirer philosophy is the caretaker of our self-liberation through culture, for Heidegger it ought to help us reconcile with our ineradicable shortcomings – the latter view is therapeutic in the psychoanalytic sense; it has no affinity with Wittgenstein's notion of philosophy as therapy (10.2).

The **Conclusion** of this book, **The *Terminus a Quo* and *Terminus ad Quem* of the Davos Debate,** reconsiders the stakes of the Davos debate on the basis of my previous findings. I first summarize the established similarities and differences between Cassirer and Heidegger's philosophical projects. Next, I reinterpret their issues of contention in light of the starting point and aim (the 'terminus a quo' and 'terminus ad quem', as they put it in Davos) of their philosophies, which, I argue, Cassirer and Heidegger failed to accurately compare. In this way, I show that Cassirer's and Heidegger's thought, despite being grounded in irreconcilable ontological and methodological assumptions, can nevertheless positively incite each other. After all, they share a philosophical concern: to comprehend and aid the human being's capacity to orient itself in and towards the world. This means that the Davos debate was an elaborate disagreement about a shared interest of profound significance for human life after all, or in other words a true philosophical debate.

1   Reconstructing the Davos Debate

1.1   Preliminary Remarks

The philosophical dispute between Cassirer and Heidegger covers much more than the public discussion, or *Arbeitsgemeinschaft*, that took place on 2 April 1929, during the second meeting of the *Internationale Davoser Hochschulkurse* (17 March–6 April). Their philosophical relationship dates back to at least 1923 and only came to an end with the posthumous publication of Cassirer's *The Myth of the State* in 1946. During these twenty-three years, Cassirer and Heidegger repeatedly commented, with varying praise and scorn, on the other's philosophical project: not only their reviews of each other's works, but also a number of explicit and implicit references in (footnotes to) their own works and lectures attest to an enduring concern with regard to the other thinker. In what follows, I will refer to the whole of this interaction as the 'Cassirer-Heidegger dispute'. This dispute can be divided into three phases, of which the 1929 public 'Davos debate' thus marks only one moment.

First, Heidegger commented on Cassirer's work four times prior to 1929, namely in a footnote in *Being and Time*, an unpublished letter to Karl Jaspers, a brief historical overview of Marburg Neo-Kantianism, and most importantly a review of the second volume of the *Philosophy of Symbolic Forms*.[1] In this phase, he values Cassirer's attempt to develop a transcendental philosophy of mythology, and suggests their shared interested in an 'existential analytics'. He wonders, however, whether Cassirer is not too loyal to the letter of Kant's texts. We here find the seeds for both Heidegger's continuing interest in and impending discontent with Cassirer's thought.

Second, during the *Davoser Hochschulkurse*, the Davos debate was preceded and followed by a series of independent lectures by Cassirer and Heidegger. I will consider these lectures in close connection to the transcript of the debate, which was composed by Cassirer and Heidegger's respective students Joachim Ritter and Otto Friedrich Bollnow. These lectures after all had the clear purpose of preparing both themselves and the audience for the

---

[1] See *BT* 51; *KPM:VI* 304–311; and *KPM:II* 255–270.

actual debate: Cassirer and Heidegger here engaged, if not directly with each other's thought, at least with each other's area of specialization.[2] While Cassirer was the publisher of Kant's works and widely considered as *the* Kant expert of his time, Heidegger had recently, and very quickly, become famous for his original theory of the human being and the philosophically most accurate way to analyse it. Nevertheless, Cassirer held three one-hour sessions on 'Foundational Problems of Philosophical Anthropology' and one, the day after the debate, on 'The Opposition between 'Spirit' and 'Life' in Scheler's Philosophy'.[3] Heidegger, in turn, spoke for four hours about 'Kant's *Critique of Pure Reason* and the Task of a Laying of the Ground for Metaphysics'.[4]

This crossover of interests may have been motivated by the general theme of the *Hochschulkurse*: the relationship between philosophy and the humanities or, more generally, the question "What is the human being?" We now know, however, that the topics of Cassirer and Heidegger's independent lectures also

[2] According to Toni Cassirer, her husband for the first time seriously studied *Being and Time* when preparing for these lectures (*Mein Leben mit Ernst Cassirer*, 187).

[3] *ECN:17* 3–73; *ECW:17* 185–205.

[4] Heidegger's notes of these talks, which were first published in the *Davoser Revue* IV/7, 1929, 194–196, form another appendix to the recent editions of *Kant and the Problem of Metaphysics* (*KPM:III* 271–273). The first preface to this work informs us that Heidegger had given these lectures before, "in a four-hour lecture during the Winter Semester of 1927/1928 and later [. . .] at the Herder Institute in Riga in September [1928]" (*KPM* xix). Heidegger's 1928–1929 Winter Seminar *Einleitung in de Philosophie* also contains a very similar discussion of Kant's thought (*GA 27* 258–275). We may further assume that his research on Kant had already far advanced by the time he faced Cassirer in Davos: according to a letter to his wife Elfride, he managed to lecture at Davos without any manuscript (*'Mein liebes Seelchen!'*. *Briefe Martin Heideggers an seine Frau Elfride (1915–1970)*, hrsg. von Gertrud Heidegger, München: Deutsche Verlag-Anstalt, 2005, 161), and he finished *Kant and the Problem of Metaphysics* merely two months after their encounter. A quick glance at the lecture notes confirms that the structure of Heidegger's *Davoser Vorträge* is almost identical to that of *Kant and the Problem of Metaphysics*. The threefold division of these notes, which assumedly refers to the topics of his three lectures, mirrors the composition of the 'Kant book'. The three steps of his argument in Davos are: "(1) the laying of the ground for metaphysics in the point of departure, (2) the laying of the ground for metaphysics in the carrying-through, (3) the laying of the ground for metaphysics in its originality" (*KPM:III* 271). These return almost verbatim in *Kant and the Problem of Metaphysics* as the titles of its first three parts: "The Starting Point for the Laying of the Ground for Metaphysics" (3–12), "Carrying Out the Laying of the Ground for Metaphysics" (*KPM* 13–88), and "The Laying of the Ground for Metaphysics in Its Originality" (89–142). Twice, Heidegger interprets the *Critique of Pure Reason* as a treatise on the possibility and ground-laying of ontology and on the finitude of human reason, and he ultimately presents Kant's account of the power of transcendental imagination as the key to this interpretation. Further, the subchapters of the second part also correspond to a division Heidegger already makes in Davos (*KPM:III* 272–273). He announces in his notes and then develops in his 'Kant book' that in order to 'lay the ground for metaphysics', one must (a) determine the elements of pure knowledge, and explain (b) the essential unity thereof, (c) the inner possibility thereof, and (d) the ground for the possibility of ontological knowledge. *Kant and the Problem of Metaphysics* adds a fourth part, called "The Laying of the Ground for Metaphysics in a Retrieval" (*KPM* 143–173), to Heidegger's overall investigation, and a (sub-)chapter, on the 'full essential determination of ontological knowledge', to its second part.

reflect their own research interests around the time of the debate. In 1929, Cassirer was working on an essay that was initially meant to conclude the third volume of the *Philosophy of Symbolic Forms: The Phenomenology of Knowledge*, but was first collected in 1995 in the so-called fourth volume, *The Metaphysics of Symbolic Forms*. In this essay, likewise titled 'On the metaphysics of symbolic forms', Cassirer tries to position his philosophy of culture within the contemporary philosophical scene. To this end, he critically engages with the then popular *Lebensphilosophie* (Dilthey, Klages, Bergson, Simmel) and with new theories in philosophical anthropology (Scheler, Plessner, Uexküll, Spengler). Although Cassirer struggled to breach out of his usual transcendental approach and never published these reflections, his attempt nevertheless indicates a genuine interest in these topics.[5]

Heidegger, in turn, had already in *Being and Time* announced his interest in Kant's philosophy in the context of a "destruction of the history of ontology" (*BT* 39–40). While this phrase at first sight suggests that Heidegger did not hold Kant in high esteem, his 1927/1928 Winter Seminar in Marburg, *Phenomenological Interpretation of Kant's Critique of Pure Reason*, actually reveals a rather positive assessment of Kant's thought. Although Heidegger eventually holds that Kant remained trapped in the discourse of traditional metaphysics, he nevertheless interprets the Transcendental Analytic of the *Critique of Pure Reason* as the first, albeit hesitant, attempt to develop a phenomenological analysis of subjectivity that lays the ground for a new ontology. For Heidegger, then, the meeting in Davos offered an excellent opportunity to advertise his original perspective on Kant, confirm the central thesis of *Being and Time*, and end the dominance of Neo-Kantianism over the European philosophical scene in the early twentieth century.

Third, after the Davos debate especially Cassirer remained explicitly concerned with Heidegger's thought. In the immediate aftermath of their encounter, he added a number of trying footnotes on *Being and Time* to the otherwise finished manuscript of the third volume of the *The Philosophy of Symbolic Forms*.[6] Heidegger, on the other hand, wrote *Kant and the Problem of*

---

[5] First in his seminars at Göteborg (1939/1940) and Yale (1941/1942) would Cassirer manage to develop a philosophical anthropology that supports his philosophy of culture on a transcendental basis (*ECN:6* 1–187; 189–343). The latter seminar forms the basis for *An Essay on Man* (1944), which is often considered an anthropological introduction to Cassirer's thought for his new, English-speaking, audience. For an excellent explanation of Cassirer's attempts to restore, after Heidegger's critique, the possibility of philosophical anthropology by reconciling it with an idealistic philosophy of culture, see Gerald Hartung, *Das Maß des Menschen. Aporien der philosophischen Anthropologie und ihre Auflösung in der Kulturphilosophie Ernst Cassirers*, Birkach: Velbrück Wissenschaft, 2003, 309–356.

[6] The manuscript of *The Phenomenology of Knowledge* that was published in 1929 was actually already completed in 1927, but Cassirer postponed its publication to include a "final, critical, chapter" on contemporary philosophy (*PSF:III* xvii). However, once he realized that this part

Metaphysics, which still criticizes the Neo-Kantian interpretation of the first *Critique* but does so in a much less prominent manner than *Phenomenological Interpretation*. Two years later, in 1931, Cassirer published a highly critical commentary on this book in *Kant-Studien*.[7] At the same time, Heidegger attempted to review *The Phenomenology of Knowledge*, but he admitted to Cassirer that he could not come to grips with it.[8] Despite this increased animosity, Heidegger invited Cassirer to give a lecture in Freiburg in 1932, which would be the last time that these eminences of twentieth-century philosophy met. However, after almost a decade of silence following his emigration from Germany, Cassirer launched a new, ethically charged critique of Heidegger: after characterizing Heidegger's thought as founded on religious rather than philosophical motives in unpublished notes from 1928, in *The Myth of the State* (1946) he connects these motives to the rise of Nazism.

The Cassirer–Heidegger dispute is marked, then, by two evolutions. First, Cassirer and Heidegger's interest in each other's thought piqued at different moments. Prior to the Davos debate, the rising philosophical star Heidegger engaged on two important occasions with Cassirer, a leading Kant scholar and one of the most respected thinkers of the moment. After 1929, he however seemed to have lost interest in Cassirer: he never finished his review of *The Phenomenology of Knowledge*, nor did he respond to Cassirer's elaborate review of *Kant and the Problem of Metaphysics*. Cassirer, on the other hand, acknowledged the philosophical challenges of his younger colleague only after the latter had turned out to be a serious match in Davos. From then on until his death, he commented on Heidegger's philosophy with ever-increasing (moral) disapproval. Second, the Cassirer–Heidegger dispute thus quickly abandoned initial suggestions of philosophical agreement and evolves into a seemingly unsurpassable conflict. The Davos debate played a crucial role in these evolutions, and is therefore rightfully recollected as the most famous moment of this dispute.

1.2   The Davos Debate: Analysis of a Coherent Discussion

The 1929 Davos debate between Cassirer and Heidegger hinges on three interrelated themes. Provoked by Heidegger's criticism of Neo-Kantianism in his independent lectures, the debate initially focuses on the proper meaning of Kant's philosophy. At this point, Cassirer and Heidegger's disagreement

---

would render the third volume too long, he reserved it for a separate volume – *The Metaphysics of Symbolic Forms* – and instead added a few footnotes on the most significant works that had appeared in the meantime, including *Being and Time*.

[7] *KPMR* 221–250. Heidegger's notes on this review are published in *KPM:V* 297–303. See also Gordon, *Continental Divide*, 265–268, 403.

[8] See Toni Cassirer, *Mein Leben mit Ernst Cassirer*, 189.

famously concerns the question whether transcendental philosophy should be understood as ontology (Heidegger) or epistemology (Cassirer). Because the debate addresses Kant's account of transcendental imagination in particular, it is also often considered a discussion about the receptive (Heidegger) or spontaneous (Cassirer) character of Kant's conception of transcendental subjectivity. However, as the conversation proceeds, it becomes clear that they are actually debating the finite (Heidegger) or infinite (Cassirer) character of the human condition as such. In hindsight, this second theme of the Davos debate, the human condition, motivated the first one, the proper interpretation of Kant's thought. However, Cassirer and Heidegger's positions with regard to the second issue are in turn propelled by a third and final disagreement concerning the task of philosophy: they ultimately debate whether philosophy is supposed to enlighten the human being (Cassirer), or can only have a 'therapeutic' function (Heidegger). Deliberately or not, this issue set the stakes for the entire Davos debate – as Heidegger also indicates towards the end:

I would like once more to place our entire discussion in terms of Kant's *Critique of Pure Reason* and to fix once more the question of what the human being is as the central question. [This question] only makes sense and is only justifiable insofar as it derives its motivation from philosophy's central problematic itself, which leads the human being back beyond itself and into the totality of beings. (*DD* 291)

1.2.1   Two Readings of the Critique of Pure Reason

The public debate between Cassirer and Heidegger commences as a discussion on the proper reading of Kant's thought: Cassirer starts off this public encounter by asking two questions: "What does Heidegger understand by Neo-Kantianism? Who is the opponent to whom Heidegger has addressed himself?" (*DD* 274). These questions clearly do not arise out of thin air: they directly react to Heidegger's lectures from the days leading up to the debate. Claiming that the *Critique of Pure Reason* offers a novel foundation for metaphysics, Heidegger had rejected the Neo-Kantian reading of this work as a theory of knowledge in general and of mathematical or physical knowledge more particularly:

These lectures are to demonstrate the thesis: Kant's *Critique of Pure Reason* is a, or rather the first, express ground-laying for metaphysics. (Negatively, and in opposition to the traditional interpretation of Neo-Kantianism, that means: it is no theory of mathematical, natural-scientific knowledge – it is not a theory of knowledge at all.) (*KPM:III* 271)

Heidegger repeats this claim when responding to Cassirer's first question. First, he holds that what unites the Neo-Kantian movement is its search for the epistemological task that is left for philosophy by the end of the nineteenth century, given the success of both the natural and cultural sciences: "We can only understand what is common to Neo-Kantianism on the basis of its origin. [Its] genesis lies in the predicament of philosophy concerning the question of what properly remains of it in the whole of knowledge" (*DD* 274). Then, Heidegger rephrases his twofold thesis that the first *Critique* is in essence neither concerned with the natural sciences, nor even with a theory of knowledge as such:

I understand by Neo-Kantianism that conception of the *Critique of Pure Reason* which explains, with reference to natural science, the part of pure reason that leads up to the Transcendental Dialectic as theory of knowledge. For me, what matters is to show that what came to be extracted here as theory of science was nonessential for Kant. Kant did not want to give any sort of theory of natural science, but rather wanted to point out the problematic of metaphysics, which is to say, the problematic of ontology. (275)

For Heidegger, the Transcendental Analytic does not explain how we can acquire scientific knowledge of objects, but rather how we can have access to other beings at all: "What I want to point out is that the analytic is [...] a general ontology, a critical, well-established *metaphysica generalis*" (279).

Cassirer clearly does not feel addressed by this critique. It is well known that his philosophy of culture programmatically transcends the focus on the natural sciences that is commonly ascribed to the Marburg Neo-Kantians: Cassirer aims to account not only for our scientific understanding of the world, but he investigates with equal interest our mythological, linguistic, religious, artistic, and political apprehension thereof. The philosophy of symbolic forms affirms, then, only the methodological primacy of the natural sciences, whose reliance on hypotheses and experiments most clearly reveals that objective meaning is grounded in the structure of human subjectivity. In response to Heidegger, Cassirer holds that the latter view is, in fact, consistent with Marburg Neo-Kantianism:

One only understands Cohen correctly if one understands him historically, not merely as an epistemologist. I do not conceive of my own development as a defection from Cohen. Naturally, in the course of my work much else has emerged, and, indeed, above all I recognized the position of mathematical natural science. However, this can only serve as a paradigm and not as the whole of the problem. And the same goes for Natorp.[9]

---

[9] *DD* 275. Cassirer's teachers and founders of the *Marburger Schule*, Hermann Cohen and Paul Natorp, were indeed also interested in much more than just the natural sciences: Cohen's *Kants Theorie der Erfahrung* (1871) is the first volume of a trilogy completed by *Die Begründung der Ethik* (1877) and *Die Begründung der Aesthetik* (1889), and Natorp's late research resulted in the publication of *Philosophische Systematik* (1923) and *Vorlesungen über praktische Philosophie* (1925). Cassirer repeatedly praises Cohen's pioneering focus on the transcendental method in

The real core of Neo-Kantianism lies, then, not in its interest in scientific knowledge but in its validation of Kant's transcendental method, namely to investigate the subjective conditions of possibility of our ways of understanding of the world: "The term 'Neo-Kantianism' must be determined functionally rather than substantially. It is not a matter of the kind of philosophy as dogmatic doctrinal system; rather, it is a matter of a direction taken in question-posing".[10] Hence, according to Cassirer, Heidegger's claims about the dominant role of the natural sciences in Neo-Kantian thought must be severely nuanced. On the basis of his 'functional definition', he even characterizes Heidegger's independent lectures as Neo-Kantian in spirit: "Contrary to what I expected, I must confess that I here found a Neo-Kantian in Heidegger".[11]

Although Heidegger would eventually become annoyed by such attempts at reconciliation – which, as we now know, did not win the audience over either – this early in the debate, he still politely answers Cassirer's questions. The list of thinkers that he, in response to Cassirer's second question, identifies as his Neo-Kantian opponents is however quite remarkable. On the one hand, besides the inevitable Cohen and the now largely forgotten thinkers Benno Erdmann and Alois Riehl, Heidegger also lists some of his own teachers, namely Wilhelm Windelband and Heinrich Rickert from the *Südwest-Deutsche* Neo-Kantian school that competed with the *Marburger Schule*, and his mentor Edmund Husserl (274–275). This means that Heidegger considers all these thinkers to support a flawed, epistemological reading of the *Critique of Pure Reason*. On the other hand, he mentions neither Natorp nor Cassirer. This is surprising, for one, because most commentators take Heidegger to have mainly

'Hermann Cohen und die Erneuerung der Kantischen Philosophie' (*ECW:9* 122, 138), 'Hermann Cohen, Worte and seinem Grabe' (493), 'Zur Lehre Hermann Cohens' (494), and 'Hermann Cohen' (503–504). Following Cohen and Natorp, Cassirer also identifies this method as the systematic core of Kant's philosophy (*KLT* 3; *Determinismus and Indeterminismus in der modernen Physik. Historische und systematische Studien zum Kausalproblem*, in: *ECW:19* 6). Rather unexpectedly, then, he admits towards the end of the Davos debate that Cohen did not realize the independence of this method from the activity of the mathematical sciences of nature after all (*DD* 294–295; see also 'Von Hermann Cohens geistigem Erbe', in: *Aufsätze und kleine Schrifte 1922–1926, ECW:16* 482–484).

[10] *DD* 274. Cassirer's functional definition of Neo-Kantianism as a method rather than a doctrine allows him to identify as a Neo-Kantian while severely disagreeing with other members of this philosophical school ('Was ist 'Subjektivismus'?', in: *ECW:22* 169). It must be said, however, that Cassirer's suggestion of methodological affinity was mostly rejected by his acclaimed fellow Neo-Kantians – Cohen publicly expressed his regret about the way in which Cassirer, already in *Substance and Function*, digressed from the Neo-Kantian tradition. For an overview of the discussion of this topic in secondary literature, see Sebastian Luft, 'Cassirer's Philosophy of Symbolic Forms: Between Reason and Relativism; a Critical Appraisal', in: *Idealistic Studies*, 34/1, 2004, 46.

[11] *DD* 274; translation modified.

targeted Natorp's version of Neo-Kantianism.[12] Further, his refusal to identify Cassirer as a Neo-Kantian here is rather unhelpful for the debate. Ironically, it leads to a situation in which Cassirer identifies Heidegger as a Neo-Kantian, but not the other way around.

It is, therefore, quite clear that Cassirer and Heidegger so far try to remain gentle with regard to each other: Cassirer tries to bridge their positions, while Heidegger refrains from specifically criticizing his conversation partner. Cassirer takes this as an opportunity to leave aside the differences among the Neo-Kantians and instead focus on the "basic systematic problem" of Kant's thought that interests both him and Heidegger: "On one point we agree, in that for me as well the productive power of imagination appears in fact to have a central meaning for Kant" (275–276). In his independent lectures, Heidegger had indeed presented this faculty as the "unknown root" of sensibility and the understanding, and thus as a "third basic source of mind" (*KPM:III* 272–273). During the public encounter, Cassirer in turn holds that the "extraordinary significance of the schematism [of transcendental imagination] cannot be overestimated" (*DD* 276–277). It is remarkable how two thinkers who seem to hold such opposed views on the original message of Kant's philosophy, nevertheless both consider a then mostly overlooked passage from his writings as the key to his thought.

Kant invokes the power of transcendental imagination in the *Critique of Pure Reason* in order to mediate between the two sources of knowledge: sensibility and the understanding. Having defined the former as a receptive faculty that provides the concrete, empirical, material for our judgements, and the latter as a spontaneous faculty that alone can account for their intelligible and universal validity, the question arises how there can be any affinity and

---

[12] Heidegger's 1927 lecture on the history of Marburg Neo-Kantianism may help us understand why he does not list Natorp as a Neo-Kantian during the Davos debate. Here, Heidegger speaks positively of Natorp's later thought, claiming that the latter saw "the essential gaps and one-sided aspects of" Cohen's systematic philosophy and brought it "to a more originally grounded, independent level of development". In particular, Natorp's revision of Cohen's thought allowed for "the positive evaluation of the fundamental meaning of a phenomenological categorical analysis of 'subjective' and 'objective' spirit" (*KPM:VI* 307–309). Several scholars have confirmed that Heidegger and Natorp's weekly meetings during their shared Marburg period revealed or established substantial parallels between their philosophies. Most importantly, both thinkers aimed at a conception of 'being' that precedes the distinction between objectivity and subjectivity. Consult, in this regard, Christoph von Wolzogen, *Die autonome Relation. Zum Problem der Beziehung im Spätwerk Paul Natorps. Ein Beitrag zur Geschichte der Theorien der Relation*, Würzburg: Königshausen und Neumann, 1984, 144–163; Éric Dufour, *Paul Natorp, de la Psychologie générale à la Systématique philosophique*, Paris: Vrin, 2010, 236–237; and Sebastian Luft's introduction to Natorp's *Allgemeine Philosophie nach kritischer Methode*, Darmstadt: Wissenschaftliche Buchgesellschaft, 2013, xxxiii–xxxv. Massimo Ferrari further suggests that Natorp's presence in Davos could have been fruitful for exposing the shared ground between Cassirer and Heidegger – Natorp died, however, in 1924 ('Paul Natorp. 'The Missing Link' in der Davoser Debatte', in: *70 Jahre Davoser Disputation*, 215–233).

cooperation between these faculties.[13] At this point, Kant calls upon the transcendental power of imagination: by producing 'transcendental schemata' that are sensible and intellectual at once, this faculty accomplishes the unity between intuitions and pure concepts that Kant deems necessary for objective experience (*CPR* A139–141/B177–180).

In 1929, there was little support left for either Kant's discourse on the faculties of the human mind or the dualisms that it entails. For the Neo-Kantians, the oppositions between sensibility and the understanding, or receptivity and spontaneity, are remnants of pre-critical metaphysics. The phenomenological movement, on the other hand, rejects the language of faculties as a characteristic of psychologism. Both movements thus recognize in Kant's account of the faculties a feature of their own philosophical adversary. Given this philosophical climate, it seems surprising that Cassirer and Heidegger positively value Kant's account of transcendental imagination as the heart of his Transcendental Analytic. They do so, however, because they interpret it as a modest attempt to distort, rather than consolidate, the discourse of faculties, thus suggesting a new framework for explaining our understanding of objects.

In order to conceive of our cultural world in terms of symbolic forms, Cassirer posits that human beings instantaneously and continuously perceive intellectual meaning in empirical data because they are capable of 'symbolic imagination'. Accordingly, Cassirer transforms Kant's notion of the 'schemata' into the idea of 'symbols of consciousness' that likewise consist of inseparable sensible and intelligible components but that moreover recur in each cultural domain. Hence, in Davos he holds that

one cannot unravel the symbolic without referring it to the faculty of the productive power of imagination. The power of imagination is the connection of all thought to the intuition. Kant calls the power of imagination *synthesis speciosa*. Synthesis is the basic power of pure thinking [...] but the problem of the species leads into the core of the concept of image, the concept of symbol. (*DD* 276; *ECW:17* 198)

In his independent lectures, Heidegger in turn argues that transcendental imagination is not an auxiliary faculty that mediates between sensibility and the understanding, but rather constitutes their common root:

The ground for the possibility of a priori synthetic knowledge is the transcendental power of imagination. In the course of the ground-laying, Kant introduced a third basic source of the mind, contrary to the operative point of departure. This does not lie 'between' both of the previously cited stems, but rather is their root. This is indicated by

---

[13] Immanuel Kant, *The Critique of Pure Reason*, in: *The Cambridge Edition of the Works of Immanuel Kant*, ed. by Paul Guyer and Allen W. Wood, New York: Cambridge University Press, 1998, A19/B33; A51/B75 – hereafter indicated as '*CPR*'.

the fact that pure sensibility and pure understanding lead back to the power of imagination. (*KPM:III* 273)

Heidegger does not repeat this claim during the debate with Cassirer, but it would become the central argument of *Kant and the Problem of Metaphysics*: through a meticulous reading of the Transcendental Analytic, he there argues that transcendental imagination, if properly understood as "the original unity of receptivity and spontaneity", constitutes "the ground of the possibility of ontological knowledge" (*KPM* 153, 88). Hence, Cassirer and Heidegger both focus on this faculty because it undercuts a sharp distinction between sensibility and the understanding, receptivity and spontaneity, or the concrete and the universal, and, as such, establishes our initial relation to the world.

Yet, as soon as this agreement is established, Cassirer points out to Heidegger that the importance of transcendental imagination is limited to Kant's theoretical philosophy. As said, Kant invokes this faculty in order to unite the empirical and intelligible realm and thus acquire theoretical knowledge of objects. The possibility of moral behavior, on the other hand, coincides for Kant with that of *pure* practical reason, or with the possibility to act according to motives that are completely independent from the empirical world. Hence, the sensible or receptive moment that is crucial to Kant's account of theoretical cognition is rigorously excluded from his foundation of ethics: he conceives of the categorical imperative as a law that the rational being gives to itself, and accordingly describes the ethical subject as gifted with pure practical spontaneity or autonomy. Cassirer concludes from this that there is no role left for transcendental imagination in Kant's practical metaphysics: "In the ethical, however, [Kant] forbids the schematism. There he says: our concepts of freedom, etc. are insights (not bits of knowledge) that no longer permit schematizing. There is a schematism of theoretical knowledge, but not of practical reason" (*DD* 277).

Cassirer finds this limited function of the power of imagination important because he regards the possibility of practical freedom as the main problem of Kant's philosophy (276). Kant indeed indicates, in both the first and second *Critique*, that his interest in metaphysical problems like that of freedom made him turn away from the theoretical towards the practical sphere.[14] This means, according to Cassirer, that the schematism marks the starting point but not the goal of Kant's thought:

It is necessary to understand that one cannot proceed if one does not give up the schematism here. For Kant, the schematism is also the *terminus a quo*, but not the

---

[14] See *CPR* Bxxv, Bxxx, A799–800/B827–828; and *The Critique of Practical Reason*, in: *Practical Philosophy*, tr. by Mary J. Gregor in *The Cambridge Edition of the Works of Immanuel Kant*, New York: Cambridge University Press, 1996, 5:119–121.

terminus ad quem. New problems arise in the *Critique of Practical Reason*, and Kant indeed always adheres to this point of departure in the schematism, but it is also expanded upon. (277)

Cassirer finds this relevant to the Davos debate, further, because it "ties in with Heidegger's arguments" (*DD* 276) from his independent lectures. The final notes of these lectures after all mention that "theoretical *and* practical reason in their separateness and their unity [. . .] lead back to the power of imagination" (*KPM:III* 273). For Heidegger, transcendental imagination thus not only constitutes the 'common root' of the two stems of theoretical knowledge, but also of the theoretical and practical uses of reason. On Cassirer's view, Heidegger hereby lends too much weight to what is merely the point of departure of Kant's thought. He thus objects to Heidegger's assertion of a practical function of transcendental imagination by saying that "Kant certainly always maintained the starting point of the schematism, but also broadened it. Kant started from Heidegger's problem, but expanded upon this sphere".[15]

One could object here that Kant expands upon Cassirer's problem as well. The philosophy of symbolic forms after all considers symbolic imagination as the constitutive power of *all* our cultural domains, and thus not as a starting point that needs to be overcome. There is for Cassirer no sphere of human culture in which the human subject achieves complete autonomy. Hence, his attempt to downplay the role of transcendental imagination seems inconsistent with the way he values it in his own written work. However, Cassirer invokes Kant's practical philosophy here not in order to contrast it with Kant's theoretical philosophy, but rather to reveal their common 'direction of question-posing', a direction that they moreover share with his own philosophy of culture. Cassirer's interest in both transcendental imagination and the moral law is motivated, then, by the idea of a 'breakthrough' (*Durchbruch*) or a 'transition' (*Übergang*) to the *mundus intelligibilis* (276). Accordingly, he asks if

Heidegger wants to renounce this entire sphere of objectivity, this form of absoluteness that Kant advocated in the ethical and the theoretical, as well as in the *Critique of Judgment*? Does he want to withdraw completely to the finite creature or, if not, where for him is the breakthrough to this sphere? (278)

This passage is revealing in another way as well. It is commonly accepted that neither Cassirer nor Heidegger truly maintains the 'neutral' conception of the power of transcendental imagination, but in the end emphasize its respective spontaneous or receptive moment after all.[16] In *Kant and the Problem of*

---

[15] *DD* 277; translation modified.
[16] Consult, in this regard, Jeffrey Andrew Barash's extensive assessment of Gordon's *Continental Divide* in 'Ernst Cassirer, Martin Heidegger, and the Legacy of Davos'.

Metaphysics, Heidegger indeed advocates the primarily receptive nature of transcendental imagination. Cassirer's writings, on the other hand, time and again emphasize the spontaneous character of symbolic imagination when explaining our capacity to bring forth a variety of cultural expressions. His turn towards Kant's account of pure practical reason would confirm this interest. However, *in Davos*, Heidegger only once suggests that Kant's account of transcendental imagination reveals "a dependency on a receptivity" (280), while Cassirer at no point explicitly favors its spontaneous moment. Furthermore, as we just saw, the Kantian language of receptivity and spontaneity quickly gives way to the broader terms 'finitude' and 'infinity', and their comments on Kant's thought become interlaced with more general claims about the human being or 'Dasein'. Hence, as the Davos debate proceeds, it becomes more and more clear that Kant's philosophy is not really Cassirer and Heidegger's main concern. Cassirer's turn to Kant's ethics does not so much serve a discussion of the correct reading of his oeuvre, as it aims to articulate a view of the human condition as such.

1.2.2   The (In)finite Character of the Human Condition

In line with the general theme of the 1929 *Davoser Hochschulkurse* – 'What is the human being?' – Cassirer's independent lectures address 'the problem of philosophical anthropology'. After a brief historical introduction, he focuses on the two contemporary thinkers whom he considers to represent this problem most sharply: he reflects on Heidegger's accounts of space, language, and death from *Being and Time* in the three lectures prior to their public encounter, and discusses Scheler's thought on the day after. These lectures not only set the stage for the second topic of the Davos debate, the human condition, but as such also motivated the earlier discussion on Kant's thought.

Cassirer's 'Heidegger lectures' follow a clear pattern: they first summarize Heidegger's analyses of the aforementioned issues and then each time conclude that, although we should not reject his position as such, he merely lays down a philosophical problem without indicating a solution to it. Thus, after considering Heidegger's conception of space as "the sphere of what is ready-to-hand, what we are concerned with", Cassirer challenges the primacy of this "pragmatic space" over a symbolic one: "We do not deny this point of departure as such – we only maintain that the anthropological space in which the human being lives, is first captured if one leaves and *overcomes* this point of departure" (*ECN:17* 15). Cassirer, likewise, counters Heidegger's account of 'idle talk' as a "lapse, Fall of man, deficiency" and as an "uprooted mode of understanding existence", asking if the achievement of natural language "is not rather the beginning of all *true spiritual* behavior" (37, 51). With regard to the phenomenon of death, finally, he holds that Heidegger "once again designates only the point of departure, the *terminus a quo* but not the *terminus ad quem*.

Not our fear for death as such, but our overcoming of this fear [. . .] characterizes the Dasein of human beings" (71). In sum, Cassirer challenges the idea that a philosophical anthropology can rest content with the analysis of Dasein developed by *Being and Time*:

We grant Heidegger this 'analysis of worldliness [. . .], but we ask: can we *stick to this beginning* – or is not rather the 'transcendence' beyond it, [. . .] the move from the 'ready-to-hand' towards the 'present-at-hand', the real *problem*? Does the capacity to 'turn towards the idea' not reveal the 'essence' of the human being [. . .] rather than indicating a decline from its original nature? (29)

With these rhetorical questions, Cassirer suggests that Heidegger's existential analytic advocates a view of the human being that deprives it of its characteristic humanity and reduces it to its biological condition.

Cassirer perceives the same structural problem in Heidegger's independent lectures on the *Critique of Pure Reason*. Analogous to the emphasis that *Being and Time* puts on Dasein's temporal nature as the ultimate precondition for its understanding of being, these lectures proclaim that Kant's philosophical project presupposes the finitude of human reason:

To understand the carrying-through of the ground-laying [of metaphysics], it is crucial to make clear that and how the purely *human*, i.e., *finite* reason, alone delimits the sphere of the problematic in advance. To this end, it is necessary to emphasize the essence of finite knowledge in general and the basic character of finitude as such. (*KPM:III* 272)

After summarizing this position, Cassirer concludes that "here the whole problem erupts once again" (*DD* 277). On his view, Heidegger once more manages to pinpoint the crucial philosophical problem but then fails to recognize it as such: rather than denoting Kant's definitive insight, Cassirer holds, the finitude of human reason is merely the problematic starting point that Kant wishes to overcome. He counters that Kant's entire philosophical endeavor precisely aims to show that the finite human reason is nevertheless capable of achieving infinite truths:

For Kant, the problem was precisely this: despite the finitude that he had himself exhibited, how can there nevertheless be necessary and universal truths? How are synthetic, a priori judgments possible – judgments that are not simply finite in their content, but which are necessarily universal? [. . .] How does this finite creature come to a determination of objects that as such are not bound to finitude?[17]

Hence, Cassirer understands the Kantian question 'How are synthetic a priori judgments possible?' as 'How can a finite being nevertheless gain access to the intelligible realm?' As the capacity to synthesize sensible intuitions under the universally valid concepts of the understanding, the power of transcendental

---

[17] *DD* 277–278; translation modified.

imagination plays a crucial role in answering this central question of the first *Critique* – and thus in establishing a transition to the *mundus intelligibilis*. In Kant's practical philosophy, this transition is of course enacted, in a more radical manner, through the moral law, which secures the possibility of a 'kingdom of ends'. Cassirer explains that

> the categorical imperative must exist in such a condition that the law is not valid by chance just for human beings, but for all rational entities in general. Here suddenly is this remarkable transition. The restrictedness to a determinate sphere suddenly falls away. The ethical as such leads beyond the world of appearances. [...] In the ethical a point is reached which is no longer relative to the finitude of the knowing creature. Rather, an absolute has now been set in place. [...] The problem of freedom has been posed in this way, that it breaks through the original sphere. (276)

On Cassirer's view, Kant's account of the moral law then provides the answer to the question: 'How can the sensible human being nevertheless act in a purely rational – and therefore good – manner?' Hence, the lasting insight of Kant's thought, whether in his theoretical or practical philosophy, lies in his attempt to account for the breakthrough to a rational sphere.

As was to be expected, Heidegger is not startled by this rather traditional presentation of Kant's philosophy. During the Davos debate and in *Kant and the Problem of Metaphysics*, he continues to develop an alternative reading of Kant that is more in line with his own existentialist interests. With regard to Kant's theoretical philosophy, Heidegger holds in his independent lectures that "because the intuition of human beings is finite, it requires thinking, which as such is finite through and through" (*KPM:III* 272). On his view, the reliance of the understanding on receptive or finite sensibility significantly downplays its spontaneous character. In the debate with Cassirer, Heidegger therefore argues that the account of transcendental imagination precisely signals the unsurpassable finite nature of the thinking human subject:

> Kant describes the power of imagination of the schematism as *exhibito originara*. But this originality is an *exhibitio*, an *exhibitio* of the presentation of the free self-giving in which lies a dependency upon a receptivity. So in a certain sense this originality is indeed there as creative faculty. As a finite creature, the human being has a certain infinitude in the ontological. But the human being is never infinite and absolute in the creating of the being itself; rather, it is infinite in the sense of the understanding of being. But as Kant says, provided that the ontological understanding of being is only possible within the inner experience of beings, this infinitude of the ontological is bound essentially to ontic experience so that we must say the reverse: this infinitude which breaks out in the power of imagination is precisely the strongest argument for finitude, for ontology is an index of finitude. God does not have it. And the fact that the human being has the *exhibitio* is the strongest argument for its finitude, for only a finite creature requires ontology.[18]

---

[18] *DD* 280; translation modified.

In the same spirit, Heidegger counters Cassirer's assessment of Kant's account of the moral law. On this issue as well, Cassirer and Heidegger demonstrate a clear interest in the same moment of Kant's thought, but nevertheless interpret it in radically diverse ways. Where Cassirer focuses on the purely rational sphere that Kant postulates in order to metaphysically found the possibility of ethical behavior, Heidegger reflects on the existential meaning of the moral law by focusing on Kant's corresponding account of our respect for it. On his view, the human being appears not so much as the author of the moral law but rather 'finds itself under it', experiencing this law as imposed from without. Only from this perspective, Heidegger holds, does it make sense to speak of an imperative: "In the categorical imperative we have something that goes beyond the finite creature. But precisely the concept of the imperative as such shows the inner reference to a finite creature" (279). For Heidegger, Kant's philosophy thus remains a story of the human being's limits even after its turn towards practical reason:

Cassirer wants to show that finitude becomes transcendent in the ethical writings. [But] this transcendence too still remains within the sphere of finitude. [...] We proceed mistakenly in the interpretation of Kantian ethics if we first orient ourselves to that to which ethical action conforms and if we see too little of the inner function of the law itself for Dasein. We cannot discuss the problem of the finitude of the ethical creature if we do not pose the question: what does law mean here, and how is the lawfulness itself constitutive for Dasein and for the personality? (279–280)

Based on these reports about Kant's philosophy, the Davos debate seems to make no progress at all, and one could indeed wonder if Cassirer and Heidegger are not just talking past each other, as Hendrik Pos at one point suggests (287). However, they subsequently also address each other directly, thus rendering the exchange more personal. Cassirer explains that his digression about Kant was necessary because of the following problem: "Heidegger has emphasized that our power of knowledge is finite. It is relative and it is fixed. But then the question arises: how does such a finite creature in general come to have knowledge, to have reason, to have truth?" (277). We have further seen that he wonders, after defending the 'breakthrough' at stake in both Kant's theoretical and practical philosophy, if "Heidegger wants to renounce this entire sphere of objectivity". Heidegger also concludes his interpretation of the moral law with a question: "It is not to be denied that something that goes beyond sensibility lies before the law. But the question is: How is the inner structure of Dasein itself, is it finite or infinite? (280). Later on, he raises two more 'questions for Cassirer': "1. What path does the human being have to infinitude? And what is the manner in which the human being can participate in infinity? 2. Is infinitude to be attained as privative determination of finitude, or is infinitude a region in its own right?" (285). For a significant amount of time, one-third of the debate, Cassirer and Heidegger thus discuss the human condition; more precisely, the question if and how the human being can transcend its finite nature.

We find a first attempt to answer this question in Cassirer's 'Heidegger lectures'. There, Cassirer somewhat vaguely explains that the human being overcomes its finite nature simply by becoming aware of this finitude, and as such taking a certain reflective distance to it. When discussing Heidegger's account of space, he holds that

> it is precisely this phenomenon of '*knowing* the limit' that first arises in the human world. The human being is that being which does not just, like all others, *has* limits, but that arrives at an *awareness* of these limits – that even lays down this limits for itself. For this reason, the human *Lebensraum* is also distinct from every animalistic space. This space has its own specific 'objectivity' in that it is not just lived, but at the same time also 'objectified'. (*ECN:17* 21)

Hence, Cassirer continues, our action radius transforms into a spiritual horizon or 'symbolic space' merely by a change of perspective (23). With regard to the phenomenon of death, he likewise maintains that "the human being is the finite being that *knows* about its finitude and that, through this knowing, overcomes its finitude and becomes aware of its infinity" (73).

During the public debate, Cassirer further specifies what kind of infinity is hereby established. Addressing Heidegger's first question, he explains that when the human being

> transposes everything that is lived experience into some objective shape in which it is objectified [. . .] it does not thereby become radically free from the finitude of the point of departure (for this is still connected to his particular finitude). Rather, while it arises from finitude, it leads finitude out into something new. And that is immanent infinitude. [. . .] The spiritual realm is not a metaphysical spiritual realm; the true spiritual realm is just the spiritual world created from itself. That the human being could create it is the seal of its infinitude. (*DD* 286)

In response to Heidegger's second question, Cassirer adds that such "infinitude does not just constitute an opposition to finitude". Instead, "it is the totality, the fulfillment of finitude itself. [. . .] As finitude goes in all directions, it steps out into infinitude. This is the opposite of privation, it is the perfect filling-out of finitude itself".[19] This 'going out in all directions' assumedly refers to the variety of cultural expressions through which the human being constitutes its particular 'symbolic universe'. The philosophy of symbolic forms elaborates on these different ways of establishing a breakthrough to an objective realm in the cultural domains of myth, art, language, science, etc. At one point, Cassirer's 'Heidegger lectures' indeed hold that "the medium that leads us from the world of mere ready-to-hand to that of presence-at-hand, from mere

---

[19] *DD* 286; translation modified.

'equipment' to real 'objectivity'" is generally speaking "the world of symbolic forms" (*ECN:17* 33). Cassirer maintains this transcendental viewpoint during the debate with Heidegger, when he claims that the 'path to infinitude' can take us "no way other than through the medium of form" (*DD* 286). He therefore posits that the human being must possess a 'metabasis' – the power of symbolic imagination – that "leads it from the immediacy of its existence into the region of pure form".

Cassirer's 'Scheler lecture', finally, explains the breakthrough to an infinite sphere in yet another, more anthropological, manner. For one, Cassirer here repeats that

> language and art, myth and theoretical knowledge [...] all contribute, each according to its own constitutive laws, to this process of the spiritual distantiation: they are the important stages on the road that leads from the space of labor, in which the animal lives and to which it is condemned, to the space of perception and thought, or to a spiritual 'horizon'. (*ECW:17* 200)

He further describes the capacity to mediate between ourselves and our environment as the *differentia specifica* of the human species. While animal behaviour can be explained according to a stimulus–response model, human behaviour is uniquely marked by the capacity to take a distance from the world (197), see the possible in the real (198), or ask questions (203). The resulting "intermediate realm of symbolic forms in between the human being and reality" (200) indicates our spontaneity or freedom. Cassirer would develop this way of explaining the *Sonderstatus* of the human being in his late lectures on anthropology and in *An Essay on Man* (1944).

Heidegger could not respond to these final thoughts, which Cassirer uttered after their public debate. He does, however, object to Cassirer's initial claim that the human being reaches a certain infinity by becoming aware of its own finitude: "It does not say much [to] simply formally argue: as soon as I make assertions about the finite and as soon as I want to determine the finite as finite, I must already have an idea of infinitude" (*DD* 280). In contrast to this 'formal' conception of infinity, he proposes an existentialist conception of transcendence, thereby explicitly addressing Cassirer's question about the infinity that is reached by attaining truth. Heidegger distinguishes between a rational notion of truth as validity – which he ascribes to Cassirer – and the phenomenological idea of being-delivered-to being. Echoing *Being and Time*, he thus argues that, more fundamental than the phenomenon of truth as correspondence, the "trans-subjectivity of truth, the breaking-out of the truth concerning the particulars themselves, as being-in-truth, already means to be at the mercy of the being itself" (281–282). On this basis, Heidegger develops an alternative idea of transcendence that does not point towards a purely intelligible realm, but is rather grounded in time itself.

We can conclude from this that, even while Cassirer and Heidegger continue to discuss Kant's philosophy, the Davos debate in fact revolves around the issue of the infinite or finite character of the human condition as such. Here as well, Cassirer and Heidegger may seem to meet each other halfway in so far as they revert to terms like 'immanent infinitude' and 'inner transcendence of time itself', yet it is clear that they interpret the human being's 'finite infinitude' in radically different manners. In fact, Heidegger remarks that Cassirer seems to have completely misunderstood "the proper kernel of intent" of *Being and Time* (284). He admits that, if one simply takes this work as a treatise on the human condition and subsequently inquires how this work explains our capacity to bring forth culture, his *magnum opus* would indeed have little to offer. However, he holds, such a question is completely "inadequate with respect to my central problem". What interests Heidegger is "not a philosophical anthropology", but "a metaphysics of Dasein that has the ground for its determination in the problem of winning the foundation for the problem of the possibility of metaphysics". To this goal, his existential analytic aims to demonstrate the temporality of Dasein, and Heidegger stresses that it is only within this context that his analyses of death and anxiety can be understood (283). In this way, Cassirer and Heidegger's discussion about the human condition also appears to be motivated by an even broader issue of contention, namely the task of philosophy. As Heidegger puts it, "the question of what the human being is must be answered not so much in the sense of an anthropological system, but instead it must first be properly clarified with regard to the perspective from within which it wants to be posed" (288).

1.2.3   The Davos Debate as a Dispute on the Task of Philosophy

In the end, Cassirer and Heidegger's disagreement about the finite or infinite human condition reveals a fundamental difference between their philosophical attitudes: while Heidegger sets out to show the true depth of certain philosophical problems, Cassirer searches for ways to solve and overcome them. This becomes especially clear in relation to the issue of anxiety. Picking up on Cassirer's lectures, Heidegger raised one more question to Cassirer: "3. To what extent does philosophy have as its task to let become free from anxiety? Does it not rather have as its task to surrender the human being, even radically, to anxiety?"[20]

As Cassirer's lectures imply, he considers it the task of philosophy to help us overcome the boundaries that are set by nature, be they of a physical (spatial or temporal), communicative, or psychological kind. Cassirer thus views

---

[20] *DD* 286; translation modified.

anxiety as a biological phenomenon that we, as rational beings, can and must surpass: 'Philosophy should allow the human being to become as free as he possibly could. In so far as it does this, I believe that it in any case frees the human being in a certain radical sense from anxiety as a mere mood'.[21] For Heidegger, by contrast, the *raison d'être* of philosophy is not to change our natural condition, but to help us come to terms with the peculiar finitude of our Dasein: "This setting-free of the Dasein in the human being must be the sole and central thing that philosophy can perform" (285). On Heidegger's view, our anxiety is not a psychological state, but one of the most radical expressions of our ontological attunement to being. Philosophy, he holds, should aim to further radicalize this transcendence of Dasein:

The freeing of the inner transcendence of Dasein is the fundamental character of philosophizing itself. [The] authentic sense of this freeing is not to be found in becoming free to a certain extent for the forming images of consciousness and for the realm of form. Rather, it is to be found in becoming free for the finitude of Dasein. (289)

Hence, whereas Cassirer maintains that philosophy should aim to free us *from* anxiety, for Heidegger it must attempt to free us *for* it. In other words, while Cassirer considers it the task of philosophy to enlighten the human being in the sense of liberating it through its own power of reason, Heidegger argues that philosophy can only have reconcile us with our ineradicable shortcomings. One could call this a 'therapeutic' function of philosophy, if this is understood in the psychoanalytic sense, and not as bearing affinity with Wittgenstein's notion of philosophy as therapy.

Heidegger confirms that he and Cassirer look at the human being's (in)finite nature from two opposed perspectives, or that they take an interest in the human condition for entirely different reasons. He sketches this difference in the following way:

In the first lecture, Cassirer used the expressions *terminus a quo* and *terminus ad quem*. One could say that for Cassirer the *terminus ad quem* is the whole of a philosophy of culture in the sense of an elucidation of the wholeness of the forms of the shaping consciousness. For Cassirer, the *terminus a quo* is utterly problematical. My position is the reverse: The *terminus a quo* is my central problematic, the one I develop. The question is: Is the *terminus ad quem* as clear for me? For me, this occurs not in the whole of a philosophy of culture, but rather in the question: what in general is called being? For me, it was from this question that the problematic of a metaphysics of Dasein arose. (288)

According to this picture, the goal of Cassirer's philosophy is to explain the objective sphere of cultural meaning, while its starting point or basic assumption is a conception of the human being as a 'rational animal'. Heidegger finds

---

[21] *DD* 287; translation modified.

this conception problematic, however, because he considers it "not at all self-evident to start from a concept of *logos*" (288). Although his own philosophical project also starts from the human being, for him it lies "in the essence of philosophy itself that it has a *terminus a quo* that must be made into a problem" (289). Hence, Heidegger conceives this starting point in a completely different manner as 'the Dasein in the human being'. As such, it must first be unearthed by means of an existential analytic or 'metaphysics of Dasein', the famous 'preliminary investigation' in Heidegger's retrieval of the meaning of being that ended up being the central topic of *Being and Time*. Only on this basis, he explains, can we strive towards the goal of philosophy, namely "to win a foundation for the basic problem of metaphysics" (285, 288).

This means that Heidegger conceives of his ground-laying of metaphysics as more than just an alternative project to Cassirer's philosophy of culture. In his independent lectures, he asserts the priority of his own endeavor: "A metaphysics of Dasein directed at the possibility of metaphysics as such, [poses] the question concerning the essence of human beings in a way that is prior to all philosophical anthropology and cultural philosophy" (*KPM:III* 273). During the public debate, he further holds that their projects are mutually exclusive: if one were to start from Cassirer's philosophy, there would be no way to ever arrive at 'the central question of philosophy' (*DD* 290). On this basis, Heidegger in the end calls Cassirer's philosophy of culture 'shallow' (*faul*) because it deals with a mere surface phenomenon of human existence: its *Geist* rather than its Dasein (289). True philosophy, he holds, "has the task of throwing man back, so to speak, into the hardness of his fate, from the shallow aspect of a man who merely uses the work of the spirit" (291). This fate is not found in our cultural life, but in those rare, limit experiences in which we truly face – rather than just reflect upon – the finitude of our Dasein, like anxiety or the advent of our death:

The highest form of the existence of Dasein is only allowed to lead back to very few and rare glimpses of Dasein's duration between living and death. [It is] so accidental that man exists only in very few glimpses of the pinnacle of his own possibility, but otherwise moves in the midst of his beings. (290)

Cassirer's comeback may not be as sharp, but is meant as an equally devastating critique: it implies that the *terminus ad quem* of Heidegger's philosophy is a completely outdated conception of being. The philosophy of symbolic forms sets out to continue the critical message of Kant's philosophy by implementing the 'Copernican revolution' in all cultural domains alike (294). Cassirer's entire thought relies, then, on the conviction that being can no longer be thought of as something that persists independently from us. Instead, it is the product of our symbolic understanding of the world: "Being in ancient metaphysics was substance, what forms a ground. Being in the new metaphysics is, in my language, no longer the being of a substance, but rather the being that starts from a variety of functional determinations and meanings" (294). Hence, when Heidegger holds that "the problematic of the metaphysics of Dasein arose from the question what in general is called being?", Cassirer views this as a retreat to traditional, pre-critical, metaphysics. Whereas Heidegger rejected Cassirer's overly rationalistic conception of the human being, Cassirer now dismisses Heidegger's idea that the human condition must be examined on the basis of a pre-given idea of 'being in general'. For Cassirer, only the human subject determines what being is – in various forms – and not also the other way around. In retrospect, these different conceptions of being may explain Cassirer and Heidegger's disagreement on the respective epistemological or ontological nature of Kant's thought. More importantly, however, these conceptions also guide their entire philosophical enterprises: Cassirer holds that here lies "the essential point that distinguishes my position from Heidegger's".

With this impasse, the Davos debate inevitably comes to an end. While Cassirer and Heidegger initially seemed to find some common ground with regard to Kant's account of transcendental imagination, and soon engaged in a lively discussion on the predominant character of the human condition, their final takes on the task of philosophy reveal two irreconcilable philosophical interests. At this point, according to Cassirer the discussion with Heidegger has in fact surpassed the level of logical argumentation:

I believe that where the disagreement lies has already become clearer. It is not fruitful, however, to highlight this disagreement again and again. We maintain a position where little is to be accomplished through arguments that are merely logical. Nobody can be compelled to take up this position, and no such purely logical compulsion can force someone to begin with the position that appears to me to be the essential one. (292)

Yet, Cassirer also holds that in light of such fundamental difference in viewpoint, one should still try to "see not only oneself but the other as well". The only way to do this is, however, through the shared media of science (293), art (295), and especially language. In this way, Cassirer reaffirms the validity of his philosophy of symbolic forms as the only way to overcome the relativism of individual standpoints:

Each of us speaks his own language, and it is unthinkable that the language of one of us is carried over into the language of the other. And yet, we understand ourselves through the medium of language. Hence, there is something like *the* language. And hence there is something like a unity that is higher than the infinitude of the various ways of speaking. Therein lies what is for me the decisive point. And it is for that reason that I start from the objectivity of the symbolic form. (292–293)

Heidegger, in turn, affirms that "authentic activity takes place only where there is opposition" (291), and that "mere mediating will never amount to anything productive" (295). Concluding the debate, he subsequently addresses the audience directly, asking each member to "not orient yourselves to the variety of positions of philosophizing human beings, and not occupy yourselves with Cassirer and Heidegger" (296). Instead, he expresses the hope that "you have felt that we are on the way toward once again getting down to business with the central question of metaphysics". Heidegger thus invites everyone to assess the philosophical confrontation with Cassirer solely on the basis of how well it answered the question of being as such. In this way, the Davos debate results in a complete deadlock.

1.3   The Cassirer–Heidegger Dispute: An Echo of the Davos Debate

This reading of the Davos debate as a philosophical, coherent debate – despite its occasional hiccups – is corroborated by the development of the entire Cassirer–Heidegger dispute. Most importantly, the three key themes of Cassirer and Heidegger's public debate – Kant's thought, the human condition, and the task of philosophy – also structure, in more or less the same order, the other moments of this decade-long dispute. Furthermore, the overall conversation likewise quickly abandons initial suggestions of philosophical agreement to evolve into an unsurpassable conflict.

1.3.1   Before Davos: Heidegger's First Criticism (1923–1928)

Based on a footnote in *Being and Time*, we can trace back the relationship between Cassirer and Heidegger to 1923:

> In a conversation that I was able to have with Cassirer on the occasion of a lecture before the Hamburg section of the *Kantgesellschaft* in December 1923 on 'Tasks and Pathways of Phenomenological Research', it was already apparent that we agreed in demanding an existential analytic such as it was sketched in that lecture. (*BT* 51)

This remark gives the impression that Heidegger held Cassirer in high regard prior to the Davos debate. For one, it looks like he considered it beneficial to the reception of *Being and Time*, the monograph that was meant to cement his fame, to mention an endorsement by Cassirer. More importantly, he here also expresses his appreciation for the second volume of the *Philosophy of Symbolic Forms* (1925), which Cassirer dedicated to mythical thinking or, as Heidegger takes it, to "the mythical Dasein". Heidegger supports Cassirer's efforts in this work to show the philosophical importance of ethnology, and applauds his phenomenological approach to the mythical human being. However, he also expresses a concern about Cassirer's reliance on the architectonics of Kant's philosophy, a framework that he does not deem fit for this task.[22]

---

[22] In an unpublished letter to Karl Löwith from 30 June 1925, Heidegger makes the same assessment of Cassirer's account of mythical thinking: "The same schema as in Volume I,

Heidegger voices the same appreciation *and* critical reservation in his 1928 review of Cassirer's volume on mythology. After summarizing Cassirer's account of 'mythical thinking', he proposes three ways to assess it:

> Our approach to the philosophy of myth outlined here must pursue three points. First, it must be asked: What does this interpretation achieve for the grounding and guiding of the positive sciences of mythical Dasein (ethnology and the history of religion)? Then it becomes necessary to examine the foundations and methodological principles that support the philosophical analysis of the essence of myth. And finally, the basic question arises concerning the constitutive function of myth in human Dasein and in the totality of beings as such. (*KPM:II* 264)

In light of the first criterion, Heidegger positively values Cassirer's research: his earlier summary already emphasized that Cassirer successfully establishes mythical thinking as "an original possibility of human Dasein that has its own proper truth" (255). In so far as the immediate, concrete, and praxis-oriented *Lebensform* of the mythical worldview resembles Dasein's primordial way of 'being-in-the-world', Heidegger even implies that the second volume of the *Philosophy of Symbolic Forms* considers "the elementary Dasein-relations of the human to its world" (262) that are also the topic of *Being and Time*. He therefore concludes that Cassirer's account of mythical thinking provides a 'secure guideline' for "the initial appropriation and interpretation of newly discovered material as well as for the elaboration and exploration of already established results" in the field of ethnology (264).

Heidegger is less enthusiastic about the second criterion: he questions whether "the predetermination of myth as a functional form of creative consciousness [is] adequately grounded on its own terms", where "the foundations for such an admittedly unavoidable grounding [are] to be found", and whether these foundations are "themselves sufficiently secured and elaborated" (264–265). Cassirer clearly relies on Kant's 'Copernican revolution' for this, arguing that "all 'reality' is to be considered as a formation of productive consciousness" (265). However, according to Heidegger it is unclear what this means, since Cassirer alternatively describes this consciousness as 'life', 'spirit', and 'reason'. Before any attempt to broaden Kant's critical approach to other domains of culture, Cassirer should thus have first clarified the nature of his starting point: on Heidegger's account, "the interpretation of the essence of myth as a possibility of human Dasein remains random and directionless as

---

although probably a bit better – I could only read it diagonally. Cassirer especially fails when it comes to the positive analysis of the primary phenomena, and he perceives everything that he considers, which is often not little, from the high ground of Kant's concepts". In his 1927 address on the history of Marburg Neo-Kantianism, Heidegger however distinguishes, albeit without any further explanation, between Natorp's interest "in the universal categorial founding of a system" and Cassirer's search for "the concrete interpretation of the individual 'symbols' of spirit" (*KPM:VI* 310).

long as it cannot be grounded in a radical ontology of Dasein in light of the problem of being in general" (265).

As a consequence, Cassirer's account of mythical thinking entirely fails to meet Heidegger's third criterion, which concerns the pathway to an account of 'the totality of beings as such'. Since Heidegger exclusively locates this passage in an existential analytic of Dasein, he regrets Cassirer's focus on consciousness, whether understood as reason or spirit: "The preoccupation with the Neo-Kantian problem of consciousness is of such little help that it actually prevents gaining a grasp on the central problem" (266). At the end of his review, Heidegger adds that it make no difference if Cassirer conceives of consciousness in an encompassing manner: what we need is not that "*all* 'symbolic forms' are presented, but rather above all [that] also the basic concepts of this system are thoroughly elaborated and brought back to their ultimate foundations". As long as the finite or temporal nature of the human being is not properly addressed, "even such a rich presentation of the phenomena of spirit is not yet philosophy itself" (269–270). Ultimately, Heidegger concludes with a backhanded compliment: he holds that Cassirer's work on mythical thought remains "a valuable starting point for a renewed philosophy of myth, even if it is not joined to his philosophy of symbolic forms" (270).

In this concluding assessment, Heidegger does identify Cassirer as a Neo-Kantian:

An orientation guided by the phenomenon of the transcendental power of imagination, and its ontological function within the *Critique of Pure Reason* and the *Critique of Judgment*, an orientation that admittedly would lie far from Neo-Kantianism, could have at least made it clear that an interpretation of the mythical understanding of being is much more labyrinthine and abysmal than is suggested by Cassirer's presentation. (269)

Heidegger does not yet explain his own interest in Kant's account of transcendental imagination here, but this remark may have motivated Cassirer to emphasize their shared appreciation for this account during the Davos debate. In any case, Heidegger's review of the second volume of *The Philosophy of Symbolic Forms* critiques Cassirer's view of the mythical human condition by criticizing his understanding of Kant. Furthermore, this critique is based on a specific understanding of the ultimate task of philosophy.

1.3.2   *After Davos: Cassirer's Comeback (1929–1946)*

After the Davos debate, Heidegger seems no longer concerned about how his philosophy relates to Cassirer's. This may be because he no longer desired Cassirer's support, no longer valued his thought, or simply because his own philosophical interests shifted from the early 1930s on. Either way, *Kant and the Problem of Metaphysics* never refers to Cassirer,[23] and Heidegger abandoned his initial plan to review the third volume of the *Philosophy of Symbolic Forms* (1929), allegedly because he could not relate it to his own inquiries.[24] One exception to this silence is Heidegger's 1929–1930 lecture course *The Fundamental Concepts of Metaphysics*, which however only repeat his earlier critique of Cassirer's philosophy of culture. Heidegger here remarks that "it is a widespread opinion today that both culture and the human being can only be properly and philosophically comprehended through the idea of expression or symbol. We have today a philosophy of culture concerned with expression, with symbol, with symbolic forms" (*FCM* 113). As before, he expresses his doubts whether the understanding of the human being as a spirit that comes to expression in forms, is an essential one that "concerns and grips his Dasein". There is a fundamental difference, Heidegger explains, "between setting out our spiritual situation and awakening a fundamental attunement" (114), the latter being the central topic of his 1929–1930 lectures.

Cassirer, in the meantime, added four footnotes on Heidegger's investigations into the nature of space and time from *Being and Time* to said volume of *The Philosophy of Symbolic Forms: The Phenomenology of Knowledge*.[25] The message of these notes is each time the same: although 'sharp' and 'profound', Heidegger's accounts of space and time as something that is lived, rather than intellectually grasped, have no affinity with the central concern of the philosophy of symbolic forms, which Cassirer here describes as the transition "from the meaning of existence to the objective meaning of the 'logos'" (*PSF:III* 163). Cassirer does not hold that his and Heidegger's views of space and time should be perceived as mutually exclusive, but rather that Heidegger halts where his own thought begins:

What distinguishes our own undertaking from that of Heidegger is above all that it does not stop at this stage of the at-hand and its mode of spatiality, but without challenging Heidegger's position goes beyond it; for we wish to follow the road leading from spatiality as a factor in the at-hand to space as the form of existence, and furthermore to show how this road leads right through the domain of symbolic formation. (149)

In Chapter 2, we find the same assessment of Heidegger's conception of time:

The Philosophy of Symbolic Forms does not question the temporality that Heidegger elaborates as the original *Seinsinn des Daseins*. But our inquiry begins *beyond* this sphere, at precisely the point where a transition is effected from this existential

---

[23] While Heidegger's 1927–1928 lectures *Phenomenological Interpretation of Kant's 'Critique of Pure Reason'* repeatedly contrast his phenomenological reading of Kant's magnum opus to the then dominant 'epistemological' one promoted by the Neo-Kantians, in *Kant and the Problem of Metaphysics* (1929), even these references to Cassirer's philosophical kin are left out, indicating that Heidegger had entirely moved on from the conversation with Cassirer.
[24] Toni Cassirer, *Mein Leben mit Ernst Cassirer*, 189.   [25] *PSF:III* 149, 163, 173, 189.

temporality to the *form* of time. It aspires to show the conditions under which this form is possible, the conditions for the postulation of a 'being' that goes beyond the existentiality of 'being-there'.[26]

Hence, Cassirer's criticism of Heidegger also remains the same after their public encounter.

Moreover, Cassirer once again applies the same critique to Heidegger's interpretation of Kant. His 1931 review of *Kant and the Problem of Metaphysics* immediately states that the central issue of this interpretation is in fact the human condition: "Heidegger designates the problem of the *finitude* of human cognition as the central theme of Kant 'critique of reason'" (*KPMR* 226). In particular, Cassirer explains, Heidegger interprets both the reliance of the understanding on receptive sensibility and the failure of pure reason to answer its own metaphysical questions as indicative of the finitude of human reason (7). The distinction between these faculties, as well as between the Transcendental Aesthetic and Transcendental Logic, is on this account merely pedagogical, since in truth the power of the imagination is their common source. Concluding his summary of the 'Kant book', Cassirer therefore holds that this power forms "the actual constitutive center of the *Critique of Pure Reason*", and that "the proof of the basic relations [between the faculties] constitutes the chief task and the actual core of Heidegger's analysis" (8).

Like in Davos, Cassirer decides to abstain from any polemical discussions about the merits of Neo-Kantianism and Hermann Cohen in particular, but instead assesses the "systematical truthfulness" of Heidegger's reading of Kant.[27] Once again, he commences by endorsing Heidegger's emphasis on the power of imagination:

I myself can, at *this* point, only express my complete consent and principle agreement with Heidegger's interpretation, since the doctrine of the 'productive power of imagination' plainly appears – albeit from a completely different systematic viewpoint – as a simply indispensable and continuously fruitful motive of Kant's teachings and of 'critical philosophy' as a whole. (8–9)

---

[26] *PSF:III* 163. Remarkably, Cassirer subsequently suggests that the postponed second and third parts of *Being and Time* may move on to the sphere of symbolic forms: "Here I shall not attempt a detailed critical discussion of this analysis. Such a discussion will be possible and fruitful only when Heidegger's work is available as a whole. For the basic problem of the 'Philosophy of Symbolic Forms' lies precisely in that territory which Heidegger expressly and intentionally excluded from the first volume of his book". Obviously, neither *Being and Time* nor *Kant and the Problem of Metaphysics*, which partly undertakes the destruction of the history of ontology that was planned for part two of *Being and Time*, gives any suggestions in this direction.

[27] *KPMR* 225. Heidegger's scattered notes on Cassirer's review of *Kant and the Problem of Metaphysics* thereupon hold that Cassirer gets lost in the letter of Kant's texts (*KPM:V* 300). Heidegger here also continues to argue that Cassirer misjudges the role of the understanding in Kant's theoretical philosophy (299–300).

However, even though he further agrees with Heidegger that human reason does not create objects, Cassirer also once more rejects the view that this implies the finitude of our cognition. Kant's critical philosophy, he holds, was after all never concerned with the origin of objects, but only with our mode of understanding objectivity as such (9). In this light, the understanding does "possess a thoroughly creative character within the realm of experience": it is a synthetic and constructive capacity that serves sensibility not by following it but by subsuming and therefore guiding it (10). Cassirer concludes, then, that

the portrayal of the understanding as a 'finite' power of cognition concerns only *one* moment of its usage. [...] The understanding may be finite insofar as it never grasps absolute objects, let alone that it creatively produces these objects from itself – but it is 'infinite' insofar as the 'absolute totality in the synthesis of conditions' belongs to its actual and essential task. (12)

On Cassirer's view, the understanding not only relates to finite sensibility through the power of imagination, but also partakes in the realm of infinity through its equally essential relation to pure theoretical reason, which has no direct relation to intuitions and reaches for the unconditioned. The case is then also clear with regard to the latter faculty: in theoretical reason "the spell of mere 'receptivity' is at last broken". The same goes, a fortiori, for Kant's practical philosophy, "for with the unconditional character of the idea of freedom, the move towards the purely intelligible, the extrasensory, and the eternal is henceforth definitively made" (13). As we have seen, Heidegger finds another sign of reason's finitude in the reliance of the moral law on a feeling of respect. Cassirer now rejects this reading of the second *Critique* by claiming that "the moral law is not at all *grounded* in the feeling of respect, and the meaning of the former is not constituted by the latter. Rather, this feeling merely indicates the way in which the law, which is unconditioned, is *represented* in empirical, finite, consciousness" (14–15). In this way, he reaffirms the infinite character of the moral law.

What is at stake here is Cassirer's renewed rejection of Heidegger's 'monism of the power of the imagination' (16), that is, of the idea that all faculties of reason relate to and derive from this power. This view, he explains, does no justice to either the letter or the spirit of Kant's thought. For one, the role of transcendental imagination is clearly limited to the topic of the Transcendental Analytic:

I am the last person to deny or diminish the systematic meaning and importance of the schematism chapter [...] However, the schematism and the doctrine of 'transcendental imagination' may be at the center of Kant's *Analytic*, but are not the focal point of Kant's *system*. This system is only fixed and completed in the Transcendental Dialectic – and further in the *Critique of Practical Reason* and in the *Critique of Judgement*. (17–18)

Most importantly, Heidegger's 'monism' also overlooks the crucial Kantian distinctions between 'phenomenal' and 'noumenal', 'is' and 'ought', experience and idea, and psychology and ethics: it denies, in other words, Kant's 'radical dualism of the sensible (*mundus sensibilis*) and intelligible (*mundus intelligibilis*) world' (14, 16). According to Cassirer, while Kant is interested in our access to the latter, Heidegger's conception of Dasein remains caught in the former: "Kant's 'doctrine of human beings' [places] human beings from the outset under the 'idea of humanity', and consider them from the viewpoint of this idea. Its true goal is not the Dasein of the human being, but its 'intelligible substrate of humanity'" (18).

Hence, following Cassirer, Heidegger oddly enough reads an ontological message in the one part of Kant's thought that is not concerned with metaphysics. It is indeed remarkable how Cassirer locates the metaphysical core of Kant's philosophy in his theoretical and especially practical accounts of the traditional objects of *metaphysica specialis*: the ideas of world, freedom, and God, while Heidegger situates it in the 'Transcendental Analytic', which reconsiders the possibility of general ontology or *metaphysica generalis*. Moreover, Heidegger is said to focus on an element of the first *Critique* that deals with the problem of objectivity rather than subjectivity:

Kant's doctrine of the schematism and transcendental imagination [. . .] is not a part of the Kantian metaphysics, but a true and necessary moment of his *theory of experience*. It does not immediately and originally deal with the Dasein of the human being, but with the constitution, status, and conditions of empirical objects. (18, 19)

On this basis, Cassirer concludes that Heidegger's "entire problematic of the temporality of subjectivity [. . .] is not just factually, but principally foreign" to Kant's thought (19). Although he does not reject Heidegger's approach outright, he nevertheless firmly holds that it may not be presented as delivering Kant's actual intentions.[28]

The second, much shorter, part of Cassirer's review of the 'Kant book' further addresses the issue of Heidegger's style of interpretation. An outstanding feature of Heidegger's writings on Kant is that they deliberately attempt to 'understand Kant better than he himself did': based on the differences between the 1781 'A-edition' and 1787 'B-edition' of the *Critique of Pure Reason*, they claim that Kant initially grasped the significance of transcendental imagination, but later recoiled from his groundbreaking insights (20). Cassirer not only denies such inconsistency in Kant's writings (21–23), but

---

[28] *KPMR* 239: "'From the point of view of his fundamental ontology, Heidegger had the right to *question* this dualism – but he should not have denied and repudiated it'". In other words, Cassirer accuses Heidegger of not approaching the first *Critique* as an objective commentator, but as its 'usurper' (240).

he also deplores Heidegger's usage of a "subjective and psychological", rather than an "objective and systematic", criterion for assessing Kant's thought (21). As he sees it, this approach allows Heidegger to shroud "all of Kant's concepts [. . .] from the outset in an altered spiritual *atmosphere*" that bears no witness to his particular style of Enlightenment thinking: what Kant is after is the 'light of reason', not the 'abyss of human Dasein' (24). In a concluding remark that resembles that of Heidegger's earlier review, Cassirer thus thanks Heidegger for clarifying "the 'event' of Kant's foundation of philosophy", but regrets that he failed to recognize the bigger picture of Kant's transcendental idealism (25).

Cassirer's final concerns about Heidegger's thought correspond to the ultimate topic of the Davos debate. In "'Geist' and 'Life': Heidegger', scattered notes that are gathered in *The Metaphysics of Symbolic Forms*, Cassirer basically repeats his 'Heidegger lectures', but frames his critique in light of the task of philosophy.[29] He begins by stating that Heidegger "comes from the philosophy of religion", and that this background determined the existential analytic: "For him all temporality [is] seen in a religious sense – for it is constituted through 'care' and through the basic religious phenomenon of death – and anxiety" (*PSF:IV* 201). Repeatedly comparing Heidegger to Kierkegaard and Luther, and emphasizing his view of inauthenticity as a 'Fall' as well as his insistence on the individual person, Cassirer leaves little doubt about where the fundamental difference between their thought lies: "This religious attitude toward death that reduces life as a whole to anxiety and dissolves it into care it not the only one possible – nor is it the authentically philosophical one" (207). Although we must take into account that Cassirer never published this assessment, we cannot ignore its implications: by identifying Heidegger as a religious thinker, he actually excludes the possibility of a philosophical conversation.

After his forced emigration from Germany, Cassirer turns to the specifically ethical task of philosophy. His final monograph, *The Myth of the State* (1946), discusses an age-old struggle between politics and persisting elements of mythical thinking.[30] According to Cassirer, these elements recur in a most dramatic form in National Socialism, partly thanks to the new technological means to advertise them. In light of this situation, Cassirer considers it the task of the philosopher to sabotage the successful but illegitimate merging of the symbolic forms of myth, politics, and technology, and to soothe the ancient fears that it arouses and thrives upon. He admits that this will require the

---

[29] See *PSF:IV* 202 on language, 203–204 on anxiety, 206 on eternal truths, and 208 on death.
[30] Cassirer introduces the ethical vocation of the philosophy of symbolic forms in 'The Problem of Jean-Jacques Rousseau', a lecture in Freiburg in 1932 that Heidegger organized and attended – the last time they met each other (*ECW:18* 3–82).

"intellectual and moral courage [. . .] to think beyond and against [one's] time" (*MS* 296).

Over against this active, Enlightening conception of the task of philosophy, Cassirer posits what I have called Heidegger's 'therapeutic idea of philosophy', according to which 'we can try to understand, but not change, the historical conditions of our existence' (293). Although Heidegger's thought may have no "direct bearing on the development of political ideas in Germany", according to Cassirer it has been a tacit ally in the downfall of European culture: by giving up "all hopes of an active share in the construction and reconstruction of our cultural life, such philosophy renounces its own fundamental theoretical and ethical ideals and becomes a pliable instrument in the hands of the political leaders".[31] Hence, by the end of his life Cassirer regards Heidegger's thought as a failure to think truly philosophical *and* as danger to human culture.

The Cassirer–Heidegger dispute thus echoes both the content and the structure of the Davos debate. The remainder of this book will augment the stakes of the Davos debate even further by showing that its key issues – Kant, the human condition, and the task of philosophy – do not merely propel Cassirer and the early Heidegger's direct engagement with each other, but also animate their respective philosophical projects.

---

[31] *MS* 293; translation modified.

Part I

The Lasting Meaning of Kant's Thought

2   Cassirer's Transformation of the Critique of Reason into a Critique of Culture

Although Cassirer is one of the most eclectic philosophers of the twentieth century, it is safe to say that his allegiance lies first and foremost with Kant and the project of transcendental philosophy.[1] In his own words, Cassirer's philosophy of symbolic forms develops 'the critique of reason into a critique of

---

[1] "The approach of the philosophy of symbolic forms [...] goes back to Kant's 'critical' question, but it gives it a broader content" (*PSF:IV* 165, 189). See also Cassirer's "Was ist 'Subjektivismus'?": "I myself have often been characterized as a 'Neo-Kantian', and I accept this label in this regard, that my entire work in the domain of theoretical philosophy presupposes the methodological foundation that Kant established in the *Critique of Pure Reason*" (*ECW:22* 169). Accordingly, even when scholars questioned Cassirer's debt to his Neo-Kantian teachers Cohen and Natorp, his Kantian inspiration remained uncontested, and even emphasized (Recki, *Cassirer*, 94–99). While being one of the first scholars to defend the enduring relevance of Cassirer's philosophy in a long time, Krois also supported the reasons for the falling out of grace of Neo-Kantianism some decades earlier, for example, its focus on epistemology and reputation as solipsistic subject-philosophy (John Michael Krois, *Cassirer: Symbolic Forms and History*, New Haven: Yale University Press, 1987, 42, 115; 'Aufklärung und Metaphysik. Zur Philosophie Cassirers und der Davoser Debatte mit Heidegger', *Internationale Zeitschrift für Philosophie*, Heft 2, 1992, 274, 280; and 'Cassirer, Neo-Kantianism and Metaphysics', in: *Revue de métaphysique et de morale*, 97/4, 1992, 453). Krois' emphasis on Cassirer's disagreements with Neo-Kantianism on these issues led a number of other influential scholars to isolate the latter's position from Cohen and Natorp's (Gunther Figal und Enno Rudolph, 'Editorial', in: *Internationale Zeitschrift für Philosophie*, Heft 2, 1992, 164; Heinz Paetzold, *Die Realität der symbolischen Formen. Die Kulturphilosophie Ernst Cassirers im Kontext*, Darmstadt: Wissenschaftliche Buchgesellschaft, 1994, 97). Cassirer, however, always acknowledged their lasting influence on his thought (*KLT* 3; *DD* 275; 'Beiträge zu: Hermann Cohen. Schriften zur Philosophie und Zeitgeschichte', *ECW:17* 290; 'Beiträge für die Encyclopedia Britannica', *ECW:17* 308; *Determinismus and Indeterminismus*, *ECW:19* 6–7; and "Was ist 'Subjektivismus'?", *ECW:22* 169). Even Donald Phillip Verene, who stresses the Hegelian elements in Cassirer's philosophy and thereby bypasses the role of the Marburg Neo-Kantians in its conception, acknowledges Cassirer's kinship to Kant ('Kant, Hegel, and Cassirer: The Origins of the Philosophy of Symbolic Forms', in: *Journal of the History of Ideas*, 30/1, 1969, 33–46; and 'Introduction', in: *Symbol, Myth, and Culture. Essays and Lectures of Ernst Cassirer 1935–1945*, New Haven: Yale University Press, 1979, 6). Especially his monograph *The Origins of the Philosophy of Symbolic Forms. Kant, Hegel, and Cassirer* defends a well-balanced view on the Kantian and Hegelian elements in Cassirer's philosophy (Evanston: Northwestern University Press, 2011, xvii, 47–48, 59). Today, however, most commentators accept the decisive influence of Neo-Kantianism on Cassirer (Massimo Ferrari, *Ernst Cassirer. Stationen einer philosophischen Biographie. Von der Marburger Schule zur Kulturtheorie*, tr. by Marion Lauschke, Hamburg: Meiner, 2003, 7–14; Friedman, *A Parting of the Ways*, 25–37; Gordon,

culture' (*PSF:I* 80). Nevertheless, the steadily growing community of Cassirer scholars still seems puzzled about the way that the symbol, the most famous concept of his philosophy, relates to Kant: it is often regarded as a simple modification of Kant's categories of the understanding, but also frequently as echoing both the categories and the schemata produced by the imagination indiscriminately.[2] This overlooks the significant differences between Cassirer's idea of a symbol and these key notions from the *Critique of Pure Reason*. Only if we shift to Kant's account of the schemata in the *Critique of Judgment* can we follow Cassirer's attempt to expand the scope of transcendental philosophy to include all cultural domains.

2.1   Categories, Schemata, and Symbols

In the second volume of the *Philosophy of Symbolic Forms*, Cassirer describes the symbols as 'categories of consciousness', by means of which we understand and shape the world in a variety of ways:

> The *Philosophy of Symbolic Forms* [...] seeks the categories of the consciousness of objects in the theoretical, intellectual sphere, and starts from the assumption that such categories must be at work wherever a cosmos, a characteristic and typical worldview, takes form out of the chaos of impressions.[3]

    Continental Divide, 52–56; and Guido Kreis, *Cassirer und die Formen des Geistes*, Berlin: Suhrkamp, 2010, 179–183, 188, 228–231).

[2] Within the first group of scholars we find Ferrari (*Stationen einer philosophischen Biographie*, 17, 198, 203; and 'Is Cassirer a Neo-Kantian Methodologically Speaking?', in: *Neo-Kantianism in Contemporary Philosophy*, 298–304), Friedman (*A Parting of the Ways*, 116), Kreis (*Cassirer und die Formen des Geistes*, 179–183, 188, 228–231), and Skidelsky (*The Last Philosopher of Culture*, 66). The second group includes Gordon (*Continental Divide*, 122, 147), S. G. Lofts (*Ernst Cassirer: A 'Repetition' of Modernity*, Albany: State University of New York Press, 2000, 20, 78), and Verene (*The Origins of the Philosophy of Symbolic Forms*, xv, xvii, 5–6, 15, 42, 54, 73). The inconsistent portrayal of the symbol in secondary literature on Cassirer points to a general characteristic of his philosophy: although often intuitively convincing, it does not always excel in conceptual clarity (see Susanne K. Langer, *Philosophical Sketches*, Baltimore: Johns Hopkins University Press, 1962, 56; and Iredell Jenkins, 'The Philosophy of Ernst Cassirer' (Book Review), in: *The Journal of Philosophy*, 47, 1950, 43–55).

[3] *PSF:II* 29. The only other passage in which Cassirer ascribes to Kant's concept of category is in *Das Erkenntnisproblem in der Philosophie und Wissenschaft der neueren Zeit* (*EP:1* 18). Additionally, Cassirer aligns his own conception of a symbol with Natorp's theory of categories in *Vorlesungen über praktische Philosophie* (Erlangen: Verlag der philosophischen Akademie, 1925, 2, 221–222, 251; see also Ernst Cassirer, 'Paul Natorp. 24 January 1854–17 August 1924', *ECW:16* 223–224). However, Natorp's conception of categories differs significantly from Kant's, which renders his and later also Cassirer's use of the term 'category' misleading. Conversely, Kant talks about symbols in the *Critique of Judgment*, but, given their 'indirect' and 'analogical' character, they have no affinity with Cassirer's concept thereof (Immanuel Kant, *Critique of Judgement*, tr. by James Creed Meredith, Oxford: Oxford University Press, 2007, 351–353 – hereafter indicated as '*CJ*').

On this basis, one might be tempted to regard the symbol as a multi-applicable variant of what Kant calls the categories of the understanding, namely as purely rational conditions of possibility of our experience that are also conditions of possibility of the objects of this experience (*CPR* A158/B197). However, with the exception of causality, none of the categories from the *Critique of Pure Reason* returns in Cassirer's list of symbols. Instead, this list includes space and time, the 'forms of intuition' that Kant sharply distinguishes from the categories of the understanding.[4] This is indicative of Cassirer's rejection of an actual distinction between the faculties of sensibility and the understanding; throughout the three volumes of *The Philosophy of Symbolic Forms*, he time and again affirms the impossibility of separating concepts from even our most fundamental intuitions: "There cannot be any such thing as an isolated, 'merely sensory' consciousness – that is, a consciousness remaining outside of any determination by the theoretical functions of signification and preceding them as an independent datum".[5] Cassirer regards the distinction between pure concepts and pre-conceptual or a-conceptual intuitions as merely methodological: the matter and form of our cognition are "members of a methodic opposition which is at the same time a methodic correlation" (*PSF:III* 10). In reality, they are 'reflected in each other', "and only in this reciprocal reflection does each disclose its own meaning" (*PSF:II* 99).

It seems, then, that Cassirer is interested not in Kant's account of the categories of the understanding[6] but rather in the 'schemata' that unite the a priori and temporal characteristics of the pure understanding and sensibility, respectively (*CPR* A140/B179). Early on in the first *Critique*, Kant famously claims that our intuitions remain blind and our concepts empty when they are not related to each other (A5/B75). He later invokes the power of imagination as the mediating third faculty that provides images (schemata) for concepts (A138–140/B177–180), or the capacity to synthesize the manifold of intuitions under the unity of a concept (A119/B130). The possibility of objective experience is thus first disclosed or established by transcendental imagination. As we have seen, Cassirer proclaims his interest in this faculty in an attempt at reconciliation with Heidegger during the Davos debate, and he speaks of

---

[4] Cassirer's 'list' of symbols, which the reader must actually deduce from the tables of contents of the three volumes of the *Philosophy of Symbolic Forms*, contains time, space, number, causality, and 'self'.

[5] *PSF:III* 8. See also, for example, *PSF:I* 303, 319; *PSF:II* 34–35; and *PSF:III* 14–15, 28, 32, 199; as well as *EP:II* 684, 722; and *EP:III* 6.

[6] For the same reason, Cassirer's notion of a symbol will differ significantly from the Kantian one: in §59 of the *Critique of Judgment*, Kant distinguishes between a schema – here referring to those discussed in the first *Critique* – and a symbol – like the ideas of beauty and the sublime – and characterizes the latter as an intuitive type of representation "which only reason can think, and to which no sensuous intuition can be adequate" (*CJ* 351).

'symbolic imagination' as a typically human feature in *An Essay on Man* (*EM* 33). Charles W. Hendel, a personal friend of Cassirer and the publisher of his posthumous monographs, even holds that the schema is "the thing that caught the imagination of Cassirer" and that 'his own philosophy of symbolic forms was a development of the possibilities of this new concept of form' (*PSF:I* 14–15).

We should note at this point that Kant's critical philosophy distinguishes two types of schemata of the imagination. In the *Critique of Pure Reason*, Kant discusses the possibility of 'determining judgements', or judgements that impose general, a priori fixed, concepts (the categories) onto appearances and thus ground a deterministic understanding of the laws of nature. The imagination here follows the rules of the understanding and applies them to our perceptions. In the *Critique of Judgment*, by contrast, Kant defends the legitimacy of 'reflective judgments' that allow for an additional, teleological interpretation of nature on the basis of the a priori principle of purposiveness (*CJ* 180, § 78). Because these judgements infer the general from the particular, the imagination is here not guided by, or bound to, the rules and concepts of the pure understanding (179). Drawing on the content of our perceptions, imagination can now perceive a harmony between natural events that complements their a priori determination by the understanding (287). Hence, rather than expressing rigid and universal laws, reflective judgements are grounded on a 'free play' of the imagination that results in a dynamic and revisable communion between concept and intuition, form and matter, or subject and object.[7]

Cassirer's conception of the symbols bears close resemblance to Kant's position in the *Critique of Judgment* in at least three regards. First, whereas in the first *Critique* Kant derives the schemata from a fixed and limited table of categories (*CPR* A142/B181), this restriction has disappeared in the third *Critique*: through reflective judging, our perceptions can give rise to an in principle unlimited number of schemata that characterize objects in an a priori manner. Likewise, Cassirer never even entertains the idea of a logical and systematic deduction of the symbols. He rather discovers them through anthropological research, by analysing the syntax of diverse natural languages, or by seeking the patterns in both ancient and contemporary mythological stories.[8]

---

[7] On this basis, Rudolf A. Makkreel argues in *Imagination and Interpretation in Kant. The Hermeneutical Import of the Critique of Judgment* (Chicago: The University of Chicago Press, 1990) that, unlike the *Critique of Pure Reason*, the *Critique of Judgment* allows for a hermeneutical comprehension of nature.

[8] See the original draft of *An Essay on Man* (*ECN:6* 397). In the introduction to the first volume of the *Philosophy of Symbolic Forms*, Cassirer announces that the following study "will not deal with this general logical significance ["a kind of critical 'deduction'"] of the representative function". Rather, it "shall seek to pursue the problem of signs, not backward to its ultimate

This empirical approach implies that any further research, be it into cultural fields that Cassirer already investigated (e.g. language), to which he merely refers (e.g. economics), or that have only developed later (e.g. ecology or social media), may reveal symbols that he had overlooked: "The *forms of judging* signify only unitary and lively *motives* of thinking, which penetrate the manifold of its particular shapes and actively cause the creation and formulation of ever new categories" (*EP:I* 18).

Second, like the schemata discussed in the *Critique of Judgment*, the symbols have an a priori determined direction but no a priori determined form. Hence, not only the extent of the list of symbols but also the meaning of those that Cassirer had already discovered can be revised on the basis of new empirical data. In a hermeneutical fashion, the general – and not the universal – orders the particular, but the latter in turn affects the outlook of the former. As Cassirer writes, 'in the development of our knowledge, the symbols are subject to metamorphosis'.[9]

Third, both Kant's third *Critique* and Cassirer's thought as a whole reject the idea of an opposition between intuition and concept, or particular and universal, that dominates the argumentation of the first *Critique*, and instead argue for their intrinsic mutual relation. Already in the *Critique of Pure Reason*, Kant defines the 'schematism' as the 'procedure of the imagination for providing a concept with its image' (*CPR* A140/B179–180). As such, it offers an a priori 'rule of synthesis' (A141/B180) for ordering our perceptions under the concepts of the pure understanding. The 'schemata', or schematized concepts, are thus the sensible representations of this procedure or rule. Cassirer complains, however, that the schematism establishes a

merely external mediation that may very well render intelligible a 'cooperation' between sensibility and thought, but which sharpens rather than reconciles their essential 'heterogeneity'. The category here appears as a construct of independent origin that is first through its application, as if by an external force, restricted by the foreign element of sensibility. (*EP:III* 11)

Despite the important role that Kant ascribes to the faculty of the imagination in the *Critique of Pure Reason*, this work fails, in Cassirer's view, to overcome the dualism of sensibility and thinking (*PSF:I* 104).

In the *Critique of Judgment*, on the other hand, Kant explains that in reflective judging, "the freedom of the imagination consists precisely in the fact that it schematizes without a concept" (*CJ* 287, 214, 229), meaning that in this case the understanding does not prescribe the guideline for the

---

'foundation', but forward to its concrete unfolding and configuration in the diverse cultural spheres" (*PSF:I* 105).

[9] Cassirer, 'Erkenntnistheorie nebst den Grenzfragen der Logik und Denkpsychologie', *ECW:17* 53.

schematism. Hence, the third *Critique* centers on the a priori relations between perceptions rather than on the concepts that express them. This matches Cassirer's view that the symbol is "the pure relation that governs the building of consciousness and that stands out in it as a genuine a priori, an essentially first factor" (*PSF:III* 202–203). In the symbols, a sensible and a conceptual or intellectual moment 'reciprocally reflect each other'; they merely exist as two components of a single relation. Mainly for this reason, Cassirer regards Kant's doctrine of transcendental imagination as coming to maturity only in the *Critique of Judgment*, where

understanding and intuition are no longer in opposition as things totally dissimilar, so that they have to be brought together through the agency of a foreign mediator and conjoined through a cunning schematism, but they are truly blended and absorbed in each other.[10]

In *The Phenomenology of Knowledge*, Cassirer explains this intimate and reciprocal relation between intuitions and concepts by means of the idea of 'symbolic pregnancy'.[11]

Kant defined the imagination as "the faculty for representing an object even without its presence in intuition" (*CPR* B151). Cassirer endorses this definition and emphasizes that this mechanism is at work not only in our scientific experience but in all our experience; we always perceive more than what is, literally speaking, present: "It lies in the very nature of consciousness that it cannot posit any content without, by this simple act, positing a complex of other contents" (*PSF:I* 97, 98, 108). Our immediate experience thus always points beyond itself to a meaningful whole within which it can first be understood: "the now is filled and saturated with the future" (*PSF:III* 202), just like the awareness of a 'here' is always accompanied with that of a 'there': "The particular place is not given prior to the spatial system but only in reference to it and in correlation with it" (*PSF:I* 101). This fundamental

---

[10]   *KLT* 315; see also *PSF:III* 7 and 'The Concept of Group and the Theory of Perception', *ECW:24* 246. Ferrari (*Stationen einer philosophischen Biographie*, 73–98), and Ernst Wolfgang Orth ('Zur Konzeption der symbolischen Formen', in: *Von der Erkenntnistheorie zur Kulturphilosophie. Studien zu Ernst Cassirers Philosophie der symbolischen Formen*, Würzburg: Königshausen & Neumann, 2004, 68–99) also convincingly highlight Cassirer's particular interest in the *Critique of Judgment*.

[11]   Cassirer borrows this concept from 'Gestaltpsychologie', with which he was familiar through Kurt Goldstein (see John Michael Krois, 'Problematik, Eigenart und Aktualität der Cassirerschen Philosophie der symbolischen Formen', in: *Über Ernst Cassirers Philosophie der Symbolischen Formen*, 23–26; and Martina Plümacher, 'Die Erforschung des Geistes – Cassirers Auseinandersetzung mit der zeitgenössischen Psychologie', in: *Kultur und Symbol. Ein Handbuch zur Philosophie Ernst Cassirers*, hrsg. von Hans Jörg Sandkühler und Detlev Pätzold, Stuttgart: Verlag J. B. Metzler, 2003, 85–110). In the meaning that Cassirer lends this concept, it in turn influenced the thought of Maurice Merleau-Ponty (see *Phenomenology of Perception*, tr. by Colin Smith, London and New York: Routledge, 2002, 147).

structure of our experience is most evident in the way we perceive a melody or a sentence, an example that returns a few times in Cassirer's writings. We clearly do not at first perceive individual notes or words that we subsequently connect to each other in a cumulative way, but anticipate our future perceptions as a necessary condition for understanding our momentaneous ones (94, 303).

According to Cassirer, we do not, however, arbitrarily impose a surplus of meaning upon our perceptions: "Here we are not dealing with bare perceptive data, on which some sort of apperceptive acts are later grafted, through which they are interpreted, judged, transformed" (*PSF:III* 202). Rather, the cultural meaning that is embodied by the symbols is 'born into' these perceptions: "It is perception itself which by virtue of its own immanent organization takes on a kind of spiritual articulation." Our perceptions are, in other words, 'pregnant with meaning':

By symbolic pregnancy we mean the way in which a perception as a sensory experience contains at the same time a certain non-intuitive meaning that it immediately and concretely represents. [...] It is this ideal interwovenness, this relatedness of the single perceptive phenomenon, given here and now, to a characteristic total meaning that the term 'pregnancy' is meant to designate.[12]

Symbolic imagination is the capacity to be perceptive of the 'symbolic pregnancy' of our perceptions, and – at once – to actualize their potential meaning by means of the symbols.[13]

---

[12] Many commentators have stressed the significance of 'symbolic pregnancy' for Cassirer's thought: Verene regards it as "the principle, reached phenomenologically, whereby Cassirer unlocks the mystery of the Kantian schematism" (*The Origins of the Philosophy of Symbolic Forms*, 54), and Krois calls it "the highest point of Cassirer's *Philosophie der symbolischen Formen*" ('Cassirer, Neo-Kantianism and Metaphysics', 448). More specifically, in *Symbolic Forms and History*, Krois subsequently characterizes symbolic pregnancy as "the condition of the possibility of all Sinngebung and Zeichengebung" (54); "the condition of the possibility of a consciousness and of the symbolic forms of culture" (56); "the necessary condition for the separation of the ego from the 'other' and the world, a separation which, in turn, is the necessary condition that the ego not only exists, but knows of itself" (58); and "the condition of possibility of *Weltverstehen*" (62).

[13] *PSF:I* 108. Recki concludes from this that Cassirer's account of our symbolic understanding of the world has a partly hermeneutic and a partly pragmatic character (Birgit Recki, *Kultur als Praxis. Eine Einführung in Ernst Cassirers Philosophie der symbolischen Formen*, in: *Deutsche Zeitschrift für Philosophie*, Sonderband 6, Berlin: Akademie Verlag, 2004, 36). This view is endorsed by Kreis (*Cassirer und die Formen des Geistes*, 251), Heinz Paetzold ('Die symbolische Ordnung der Kultur. Ernst Cassirers Beitrag zu einer Theorie der Kulturentwicklung', in: *Ernst Cassirers Werk und Wirkung*, hrsg. von Dorothea Frede und Reinold Schmücker, Darmstadt: Wissenschaftliche Buchgesellschaft, 1997, 170), and Nicolas de Warren ('Reise um die Welt. Cassirer's Cosmological Phenomenology', in: *New Approaches to Neo-Kantianism*, ed. by Nicolas de Warren and Andrea Staiti, Cambridge: Cambridge University Press, 2015, 102–104). Rudolf Bernet further argues that Cassirer's position on this matter mediates between Husserl's doctrine of categorial intuition and Heidegger's existential hermeneutics ('Perception et herméneutique (Husserl, Cassirer et Heidegger)', in: *La vie du sujet*, Paris: PUF, 1994, 147–153). Cassirer's account of symbolic pregnancy indeed entails an

2.2   The Diversity of the Cultural World

We still have not addressed the most obvious difference between Cassirer's conception of the symbol and Kant's account of the categories. Following Kant, Cassirer searches for the conditions of possibility for the objective status of our truth claims. He goes beyond Kant, however, by expanding this search to all cultural domains of the human world, including not only science, ethics, and aesthetics but also, for example, history, linguistics, mythology, and religion:

> The Copernican revolution, with which Kant began, takes on a new and amplified meaning. It refers no longer solely to the function of logical judgment but extends with equal justification and right to every trend and every principle by which the human spirit gives form to reality.[14]

Cassirer thus wants to uncover the rational constituents of culture as a whole. In this way, he asserts, "the critique of reason becomes the critique of culture" (*PSF:I* 80). Throughout his oeuvre, Cassirer discusses or at least acknowledges the cultural domains of myth, language, art, religion, science, history, law, economy, technology, and politics. He calls the transcendental frameworks that constitute these domains 'symbolic forms'.[15]

Cassirer realizes, however, that the acceptance of "the 'poly-dimensionality' of the cultural world" (*PSF:III* 13) significantly complicates the systematic aim of transcendental philosophy. If we acknowledge a variety of cultural spheres, can we still conceive of a formal principle that guarantees the intelligible unity of the whole of our cultural life? Most commentators agree that Kant never managed to satisfactorily present theoretical, practical, and teleological thinking as different uses of the same reason. Cassirer, on the other hand, seems determined to solve this "strange dilemma":

> If we hold fast to the postulate of logical unity, the universality of the logical form threatens ultimately to efface the individuality of each special province and the specificity of its principle – but if we immerse ourselves in this individuality and persevere in our examination of it, we run the risk of losing ourselves and finding no way back to the universal. An escape from this methodological dilemma is only possible if we can discover a factor that recurs in each basic cultural form but in no two of them takes

---

explicit critique of Husserl's dualist theory of the hyletic and noetic moments of intuition (*PSF: III* 198–201), one that was uttered earlier by Cohen (*Das Prinzip der Infinitisimal-Methode und seine Geschichte: Ein Kaptiel zur Grundlegung der Erkenntniskritik*, Hildesheim: Olms Verlag, 1984) and Natorp ('Zur Frage der logischen Methode. Mit Beziehung auf Edmund Husserl's 'Prolegomena' zur reinen Logik', in: *Kant-Studien*, VI, 1901, 270–283; and 'Husserl's Ideen zu einer Reinen Phänomenologie', in: *Logos*, VII, 1917/1918, 224–246).

[14] *PSF:I* 79. See also *PSF:III* 13; *CIPC* 70–71; and *CPPP* 55–56.

[15] See *PSF:I* 111; and 'Der Begriff der symbolischen Form in der Aufbau der Geisteswissenschaften', *ECW:16* 79.

exactly the same shape. Then, in reference to this principle, we might assert the ideal relation between the individual provinces – between the basic functions of language and cognition, of art and religion – without losing the incomparable particularity of any one of them. (*PSF:I* 84)

Cassirer finds this 'recurring factor' in the symbol, which resembles the schemata of the third *Critique*. However, for Kant these schemata are typical of teleological thinking, whereas Cassirer understands the symbol as 'a medium through which all the configurations effected in the separate branches of cultural life must pass, but which nevertheless retains its particular nature, its specific character'. In this way, the symbols provide 'the necessary intermediary link for an inquiry which will accomplish for the *totality* of cultural forms what the transcendental critique has done for pure *cognition*'. The same symbols thus return in all symbolic forms but appear in a different 'modality'[16] or 'tonality'[17] in each one of them.

Cassirer most famously illustrates the interpretative flexibility of the symbols by referring to the drawing of a line (*Linienzug*). We can perceive a line, which is itself already a spatial construct (symbol), in very different and yet equally meaningful ways, depending on the cultural context (symbolic form): as a geometrical figure, a geographical border, an aesthetic ornament, a mythical dividing line between the profane and divine, or a religious symbol (*PSF:III* 202–204). Likewise, causal relationships are constitutive of both the scientific and mythological worldview, even though these views promote a respective genetic and teleological conception of causality (*PSF:II* 20), and even though they express universal laws in the former and magical inferences in the latter case (48; *PSF:I* 96–97). 'Here again', Cassirer holds, 'it is not the concept of causality as such but the specific form of causal explanation which underlies the difference and contrast between the two spiritual worlds'.[18]

The symbols consequently appear to have two faces: they are simultaneously 'extremely versatile' and universal (*EM* 36). On the one hand, in our lived cultural experiences we always encounter the symbols in a modality that is *particular* to one of the symbolic forms, namely as mythological space, scientific time, etc. Kreis therefore holds that we should understand the

---

[16] 'Modalität': *PSF:I* 31; *PSF:II* 60; *PSF:III* 13.   [17] 'Tönung': *PSF:II* 61, 258; *PSF:III* 13.

[18] *PSF:II* 48, 60. One could argue that Kant also distinguishes between a theoretical, practical, and aesthetic perspective on the world – ruled by the faculty of the understanding, pure practical reason, and the imagination, respectively (*CJ* 174, 197) – and that these perspectives are constituted by different modalities of the concept of causality: a law of natural science, moral freedom, and the principle of teleology. Kant, however, never thematized this structural relation between the different uses of reason or drew any conclusions from it with regard to the unity of reason. Consult on this topic Angelica Nuzzo's *Kant and the Unity of Reason* (History of Philosophy Series, West Lafayette: Purdue University Press, 2005); and Susan Neiman's, *The Unity of Reason. Rereading Kant* (Oxford: Oxford University Press, 1994).

symbols as "the phrases, images, institutions, artifacts and the cultic or religious or in some other way meaningful acts that occur in our world".[19] In this regard, the idea that the *same* symbols (space, time, etc.) return in each symbolic form is a mere construct of transcendental philosophy: we never perceive a spatial object 'as such', since it is always already taken up by a certain cultural point of view. Hence, the three key concepts of the philosophy of symbolic forms – 'symbolic pregnancy', 'symbol', and 'symbolic form' – refer to the same phenomena:

It is the perception itself which by virtue of its own immanent organization [symbolic pregnancy], takes on a kind of spiritual articulation [symbol] – which, being ordered in itself, also belongs to a determinate order of meaning [symbolic form]. (*PSF:III* 202)

On the other hand, Cassirer considers the particular shapes of the symbols as modalities *of* a type of relationship between perceptions that returns in each form; he sees sufficient formal similarity between, for example, the idea of a scientific causal law and that of magical inference to identify both as instances of the symbol of causality. In this regard, the symbols appear as "a principle of universal applicability which encompasses the whole field of human thought" (*EM* 35). This perspective is of crucial importance for Cassirer, whose goal is to provide "a general plan of ideal orientation, in which we can [...] mark the position of each symbolic form".[20] The philosophy of symbolic forms after all aims to explain not only the internal constitution of our different symbolic forms, but also their mutual relation and coherence. For this reason, Cassirer must assume an ideal element that is common to all the symbolic forms and that accounts for their structural relatedness:

If we approach spiritual life, [...] we shall find certain common and typical principles of formation, diverse and dissimilar as the forms may be. If the philosophy of culture succeeds in apprehending and elucidating such basic principles, it will have fulfilled, in a new sense, its task of demonstrating the unity of the spirit as opposed to the multiplicity of its manifestations – for the clearest evidence of this unity is precisely that the diversity of the *products* of the human spirit does not impair the unity of its *productive process*, but rather sustains and confirms it. (*PSF:I* 114)

But here a problem arises within this project because of the dual nature of the symbols. By ascribing a universal status to the symbols in their abstract shape, Cassirer lends them a certain ideal independence. As a consequence, despite his continuing efforts to overcome the dualism in Kant's account of the faculties of sensibility and the understanding, Cassirer in the end seems to install a new dualism between a variety of concrete symbols and a small

---

[19] Kreis, *Cassirer und die Formen des Geistes*, 19; see also Recki, *Kultur als Praxis*, 32.
[20] Cassirer, 'Das Symbolproblem und seine Stellung im System der Philosophie', in: *ECW:17* 262.

number of their ideal templates.[21] A desire to downplay or even conceal this
unwanted consequence could perhaps explain why most of Cassirer's works
offer predominantly descriptive overviews of the different domains of our
cultural world, focusing almost exclusively on the symbol's modalities. This
fragmentary approach fails, however, to satisfy his repeated interest in
developing a 'morphology of spirit' in its systematic unity (*PSF:I* 69).

2.3   The Two Kantian Conceptions of Objectivity in Cassirer's Philosophy of Culture

The idea of 'symbolic pregnancy' implied that it is impossible for us to
perceive an object independently of any symbolic meaning. Further,
Cassirer's emphasis on the variety of rational worldviews suggested that what
is true is always relative to the viewpoint of one of the symbolic forms. It
should not surprise, then, that Cassirer considers the concept of a 'thing in
itself' nonsensical ("a fallacy in formulation, an intellectual phantasm", *PSF:I*
11). Nevertheless, his early deconstruction of this Kantian notion gives insight
into the conception of objectivity that supports his mature philosophy of
symbolic forms. By adopting both a constitutive and a regulative conception,
Cassirer legitimizes the duality on which this philosophy hinges.

In the second volume of *The Problem of Knowledge*, Cassirer at length
discusses the development of the concept of the 'thing in itself' in the first
Critique.[22] Although he regards it as a key concept in this work (*EP:II* 613,
635), he also admits that it is a particularly difficult notion to understand. The
reason for this, he holds, is that Kant had not yet fixed its meaning when he
began his critical inquiry: "The actual difficulty related to this concept is
grounded in the fact that it was for Kant himself not in advance determined
in a rigid, once and for all fixed meaning, but that he first needed to gain it from
the critical analysis of the problem of objectivity". We should not understand
this as a critique that Cassirer addressed at Kant, as if the latter was badly
prepared when he started writing his magnum opus. Cassirer rather regards
Kant's initial abeyance as a deliberate choice: what sets apart his critical
approach from a dogmatic one is precisely that it does not presuppose an

---

[21] We could now understand the concrete symbols as schemata of the ideals templates, whereby
the mechanism of schematization is different in each symbolic form. This means, however, that
these templates resemble the categories of the pure understanding as Kant described them after
all – and that the confusion among Cassirer scholars regarding the relation between the concepts
of 'category' and 'symbol' is quite understandable. Cassirer indeed uses the term 'category' in
this way, albeit not in a systematic manner, for example, on *PSF:II* 60.

[22] All following quotes from the first three volumes of *The Problem of Knowledge* (1906, 1907,
1920) present my own translations from the original German.

understanding of objectivity, but that it aims to obtain one through an investigation of the structure of reason.[23]

Cassirer subsequently argues that Kant's critical method also explains why the remarks about objectivity and the 'thing in itself' in the *Critique of Pure Reason* not always seem coherent. This incoherence would be unacceptable if one understands objectivity as that which "exists independently of every relation to our knowledge" (621), but Cassirer holds that the meaning of Kant's notion of the 'thing in itself' legitimately alters throughout the first *Critique*. More specifically, he claims that a generically different understanding of this concept corresponds to each stage of the constitution of our knowledge:

> The different steps on the way towards a critical concept of objectivity must necessarily correspond to equally different formulations of the 'thing in itself'. [If] one considers the 'thing in itself' from the very outset in relation to its logical and epistemological function, it is clear that this function, in accordance with the viewpoint that our knowledge has attained in its positive construction, appears in a different light.

Hence, for Cassirer, the Transcendental Aesthetic, Transcendental Analytic, and Transcendental Dialectic deal with three generically different conceptions of the 'thing in itself': "It can first function as the correlate of the 'passivity' of our sensibility, to then become the counterpart of the objectifying function of the pure concept of the understanding, and finally the schema of the regulative principle of reason."[24]

While discussing the receptive nature of the faculty of sensibility in the Transcendental Aesthetic, Cassirer points out, Kant presents the 'thing in itself' still in a pre-critical fashion, as the real or independent cause of our perceptions (*EP:II* 622–626). He, for example, defines sensibility as "the receptivity of our mind to receive representations, insofar as it is affected in some way" (*CPR* A51/B75), and holds that "the receptivity of the subject to be affected by objects necessarily precedes all intuitions of these objects" (A26/B42).[25] These 'affecting objects' could correspond to what Kant later

---

[23] See also *CIPC* 69.

[24] *EP:II* 635. Karin de Boer also argues that "the term 'thing in itself' receives a different meaning in the various parts of the *Critique of Pure Reason* and that these meaning cannot be reduced to a single one" ('Kant's Multi-Layered Conception of Things in Themselves, Transcendental Objects, and Monads', in: *Kant-Studien*, 105/2, 2014, 3). These 'various parts', she further agrees with Cassirer, are "the passages that concern the issue of affection" (10; i.e. the Transcendental Aesthetic), those that concern "Kant's conception of the transcendental object and related terms in light of his intended reform of Wolffian general metaphysics" (18; i.e. the Transcendental Analytic), and "the context of former special metaphysics" (30; i.e. the Transcendental Dialectic). While De Boer's – convincing – account of Kant's concept of the 'thing in itself' in the *Critique of Pure Reason* is much more elaborate than Cassirer's, the latter extends to the *Critique of Practical Reason* (*EP:II* 635–637).

[25] See also *CPR* A35/B51 and B72.

calls 'a noumenon in the negative sense': "a thing *insofar as it is not an object of our sensible intuition*, because we abstract from the manner of our intuition of it" (*CPR* B307). Kant must define the traditional conception of objectivity in this negative way here because, seen from a transcendental viewpoint, we have no access to objects as they are apart from the way we intuit them in space and time. In the Transcendental Aesthetic, the 'thing in itself' is thus a problematic concept whose only useful role is to indicate the boundaries of our experience.[26]

When Kant considers the faculty of pure understanding in the Transcendental Analytic, however, the idea of a mind-independent object is dropped entirely. Having arrived at the heart of his critical investigation, he now conceives of the 'thing in itself' as the unity of the objective determinations of our perceptions by the understanding (*EP:II* 626–628). In this regard, Cassirer remarks, Kant refers to the 'thing in itself' as the 'transcendental object': it is "a correlate of the unity of apperception for the unity of the manifold in sensible intuition" (cf. *CPR* A250). At this point in the *Critique of Pure Reason*, objects are the product rather than the foundation or source of our knowledge.

Turning to the faculty of pure reason in the Transcendental Dialectic, finally, Kant conceives of the concept of the 'thing in itself', according to Cassirer, as the regulative idea of the 'absolute object' (*EP:II* 628–635). Pure theoretical reason strives for the complete determination of the objects constituted by the understanding, so as to bring out the systematic unity of the whole of our experience. As is well known, however, Kant regards this unity as out of reach for us who must rely on the capacity of sensible, fragmentary, intuition. Hence, in the context of the Transcendental Dialectic, the idea of the 'thing in itself' indicates neither the source nor the product of our knowledge, but its 'focus imaginarius' (*CPR* A644/B672). At this point, Kant understands it as the ultimate goal of our strife for knowledge that, even though unattainable, nevertheless functions as a continual motivation for any objective determination of our intuitions.[27] In Cassirer's words, the 'thing in itself' does not refer to a given (*ein Gegebenes*) here, but to a task (*ein Aufgegebenes*; *EP:II* 630).[28]

Cassirer concludes that Kant's concept of the 'thing in itself', "which initially seemed to take us beyond all boundaries of knowledge" turns out to be "the sharpest indication of the fact that all our knowledge moves merely

---

[26] See *EP:II* 624–626; and *CPR* A255/B310–311.   [27] See *CPR* A672/B702, A679/B707.

[28] This task, one could say, is to reach as closely as possible the viewpoint of a being that is capable of intellectual intuition. Hence, the notion of a 'thing in itself' in the Transcendental Dialectic corresponds to what Kant earlier called a 'noumenon in a positive sense': it indicates "an *object of a non-sensible intuition*" (*CPR* B307) that actually best not understood as an object, "but rather as the task that is unavoidably connected with the limitation of our sensibility" (A 287/343–344 – translation modified).

within the sphere of relating and objectifying" (634). On his reading, Kant in the first *Critique* gradually transforms the meaning of objectivity from an object of cognition into a methodological principle that directs the cognitive process: "The 'absolute', that we oppose to the appearances as their touchstone, is no new, independent, entity, but merely mirrors this pure function of objectification, which alone allows us to achieve knowledge" (635, 756–757).

Cassirer's original reading of Kant's concept of the 'thing in itself', which untangles some of Kant's seemingly contradictory claims in the *Critique of Pure Reason*, clearly informed his mature thought. Within the framework of his philosophy of culture, he retains the two conceptions of objectivity that he discerned in the Transcendental Analytic and Transcendental Dialectic, namely a constitutive and regulative one, respectively.

First, when Cassirer considers the inner constitution of the different symbolic forms, he holds on to the idea that objects are not the source or basis of our knowledge but their product. When Kant famously stated that "the conditions of the possibility of experience in general are at the same time conditions of the possibility of the objects of experience" (*CPR* A158/B197), he referred to the categories and rules of the understanding. For Cassirer, however, the dependence of objectivity on transcendental subjectivity marks the constitution of all the domains of human culture. Since these domains each have their own subjective rules of constitution, he thus acknowledges multiple rational conceptions of objectivity.[29] Already in volume two of *The Problem of Knowledge*, Cassirer holds that "the different orders of being, the domains of nature, art, or morality, originate in the different directions of our spiritual activity" (*EP:II* 637–638), and that "the 'being' of a representational content is thus not a univocal concept, but only becomes stable once we have determined the faculty to which we relate the claim" (618). In *The Philosophy of Symbolic Forms*, he reiterates this view: "Objectivity lies neither in a metaphysical nor an empirical-psychological 'reality' which stands behind it, but in what [each symbolic form] itself is and achieves, in the manner and form of *objectification* which it accomplishes".[30] Cassirer's constitutive conception of objectivity relates our heterogeneous perceptions under concrete symbols in accordance to the rational viewpoint of myth, natural science, etc. On this account, the idea of objectivity signifies a rational, coherent, and meaningful order of a variety of symbolic experiences, and corresponds to Cassirer's idea of a symbolic form.

Second, when Cassirer considers the unity of culture as a whole, and thus the relation between the different symbolic forms, he maintains Kant's

---

[29] Chapter 7 (Section 7.1) elaborates on the mutual differences between the constitutive rules of the symbolic forms.

[30] *PSF:II* 14; translation modified.

conception of objectivity as a regulative idea.[31] It follows from the manifold of cultural domains that each shows only one side of the human world. In order to achieve a *rich understanding* of objectivity, Cassirer therefore holds, we should combine the insights of these limited worldviews:

Since, according to the idealistic insight, we can grasp the 'real' nowhere but in these functions [. . .] there is for us only 'truth' in so far as we understand each of these forms in their distinctive character and simultaneously imagine the interrelatedness through which they are connected with all others.[32]

However, since the symbolic forms shape the world according to their own distinctive viewpoint and 'tonalities', they carry out generically different conceptions of objectivity that can only be measured by their own standards. A *complete determination* of objectivity, as the philosopher desires, is consequently an unreachable goal, and our culture must remain a fragmented whole of one-sided worldviews:

In human experience we by no means find the various activities which constitute the world existing in harmony. On the contrary, we find the perpetual strife of diverse conflicting forces. Scientific thought contradicts and suppresses mythical thought. Religion in its highest theoretical and ethical development is under the necessity of defending the purity of its own ideal against the extravagant fancies of myth and art. Thus the unity appears to be little more than a pious fraud which is constantly frustrated by the real course of events. (*EM* 70)

Cassirer's second conception of objectivity thus refers to neither the source nor the product of our understanding of the world, but to a task that serves as a merely regulative ideal: this idea is both the impossible goal of and the incentive for our symbolic formation of the world. This regulative conception of objectivity relates the different symbolic forms and their corresponding tonalities under the encompassing viewpoint of the "pure function of objectification" (*EP:II* 635), or the 'symbol as such'. On this account, the idea of objectivity signifies the desired harmony of *all* our experience, and translates into Cassirer's idea of human culture as a whole. This means that, for Cassirer, the unity of human culture is a regulative idea that presents us not with the stable product of our symbolic imagination, but with its never-ending task.

---

[31] See Krois, *Symbolic Forms and History*, 64: "The 'thing-in-itself' for Cassirer becomes equivalent to the concept of the world". Krois later explains how Cassirer's functional conception of truth, that is, of objectivity, avoids the pitfalls of both dogmatism and relativism (134–141).

[32] *ECW:9* 303. Accordingly, Cassirer defines the idea of 'the absolute' as "nothing but the expression and the sharpest formulation of the relativity of our knowledge" (*EP:II* 634; *PSF: IV* 227).

Heidegger's reading of the *Critique of Pure Reason* is usually labelled an 'ontological interpretation', in contrast to the 'idealistic interpretation' of the German Idealists and the 'epistemological interpretation' of the Neo-Kantians.[1] Heidegger indeed insists that the aim of Kant's transcendental project is to lay out a general ontology. Yet, this description covers only one aspect of Heidegger's appraisal of the first *Critique*. For Heidegger, "Kant took an essential step in the direction of a fundamental elucidation of the concept *and* method of philosophy" that he himself had set out in the introduction to *Being and Time* (1927).[2] Heidegger thus attributes to Kant's thought all three

---

[1] We find this description in commentaries on Heidegger (Frank Schalow, *The Renewal of the Heidegger Kant Dialogue: Action, Thought, Responsibility*, SUNY Press, 1992, 319; Christopher Macann, 'Heidegger's Kant Interpretation', in: *Critical Heidegger*, ed. by Christopher Macann, Routledge, 1996, 97–120; and Karin de Boer, 'Heidegger's Ontological Reading of Kant', in: *The Bloomsbury Companion to Kant*, ed. by Gary Banham, Dennis Schulting, and Nigel Hems, London: Bloomsbury Publishing, 2012, 324–329) as well as on Kant (Helmut Holzhey and Vilem Mudroch, *Historical Dictionary of Kant and Kantianism*, Lanham: Scarecrow Press, 2005, 199; Paul Gorner, 'Phenomenological Interpretations of Kant in Husserl and Heidegger', in: *A Companion to Kant*, ed. by Graham Bird, Oxford: Blackwell Publishing, 2010, 507).

[2] *PIK* 6; my emphasis. Heidegger's interpretation of Kant is usually labelled as an 'appropriation' of the latter's thought (William Blattner, 'Laying the ground for metaphysics: Heidegger's appropriation of Kant', in: *The Cambridge Companion to Heidegger*, ed. by Charles B. Guignon, Cambridge: Cambridge UP, 2006, 149–176; Béatrice Han-Pile, 'Early Heidegger's Appropriation of Kant', in: *A Companion to Heidegger*, ed. by Hubert L. Dreyfus and Mark A. Wrathall, Blackwell Publishing, 2005, 80–101; and Brian Elliott, 'Heidegger's appropriation of Kant', in: *Phenomenology and Imagination in Heidegger and Husserl*, Routledge, 2015, 84–98). His reading of the first *Critique* is then said to transform Kant's transcendental philosophy in a vehicle for his own philosophical project (see *KPMR* 239–240). In fact, even Heidegger gradually distanced himself from his tendentious reading of Kant once he began to abandon his early philosophical program. In 1950, he admits to the many shortcomings of his 1929 Kant book, but adds that "the possibility of going astray" is inherent to a "dialogue between thinkers" (*KPM* xvii). In 1973, however, Heidegger takes full responsibility for his 'interpretative violence': "Kant's text became a refuge, as I sought in Kant an advocate for the question of being that I posed. [This] led me to interpret the *Critique of Pure Reason* from within the horizon of the manner of questioning set forth in *Being and Time*. In truth, however, Kant's question is foreign to it" (xviii). Nevertheless, a number of scholars have nuanced this (self-)criticism: see Martin Weatherston, *Heidegger's Interpretation of Kant*, Pallgrave

moments of his own conception of philosophy, considering him as an onto-logical, phenomenological, *and* hermeneutical thinker.

Whereas Heidegger never uses the phrase 'ontological interpretation' him-self, he does speak of a 'phenomenological interpretation of the *Critique of Pure Reason*'. In fact, throughout his writings on Kant, but unnoticed by most commentators, Heidegger alternates between two definitions of transcendental philosophy: when considering the *aim* of the first *Critique*, he treats it as synonymous to ontology, and when considering the *method* of the first *Critique*, he equates it to phenomenology. Hence, Heidegger views Kant's critical method as a forerunner of his own phenomenological approach.[3] Likewise, it is often overlooked that Heidegger in the end *praises* Kant's alleged 'oscillating' between the rationalist philosophical tradition and phe-nomenological ontology. For Heidegger, Kant's struggle in fact reveals his hermeneutic sensitivity to 'the problem of metaphysics'. Hence, he even considers Kant a hermeneutic thinker in his own regard.[4] This means that we can only assess Heidegger's attempt "to grasp the coherence of the whole of the *Critique of Pure Reason*" (*PIK* 6), if we consider three moments of his Kant interpretation – ontology, phenomenology, and hermeneutics – in their mutual relation.

Macmillan, 2002, 1–8; Stephan Käufer, 'Heidegger's Interpretation of Kant', in: *Interpreting Heidegger: Critical Essays*, ed. by Daniel O. Dahlstrom, Cambridge University Press, 2011, 174–196; and Camilla Serck-Hanssen, 'Towards Fundamental Ontology: Heidegger's Phenomenological Reading of Kant', in: *Continental Philosophy Review*, 48, 2015, 217–235. I will abstain entirely from defending Kant's own intentions against this violent interpretation, and solely focus on Heidegger's motivations for developing it.

[3] In a most instructive article, Chad Engelland confirms that the recurrent theme throughout Heidegger's successive assessments of Kant's thought is not so much the latter's interest in ontology but primarily his (proto-)phenomenological methodology. Engelland distinguishes four phases in Heidegger's phenomenological interpretation of Kant: while initially bothered by Kant's non-phenomenological approach (1919), Heidegger came to appreciate Kant as a fore-runner of both Husserl's and his own phenomenological method (1925–1926), as a collaborator against Husserl's flawed conception of phenomenology (1927–1929), and again as a quasi-phenomenological precursor of his thought on par with Husserl (1930 and onwards). This chapter focuses on the third phase, during which Heidegger "sees Kant as a phenomenological partner" ('The Phenomenological Kant: Heidegger's Interest in Transcendental Philosophy', in: *Journal of the British Society for Phenomenology*, 41, 2010, 165). I endorse Engelland's general thesis with regard to the 1927–1929 phase, and further develop it in two ways: by discussing the different stages of Heidegger's phenomenological reading of the Transcendental Analytic, and by relating this reading to Heidegger's conceptions of ontology and hermeneutics.

[4] In his essay 'Heidegger's Kant interpretation', Christopher Macann accurately explains how the structure of *Kant and the Problem of Metaphysics* expresses the circular procedure of Heidegger's hermeneutic reading of the first *Critique* (*Critical Heidegger*, 103–109). He also rightly wonders how Heidegger, given his own hermeneutic principles, can nevertheless claim to lay bare 'the true sense' of Kant's thought (103, 109–110). Macann fails to notice, however, what exactly Heidegger considers to be this 'true sense' – and hence overlooks the extent of his assimilation to Kant: in the end, Heidegger identifies a hermeneutic questioning to the possibility of metaphysics as the compass of Kant's own thinking.

3.1   On Kant's Concept of Philosophy: Transcendental Philosophy as Ontology

On a number of occasions, Heidegger claims that Kant's transcendental philosophy *is* ontology.[5] Most specifically, in *What Is a Thing?* he states that "the philosophical determination of the thingness of the thing is the metaphysical center of the philosophy of Kant" (*WT* 55, 122). This may seem odd: does Kant not hold that the Transcendental Analytic is meant to *replace* "the proud name of ontology" by a "mere analytic of the pure understanding" (*CPR* A247/B303)? And does not his agnostic stance with regard to 'things in themselves' obstruct any determination of 'the thingness of the thing'? How, then, can Heidegger defend an 'ontological reading' of the first *Critique*?

(1) In order to make sense of Heidegger's ontological interpretation of Kant, it is useful to first consider the former's understanding of 'the thingness of the thing', or 'the being of beings' as he calls it in *Being and Time*. There, Heidegger distinguishes the 'phenomenological conception of a phenomenon' from a 'vulgar' or 'ordinary' conception. It eventually becomes clear that the difference between these two conceptions of phenomena is identical to the 'ontological difference' between beings and being. When defining 'phenomenological phenomena', Heidegger holds that they "remain *concealed* in an exceptional sense", and that they are, therefore, "not this or that being but rather [. . .] the being of beings" (*BT* 35). 'Ordinary phenomena', on the other hand, he defines as 'appearances', that is, beings as they appear to us or as we ordinarily encounter them (30–31). Furthermore, while Heidegger's true interest goes out to the phenomenological conception, he later adds that "the vulgar concept of phenomenon becomes phenomenologically relevant" as well, because "being is always the being of beings, [and] we must first of all bring beings themselves forward in the right way if we are to have any prospect of exposing being" (37).

Initially, however, Heidegger explains these different conceptions of a phenomenon by referring to Kant. Phenomena in their ordinary meaning, he holds, can be understood as "those things that are accessible through empirical intuition in Kant's sense" (31). Kant indeed speaks of 'phenomena' in this way, famously opposing them to 'noumena'. The 'phenomena of phenomenology', Heidegger continues, can in turn be understood in line with what Kant calls 'the forms of intuition':

In the horizon of the Kantian problematic what is understood phenomenologically by the term phenomenon (disregarding other differences) can be illustrated by saying that

---

[5] *PIK* 58–59, 186; *KPM* 88; *BPP* 208. Heidegger also presents 'transcendental' and 'ontological' as synonymous terms on *PIK* 76, 170, 242, and 373.

what already shows itself in appearances, prior to and always accompanying what we commonly understand as phenomena (though unthematically), can be brought thematically to self-showing. What thus shows itself in itself ('the forms of intuition') are the phenomena of phenomenology. For, clearly, space and time must be able to show themselves this way.[6]

Heidegger thus likens Kant's conception of space and time to his phenomenological conception of a phenomenon – being – on the basis of their universal yet unthematic way of being present in our experience of beings. In *Being and Time*, Heidegger defines the phenomenological phenomenon as "something that does not show itself initially and for the most part [. . .] but at the same time [. . .] essentially belongs to what initially and for the most part shows itself, indeed in such a way that it constitutes its meaning and ground" (35). Simultaneously hidden and pervasive, such phenomena especially call for a phenomenological investigation. Similarly, Kant holds that we can never have a perception *of* space and time even though, and precisely because, they determine the form of all our perceptions so that we always perceive objects *in* time and space (*CPR* A37/B54). The 'forms of intuition' are thus constitutive yet elusive moments of appearances whose accurate articulation requires a transcendental investigation.

This analogy forms the basis for the ontological reading of the first *Critique* that Heidegger develops in his writings on Kant. The 'always accompanying yet unthematic' moments of our phenomena that interest him are what Kant more generally calls the a priori conditions of possibility of experience. In *Phenomenological Interpretation*, Heidegger thus holds that "what in advance determines a being as a being, the constitution of being which first makes possible a being as the being that it is, is what in a certain sense is 'earlier' than a being and is *a priori*" (*PIK* 37). He confirms this analogy in *What Is a Thing?*: "The priority of the a priori concerns the essence of things. What enables the thing to be what it is *precedes* the thing in fact and 'nature', although we only grasp that which precedes after taking account of some of the most obvious qualities of the thing" (*WT* 165–166). On this ground, Heidegger considers Kant's famous question 'How are synthetic a priori judgments possible?' as "the core question within the problem of laying the foundation of a science of beings, i.e. the problem of the first *Critique*" (*PIK* 51; *WT* 181).

Kant defines transcendental knowledge as "all cognition that is occupied not so much with objects but rather with our a priori concepts of objects in general" (*CPR* A11/B25). Heidegger concludes from this that "transcendental knowledge does not investigate beings themselves, but rather the possibility of the preliminary understanding of being, i.e., the constitution of the being of

---

[6] *BT* 31; translation modified. Heidegger already interpreted Kant's conception of the forms of intuition in this way in his 1925–1926 lectures *Logic: The Question of Truth* (*Logic* 229, 330).

beings".[7] On this basis, he regards Kant's 'Copernican revolution' as an acknowledgment of the ontological difference: through this revolution in the way of thinking, Kant reorients the philosophical gaze from the ontic level of beings to the ontological level of being.[8] According to Heidegger, we can only know beings on the basis of our pre-ontological understanding of their being: "What makes the comporting toward beings (ontic knowledge) possible is the preliminary understanding of the constitution of being, ontological knowledge".[9] Kant posits the same hierarchy between transcendental or a priori knowledge and empirical knowledge: "Transcendental truth precedes all empirical truth and makes it possible" (*CPR* A147/B187). All empirical truth, or all 'agreement of our cognition with its objects', presupposes the a priori forms of intuition that allow phenomena to appear to us as well as the a priori concepts of the understanding that constitute objects of cognition. In other words, our knowledge of objects necessarily builds on our capacity to constitute objectivity as such. As Heidegger puts it: "Objects could never confront us as objects at all without synthetic judgments *a priori*; by these objects we 'then' guide ourselves in particular investigations, inquiries, and proofs, in which we constantly appeal to them" (*WT* 180).

It is clear, then, that Heidegger's 'ontological reading' does not reject Kant's departure from the naive – or 'proud' – attempt of traditional ontology to determine 'things in themselves'. His comparison of Kant's idea of a priori conditions of experience to 'the being of beings' seems far-fetched because Kant traces these conditions back to human consciousness. We must keep in mind, however, that Heidegger's writings on Kant draw on the conception of being from *Being and Time*, which considers being in so far as Dasein pre-ontologically understands it. This allows him to argue that the *Critique of Pure Reason* cares for ontology and the 'thingness of the things' precisely in so far as it turns away from concrete, empirical beings and thematizes the transcendental sphere of the 'a priori'. As Heidegger sees it, "the term 'transcendental philosophy' is only another designation for the problem of 'ontology'" (*PIK* 58).

(2) Having thus established an analogy between transcendental and ontological knowledge, Heidegger's ontological interpretation of the *Critique of Pure Reason* is, however, still only halfway. In *Being and Time*, Heidegger not

---

[7] *KPM* 16; *PIK* 57. Heidegger already suggests this interpretation of transcendental knowledge in *BT* 38.

[8] *PIK* 56; *KPM* 17, 12. On this basis, Christina Lafont holds that "Heidegger sees his own project as Kantian to the extent that it incorporates the core of Kant's Copernican revolution into the most important categorical distinction of his philosophy, namely, the *ontological difference*" ('Heidegger and the Synthetic a Priori', in: Steven Crowell and Jeff Malpas, *Transcendental Heidegger*, Stanford University Press, 2007, 105).

[9] *KPM* 11; see also *PIK* 36, 55–56, 322.

only distinguished between the ontic investigations performed by science and the ontological investigations of philosophy, but also between the ontological grounding of particular sciences or realms of being and a search for the being of beings as such (*BT* 11). Even though he later describes this in Husserlian terms as the difference between regional ontologies and a general or fundamental ontology, he unlike Husserl identifies the latter as 'the essence of philosophy' (*PIK* 35–39). In his commentaries on Kant, Heidegger argues that this fundamental philosophical interest also motivates the first *Critique*. On his reading, this work does not, as is often thought, establish a regional ontology of the natural sciences but instead aims at an account of the being of beings as such: "What I want to point out is that the transcendental analytic is not just an ontology of nature as object of natural science, but is rather a general ontology, a critical, well-established *metaphysica generalis*" (*DD* 279). Nevertheless, in *Phenomenological Interpretation* Heidegger admits that the natural sciences "play a decisively exemplary role in the problem that Kant poses, namely, the question concerning the ground of the possibility of a science of beings in general" (*PIK* 43). It should be noted, however, that he uses the term 'exemplary' in a twofold sense here, namely as 'providing a guiding model' *and* as 'non-essential'.

Heidegger does not contest that the *Critique of Pure Reason* focuses on the mathematical natural sciences when investigating the possibility of synthetic a priori judgments: "Concerned with an ontology of the present-at-hand in general, a certain realm of the present-at-hand, namely the physical material nature, shows itself for Kant as an explicit basis".[10] In the preface to the second edition of the first *Critique*, Kant indeed identifies mathematics and physics as "the two theoretical cognitions of reason that are supposed to determine their objects a priori" (*CPR* Bx). He thereupon concludes that "the concern of this critique of pure speculative reason consists in the attempt to transform the accepted procedure of metaphysics, undertaking an entire revolution according to the example of the geometers and natural scientists".[11] In this context, Kant also introduces his groundbreaking ideas of "a revolution in the way of thinking" (Bxi) and of reason as the judge of nature (Bxiii). Heidegger not only endorses such an indirect approach, but also acknowledges Kant's reason for focusing on the mathematical-physical conception of objectivity in particular: the inspirational success of the modern natural sciences stems from their insight "that there is no such thing as pure facts and that facts can only be

---

[10] *PIK* 67. Heidegger in fact holds that the 'exemplary role' of these sciences for Kant's thought is almost inevitable when considered from a historical perspective (43). In *What Is a Thing?*, he gives a detailed historical account of how the rise of the modern natural sciences informed Kant's mathematical understanding of the 'essential definition of the thing' (*WT* 65–111).

[11] *CPR* Bxxii. Kant elaborates on the instructive role of the mathematical natural sciences in chapter 2 (B3–6) and chapter 5 (B14–18) of the B-introduction to the first *Critique*.

grasped and experimented with when the realm of nature as such is circum-scribed" (*PIK* 32). The relevance of these sciences for Kant's project thus lies in their operative idea, endorsed by Heidegger, that the being of beings can only appear to us within a horizon that we delimit in advance.[12]

Still, Heidegger considers Kant's interest in the natural sciences as no more than a 'cue' (*Fingerzeig*; 45) or 'indication' (*Anzeige*) of 'the direction in which the fundamental connection between ontic experience and ontological knowledge must first be sought in order to be understood in its more funda-mental universality' (*KPM* 11). He provides a historical as well as a systematic argument for why the possibility of the natural sciences is not Kant's ultimate concern.

In the first paragraphs of both *Phenomenological Interpretation* and *Kant and the Problem of Metaphysics*, Heidegger situates Kant's thought against the background of 'the traditional concept of metaphysics': originating with Aristotle, he holds, this concept has always had a double meaning: metaphys-ics aims to understand both being in general or 'being as such' and the totality of beings. The scholastic tradition took up this distinction and systematically developed a *metaphysica generalis*, or ontology, on the one hand, and a *metaphysica specialis*, which was further divided in a rational psychology, cosmology, and theology, on the other. Heidegger points out that the compos-ition of the *Critique of Pure Reason* echoes these divisions: before the Transcendental Dialectic turns the three doctrines of special metaphysics into critical disciplines, the Transcendental Analytic rethinks the possibility of ontology (*PIK* 11–17; *KPM* 5–13). Kant indeed holds that "the proud name of an ontology, which presumes to offer synthetic a priori cognitions of things *in general* in a systematic doctrine [. . .], must give way to the modest one of a mere analytic of the pure understanding".[13] According to Heidegger, then, the proud presumptions of traditional ontology that Kant dismisses only concern the limits of finite reason: the phenomenal realm must be delineated from the noumenal one because the latter is inaccessible to theoretical knowledge (*KPM* 123). He sees no reason to also assume that Kant meant to replace traditional ontology 'of things in general' by a transcendental investigation into our scientific experience of nature alone. Heidegger thus stresses the continuity between traditional ontology and transcendental philosophy.[14]

Moreover, in two passages from the first *Critique* and *Metaphysical Foundations of Natural Science*, Kant considers it 'quite noteworthy'

---

[12] See *CPR* Bxiii and *PIK* 30–32.   [13] *CPR* A247/B303; Kant's emphasis.

[14] Heidegger further points to *CPR* A845/B873 to demonstrate this continuity: "Transcendental philosophy [. . .] considers only the understanding and reason itself in a system of all concepts and principles that are related to objects in general, without assuming objects that *would be given* (Ontologia)" (see *KPM* 124).

(*merkwürdig*) that general metaphysics relies on outer intuition, using examples taken from the sphere of material nature, for demonstrating the objectivity and intelligibility of its concepts.[15] In this way, he suggests that the link between his transcendental philosophy and the natural sciences is not an essential one. Heidegger therefore holds that whenever Kant talks about the structure of experience as the structure of nature, and thus of nature as the topic of transcendental philosophy, what is meant is not nature considered as the object of the natural sciences, but rather as the essence or being of beings *as such*: "Kant places transcendental philosophy ahead of a metaphysics of nature [. . .]. Prior to the founding of physics, [. . .] there is the founding of knowledge or the constitution of nature as such, regardless of whether there is something like a physical or psychic nature" (*PIK* 63–65). In the Architectonic of Reason, Kant confirms that transcendental philosophy aims at "a system of all concepts and principles that are related to objects in general, without assuming objects that *would be given*" (A845/B873). Heidegger concludes from this that the *Critique of Pure Reason* is in essence not concerned with a specific realm or region of beings, but with the being of beings as such: "The task of the entire *Critique* is *laying the foundation of general ontology*" (*PIK* 199).

3.2   On Kant's Philosophical Method: Critical Philosophy as Phenomenology

Heidegger furthermore recognizes his phenomenological method in Kant's 'critique of pure reason'. First, he sees the mutual dependence that he established between ontology and phenomenology reflected in the connection between Kant's transcendental project and his critical investigation of reason. Second, there's a striking similarity between Heidegger's understanding of Kant's 'transcendental analytic' and his own conception of (ontological) phenomenology. Third, according to Heidegger, Kant effectively proceeds in a phenomenological manner – analysing the essential moments of intentionality or 'transcendence' – in the crucial parts of the Transcendental Analytic: the transcendental deduction and his account of transcendental imagination.[16] On this basis, Heidegger's 'phenomenological reading of the

---

[15] See *PIK* 67–68, where Heidegger refers to *CPR* B288–291 and Immanuel Kant, *Metaphysical Foundations of Natural Science*, tr. by Michael Friedman, Cambridge University Press, 2004, 478.

[16] Heidegger states that 'the first and only goal' of *Phenomenological Interpretation* is to grasp the coherence of the whole of the *Critique of Pure Reason* (*PIK* 6). Nevertheless, like in *Being and Time*, he manages to execute only a third of his initial plan, touching only briefly on the account of the schematism that he had designated earlier as the crucial passage of the first *Critique* (*BT* 23). Therefore, Heidegger less than two years later extensively revisits this account in *Kant and the Problem of Metaphysics*. Yet, it is not until *What Is a thing?* (1935–1936), which focuses on Kant's account of the principles of the understanding, that Heidegger completes even his

Critique of Pure Reason' will gain a double meaning: it approaches Kant's writings in a phenomenological manner *and* interprets Kant's own thought as itself phenomenological.

(1) In the introduction to *Being and Time*, Heidegger argues that the founding of general ontology, his actual interest, requires a preliminary analysis of Dasein's existential constitution. This detour, he holds, is both necessary and opportune: while the philosophical tradition has consistently conflated being with beings, thus confusing the very question about the meaning of being, an implicit or 'pre-ontological' understanding thereof is actually "a determination of being (*eine Seinsbestimmtheit*) of Dasein" (*BT* 12). Hence, an 'existential analytic of Dasein' can and must take the role of a 'fundamental ontology' (13, 14), and as such occupies the entire published part of *Being and Time*.

In order to execute this analysis, Heidegger adopts a phenomenological method. In se, this originally Husserlian method has the seemingly modest task "to let what shows itself be seen from itself, just as it shows itself from itself" (34). Applied to Dasein, however, phenomenology aims to reveal our implicit understanding of being, while disregarding any theoretical preconceptions of either the human being or being as such. For Heidegger, then, ontology and phenomenology are essentially bound up with each other because they indicate the respective object and methodology of original philosophy: "Ontology and phenomenology are not two different disciplines which among others belong to philosophy. Both terms characterize philosophy itself, its object and procedure" (38, 35). In *The Basic Problems of Phenomenology* (1927), Heidegger accordingly holds that the phenomenological method essentially aims to "positively approach being" (*BPP* 29).

In his writings on Kant, Heidegger discerns a similar approach to ontology in the *Critique of Pure Reason*. In this work, he holds, Kant after all secures the possibility of ontological knowledge by investigating the structure of transcendental subjectivity, or by a 'critique of pure reason':

Insofar as the principles contained in reason constitute the possibility of a priori knowledge, the unveiling of the possibility of ontological knowledge must become an

---

reading of the Transcendental Analytic. In the third preface to *Kant and the Problem of Metaphysics* (1965), Heidegger says that *What Is a Thing?* (published in 1962) supplements the Kant book, thus indicating the continuity of his commentaries on Kant (*KPM* xxi). Engelland, however, nuances that these lectures rather "correct, supplement, and retract aspects of the 1929 book": for Engelland's detailed and insightful analysis of these further variations in Heidegger's reading of Kant, see *Heidegger's Shadow. Kant, Husserl, and the Transcendental Turn*. New York: Routledge, 2017, 125 a.f. (I will not engage with Heidegger's 1961 essay 'Kant's Thesis about Being' because it was written long after the dispute with Cassirer had ended (see *Pathmarks*, tr. William McNeill, Cambridge: Cambridge University Press, 1998, 337–363).

elucidation of the essence of pure reason. The delimitation of the essence of pure reason, however, is at the same time the differentiating determination of its non-essence and, with that, the limitation and restriction (critique) of its essential possibilities. Laying the ground for metaphysics as unveiling the essence of ontology is 'critique of pure reason'.[17]

Hence, in so far as the first *Critique* focuses on the capacities and limits of reason, Heidegger distinctively claims that it – like *Being and Time* – primarily investigates *the possibility of* ontology, rather than carrying out an actual ontological theory: "The inquiry into the ground of the possibility of onto-logical knowledge constitutes the basic inquiry of the *Critique of Pure Reason*."[18] Accordingly, in the very first sentence of *Kant and the Problem of Metaphysics* he announces that he will consider the first *Critique* as "placing the problem of metaphysics before us as a fundamental ontology".[19]

The way that Kant sets up his critical philosophy indeed seems to mirror the way that Heidegger relates philosophy's ultimate task of retrieving the mean-ing of being to its preliminary task of investigating the constitution of Dasein. On the one hand, Kant investigates the faculties of the human mind *for the sake of* affirming the possibility of metaphysics, to which, he says, all reason-able beings have a natural predisposition (*CPR* B21). Kant considers the 'critique of pure reason' as a propaedeutic for actual metaphysics, be it of nature or morals,[20] and holds that it should be understood as "*a treatise on the method*, not a system of the science [of metaphysics] itself".[21] He expresses the hope that once the limits of reason have been determined, he can develop an actual metaphysics of nature, "which will be not half so extensive but will be incomparably richer in content than this critique" (Axxi), and metaphysics of morals. According to Heidegger, Kant's critical method therefore has the fundamentally positive intent to regain our lost sensitivity for ontology (*WT* 119–120).

On the other hand, Kant deems his critical approach *necessary* because he considers metaphysics to have made almost no progress since Aristotle.[22] In order to avoid scepticism and finally safeguard the legitimacy of metaphysics as science, Kant sees no other option than to carry out the 'Copernican revolution' that puts reason at the center of philosophy.[23] Hence, Kant's

---

[17] *KPM* 14; see also *PIK* 69, 334; *KPM* 10, 205, 213; and *WT* 122, 181, 243–244.
[18] *PIK* 51; see also *PIK* 10, 15, 66, 69, 81; *KPM* 1, 10–18, 35, 40, 42, etc.
[19] *KPM* 1; seen also *PIK* 372–373.   [20] *CPR* A11–12/B25–26, A841/B869; *PIK* 61–62.
[21] *CPR* Bxxii (my emphasis), Bxliv; *PIK* 58–59.
[22] *CPR* Bxv. Heidegger addresses this in *PIK* 14–16, where he holds that Kant's critical founda-tion of metaphysics brought an end to the fundamental uncertainties that had been ingrained in the concept of ontology ever since Plato and Aristotle.
[23] Daniel Dahlstrom distinguishes between a metaphysical and a cognitive dimension of Heidegger's reading of Kant. The former, he says, dominates the introduction and conclusion to *Kant and the Problem of Metaphysics*, and the latter is found in Heidegger's interpretation of

transcendental project and critical investigation of reason can be said to relate to each other in the same way as the concept – ontology – and method – phenomenology – of philosophy do in Heidegger's view: "The *Critique of Pure Reason* lays the foundation of ontology as the fundamental discipline of metaphysics and is the treatise on the method of transcendental philosophy" (*PIK* 69). Heidegger's writings on Kant follow this procedure that is shared by the first *Critique* and *Being and Time*: while their introductions concern the possibility of 'conceiving anew the concept of ontology' (15), their main body develops the method that this purpose requires.

(2) Heidegger further endorses this analogy by claiming that Kant's philosophical method is indeed phenomenological: "In its basic posture the *method* of the *Critique* is what we, since Husserl, understand, carry out, and learn to ground more radically as *phenomenological method*" (*PIK* 71, 431). In *Being and Time*, Heidegger defines phenomenology as a purely descriptive method (*BT* 34–35) and distinguishes between its formal and its philosophical or ontological task. The formal task of phenomenology, he explains, is to indiscriminately scrutinize *all* phenomena that are, for various reasons, "initially and for the most part not given" (36). The ontological task of phenomenology, on the other hand, is to specifically thematize "what is concealed but at the same time essentially belongs to what initially and for the most part shows itself, indeed in such a way that it constitutes its meaning and ground".[24] By this constitutive yet predominantly elusive moment of all our appearances, Heidegger after all means the being of beings: "What remains *concealed* in an exceptional sense, or what falls back and is *covered up* again, or shows itself only in a *disguised*' way, is not this or that being but rather [. . .] the being of beings" (35). 'Ontological phenomenology' or 'phenomenological ontology' searches, then, for being understood as the naturally undisclosed ground of the beings that evidently surround us.

Heidegger's discussion of Kant's concepts of 'analytic' and 'transcendental analytic' in §18 of *Phenomenological Interpretation* clearly echoes these respective conceptions of phenomenology. Heidegger defines Kant's term 'analytic' as 'clarifying thinking and what is thought' by "isolating the moments that constitute the contents of a given concept", and adds that "in this context, it is of no concern whatsoever what the concept is a concept of,

---

Kant's account of transcendental imagination ('The *Critique of Pure Reason* and Continental Philosophy: Heidegger's Interpretation of Transcendental Imagination', in: *The Cambridge Companion to Heidegger*, 385–389). While I endorse this distinction, and argue that it returns in Heidegger's other writings on Kant, I find the term 'cognitive' rather unfit in this context: given Heidegger's staunch criticism of any epistemological reading of the first *Critique* and his own carefully developed philosophical methodology, the term 'phenomenological dimension' seems more accurate.

[24] *BT* 35; my translation.

what kind of being the concept indicates, [...] in what way the concept indicates a being[, or] in what course of thinking the concept is obtained" (*PIK* 217). A 'transcendental analytic', on the other hand, "is not concerned with whatever concepts that are somehow given". Instead, Heidegger holds, it aims at a "clarification of the faculty of the understanding itself [...] with the intention of rendering visible this comportment of thinking as the birthplace of those concepts that determine a priori the objectivity of objects".[25] By 'rendering visible' the a priori concepts of the understanding, Kant's Transcendental Analytic reveals the constitutive conditions of possibility of our experience of objects that otherwise necessarily remain unthematic. In Heideggerean terms, it offers a phenomenological analysis of Dasein's understanding of the being of beings, or a phenomenological ontology (69–70).

(3) On this basis, we can understand Heidegger's alternating between two definitions of transcendental philosophy. We have seen earlier that, when first explaining the *goal* of Kant's thought, Heidegger holds that transcendental philosophy is synonymous with general ontology. When he later considers Kant's critical *method* for grounding ontology, by contrast, he defines transcendental philosophy as an "essential unveiling of transcendence".[26] Likewise, Heidegger determines the theme of the Transcendental Analytic – 'the positive part of the critique' (280, 429) – as 'the transcendence of Dasein'.[27] If, according to Heidegger, being is the topic of Kant's thought considered from an ontological perspective, then Dasein's transcendence, or its capacity to understand the being of beings, is its topic from a phenomenological one: "The task of an 'analytic of transcendence' [is that] of a pure phenomenology of the subjectivity of the subject".[28] Hence, he claims, "the insight into the full structure of transcendence makes it possible for the first time to have a clear view of the complete range of characteristics peculiar to ontological knowledge" (*KPM* 120, 76, 117). Heidegger shows no interest in actually uncovering this 'complete range of characteristics'. More important is where and how the Transcendental Analytic contains an argument for 'the transcendence of Dasein'. In these questions lies the real test for Heidegger's phenomenological reading of Kant.

---

[25] *PIK* 218 (based on *CPR* A65–66/B90); *KPM* 41.
[26] *KPM* 124, 166. See also *WT* 176; Martin Heidegger, 'On the Essence of Ground', in: *Pathmarks*, tr. by William McNeill, Cambridge: Cambridge University Press, 1998, 109; and *GA 27* 207. For more on Heidegger's use of the term transcendental, see Adam R. Tate, 'On Heidegger's Root and Branch Reformulation of Transcendental Psychology', *The Journal of the British Society for Phenomenology*, 46(1), 2015, 61–78.
[27] *PIK* 219; see also Martin Heidegger, *The Metaphysical Foundations of Logic*, tr. by Michael Heim, Bloomington: Indiana University Press, 1984, 164–165.
[28] *KPM* 87. Heidegger also presents 'transcendental' and 'phenomenological' as synonymous terms on *PIK* 355.

The 'transcendence of Dasein' is another designation for what Heidegger in *Being and Time* calls Dasein's 'being-in-the-world', and thus another attempt to rethink Husserl's concept of 'intentionality' – a, if not *the*, central idea of their respective phenomenological research. According to Husserl, consciousness is fundamentally characterized by intentionality in the sense that it is never isolated from its objects but rather always already engages with them. This engagement is further marked by an 'intentional horizon' that includes not only what we actually perceive but also, implicitly, what we perceived earlier or could potentially perceive next.[29] Heidegger's concept of 'being-in-the-world' likewise indicates that Dasein is essentially among other beings and always situated in a meaningful context, namely the world within which it understands the being of these beings (*BT* 62). Accordingly, Dasein's transcendence consists not only in its capacity to 'go beyond' itself towards the beings that it encounters, but also in its capacity to transcend concrete being*s* and understand their being.[30]

In *Kant and the Problem of Metaphysics*, Heidegger thus holds that transcendence is fully determined by two conditions: "In itself, transcendence is ecstatic-horizonal" (*KPM* 118–119). We have already implicitly touched upon the idea of horizonality in the previous section, when explaining that ontological (transcendental) knowledge of being as such (objectivity as such) is a condition of possibility of ontic (empirical) knowledge of beings (objects). According to Heidegger, ontological knowledge thus establishes the a priori horizon within which we can first encounter objects: in order for knowledge of objects to be possible, there "must open up in advance the distinct horizon of the standing-against that regulates its possible accordance with objects by giving a standard. This horizon is the condition for the possibility of the object with respect to its being-able-to-stand-against".[31] Heidegger now explains that Dasein's transcendence brings about this horizon: "Transcendence constitutes knowledge, and this constitution is nothing other than the holding-open of the horizon within which the being of beings becomes discernable in a preliminary way".[32] As such, transcendence is the condition of possibility of the onto-logical – or 'transcendental' – knowledge of the being of beings (114).

---

[29] Edmund Husserl, *Cartesian Meditations: An Introduction to Phenomenology*, tr. by Dorion Cairns, The Hague: Martinus Nijhoff, 1973, 44–46 (§19).

[30] Consult, in this regard, *PIK* 334; *GA 27* 210; or *EG* 109.

[31] *KPM* 118; translation modified, 108.

[32] *KPM* 123, 127. The way that Heidegger each time phrases this constitutive relation ("Die ontologische Erkenntniss 'bildet' die Transzendenz") occasions misinterpretation and faulty translation, yet there can be no doubt that transcendence is the constitutive condition of possibility of ontological knowledge, rather than the other way around. Heidegger confirms this on *GA 27* 207, 209.

In order to 'hold open' this horizon, Dasein must however have an 'ecstatic' nature; it must be 'open to the world', even if it is so unthematically: "In order for an object to be able to give itself, there must in advance already be a turning-toward such an occurrence, which is capable of being 'summoned'. This preliminary turning-one's-attention-toward something [...] is the condition for the possibility of experiencing".[33] The 'full structure of transcendence' lies, then, "in the fact that the *turning-itself-toward* constitutes the horizon of objectivity in general by allowing the *letting-stand-against as such*".[34] Heidegger recognizes this structure in Kant's famous claim that "the conditions of the possibility of experience in general are at the same time conditions of the possibility of the objects of experience, and on this account have objective validity in a synthetic judgment a priori".[35] This claim, Heidegger holds, "is the expression of the most original phenomenological knowledge of the innermost, unified structure of transcendence" (119).

For a more detailed account of the ecstatic-horizonal structure of transcendental subjectivity, we must turn to the heart of Heidegger's writings on Kant, which consists of meticulous but highly provocative readings of the transcendental deduction and Kant's account of transcendental imagination. Heidegger interprets the transcendental deduction of the categories of the understanding as establishing the horizonal character of transcendental knowledge, and the transcendental power of imagination as accounting for the ecstatic character of transcendental subjectivity.[36]

In the second section of the 'A-deduction' of the categories, Kant discusses the pure syntheses of apprehension in intuition, of reproduction in the

---

[33] *KPM* 118; see also *PIK* 309, 408–409.   [34] *KPM* 119; my translation and emphasis.
[35] *CPR* A158/B197; *KPM* 160.
[36] Kant distinguishes between showing "*that* the categories contain the grounds of the possibility of all experience in general" and explaining "*how* they make experience possible, and which principles of its possibility they yield in their application to appearances" (*CPR* B167; my emphasis). While he identifies the former accomplishment as the result of the transcendental deduction, for the latter, twofold, task he refers to "the following chapter on the transcendental use of the power of judgment". This chapter first discusses the schematizing of the categories by the transcendental power of imagination and subsequently offers a systematic overview of the synthetic principles of pure understanding. Heidegger repeatedly relies on the distinction between exposition and foundation for explaining the argumentative, phenomenological, thread of the Transcendental Analytic (*PIK* 365, 430–431; *KPM* 118, 135). Moreover, this distinction also directs the overall structure of *Kant and the Problem of Metaphysics*: in this work, Heidegger dissects the transcendental deduction when discussing "the *inner possibility* of the essential unity of ontological synthesis" (the 'third stage of the ground-laying of metaphysics'; *KPM* 69–88), and rethinks the status of transcendental imagination when exploring "the *ground* for the possibility of ontological knowledge" (the 'fourth stage'; 88–113). His definition of the 'full structure of transcendence' follows, then, in the subsequent, summarizing section on "the full essential determination of ontological knowledge" (the fifth stage; 113–125). Once this is covered, Heidegger holds that "we have only to be concerned with presenting concretely the synthetic principles a priori in their system" (*PIK* 429; *GA* 27 273). He then discusses these principles at length in *What Is a Thing?* (*WT* 184–243).

imagination, and of recognition through concepts in apperception (*CPR* A98–110). Heidegger interprets these syntheses as three horizons that are required for the knowledge of objects: he explains the synthesis of apprehension as "the horizon in which the manifold *as such* can be offered" (*PIK* 345–346), that of reproduction as "an open horizon of the past" that enables us to 'go back into the past and retain what we perceived earlier' (352), and the synthesis of reproduction as an 'a priori projection of a whole' (*vorwegnehmende Entwurf eines Ganzen*; 364) that allows us to identify objects of experience. Heidegger further argues that these horizons presuppose each other (361). On his reading of the transcendental deduction, we can only intuit something on the basis of an apprehensive horizon within which our current intuition is juxtaposed to previous ones. In order to distinguish between the now and the 'no-longer-now', we must however be able to recall or re-intuit our earlier intuitions – or to imagine what is not currently given: "Apprehension is not itself possible without reproduction. Already in seizing what is immediately given as intuitive there occurs a reaching beyond and reaching back" (353). This reproduction of intuitions is, in turn, only possible "if we can recognize what we previously intuited as *the same* as what we intuit now" (361) and identify their unity by means of a pure concept in appercep-tion. Hence, even our mere intuitions presuppose the horizon established by the categories, which therefore have objective reality.[37]

In the third section of the 'A-deduction', Kant subsequently ascertains the intimate connection between the 'three subjective sources of cognition on which the possibility of an experience in general rests', first by arguing from the role of pure apperception (*CPR* A116–119), and then also from intuition (A119–124). On the whole, he concludes that

we have a pure imagination, as a fundamental faculty of the human soul, that grounds all cognition a priori. By its means we bring into combination the manifold of intuition on the one side, and the condition of the necessary unity of apperception on the other. Both extremes, namely sensibility and understanding, must necessarily be connected by means of this transcendental function of the imagination, since otherwise the former would surely yield appearances but no objects of an empirical cognition, hence there would be no experience. (A124; *KPM* 77, 84, 134)

Heidegger infers from this that the transcendental power of imagination is the ultimate subjective ground of ontological knowledge.[38] On his reading, this

---

[37] For a more detailed account and critical assessment of Heidegger's reading of the A-deduction, see Weatherston, *Heidegger's Interpretation of Kant*, 85–165. Also instructive in this regard are Elliott, 'Heidegger's appropriation of Kant', 111–116; and Käufer, 'Heidegger's Interpretation of Kant', 187–193.

[38] *PIK* 281, 332, 338, 411, 420. At the end of *Phenomenological Interpretation*, Heidegger even holds that "in the way in which we set out to interpret [...] the transcendental deduction, we

power represents the ecstatic moment of transcendence in Kant's thought: "The productive power of imagination is the root of the faculties of subjectivity; it is the basic *ecstatic constitution of the subject*, of *Dasein* itself" (*PIK* 417–418, 412, 414). Kant holds that the specific capacity of imagination consists in synthesizing (*CPR* A78/B103). On this basis, Heidegger conceives of transcendental imagination as producing the 'original, pure, synthesis' (*KPM* 127) from which all other syntheses are derived: "The transcendental power of imagination is in general the origin of all that is 'synthetic'. 'Synthesis' must be taken here in a way that is quite wide enough to encompass the synopsis of intuition and the 'synthesis' of the understanding".[39] Furthermore, Kant defines imagination as "the faculty for representing an object even without its presence in intuition".[40] Unbound to particular objects, the transcendental power of imagination is, then, for Heidegger the original, ecstatic, force of the mind to constitute the horizon of transcendence (89, 90, 131, 198). He concludes that the transcendental power of imagination is the "root" (140) and "essential unity of transcendence as a whole" (134), and "the ground for the inner possibility of ontological knowledge" (108, 111, 127).

Kant and the Problem of Metaphysics suggests at least two additional points of analogy between Kant's account of transcendental imagination and Heidegger's phenomenological analysis of Dasein. First, Heidegger characterizes this faculty, now understood as the common root of (the syntheses of) sensibility and the understanding, as "structural, unified, receptive spontaneity" (153–155). This echoes his view of Dasein's being-in-the-world as a simultaneously thrown and projective condition (*BT* §29, §31). Second, Heidegger ultimately identifies the structure of 'original temporality' as the

---

already fundamentally dealt with the problem of the schematism" (431, *KPM* 127, 163). As Alberto Moreiras puts it, for Heidegger "the transcendental deduction of the categories is the analytical revelation of the structure of the pure synthesis of the imagination" ('Heidegger, Kant, and the Problem of Transcendence', in: *The Southern Journal of Philosophy*, 34(1), 1986, 88).

[39] *KPM* 142. Heidegger further stresses that Kant, at least in de A-edition, repeatedly identifies three instead of two basic sources of cognition: sensibility, imagination, and the apperception (*KPM* 135–137; see *CPR* A94(fn), A115, A124). According to Heidegger, Kant only invokes this threefold distinction when he is concerned with the 'dimension of the origin' of ontological knowledge (*PIK* 407). He thus connects Kant's claim that the faculties of sensibility and the understanding "may perhaps arise from a common but to us unknown root" (*CPR* A15/B29, A835/B863) to the descriptions of imagination as "an indispensable function of the soul [. . .] of which we are seldom even conscious" (A78/B103), and of the schematism as "a hidden art in the depths of the human soul" (A141/B180). On this basis, Heidegger proclaims the transcendental power of the imagination the most fundamental ground of ontological knowledge (*KPM* 160; see also 37, 63, 101, 137). Concerning this notorious part of Heidegger's reading of Kant, see Dahlstrom, 'Heidegger's Interpretation of Transcendental Imagination', 387–398.

[40] *CPR* B151; *KPM* 131. On *PIK* 413 and *KPM* 128, Heidegger refers to a similar definition of the power of imagination that Kant offers in §28 of his *Anthropology from a Pragmatic Point of View*.

ground of the three syntheses discussed in the A-deduction (*KPM* §33) as well as of transcendental imagination (§34). This reflects the final step ('Division Two') of the published part of *Being and Time*, which traces Dasein's *existentiale* of being-in-the-world and care back to the ecstatic structure of temporality.[41] Without going into these matters here, we can conclude that Heidegger's reading of Kant engages most extensively with the transcendental deduction and Kant's account of transcendental imagination because he takes these passages to explain and ground the idea of transcendence that is central to his own analysis of Dasein: "What occurs in the Kantian ground-laying? Nothing less than this: the grounding of the inner possibility of ontology is brought about as an unveiling of transcendence, i.e., of the subjectivity of the human subject" (205). On this basis, we can understand why Heidegger interprets the Transcendental Analytic as an exercise in phenomenology.

3.3   On Kant's Hermeneutical Situation: The Problem of Metaphysics

We can now understand on which grounds Heidegger considers Kant to take "an essential step in the direction of a fundamental elucidation of the concept and method of philosophy" (*PIK* 6). Notwithstanding this appraisal, Heidegger however also severely criticizes Kant for remaining caught under the spell of traditional philosophy. This ambiguous evaluation should, of course, not surprise us: as a part of Heidegger's 'phenomenological destruction of the history of philosophy', his reading of Kant has both a constructive element – as displayed in the two previous sections – and a destructive one.[42] More surprising is that Heidegger in the end *praises* Kant *precisely because* his transcendental philosophy oscillates between the rationalist tradition and phenomenological ontology. This is the case because Heidegger also perceives a hermeneutic moment in Kant's thought.

Heidegger repeatedly remarks that Kant did not fully endorse the project of a phenomenological ontology. Already in *Being and Time*, he lauds Kant for being "the first and only one who traversed *a stretch of the path toward* investigating the problematic [of temporality]", but immediately adds that this problem "had to remain closed to Kant in its *real* dimensions and its *central* ontological function".[43] The reason for Kant's eventual failure, Heidegger explains, is twofold: the *Critique of Pure Reason* lacked the philosophical compass of the question of being as such, and it accordingly also "failed to provide [...] a preliminary ontological analytic of the subjectivity of the subject". Because of his traditional understanding of subjectivity, Kant did

---

[41] See f.e. *BT* 329–331, 360, and 365–366; and *BPP* 429.
[42] Chapter 9 elaborates on the general nature of this 'historical destruction'.
[43] *BT* 23; my emphasis; see also *Logic* 224, 312.

not come to terms with Dasein's fundamentally temporal nature, and therefore "could never gain insight into the problem of temporality" (*BT* 24).

Heidegger's writings on Kant revisit this criticism, but here his tone changes twice. In the introductions and conclusions to these works, Heidegger no longer questions the first *Critique*'s accomplishment but rather Kant's own understanding thereof. In his 1927 lectures, he claims that "Kant's actual procedure is far better than his own knowledge of it" (*PIK* 324, 71, 425–426). In *Kant and the Problem of Metaphysics*, Heidegger in turn holds that "whether Kant himself achieves the full clarification of this problem [of ontological knowledge] remains a subordinate question. It is enough that he recognized its necessity and, above all, that he presented it" (*KPM* 12, 230). However, when discussing the key passages from the Transcendental Analytic, Heidegger argues that Kant *did* recognize the implications of his insights, but ultimately recoiled (*zurückweichen*) from them because he could not forsake traditional metaphysics entirely.[44] These assessments do not contradict each other: as their location in Heidegger's writings signals, they respectively concern the aim and methodology of Kant's philosophy.

With regard to the *aim* of transcendental philosophy, we have seen that Heidegger nuances Kant's focus on the mathematical-natural sciences in the *Critique of Pure Reason*: these sciences, he holds, served as a mere guideline for the account of ontological knowledge as such that Kant attempted to establish:

Because Kant considers as unshaken and self-evident the traditional science of beings as the science of what is present-at-hand, because in a way beings are taken to be identical with the beings that belong to extant nature, therefore natural science is inevitably given a priority in the fundamental discussion of the possibility of a science of beings in general. (*PIK* 44)

Nevertheless, Heidegger still takes issue with Kant's conception of being: "However, because Kant, following the tradition, identifies beings with what is present-at-hand [. . .] his posing of the [ontological] problem suffers from a significant contraction (*Verengung*)". According to Heidegger, then, even though Kant's thought concerns the possibility of a general ontology, his uncritical attitude with regard to 'the traditional science of beings' causes him to conflate the being of beings as such with 'being-present-at-hand' (62–65, 200). In *Being and Time*, Heidegger argued that presence-at-hand is neither the sole nor the ontologically most original mode of being: Dasein's 'existence' precludes any definition in terms of actuality or presence (*BT*

---

[44] See *KPM* §31, 214, 244. In 'Heidegger's Kantian Turn: Notes to His Commentary on the 'Kritik der reinen Vernunft', Dahlstrom offers an overview of the different issues on which Kant wavers according to the *Phenomenological Interpretation* (*The Review of Metaphysics*, 45 (2), 1991, 335–336).

42–43, 143–144), and the beings through which it primarily understands being are tools that are 'ready-to-hand', that is, beings that Dasein encounters as 'actively' involved in its world (67–72). In contrast, the 'present-at-hand' indicates the type of objects that we cognize by means of logical judgements and that belong to the theoretical, detached, realm of the sciences that Heidegger considers ontologically derivative (69, 138, §33). In so far as Kant's account of the categories and synthetic judgements a priori matches the latter conception of being (*WT* 122, 181), his attempt to ground a general ontology must therefore remain confused in Heidegger's eyes.[45]

With regard to the *method* of the *Critique of Pure Reason*, Heidegger accordingly holds that Kant wavers between a phenomenological and a logical account of transcendental subjectivity (*PIK* 318, 324). Kant's fundamental flaw, he now counters his initial appraisal, consists in "misconstruing the problem of transcendence – or better said, in failing to see transcendence as an original and essential determination of the ontological constitution of Dasein".[46] More specifically, Heidegger claims that the B-edition of the first *Critique* reverts to a more traditional, rationalistic, approach to general ontology.[47]

As we have seen, in the A-deduction Kant establishes the objective reality of the categories by investigating the structure of the subjectivity of the subject, that is, by explaining the coordination and unity of the transcendental faculties of the mind. Heidegger considers this approach a forerunner of his own phenomenological analysis of Dasein. In the B-deduction – albeit not exclusively there – he however discerns a different approach: on his view, Kant here assumes the subjective conditions of our thinking from the outset, and questions how they can have objective validity as well. As Heidegger puts it, the transcendental deduction now deals with the 'juridical' issue of the logical

---

[45] *WT* 128–129. Heidegger likewise criticizes Kant's conception of time, as a form of intuition, for being modeled after the Newtonian conception thereof that is exclusively oriented towards the present time. In contrast, his account of transcendental imagination as the ground of the three syntheses aims to lodge his own conception of original temporality, as the unity of the ecstases of past, present, and future, in the heart of the first *Critique* (*PIK* 364, 395).

[46] *PIK* 315, 319. Already in *Being and Time*, Heidegger considers it a crucial shortcoming of Kant's thought that he understood the self as an 'I think' but not yet as an 'I think something' (*BT* 321). This means, Heidegger explains, that "Kant did not see the phenomenon of the world, and [that] the 'I' was forced back again to an *isolated* subject".

[47] On Heidegger's view, the "first edition is only more difficult, while at the same time more genuine and more radical in its inquiry" (*PIK* 216), and we should, thus, "place the major emphasis on the elaboration of the first edition, which is a sample of the force of Kant's phenomenological seeing" (324). In *Kant and the Problem of Metaphysics*, Heidegger confirms that the 1981 edition of the *Critique of Pure Reason* "remains closer to the innermost thrust of the problematic of a laying of the ground for metaphysics" (*KPM* 197), and in *What Is a Thing?*, he says that "in terms of content all decisive insights had been achieved in the first edition" (*WT* 151).

validity of the categories rather than the phenomenological concern about their
ontological meaning: "The problem of the objective reality of the categories as
the disclosure of the inner possibility of their content becomes the problem of
objective validity, in the sense of a juridical justification of the validity of
something subjective as something objective".[48] For Heidegger, however, it is
"absurd to begin with categories and then to inquire into their valid application
to objects" (400). To do so, means to have misunderstood the problem at hand,
since the categories are not logical concepts of the pure understanding, but
ontological determinations of beings.[49] As a consequence, their objective
reality should already be clear once we grasp the transcendent, ecstatic, nature
of subjectivity:

With the working out of the original dimension [of subjectivity] the ontological essence
of categories must *eo ipso* already be established. [...] From this we infer that a
juridical inquiry makes no sense and that we can no longer ask how a pure concept
of the understanding is to have objective validity now that we are clear about the nature
of subjectivity. *For belonging to subjectivity sufficiently disclosed is just the elucidation
of the manner and possibility of the objective reality of categories.* (384–385)

This original dimension is lost, however, when the B-deduction also downplays the role of transcendental imagination for the grounding of ontological
knowledge. In 1787, Kant indeed seems to reform his original, threefold,
account of the faculties of the mind into the classical twofold distinction
between sensibility and the understanding: he omits the passages from the
A-edition that identify 'three original sources, capacities, or faculties of the
soul', and redefines transcendental imagination from an 'indispensable function of the soul' to a 'function of the understanding'.[50] On this basis,
Heidegger notes that "in the second edition of the *Critique of Pure Reason*,
the transcendental power of imagination as it came to light in the impassioned
course of its first projection was thrust aside and given a new interpretation –
one favoring the understanding" (*KPM* 161). Once apperception becomes the
focal point of interest, the power of imagination is no longer considered the
common root of sensibility and the understanding, but "just an external bond
that fastens together two ends" (137, 164; *PIK* 418). Ultimately, Heidegger
holds that the rather one-sided focus of the B-deduction on the transcendental

---

[48] *PIK* 323 (my translation); *CPR* A84–85/B116–117.
[49] *PIK* 402; *KPM* 86. In *Phenomenological Interpretation* Heidegger time and again claims that
Kant did not truly understand the task he was facing: see *PIK* 308, 309, 385, and 401. Kant's
misunderstanding of the phenomenological problem of transcendence forms the topic of David
Carr's excellent essay 'Heidegger on Kant on Transcendence' (in: *Transcendental Heidegger*,
28–42).
[50] See *CPR* A94(fn), A115, A78, B103; discussed by Heidegger on *KPM* 161–164.

unity of apperception (*CPR* B131–142; *PIK* 412) obscures Dasein's ecstatic character because it severs the intimate bond between the 'I think' and time.[51]

As Heidegger sees it, these revisions at the heart of Kant's thought signal a retreat to a rationalist approach to ontology. With regard to the transcendental deduction, he explains that "Kant's polemical orientation toward theoretical metaphysics is the motivation for the juridical approach to the problem of the possibility of ontological knowledge".[52] Concerning transcendental imagination, he in turn holds that

> Kant came upon the central function of the power of imagination, but did not come to terms with an interpretation of this power in terms of fundamental ontology; for this he was much too strongly tied to the traditional doctrine of the faculties of the soul and even more so to the division – still prevalent today – of the basic faculty of knowledge into intuition and thinking. (*PIK* 280; *KPM* 169)

Near the end of *Kant and the Problem of Metaphysics*, Heidegger even concludes that the true outcome (*das eigentliche Ergebnis*) of Kant's philosophy is not his insight that general ontology must be founded in the transcendent character of subjectivity, but his refusal to fully endorse this insight:

> What has actually resulted from the occurrence of the Kantian ground-laying? Not that the transcendental power of imagination is the ground, and not that this ground-laying becomes a question of the essence of human reason, but rather that, as a result of unveiling the subjectivity of the subject, Kant recoils from the ground that he himself had laid.[53]

It seems, then, that Heidegger in the end chooses to emphasize the shortcomings of Kant's philosophy over its affinity to his own.

Yet, in so far as Heidegger explains Kant's wavering "as a result of unveiling the subjectivity of the subject", he does not withdraw his interpretation of Kant as a phenomenological thinker entirely. For one, he still insists that Kant initially grasped the essential role of transcendental imagination for the ground-laying of general ontology, and only later "shrank back from this unknown root" (*KPM* 160, 165). More importantly, he holds that Kant oscillated between traditional, rationalistic, metaphysics and phenomenological ontology *precisely because* he had truly understood the distinctive nature of the 'ground-laying' that occurs in the latter:

> That much is clear, that Kant at the heart of his own problem and under the title of the transcendental power of the imagination comes across a phenomenon that – as he also noticed – completely runs against that which according to the tradition and his own view should be fixed as the fundamental phenomenon of human Dasein. As soon as one

---

[51] *PIK* 358, 393; see also *Logic* 335–337; and *BT* 427–428.

[52] *PIK* 308. In *Einleitung in de Philosophie*, Heidegger remarks that 'transcendental' was for Kant a rather 'critical-negative concept' meant to distinguish his position from 'theological-dogmatic metaphysics', whereas he himself understands it positively 'on the basis of the essence of transcendence itself' (*GA 27* 208).

[53] *KPM* 214; my translation.

establishes the power of imagination of the central power, the entire previous idea of philosophy collapses – hence Kant's evasion.[54]

The division of the first *Critique* in a Transcendental Aesthetic and Transcendental Logic reflects the traditional view of sensibility and reason as the two basic sources of cognition. Imagination – which was traditionally related to fantasy (*PIK* 279) and illusion – has no clear place in this architectonics: it is, as Heidegger puts it, 'homeless' (*heimatlos*).[55] This is, in fact, the main reason for his interest in this power: as the capacity to go 'beyond oneself' and be amidst other beings, transcendental imagination is indeed at home in neither the self nor the world but rather forms their common ground that cannot itself be located and fixed.[56] As such, this force threatens the very idea of a stable foundation for metaphysics: rather than a ground, Heidegger holds, Kant found an abyss (*Ab-grund*) at the heart of subjectivity, and thus at the root of metaphysics: "'In attempting to lay the ground for metaphysics, Kant was pressed in a way that makes the proper foundation into an abyss" (*DD* 288). Not willing to risk the fate of metaphysics in this way, Kant however recoiled, and reinforced 'the mastery (*Herrschaft*) of reason' (*KPM* 243–244):

Will not the *Critique of Pure Reason* have deprived itself of its own theme if pure reason reverts to the transcendental power of imagination? Does not this ground-laying lead us to an abyss? In the radicalism of his questions, Kant brought the 'possibility' of metaphysics to this abyss. He saw the unknown. He had to shrink back. (*KPM* 167–168; *PIK* 213–214)

Heidegger thus interprets Kant's hesitation in the first *Critique* not as a sign of his weakness but rather as a proof of his profound insight: "It is just this hesitation by Kant in this central dimension that is productive and instructive – and by no means a deficiency of his philosophical research".[57] According to

---

[54] *GA 27* 269; my translation.
[55] *KPM* 136, 167. Heidegger further holds that the problems of the pure synthesis and the categories, if properly understood, likewise belong in neither the Transcendental Aesthetic, nor the Transcendental Logic (66).
[56] In *Einleitung in die Philosophie*, Heidegger holds that the transcendence of Dasein expresses itself as a 'lack of bearing' (*Haltlosigkeit; GA 27* 337).
[57] *PIK* 216, 68. Heidegger adds that "only Kant and, by way of comparison, Aristotle – who both aimed so clearly at a radical and fundamental goal – could have and had to hesitate in this clumsy manner" (217). Both the reference to Aristotle, the other main target of Heidegger's destruction of the history of philosophy, and the contention that Kant *had to* hesitate, affirm Heidegger's positive assessment of Kant's wavering. Heidegger in this way also discredits Cassirer's later criticism of his Kant interpretation: the claim that Kant 'shrank back' does not provide a psychological explanation of the twists in Kant's thought, as Cassirer suggests (*KPMR* 244), but a philosophical argument pertaining to the possibility of metaphysics as such. In fact, in the *Phenomenological Interpretation* Heidegger relates this hesitation to Dasein's fallenness (*PIK* 68), and in *Einleitung in die Philosophie* he holds that Kant suffered from 'metaphysical anxiety' (*GA 27* 269). In either case, Kant's wavering is once again not ascribed to a psychological flaw, but to a philosophical sensitivity for the lack of bearing that marks 'the subjectivity of the subject'.

Heidegger, Kant's wavering is *instructive* because it reveals 'the problem of metaphysics', namely that it is without a ground:

> Kant's recoiling from the ground that he himself unveiled, from the transcendental power of imagination – for purposes of the rescue of pure reason, i.e., of holding-fast to the proper foundation – is that movement of philosophizing which makes manifest the breaking-open of the foundation and thus makes manifest the abyss of metaphysics.[58]

Genuine philosophy, Heidegger holds, 'must constantly balance on the edges of the abyss'.[59]

He considers Kant's wavering to be *productive*, further, because it points to "a fundamental methodological question that decides the possibility of philosophy in general" (397). Heidegger's thesis that Kant recoiled from his own insights is usually, and correctly, related to his hermeneutic attempt to go beyond the letter of the first *Critique* and "concentrate on what Kant wanted to say" (3). However, in so far as Heidegger applauds Kant's oscillating between a rationalistic and a phenomenological approach to the ground-laying of metaphysics, he also seems to interpret Kant as a hermeneutical thinker in his own right, fundamentally struggling with the 'fore-structure' of the *Seinsfrage*.

---

[58] *KPM* 215, 214. The 'abyss of metaphysics' then constitutes what Heidegger calls 'the problem of metaphysics': "The title of [the Kant book] is not precise and therefore easily leads to the misunderstanding that *The Problem of Metaphysics* is concerned with a problematic whose overcoming was the task of metaphysics. Rather, *The Problem of Metaphysics* indicates that metaphysics as such is questionable" (*WT* 125; *KPM* xxi).

[59] *PIK* 279. For Heidegger, then, it is precisely on the basis of Kant's own wavering that "the original interpretation of the Kantian ground-laying, carried out above, first acquires its justification and the grounding of its necessity" (*KPM* 215).

4   Receptivity or Spontaneity

Two Readings of the Critique of Pure Reason

At the beginning of the Davos debate, Cassirer and Heidegger touch upon two issues pertaining to the meaning and enduring significance of Kant's philosophical project. First, Heidegger distinguishes his own 'ontological reading' of the first *Critique* from the 'epistemological reading' advanced by Neo-Kantianism. Second, after Cassirer points out their shared appreciation for Kant's account of transcendental imagination, he and Heidegger quickly enter into a disagreement about the primordially spontaneous or finite nature of this faculty. The Davos debate does not dwell on these issues for very long, and neither Heidegger nor Cassirer spells out how they relate to each other. Having discussed in the previous chapters Cassirer and Heidegger's respective readings of Kant's transcendental philosophy, we can now elucidate these two points of contention and settle the philosophical stakes of the first part of the Cassirer–Heidegger dispute.

4.1   Transcendental Philosophy as Ontology or Epistemology

When Cassirer asks Heidegger at the beginning of the Davos debate what he opposes in Neo-Kantianism, Heidegger answers in the following way:

> I understand by Neo-Kantianism that conception of the *Critique of Pure Reason* which explains, with reference to natural science, the part of pure reason that leads up to the Transcendental Dialectic as a theory of knowledge. For me, what matters is to show that what came to be extracted here as theory of science was non-essential for Kant. Kant did not want to give any sort of theory of natural science, but rather wanted to point out the problematic of metaphysics, which is to say, the problematic of ontology. (*DD* 275)

Heidegger's critique of the Neo-Kantian interpretation of transcendental philosophy is not incidental to his encounter with Cassirer in Davos, but returns in many of his writings and lectures on Kant.[1] In order to show the

---

[1] *PIK* 66–67, 77–78, 122–123, 156, 185, 211–213, 303; *WT* 145–146; *BT* 10–11; *Logic* 225–226, 230, 234, 244, 269; *BPP* 174, 181, 183, 216, 253, 286; *GA 27* 145, 250, 255–256, 259, 269; *GA56/57* 83–84. It is remarkable that Heidegger no longer refers to the Neo-Kantian movement when he continues to defend his 'ontological interpretation' of Kant after the Davos debate in

affinity between Kant's thought and his own phenomenological ontology, Heidegger must after all not only tackle Kant's flawed self-understanding, but also refute the Neo-Kantian tradition that dominates early twentieth-century Kant scholarship. Heidegger's rejection of the Neo-Kantian or 'epistemological' reading of the *Critique of Pure Reason* forms, then, the reverse side of his own appreciation of Kant.

As we have seen, Heidegger's 'ontological interpretation' consists of two moments. He not only argues that the first *Critique* is a treatise on the ground-laying of ontology, but he specifies that this work is concerned with the possibility of *general* ontology. Despite focusing on the natural sciences, he argues, Kant is actually interested in our understanding of the being of beings as such. Voiced as a critique, Heidegger thus holds that

> the interpretation of the *Critique* as an epistemology of the mathematical natural sciences fails fundamentally in two respects. First, this interpretation fails to see that the *Critique* is concerned with ontology and not with epistemology. Second, it fails to see that this ontology of nature is not an ontology of material nature but an ontology of what is present-at-hand in general. (*PIK* 66)

The first thesis, concerning the *intention* of the first *Critique*'s Transcendental Analytic, has always taken centre stage in discussions about Heidegger's feuds with Neo-Kantianism. In fact, contemporary Kant scholarship is still divided between epistemological and ontological (or metaphysical) readings of Kant's transcendental philosophy. The second thesis, concerning the *scope* of Kant's transcendental project, has received considerably less attention. This is quite remarkable, since Heidegger clearly states that this thesis constitutes the heart of his ontological interpretation of the first *Critique*:

> If one generally could allow the interpretation of the *Critique of Pure Reason* as a theory of knowledge, then that would be to say that it is not a theory of ontic knowledge (experience), but rather a theory of ontological knowledge. *But even with this conception*, already far removed from the prevailing interpretation of the Transcendental Aesthetic and Transcendental Analytic, *we have not encountered what is essential: that ontology as metaphysica generalis*, i.e., as the basic part of metaphysics as a whole, *is grounded here for the first time*; that the inner possibility of ontology is questioned.[2]

Hence, in order to comprehend the conflict between Heidegger and Cassirer's readings of Kant, we must consider both the scope and the aim of the Transcendental Analytic.

(1) It would obviously be absurd to criticize Cassirer's philosophy of culture for having too narrow a scope. The philosophy of symbolic forms

---

Kant and the Problem of Metaphysics and *What Is a Thing?* Assumedly, Heidegger felt that he had won this argument and therefore no longer needed to bother with competing readings.

[2] *KPM* 17 (my editing and emphases); *PIK* 66.

programmatically transcends Kant's focus on the natural sciences: with equal interest and extensive care for detail, Cassirer investigates also our mythological, linguistic, religious, artistic, and political understanding of the world – applying the 'Copernican revolution' and the transcendental method to each of these domains of culture (*PSF:1* 78–79). As a consequence, Cassirer's thought aims to establish a general theory of meaning:

> More and more we have been forced to recognize that the sphere of theoretical meaning that we designate with the names 'knowledge' and 'truth' represent only one (however significant and fundamental), layer of meaning. In order to understand it, in order to see through its structure, we must compare and contrast this layer with other dimensions of meaning. We must, in other words, grasp the problem of knowledge and the problem of truth as particular cases of the more general problem of meaning.[3]

Cassirer's take on this problem will be that scientific truth is no more accurate than artistic or political expressions of meaning. Hence, the philosophy of symbolic forms only affirms the methodological primacy of the natural sciences: Kant's transcendental investigation of this domain of human culture paved the way for understanding the other symbolic forms as legitimate alternative forms of meaning constitution (*PSF:1* 76). As Cassirer claimed in Davos, "mathematical natural science [. . .] can only serve as a paradigm and not as the whole of the problem" (*DD* 274). We should further reiterate that Cassirer's transformation of the critique of theoretical reason into a critique of culture does not merely seek for the transcendental conditions of each separate cultural domain, but also addresses what grounds their mutual connection. Cassirer considers this connection essential to a philosophy of culture and therefore develops a complex notion of versatile yet universal symbols that underlie both the diversity and the unity of the different symbolic forms. Hence, his philosophy of symbolic forms does not simply horizontally expand upon the paradigmatic case of scientific truth, but grounds it in a general theory of cultural meaning.[4]

   Of course, Heidegger's critique does not concern Cassirer's own philosophy but his interpretation of Kant's thought. In fact, if Cassirer designates (the critique of) theoretical or scientific reason to one moment of a larger (critique of) culture, does this not confirm Heidegger's point? Heidegger after all disputes that the first *Critique* was ever concerned about natural science in

---

[3] Cassirer, 'Erkenntnistheorie nebst den Grenzfragen der Logik und Denkpsychologie', *ECW:17* 16; *PSF:1* 69.
[4] On separate occasions, Krois confirms that Cassirer has not "expanded the theory of knowledge but rather shifted the whole task of philosophical investigations to a new, more fundamental ground" (*Cassirer: Symbolic Forms and History*, 24), and that "Cassirer did not 'expand' the theory of knowledge with his *Philosophy of Symbolic Forms*, he subsumed the theory of knowledge under a phenomenological study of meaning" ('Cassirer's Unpublished Critique of Heidegger', in: *Philosophy and Rhetoric*, 16/3, 1983, 151).

the first place. In his view, Kant already had the more profound aim of revealing the being of beings as such: "Kant does not presuppose the fact of science but rather attempts to work out, from pure reason itself as the original faculty of knowledge, the possibility and the necessary conditions for the possibility of a science of beings in general" (*PIK* 44–45). In *Phenomenological Interpretation*, Heidegger agrees that the natural sciences "play a decisively exemplary role in the problem that Kant poses", but he defines this problem as "the question concerning the ground of the possibility of a science of beings in general" (43). He therefore differentiates between a factual (*sachliches*) and an essential (*wesentliches*) reading of this role for Kant's transcendental project (67). In Kant's time, Heidegger explains, it was common for philosophers to talk about beings in terms of natural, present-at-hand beings, even when they were actually interested in the being of beings per se. In essence, however, "the question [Kant] poses is a fundamental one, which is not directed to a specific science of beings" (43–44). Heidegger's issue with the Neo-Kantian interpretation of the first *Critique* is, then, that it sticks to the letter of the Transcendental Analytic rather than the spirit of the entire work, mistaking its source of inspiration for its sole interest.

There thus is a crucial difference between Cassirer and Heidegger's understanding of the 'paradigmatic' or 'exemplary' role of the natural sciences for transcendental philosophy. While Cassirer sees it as an instructive moment that needs to be imbedded in the larger picture of a philosophy of culture, Heidegger views it as a misleading presentation of the core philosophical issue itself, namely the possibility of ontology. For Heidegger, one needs to neither expand the scope of Kant's critique of reason nor further ground it. Instead, one should properly value the breadth and depth that Kant's thought already, implicitly, has.

(2) On this basis, we could still say that while Heidegger recognizes an exercise in general ontology in the *Critique of Pure Reason*, for Cassirer it merely establishes a 'regional ontology', that is, an ontology of natural beings in particular. Yet in Heidegger's view, their difference cuts deeper: he charges the Neo-Kantian school to which Cassirer belonged for defending an epistemological reading of the first *Critique*.

Surprisingly, Heidegger's writings on Kant never define 'epistemology'. Turning to *Being and Time*, we learn, however, that he takes '*Erkenntnistheorie*' to be concerned with truth as correspondence between an ideal subject and a physical object (*BT* 215–216). Since he subsequently contrasts this notion of truth with a (more original) ontological notion of truth (225–226), we can infer that Heidegger's distinction between epistemology and ontology matches that between an ontic and an ontological approach to beings. An ontic investigation examines the relation between distinct being*s*, in this case a knowing and a known being, or a judgement and a thing. An ontological investigation

considers the way we come to understand the *being of* beings, or what allows
that and how beings appear to us in the first place. Put differently, epistemology investigates the possibility of knowledge of particular objects and
ontology the possibility of objectivity as such.[5] Heidegger states that the latter
concern is the more fundamental one, since "being cannot be explained by
beings" (207–208).

In his writings on Kant, Heidegger holds that this primacy of ontology over
epistemology is also the original point of Kant's 'Copernican revolution'. In
Phenomenological Interpretation, he holds that "the Copernican revolution
simply states that ontic knowledge of beings must in advance be guided by
ontological knowledge. [It] elucidates for the first time the possibility of access
to objects themselves" (56). He repeats this claim in *Kant and the Problem of
Metaphysics*: "Ontic truth necessarily adjusts itself to the ontological.
Accordingly, the legitimate interpretation of the 'Copernican Revolution' is
renewed. With this revolution Kant forces the problem of ontology to center
stage" (*KPM* 17, 13). In this way, Heidegger presents Kant's claim that
transcendental truth "precedes all empirical truth and makes it possible"
(*CPR* A146/B185) as a guideline for his own attempt to ground ontic or
epistemic knowledge of beings in an ontological understanding of their being.[6]

Now that it is clear why Heidegger dismisses an epistemological reading of
the first *Critique*, we can examine whether this critique also applies to Cassirer.
Surely Cassirer does not consider either Kant or himself to be engaged in
ontology. His take on the critical development of the notion of a 'thing in
itself' throughout the first *Critique* dispenses of any traditional notion of being.
In fact, this reading is part of Cassirer's four-volume overview of the history of
the problem of knowledge (*das Erkenntnisproblem*) leading up to his own
philosophical project, which he later presents as a 'phenomenology of
knowledge'. But this project does not, therefore, match Heidegger's description of epistemology. Since Cassirer's critical stance entails a rejection of the
idea of 'matter in itself' *and* of a pure isolated consciousness[7], the philosophy
of symbolic forms does precisely not occupy itself with relations of correspondence between distinct beings. Instead, it examines how mythical, linguistic, scientific, and other modalities of objectivity are possible. Accordingly,
Cassirer likewise applauds Kant's 'Copernican revolution' for establishing the

---

[5] Heidegger therefore admits that the term 'ontological knowledge' can be misleading, as it does
not concern knowledge in the sense of "apprehending of beings", but "the holding-open of the
horizon within which the being of the being becomes discernable in a preliminary way"
(*KPM* 123).

[6] *KPM* 17. In order to further substantiate this parallel, Heidegger also refers to *CPR* A58/B82 and
A237/B296.

[7] Both points are further discussed in Chapter 5 (Section 5.2): 'The primacy of the relation and the
inaccessibility of human consciousness'.

dependency of empirical knowledge (of objects of experience) on transcendental knowledge (of the conditions of the objectivity of experience):

> We can only study the nature of things a priori by exploring the conditions and general (although subjective) laws by means of which alone such knowledge as experience (according to mere forms) is possible, and only then determine the possibility of things as objects of experience [. . .] With that, the Copernican revolution is carried out. The empirical objects are only given to us by experience and under its conditions. (*EP:II* 672, 686–687)

Hence, Cassirer also considers Kant's thought as invested in the possibility of primordial, transcendental knowledge – which Heidegger calls ontological knowledge. The question remains, therefore, what makes a transcendental investigation into the possibility of objectivity as such an exercise in either ontology or epistemology. The hierarchical distinction between ontic and ontological viewpoints does not in itself explain this, since Cassirer subscribes to it as well.

The real difference between Cassirer and Heidegger's readings of Kant lies, then, not so much in its topic but in its goal: while they agree that Kant manages to explain the constitution of objectivity through transcendental knowledge, they disagree about what this explanation is supposed to accomplish. This becomes clear when we look at their interpretations of what is usually considered the heart of Kant's first *Critique*: the transcendental deduction of the categories of the understanding.[8]

Through this deduction, Kant famously demonstrates that the understanding harbours not just the conditions of possibility of our experience but therewith also of the objects of our experience (*CPR* A111). While this may be the decisive moment in Kant's challenge to the traditional opposition between subjectivity and objectivity, in the introduction to the first *Critique*'s A-edition he nevertheless still distinguishes between a subjective and an objective moment of the transcendental deduction. The 'objective deduction' establishes the objective status of the categories, while the 'subjective deduction' grounds this objectivity in the structures of transcendental subjectivity (Axvi-ii). Alternatively, Kant's actual discussion of the transcendental deduction starts by distinguishing between "questions about what is lawful (*quid juris*) and that which concerns the fact (*quid facti*)" and designates only the former as the proper subject of a deduction (A84–87/B116–119). Kant does not connect

---

[8] Although Heidegger's interpretation of Kant is famous for its focus on, and elevation of, the account of transcendental imagination, his writings show that he in fact considers the transcendental deduction at least as significant for grasping both the meaning and the shortcomings of Kant's thought. Heidegger dedicates more than one-fourth of his 1927–1928 lectures to this 'most obscure' (*PIK* 303) passage, to conclude that "the transcendental deduction, if properly understood, would assume the central function in the positive part of the *Critique*" (429).

these distinctions, but one could infer – as Cassirer and Heidegger do – that the subjective deduction concerns the mere existence or use of pure concepts of the understanding, while the objective deduction establishes their ('juridical') legitimacy or objective validity (*objektive Gültigkeit*; A111).

Both Cassirer and Heidegger insist that the subjective and objective moments of the transcendental deduction form each other's flip sides.[9] Yet, their dispute confirms the distinction between these two moments in so far as they each highlight a different one as the essential and dominant moment. Following Kant's statement, Cassirer holds that, in the system of transcendental philosophy, the

> fundamental tendency is oriented toward the question of *quid juris*, not that of *quid facti*. Its central problem lies in the 'objective', not in the 'subjective' deduction, in the question of the nature and foundational principle of particular areas of meaning which, as is emphasized over and over, in no way is to be confused with the question of their subjective representation in 'consciousness', but something methodologically strictly differentiated from it.[10]

Heidegger, on the other hand, admits that the first *Critique* foregrounds the objective deduction, but he nevertheless makes the case that Kant "fails to see that, by radically carrying out the subjective side of the task of deduction, the objective task is taken care of", meaning that "it does not at all appear in this form" (*PIK* 331). Hence, properly understood, "we would have to say that precisely *not* a *quaestio juris* but a *quaestio facti* is at the center of the problem of the transcendental deduction. At stake here [is] a *fact* in the sense of *the ontological and essential structure of Dasein*, the transcendental constitution of the subject" (330).

Interestingly, Cassirer and Heidegger are well aware of their diverging positions on this point. Heidegger specifies that

> with the working out of the original dimension [*Ursprungsdimension*] the ontological essence of categories must *eo ipso* already be established. [. . .] From this we infer that a juridical inquiry makes no sense and that we can no longer ask how a pure concept of the understanding is to have objective validity now that we are clear about the nature of subjectivity. *For belonging to subjectivity sufficiently disclosed is just the elucidation of the manner and possibility of the objective reality of categories.*[11]

For Heidegger, the 'juridical reading' of the first Critique is that of the Neo-Kantians. In his review of the Kant book, Cassirer retorts that "here as

---

[9] For Heidegger, see *PIK* 331, 384–385, 400; *KPM* 166; and *WT* 117; while Cassirer refers to this in *PSF:III* 49–50; *ECW:9* 125; or *ECW:17* 72.

[10] *PSF:IV* 35; see also *PSF:IV* 56, *KPMR* 244–245 and *EP:II* 706.

[11] *PIK* 384–385, 303, 401; *KPM* 69. Most dramatically, Heidegger even holds that "viewed as a *quaestio juris*, the transcendental deduction is the most disastrous segment of teaching in Kantian philosophy to which one can refer" (*PIK* 309).

well, despite all his carefulness and precision when it comes to the details, Heidegger gave the whole analysis of Kant an entirely changed character. He has attempted to displace it from a basis in the 'objective deduction purely and exclusively to one in the 'subjective deduction'" (*KPMR* 242–243).

If we take Cassirer and Heidegger's readings of the transcendental deduction as indicative of their overall takes on the meaning of Kant's transcendental philosophy, we can now understand their conflict in terms of validity versus ground. On the one hand, Cassirer abides by Kant's own, logical, terminology when he states that "the fundamental question of the *Critique of Pure Reason* can be designated by means of the concept of objectivity. Demonstrating the objective validity of our a priori knowledge forms its central task" (*EP:II* 733) – and when he continues to use the phrase 'objective validity' (*objektive Gültigkeit*) throughout his commentary on the first *Critique* (664–665, 697, 721). Heidegger, however, firmly rejects this reading of transcendental logic as a *Geltungslogik*:

It is clear [. . .] how completely cut off from the actual meaning of the transcendental deduction neo-Kantianism is when it conceives the problem of this deduction as one of *validity*. [The] basic determining factor of the deduction remains the ontological disclosure of the *transcendental constitution of the subject*. A *problem of validity* is absurd in such an inquiry and in this form has never been Kant's goal. (*PIK* 330, 373; *KPM* 87)

Instead, transcendental logic – if it is truly a logic at all – is for Heidegger best understood as an *Ursprungslogik*. On his provocative view, the term *"deduction* can only mean disclosure of the origin (*Ursprungsenthüllung*) of the categories" (*PIK* 304). More broadly, the introduction to *Kant and the Problem of Metaphysics* presents the *Critique of Pure Reason* "as a laying of the ground of metaphysics" (*KPM* 1) – a phrase that returns in almost all (sub) chapter titles in this book.

For Cassirer, then, transcendental philosophy inquires how transcendental knowledge makes possible, in the sense of validates, empirical knowledge – be it in the realm of science, mythic, language, or another cultural domain. As such, one could say that it provides a guideline for an epistemology of science, myth, language, etc. Heidegger, on the other hand, insists on the difference between ontic and ontological knowledge not because he is interested in how the latter grounds the former, but so he can investigate how ontology itself is possible. He then seeks the ground of ontology in the constitution of the human subject. In conclusion, Cassirer does transcendental philosophy *for the sake of* epistemology, whereas Heidegger engages with it because of his interest in the problem of metaphysics. Each aspect of their respective readings of Kant must be understood in light of these diverging aims.

4.2   The Receptive and Spontaneous Nature
of Transcendental Imagination

Heidegger's interpretation of Kant's thought is without a doubt most famous
for emphasizing the importance of the first *Critique*'s account of transcendental imagination, which concerns the schematism and the rules of the
understanding. Already in *Being and Time*, Heidegger affirms the "central
ontological function" of Kant's "doctrine of the schematism" (*BT* 23). In his
writings on Kant, he is even more adamant about its significance, repeatedly
holding that "these eleven pages of the *Critique of Pure Reason* must constitute the central core of the whole voluminous work".[12] For Heidegger, then,
"the doctrine of the schematism of the pure concepts of the understanding is
the decisive stage of the laying of the ground for *metaphysica generalis*".[13]

Heidegger explains this importance primarily in the third part of *Kant and
the Problem of Metaphysics*. He first argues that the power of imagination is
both receptive and spontaneous in nature (*KPM* §26). To support this, he refers
to Kant's definition of this power as "a faculty of intuition, even without the
presence of the object".[14] As a 'faculty of intuition' or 'intuitive presentation',
imagination is of course a capacity for perceiving sensible or empirical images
of objects. In so far as this intuition is not bound to currently given objects, it
however displays "a peculiar non-connectedness to these beings" (128) and
itself "creates and forms the image" (129). As such, Heidegger concludes, this
formative power is

a 'forming' that simultaneously receives and creates (spontaneously). In this 'simultaneously' lies the proper essence of its structure. But if receptivity means the same as
sensibility and if spontaneity means the same as understanding, then in a peculiar way
the power of imagination falls between both.[15]

Heidegger specifies that there are in fact degrees to the spontaneity of the
power of imagination: it can merely recall previously perceived images (*exhibitio derivativa*), compose a new empirical object on the basis of such images
(*exhibitio originaria*), or it can "form the look of the horizon of objectivity as
such in advance, before the experience of the being" (131). Heidegger considers the first two, empirical, uses of the imagination to be anthropological
issues, but the third, pure or transcendental, use as key to the first *Critique*'s
attempt to lay the ground for metaphysics. Since transcendental imagination
forms images prior to any experience, here "the essence of the power of

---

[12] *KPM* 89; see also *PIK* 168, 194, 386; *Logic* 294.   [13] *KPM* 111, 127; *PIK* 431.
[14] *KPM* 128, 131; see also Kant, Anthropology from a Pragmatic Point of View, ed. by Robert
Louden, in: *Cambridge Texts in the History of Philosophy*, Cambridge: Cambridge University
Press, 2006, 54; and *CPR* B151.
[15] *KPM* 129 (translation modified), 153.

imagination – to be able to intuit without the present presence – is grasped in a way that is fundamentally more original" (132). On this level, imagination combines pure receptivity and pure spontaneity, and thus falls in between the faculties of pure sensibility and pure understanding.

Heidegger therefore argues that Kant conceived of transcendental imagination as a third 'basic faculty' of the human mind, irreducible to either sensibility or the understanding (§27). To this end, he relies on Kant's descriptions of this faculty as "a fundamental faculty of the human soul that grounds all cognition a priori", and Kant's incidental references to three 'subjective sources of cognition', including the power of imagination.[16] Subsequently, he connects this presentation of transcendental imagination as "an indispensable function of the soul, without which we should have no knowledge at all, but of which we are seldom even conscious" to Kant's earlier, otherwise puzzling, claim that there must be a "common, but to us unknown, root [of] sensibility and understanding".[17] According to Heidegger, then, Kant conceives of transcendental imagination as the common root of pure sensibility and pure understanding, such that their respective transcendental structures can only be explained in reference to this foundational faculty (134, 137–138).

Heidegger backs up this claim by arguing that both pure sensibility (§28) and pure understanding (§29) are indeed grounded in the simultaneously receptive and spontaneous power of transcendental imagination. On the one hand, he claims that pure intuition is a receptive capacity only by virtue of its ability to produce 'original presentations' that establish the horizon for intuiting. In other words, this faculty has formative power in so far as it provides the unifying forms of space and time that a priori structure our intuitions. For Heidegger, this proves that pure sensibility is grounded in transcendental imagination:

> The pure intuitions themselves are 'original', i.e., presentations of the intuitable that allow something to spring forth: *exhibitio originaria*. In this presenting, however, lies the essence of the pure power of imagination. Pure intuition, therefore, can only be 'original' because according to its essence it is the pure power of imagination itself that formatively gives images from out of itself. (141)

Kant is said to confirm this essential relationship between pure intuition and transcendental imagination when describing space and time, which are not empirically given *in* intuition but rather form it, as in a way 'imaginary': "What is intuited in pure intuition as such is an *ens imaginarium*. Hence, on the grounds of its essence, pure intuiting is pure imagination".[18]

---

[16] *CPR* A94, A115.   [17] See *KPM* 134, 135; cf. *CPR* A124, A78/B103; and *CPR* A15/B29.
[18] *KPM* 143; *CPR* A291/B347.

On the other hand, Heidegger claims that the essence of pure understanding lies somewhat paradoxically in its dependency on intuition (148). From a transcendental viewpoint, pure understanding is not so much a faculty of 'mere concepts' as it is a 'faculty of rules', that is, a capacity to a priori regulate our intuitions under a conceptual, 'pre-formed, horizon of unity'. According to Heidegger, thinking understood in this way is identical with pure imagining: "Thinking is, then, no longer called judging, but is thinking in the sense of the free, forming, and projecting (although not arbitrary) 'conceiving' of something" (151). He remarks that Kant after all speaks of "the procedure of understanding with these schemata" and the "schematism of our understanding".[19] On this basis, Heidegger concludes that "as a way of representing that forms spontaneously, the apparent achievement of the pure understanding in the thinking of the unities is a pure basic act of the transcendental power of imagination".

In sum, Heidegger claims that the opposition between receptive sensibility and spontaneous understanding only holds with regard to *empirical* intuition and the *purely logical* function of the understanding. Kant's transcendental philosophy is concerned, however, with neither of these capacities: instead, Heidegger explains, it deals with pure intuition, which "on the grounds of its purity [...] possesses the character of spontaneity" (153), and pure thinking, which "in itself, not after the fact, is capable of receiving: i.e., it is pure intuition" (154). As "pure, spontaneous, receptivity" and "structural, coherent, receptive spontaneity" these respective sources of transcendental knowledge "have their essence [and] spring forth from the transcendental power of imagination" (153–154; *PIK* 338).

In his review of *Kant and the Problem of Metaphysics*, Cassirer praises the "extraordinary sharpness and clarity" of Heidegger's reassessment of transcendental imagination (*KPMR* 229). He too considers it

a sign of the complete misconception of Kant's basic intention that the secondary literature on Kant consistently presents his doctrine of the schematism as 'artificial' – as if he invoked the 'transcendental power of the imagination' on purely external grounds of 'symmetry' and 'architectonics'.[20]

Cassirer expresses the hope that Heidegger's 'Kant book' will make an end to this 'absurd accusation', and declares his "complete consent and principle agreement with Heidegger's interpretation". While this may sound surprising, the second volume of *The Problem of Knowledge* (1907) had actually put

---

[19] *KPM* 151; see *CPR* A140/B179, A141/B180.
[20] Despite Heidegger and Cassirer's agreement on this point, this 'misconception' of Kant's account of transcendental imagination would remain popular (e.g. Henry Allison, *Kant's Transcendental Idealism: An Interpretation and Defense*, New Haven: Yale University Press, 1983, 174, 188).

forward a reading of Kant's account of transcendental imagination that bears significant similarities to Heidegger's.

In the chapter 'The Critique of Reason', Cassirer admits that, from a historical perspective, "the critical method first gained its stability and independence with regard to [previous] metaphysics" by distinguishing between the basic concepts of sensibility and those of the understanding (*EP:II* 571). Yet, in so far as these concepts do not refer to two distinctive worlds, but rather imply two different ways of representing the same objects, he also holds that "both faculties must be somehow connected in their factual root; there must be a principle through which they, while remaining clearly distinct, nevertheless methodologically concur" (572). According to Cassirer, the *Critique of Pure Reason* achieves this by rethinking the concept of 'synthesis': "The pure intuitions of space and time, like the concepts of the pure understanding, constitute only various developments and characteristics of the fundamental form of the synthetic function of unity".

Cassirer further explains that throughout Kant's critical investigation of reason, "the opposition between the forms of sensibility and those of the understanding seems to dissolve more and more" (579). Intuition after all appears to be not only receptive but also capable of a certain free activity, a 'new form of freedom and spontaneity', whereas the understanding must refer back to that which is 'given in intuition' in order to obtain cognition. And like Heidegger, Cassirer holds that if we conceive of the understanding as the transcendental 'faculty of rules' rather than a purely logical faculty of abstract, generic concepts, "it indeed ceases to be entirely dissimilar to the intuition" (599). From the critical perspective, the opposition between the understanding and sensibility can only pertain to the respective starting point (*Ausgangspunkt*) and goal (*Zielpunkt*) of synthetic judgements, namely the "logical ground of the synthesis as such" and "the condition of its objective validity" (583). The synthesis that establishes cognition is therefore equiprimordially characterized by its purely intelligible origin and its necessary connection to the intuition (582–583).

Finally, Cassirer claims that the dissimilarity between the pure concepts of the understanding and sensible intuitions is definitively lifted by "one of the most difficult chapters of the critique of reason, the doctrine of the 'schematism of the concepts of the understanding'".[21] He reads Kant's account of the schema as conclusively showing that pure concepts are the products of imaginative construction rather than logical abstraction: they do not reflect preexisting objects, but represent a fundamental process of synthesis (597–598).

---

[21] *EP:II* 596. In his contribution to the 1929 edition of the *Encyclopedia Britannica*, Cassirer thus claims that "the fundamental idea of Kant's critical rationalism is developed in his doctrine of the 'schematism of the pure concepts of the understanding'" (*ECW:17* 320).

By providing images for pure concepts, the schema first constructs them in intuition, and thereby forms the model for any possible object of experience: "In this way, the schematism indeed unites pure intuition and pure concepts, by referring both in turn back to their common logical root" (598).

Cassirer builds on this interpretation of Kant's 'critique of reason' to develop his own 'critique of culture'. In *The Phenomenology of Knowledge*, he identifies "three original sources of knowledge which according to the *Critique of Pure Reason* make all experience possible: sensibility, imagination, and understanding", and holds that these sources, "when viewed from the standpoint of the problem of symbolism, prove to be interrelated and linked to one another in a new way" (*PSF:III* 48, 9). Accordingly, Cassirer rejects the oppositions between presentation and representation, arguing that "it is only in the reciprocal movement between the 'representing' and the 'represented' that knowledge can arise" (203, 199). He likewise claims that matter and form should be conceived as "members of a methodic opposition which is at the same time a methodic correlation" (10; *EP:III* 5–10). As I explained earlier, Cassirer thereupon grounds all domains of culture in the human capacity of 'symbolic imagination', which enables us to instantly grasp the 'symbolic pregnancy' of sensations.

On this basis, we can confirm that both Heidegger and Cassirer value Kant's account of transcendental imagination because they take it to undercut the artificial opposition between receptivity and spontaneity. This explains Cassirer's attempted rapprochement to Heidegger in Davos, where he held that "on one point we agree, in that for me as well the productive power of imagination appears in fact to have a central meaning for Kant" (*DD* 275–276). Interestingly, this agreement further extends to the shared view that Kant did not, in fact, entirely succeed in unifying the faculties of sensibility and understanding. More particularly, both Heidegger and Cassirer claim that Kant could not properly carry out his critical project because he lacked a thorough understanding of the phenomenological method.

4.3 Kant's Vacillating between Logic, Psychology, and Phenomenology

The most infamous moment of Heidegger's reading of Kant is found in *Kant and the Problem of Metaphysics*, where he states that Kant ultimately recoiled from his original insight into the crucial role of transcendental imagination (*KPM* §31). Heidegger points out that the 1787 B-edition of the *Critique of Pure Reason* reinforces the traditional twofold distinction between the faculties of sensibility and the understanding that the 1781 A-edition had overcome: Kant here omits all passages that identified transcendental imagination as a third basic faculty of the human mind, and relabels this power from an 'indispensable function of the soul' to a 'function of the understanding'.[22] Heidegger concludes that Kant

did not carry through the more original interpretation of the transcendental power of imagination [...] On the contrary: Kant shrank back from this unknown root. In the second edition of the *Critique of Pure Reason*, the transcendental power of imagination as it came to light in the impassioned course of its first projection was thrust aside and given a new interpretation – one favoring the understanding.[23]

According to Heidegger, Kant feared that his account of faculties of the mind remained too close to a psychological discourse, and thus sought an alternative approach. However, since he did not have a clear conception of phenomenology, Kant ended up expressing his critical method in a traditional rationalist manner that does no justice to his original insight either:

Kant was basically not clear about the real and necessary character of his investigation. He realized that discussion of pure intuition, pure thinking, and the pure power of imagination [...] cannot and should not be psychology [and] is *not an empirical* discussion. As opposite, he knew only the *rational* discussion. But rational discussion is a *logical* one. Hence, if the discussion of the subject, the mind, the faculties and fundamental sources cannot be a psychological one, then it must be shifted to a transcendental *logic*. Kant did not yet see the essential task of a purely phenomeno-logical interpretation of *Dasein* in the sense of a *fundamental ontological explication of its basic structures*. (*PIK* 318; *KPM* 170)

Heidegger hereby introduces a distinction between the execution and the intention of Kant's critical philosophy: while Kant de facto "vacillates between psychology and logic" (324), actually "a phenomenological interpretation of the *Critique* is the only interpretation that fits Kant's own intentions, even if these intentions are not clearly spelled out by him".[24] Accordingly, Heidegger regrets Kant's 1787 presentation of the understanding as an isolated faculty – he maintains that its function and ground can only be grasped when one considers its intimate relation to the intuition.[25] If Kant had fully acknow-ledged the radical novelty of his transcendental approach, he would have further developed his original account of the foundational role of transcenden-tal imagination. However, "as much as the togetherness of receptivity and spontaneity is again and again important for Kant", because he lacked a profound understanding of the phenomenological method, "he still does not succeed in demonstrating a ground wherein both can be together" (396), namely the transcendence of Dasein.

---

[22] *KPM* 161–164; see *CPR* A94(fn), A115, A78, B103.
[23] *KPM* 160–161; see also 169; and *PIK* 280.
[24] *PIK* 71. Heidegger applies this claim to the transcendental deduction on *PIK* 318, 324, 329, 337; and *KPM* 87.
[25] *KPM* 57, 59, 67–68, 83, 148.

Cassirer does not share Heidegger's view that Kant recoiled from his own insight, if only because he dismisses a psychological assessment of an author as a legitimate tool for interpreting their writings (*KPMR* 244). Yet, he agrees in diverse writings that Kant's account of transcendental imagination in the *Critique of Pure Reason* only partly succeeds in rethinking the way that the human being achieves an understanding of other beings. More precisely, he too holds that Kant failed to develop a "true phenomenology of perception" (*PSF:III* 193) because he could not break entirely with the traditional approaches of logic and psychology.

On Cassirer's view, Kant conceived of transcendental philosophy as an alternative to both the rationalism of metaphysics and the 'sensationalism' or 'sensualism' advocated by psychology (*EP:II* 600; *PSF:I* 102–103). Nevertheless, Cassirer holds, Kant's thought preserves crucial elements of the two positions that it wished to overcome: "in the beginning of the *Critique of Pure Reason*, the antithesis between sensibility and thought, between the 'material' and 'formal' determinants of consciousness, retains its full force" (*PSF:I* 104). On the one hand, Cassirer labels this antithesis as the derivative result of logical abstraction, a methodology which fails to see that

the unity of the matter and form of consciousness, of the 'particular' and the 'universal', of sensory 'data' and pure 'principles of order', constitutes precisely that originally certain and originally known phenomenon which every analysis of consciousness must take as its point of departure.

Agreeing with Heidegger, Cassirer thus regrets the predominant focus of the first *Critique* on the concepts rather than the rules of the understanding: "In the isolation of the 'mere' concepts of the understanding [...] clearly resonates a pre-critical way of posing the problem". Actually, he counters, thinking should be "first defined by its connection to intuition, through which alone it receives objective meaning and a genuine determination" (*EP:III* 11; *PSF:III* 194).

According to Cassirer, this initial isolation of the two traditional sources of the understanding echoes throughout Kant's further argumentation. For one, it leads him to adopt an account of determining judgements, according to which intuitions are subsumed under pregiven concepts: "Kant attached his explanation to the type of judgement that he found to be dominant everywhere in traditional logic, but one easily sees that the scheme in which this logic pushes him, proves to be too narrow to grasp and adequately express his novel epistemological insights".[26] As a further consequence, transcendental imagination is presented as an additional, mediating, capacity at the service of the understanding:

---

[26] Cassirer, 'Kant und die Moderne Mathematik' in: *ECW:9* 72.

Meanwhile, precisely the theory of the schematism suffers from the shortcoming that, in the form in which it first appears, it seems to offer a merely external mediation that may very well render intelligible a 'cooperation' between sensibility and thought, but which sharpens rather than reconciles their essential 'heterogeneity'. The category here appears as a construct of independent origin that is restricted only through its application, as if by an external force, by the foreign element of sensibility.[27]

For Cassirer, all of this follows from the fact that Kant still conceived of the basic problem of the first *Critique* as a merely logical issue.

On the other hand, Cassirer argues in *The Phenomenology of Knowledge* that Kant's terminology often retains the psychological discourse of faculties of the human mind:

But there remains a difficulty and ambiguity that the *Critique of Pure Reason* did not fully elucidate and eliminate. For the new idea that it outlined did not at first find its adequate expression insofar as Kant, precisely where he most decisively attacked the methodological presuppositions of the old psychology, nevertheless continued to speak its language. The new transcendental insight that he was striving to establish is expressed in the concepts of eighteenth-century faculty psychology. Thus, here again 'receptivity' and 'spontaneity', 'sensation' and 'understanding' might seem to be conceived as 'psychological faculties', each of which exists as an independent reality and only bring forth experience through their empirical cooperation, their causal concatenation. It is evident that this would negate the meaning of the transcendental idea.[28]

Now Kant is said to remain stuck on "the same methodological plane as the attempted sensationalist explanations" (*PSF:III* 195). For Cassirer, there is thus a remarkable mismatch between Kant's project and the terminology by means of which he explains it. He takes issue with this because Kant hereby seems to deliver yet another "attempt to solve pure problems of meaning by transposing them into problems of reality". The shift from a physical explanation in terms of real objects to a psychological one in terms of faculties of the mind cannot, however, solve Kant's problem of the relation between form and matter. This problem rather calls for a more fundamental transition from the pre-critical problem of being to the critical problem of meaning.

Hence, like Heidegger, Cassirer perceives a conflict between the spirit and the letter of the *Critique of Pure Reason*. Rather than distinguishing between the two editions of the first *Critique*, however, he points to the *Critique of Judgment*.[29] Focusing on judgements rather than concepts, Kant here

---

[27] *EP:III* 11–12. In 1907, Cassirer thus admits that the architectonic of Kant's *Critique of Pure Reason* indeed nourishes the recurring 'misconception of its basic intention' that he would rebuke in his review of *Kant and the Problem of Metaphysics*.

[28] *PSF:III* 194–195; translation modified.

[29] See Cassirer, 'The Concept of Group and the Theory of Perception', in: *ECW:24* 246: "For Kant, the schemata belong to the 'transcendental doctrine of judgment'; in discussing them, he

introduces a reflective type of judgement that is formed by transcendental imagination without the guidance of pure understanding. As a consequence, Cassirer points out, here "understanding and intuition are no longer [. . .] brought together through the agency of a foreign mediator and conjoined through a cunning schematism, but are truly blended and absorbed in each other" (*KLT* 315). For Cassirer, then, the critical idea "at which the doctrine of the schematism aims only finds its decisive realization and completion in the *Critique of Judgment*" (*EP:III* 11; *PSF:III* 7–8). Further, despite their turn to different textual resources, Cassirer also endorses Heidegger's claim that a phenomenological approach would more aptly convey the intentions of Kant's transcendental philosophy. In *The Problem of Knowledge*, he holds that such an approach would have prevented the flaws resulting from the logical one:

Purely phenomenologically speaking, function and content are not separated in our immediate understanding [of reality], but can only later be isolated through reflection. For the forms of the understanding, the opposite is the case, since they, as purely logical functions of judgment, at first seem to include no necessary relation to the empirical intuition at all, and must first be relegated and tied to it by the transcendental critique. (*EP:II* 586)

In *The Phenomenology of Knowledge* – published in the same year as *Kant and the Problem of Metaphysics* – Cassirer in turn distinguishes between an 'ontic' investigation into psychological entities and the 'critical-phenomeno-logical problem' of transcendental meaning (*PSF:III* 195, 135, 199). According to Cassirer as well as Heidegger, Kant sensed the crucial distinction between these approaches but lacked the truly novel, phenomenological, method and vocabulary needed to cement his transcendental project.

4.4   The Finite or Spontaneous Nature of Human Reason

So far, we have established a rather extensive agreement between Heidegger and Cassirer: both thinkers praise Kant's account of transcendental imagination for revealing the fundamental correlation between receptivity and spontaneity, and both criticize Kant for not developing the phenomeno-logical method and terminology that would ratify this insight. They neverthe-less part ways on the implications of said correlation: while Heidegger takes transcendental imagination as the ground of human reason's finite nature, Cassirer concludes from the primacy of this faculty to the fundamentally spontaneous character of reason.

anticipates problems that find their systematic discussion and clarification only in the 'Critique of Judgment'".

According to Heidegger, the *Critique of Pure Reason* is an attempt to ground metaphysics not just in reason 'as such', but in human, finite, reason specifically (*KPM* 21, 23–24). This finitude is then not a flaw of human reason, but constitutes its very essence. Heidegger refers to the first line of the first *Critique*, which reads as follows: "In whatever way and through whatever means a cognition may relate to objects, that through which it relates immediately to them, and at which all thought as a means is directed as an end, is *intuition*".[30] Heidegger infers from this that Kant's basic premise is that human cognition is primarily intuition (21, 23). He further points out that Kant distinguishes between *intuitus orginarius*, which is usually ascribed to infinite divine knowledge, and our own *intuitus derivativus*: unlike a divine being, we do not create the objects of our knowledge, but are rather dependent on what we receive through our senses.[31] On this basis, Heidegger holds that all human cognition is marked by finitude: "Hence, the character of the finitude of intuition is found in its receptivity. [It] cannot receive something unless that which is to be received announces itself. According to its essence, finite intuition must be solicited or affected by that which is intuitable" (26).

Subsequently, Heidegger argues that our capacity for thinking does not transcend, but actually solidifies this finitude. On the one hand, the fact "that a finite, thinking creature must 'also' think is an essential consequence of the finitude of its own intuiting" (25). It is precisely because our intuition does not create objects, but receives them, that we require thinking in order to determine its sensible content. On the other hand, in so far as our thinking can only relate to objects through intuition, Heidegger asserts that is also itself intrinsically finite:

The understanding [. . .] lacks the immediacy of finite intuiting. Its representing requires the indirection of a reference to a universal by means of and according to which the several particulars become conceptually representable. This discursiveness that belongs to the essence of understanding is the sharpest index of its finitude.[32]

Hence, according to Heidegger it is due to the finite nature of our cognition that the faculties of intuition and the understanding mutually depend on each other (*KPM* 135).

This makes Heidegger further inquire about Kant's view on the "internal relationship" between sensibility and the understanding. Early in the 'Kant

---

[30] *CPR* A19/B33; quoted on *KPM* 21. While Heidegger actually quotes the first sentence of the Transcendental Aesthetic here, the introductions to both editions of the first *Critique* also begin by asserting that all our cognition grounded in intuitions (*CPR* A1, B1).

[31] *KPM* 24–25 (see also *PIK* 85–89), based on *CPR* B72.

[32] *KPM* 29–30, 75. Heidegger adds that it only makes sense to speak of both an 'ob-ject' (*Gegenstand*; 31) and a problematic 'thing in itself' (34) with regard to a being that possesses finite cognition.

book', he had pointed out that these faculties, despite their different characters, are two capacities for representing objects (22): while sensibility directly represents objects through intuitions (27), the understanding does so indirectly through concepts – thus 'conceptually representing sensible representations'.[33] On the transcendental level, Heidegger accordingly characterizes these faculties as two capacities for a priori synthesizing such representations: while pure sensibility produces the 'synopsis' of the pure forms of intuition, pure understanding establishes the 'predicative synthesis' of intuitions under a priori concepts (60–64). When asking about the 'original synthesis' that in turn grounds these two types of synthesis (37, 60), Heidegger for the first time invokes the power of transcendental imagination. Once more, he refers to Kant's claim that "synthesis in general [...] is the mere result of the *power of imagination*, a blind but indispensable function of the soul".[34] Heidegger concludes that the "essential, structural belonging-together" of intuition and thinking (64), and hence the essence of finite human reason, is grounded in the faculty of transcendental imagination. His subsequent, elaborate argumentation for the foundational role of this faculty is motivated, then, by a search for the "*essential unity* of finite, pure, knowledge" (58).

Heidegger's emphasis on the co-dependence and unity between pure intuition and pure understanding does not, however, stop him from installing a hierarchy among these capacities. In fact, he claims that the dominance of intuition over understanding is essential to their unity:

The necessary way in which sensibility and understanding belong together in the essential unity of finite knowledge does not exclude but rather includes an order of precedence in the structural grounding of thinking in intuition, which exists as the initial representing. Precisely this order of precedence concerning the reflexive belonging-together of sensibility and understanding must not be overlooked, it must not become leveled off to an indifferent correlation of content and form, if we want to come closer to the innermost course of the Kantian problematic. (35)

Throughout his commentary on the first *Critique*, Heidegger indeed consistently stresses that thinking serves intuition: he asserts that the faculty of thinking is not simply juxtaposed to, but structurally oriented towards the goal of intuition (22, 51), that its "dependency on pure intuition is not secondary or supplemental to pure thinking but belongs essentially to it" (57), and that it has a central function for ontological knowledge only because receptive intuition requires determinative thinking (51, 71). For Heidegger, the receptive side of human cognition is thus more fundamental than its spontaneous moment. Even though his subsequent account of the power of transcendental imagination

---

[33] *KPM* 28; *WT* 135–137. Heidegger here refers to Kant, who held that "judgment is the mediate knowledge of an object, that is, the representation of a representation of it" (*CPR* A68/B93).
[34] *KPM* 63; *CPR* A78/B103.

cements the idea that both moments presuppose each other, it really serves an argument for the finite nature of human reason, which originates in its dependence on receptive intuition.

When it comes to the order between intuition and understanding, Cassirer sketches an entirely different picture of the *Critique of Pure Reason*. While Heidegger ultimately considers Kant's account of transcendental imagination the heart of this work because it seals the finite nature of human reason, Cassirer praises it for showing that our perception is at all times marked by spontaneity. In *The Problem of Knowledge*, Cassirer calls it the basic insight of transcendental philosophy that "without a 'recognition through concepts', there could never arise an image of intuition, not even the purest and most original representations of space and time", meaning that "in intuition itself, the function of the concept already proves to be operative" (*EP:II* 599). As I demonstrated earlier, Cassirer argues in this work that the *Critique of Pure Reason* gradually transforms the idea of the 'thing in itself' from an empirical cause of our perception into a construct of our cognition and finally into an ideal goal towards which this cognition strives. The only 'given' that is maintained by this critical perspective is the 'synthesis of pure intuition' considered from the viewpoint of the understanding (581). In the final sentence of *The Problem of Knowledge*, Cassirer thus concludes that "the dissolution (*Auflösung*) of the 'given' in the pure functions of cognition constitutes the definitive goal and the achievement of the critical doctrine" (638).

Cassirer maintains this view in his philosophy of culture, which aims to transform the critique of reason into a critique of culture in order to establish 'the true and complete confirmation of the basic thesis of idealism' (*PSF:I* 80). Once again, he holds that sensibility and thought are not generically distinct functions of the human mind: instead, the latter merely makes explicit what was already contained in the former (*PSF:I* 319). Although this may seem to confirm the priority of intuition, what matters to Cassirer is most of all that the human mind is at all time formative:

The act of 'symbolic ideation' is no secondary and as it were accidental factor, by which vision is for the first time being partly determined, but first constitutes vision. For there is no seeing and nothing visible which does not stand in some mode of spiritual vision, of ideation. A seeing and a thing-seen outside of this 'sight', a 'bare' sensation preceding all information, is an empty abstraction. The 'given' must always be taken in a definite aspect that first lends it meaning. This meaning is to be understood neither as secondary and conceptual nor as an associative addition: rather, it is the simple meaning of the original intuition itself. There is creation in the very act of seeing, and this applies not only to the scientifically determined or the artistically formed intuition, but to simple empirical intuition as well.[35]

---

[35] *PSF:III* 134; translation modified.

Accordingly, Cassirer's philosophy of symbolic forms consistently denies the existence of "an isolated, 'merely sensory', consciousness" (*PSF:III* 8) or "naked sensation as a raw material" (15), arguing that such a "purely 'naïve' stage of empirical consciousness [...] is itself no fact but a theoretical construction" (*PSF:II* 34). In truth, Cassirer holds, all perception is "dominated and permeated through and through by definite modes of formation" – or 'pregnant' with meaning.[36] As it turns out, his account of the simultaneously sensible and intelligible nature of transcendental imagination – which Cassirer reconceives as 'symbolic imagination' – serves the view that our various ways of making sense of the world are nothing but various products of a spontaneous capacity of human cognition.

It is clear now that Cassirer and Heidegger's assessments of Kant's account of transcendental imagination, similar as they may be in a number of relevant ways, are motivated by opposing views of human reason as a whole. In order to further spell out this difference, we shall have another look at the targets of Heidegger and Cassirer's critiques of Kant's proto-phenomenological method-ology in the first *Critique*.

While Heidegger holds that Kant tried to steer clear of faculty psychology, he himself does not consider this the crucial problem of Kant's approach in the *Critique of Pure Reason*. Instead, he time and again reproaches Kant for insufficiently distinguishing between the categories and the pure 'notions' of the understanding:

Dependency on pure intuition is not secondary or supplementary to pure thinking but belongs essentially to it. If the pure concept is apprehended initially as notion, then the second element of pure knowledge has by no means been attained in its elementary character. On the contrary, it has been shorn of the decisive, essential moment, namely, the inner reference to intuition. The pure concept as notion is therefore only a fragment of the second element of pure knowledge. As long as pure understanding is not viewed with regard to its essence, i.e., its pure relatedness to intuition, the origin of the notions as ontological predicates cannot be unveiled at all.[37]

By treating the categories under the header of a 'transcendental *logic*', Kant is said to deny their proper, ontological, meaning – according to Heidegger, "the category is neither a problem of the Transcendental Aesthetic nor of the Transcendental Logic" (*KPM* 66), just as the power of transcendental imagination is not at home (*Heimatlos*) in either one of them (136). The reason why Heidegger rejects the division of the first *Critique* in a Transcendental Aesthetic and Transcendental Logic is, then, to overthrow the dominance (*Herrschaft*) of logic (68) or of the understanding and reason (243): a 'phe-nomenological interpretation "must liberate itself from the Kantian architec-tonic, and it must make the idea of a transcendental logic problematic" (67). In

---

[36] *PSF:III* 15, 48, 194, 202–203.   [37] *KPM* 57; cf. 58, 65–66, 68, 86.

a clear reference to the Neo-Kantians, he explains that this correction is pertinent because "in interpreting the *Critique of Pure Reason* the tendency to accept it as a 'logic of pure knowledge' constantly wins out".[38] While he agrees with the Neo-Kantians that Kant's account of intuition remains incomprehensible until the first *Critique* discusses the categories, Heidegger thus rejects their solution to "absorb the Transcendental Aesthetic into the Logic", because this obscures their common ground and once again assigns the task of laying the ground for metaphysics to pure logic (145; *WT* 145–146).

Cassirer, on the other hand, does not take issue with Kant's logical approach to transcendental philosophy per se. He precisely applauds that "the initial separation of intuition and concept dissolves more and more clearly in a purely logical correlation" (*EP:II* 583) throughout the first *Critique*, and that "the schematism unites pure intuition and pure concepts, by referring both in turn back to their common logical root" (598). Cassirer rather denounces the particular determining type of judgement upon which the entire structure of this work hinges. Such judgements after all presuppose a differentiation between the sensible and intelligible spheres, whereas Cassirer's own thought relies on the idea that there cannot be a separate sensible realm that is 'not yet' shaped by symbols. Building on the reflective type of judgement that is central to the third *Critique*, the first accomplishment of his philosophy of culture was thus to demonstrate the formative nature of the symbolic forms of mythical thought and language, two ways of understanding the world that fell strictly outside of Kant's conception of reason. Hence, even when criticizing what he takes to be Kant's overly logical approach, Cassirer's main target is always the sensationalist view that relies on the 'myth of the given'.

On this basis, it becomes clear that Heidegger and Cassirer actually defend different conceptions of phenomenology. Building on Husserl's thought, for Heidegger the phenomenological approach consists in thematizing our intentional, unthematic or pre-theoretical, relation to the world that is usually covered up by logical determinations of objects. Cassirer, in turn, explains in the preface to the *Phenomenology of Knowledge* that his use of the term phenomenology is not meant "in its modern sense", namely as it is used by Husserl and his followers, but refers to Hegel's *Phenomenology of Spirit*.[39] On this view, phenomenology merely strives to offer an overview of "the

---

[38] *KPM* 66. Heidegger here refers to the first part of Cohen's *System der Philosophie: Logik der reinen Erkenntnis* (Berlin: Bruno Cassirer, 1902).

[39] In the chapter on 'symbolic pregnancy', Cassirer rejects Husserl's distinction between the noetic and noematic moments of intentionality in the same way that he denounces the Kantian distinction between receptive sensibility and spontaneous understanding (196–199). Some commentators have nevertheless related Cassirer's conception of phenomenology to Husserl's (see Orth, *Von der Erkenntnistheorie zur Kulturphilosophie*, 162–175; and Christian Bermes, *Philosophie der Bedeutung – Bedeutung als Bestimmung und Bestimmbarkeit. Eine Studie zu Frege, Husserl, Cassirer und Hönigswald*, Würzburg: Königshausen & Neumann, 1997, 176–181).

totality of spiritual or cultural forms" by making visible "the transitions from one form to another" (*PSF:III* xiv). In this way, Cassirer aims to lead his readers "from the primary configurations found in the world of immediate consciousness to the world of pure knowledge" (xv). Accordingly, his review of the 'Kant book' holds that Kant's account of the schematism only supports a phenomenology of *objective* spirit (*KPMR* 241).[40]

These different conceptions of phenomenology align with Cassirer and Heidegger's disagreement about the epistemological or ontological intent of Kant's first *Critique*. Cassirer's emphasis on the spontaneity of human cognition supports his conviction that transcendental philosophy sets out to establish – or justify – the objective validity of spiritual or cultural forms. Heidegger's insistence on the finite nature of human reason matches his conception of transcendental philosophy as seeking the ground of objectivity in the ontological constitution of the human subject. These motivating concerns clearly surpass the topic of the proper meaning of Kant's thought, and lead us to a disagreement about the human condition at large.

---

[40] Luft makes an interesting case for a complementary reading Husserl and Cassirer's philosophies as examining subjective spirit and objective spirit respectively, in chapter 9 of Subjectivity and Lifeworld in Transcendental Phenomenology, Evanston: Northwestern University Press, 2011.

Part II

'What Is the Human Being?'

5   Cassirer's Functional Account
of the Animal Symbolicum

It is a remarkable feature of Cassirer's philosophy of culture that it posits the human being as the unifying factor of all cultural expressions, and yet rarely discusses this being. On the one hand, Cassirer insists that we can neither gain a systematic overview of the different symbolic forms nor even a thorough understanding of their individual functioning if we do not assume their ideal connection in the human consciousness. On the other hand, his writings are almost exclusively concerned with the inner constitution of specific symbolic forms, most famously those of language, mythical thought, and science. Even when discussing the historical and structural relations between some of these cultural domains, Cassirer never establishes a systematic account of their shared origin in human consciousness. This raises two questions: What really is Cassirer's view of the human being? And how can we, first of all, retrieve it from his writings?

5.1   The Discrepancy between the Task and the Execution
of the Philosophy of Symbolic Forms

The stated goal of Cassirer's philosophy of symbolic forms is to transform Kant's critique of reason into a critique of culture and thereby bring idealism to completion (*PSF:I* 80). In order to achieve this goal, Cassirer must not only account for the inner constitution of our various cultural domains, but also establish their mutual relations. His transcendental analyses of the symbolic forms of language, mythical thought, science, art, religion, history, law, technology, and politics therefore constitute only one moment of his project: for Cassirer, the philosopher of culture also "strives to comprehend every symbol in its place and recognize how it is limited and conditioned by every other symbol" (*PSF:IV* 227). It is, in other words, "one of the first and principal tasks of a philosophy of human culture to analyze [our] various [spiritual] functions, to show us their differences and their mutual relations, their opposition and their collaboration".[1]

---

[1] Cassirer, 'Structuralism in Modern Linguistics', in: *ECW:24* 313–314; 'Goethe und die mathematische Physik', in: *ECW:9* 307.

In *An Essay on Man* (1945), Cassirer therefore holds that "philosophy cannot be content with analyzing the individual forms of human culture. It seeks a universal synthetic view that includes all individual forms" (*EM* 70). In the first draft of this work, he even adds that "if we do not presuppose such a fundamental unity, human civilization becomes enigmatical and unintelligible" (*ECN:6* 403). The 'synthetic view' that Cassirer addresses here entails more than a merely empirical overview, as it should ground all cultural phenomena in a systematic unity:

A philosophy of culture begins with the assumption that the world of human culture is not a mere aggregate of loose and detached facts. It seeks to understand these facts as a system, as an organic whole. For an empirical or historical view it would seem to be enough to collect the data of human culture. Here we are interested in the breadth of human life. [. . .] But a philosophical analysis sets itself a different task. Its starting point and its working hypothesis are embodied in the conviction that the varied and seemingly dispersed rays may be gathered together and brought into a common focus. The facts here are reduced to forms, and the forms themselves are supposed to possess an inner unity. (*EM* 222)

As a transcendental philosopher, Cassirer evidently expects to find this unity in the structure of human subjectivity: in the same way that Kant wanted to ground the manifold of our perceptions in the transcendental unity of apperception, Cassirer aims to show that our various ways of comprehending the world through the different symbolic forms are grounded in the unity of our symbolic consciousness.[2] He expresses his hope "to come to a sort of grammar and syntax of the human mind" (*CIPC* 90), or to establish "a general plan of ideal orientation, upon which we can so to speak indicate the place of each symbolic form".[3] In sum, Cassirer holds that "only when the 'morphology' of the human spirit is established, at least in its general outline, can we hope to arrive at a clearer and more reliable methodological approach to the individual cultural sciences" (*PSF:I* 69).

Nevertheless, most of Cassirer's writings discuss the inner constitution of an individual symbolic form. His most renowned works, the three volumes of *The Philosophy of Symbolic Forms*, deal with language (1923), mythical thought (1925), and scientific thought (1929), respectively. More than a decade later, Cassirer turns to the humanities in *The Logic of the Cultural Sciences* (1942) and ultimately to politics in *The Myth of the State* (1946). Less famously, he in the meantime also discussed the symbolic forms of technology in 'Form and Technology' (1930) and of law in an essay on the Swedish philosopher Axel Hägerström (1939).[4]

[2] See *PSF:III* 13; and *CIPC* 70–71.
[3] Cassirer, 'Das Symbolproblem und seine Stellung im System der Philosophie', in: *ECW:17* 262.
[4] Cassirer, 'Form und Technik', in: *ECW:17* 139–183; and 'Axel Hägerström: Eine Studie zur Schwedischen Philosophie der Gegenwart', in: *Göteborgs Högskolas Arsskrift*, 45, 1939, 1–119.

On a few occasions, Cassirer does elaborate on the historical or structural relations between certain cultural domains: in *Language and Myth* (1925) he discusses the interwoven development of the early forms of mythical thought, religion, and language, and in *The Phenomenology of Knowledge* he reflects on the respective functions that characterize the most decisive symbolic forms of language, myth, and science.[5] Yet, while Cassirer here compares the constitutive principles of these forms, he never establishes a systematic account of their shared origin in a limited amount of symbols or, ultimately, in the symbolic imagination of human consciousness as such. Even in *An Essay on Man* – what's in a name? – Cassirer broaches this subject rather briefly, and mainly engages in a general overview of the different symbolic forms. How can we reconcile this fact with the explicit task of his philosophy, namely to "demonstrate the unity of spirit as opposed to the multiplicity of its manifestations" (*PSF:I* 114)?

5.2   The Primacy of the Relation and the Inaccessibility of Human Consciousness

The absence of a separate account of the human subject in Cassirer's published writings is not due to an exclusive interest in cultural objectivity or to mere forgetfulness. It rather follows from his view that the subjective and objective spheres cannot be separated. Cassirer advocates their intrinsic mutual relation first through his logical concept of a 'function' and later through the idea of the 'symbol'. In order to fully understand Cassirer's focus on the mediating symbol, it is useful to first consider his main sources of inspiration in this regard, namely Kant and the Neo-Kantian thinker Paul Natorp.

Kant's 'Copernican revolution' leads him to endorse empirical realism and transcendental idealism as two sides of the same coin. Kant's empirical realism results from his acceptance of a receptive faculty of sensibility as the primary source of all cognition of objects: according to Kant, it is through sensible intuition alone that we can have access to other beings.[6] His transcendental idealism implies, however, that we can only have cognition of objects thanks to the formative power of the pure sensible forms of time and space and the pure intelligible categories of the understanding.[7] In so far as these structures are in turn solely applicable to appearances[8], empirical realism and transcendental idealism are only viable positions when combined with each other.[9]

---

[5] Ernst Cassirer, *Language and Myth*, tr. by Susanne K. Langer, Dover Publications Inc., 1946; and *PSF:III* 448–453 .

[6] *CPR* B1, A19/B33, A27/B43, A50–51/B74–75, and A375.

[7] *CPR* Bxvii, A103–107, B137, B143.   [8] *CPR* A38–39/B55–56, B145, A147/B187.

[9] *CPR* A369–371. Concerning this topic, see Paul Abela's, *Kant's Empirical Realism*, Oxford: Clarendon Press, 2002, especially pp. 15–44.

Hence, Kant famously holds that "thoughts without content are empty, while intuitions without concepts are blind" (*CPR* A51/B75).

This view entails that Kant rejects the possibility of intellectual intuition of objects 'as they are in themselves', independent of the way that we perceive and judge them. At least for us human beings, no knowledge is possible of an object that is not given in experience, be it an object of external intuition[10] or our own 'soul'.[11] In this way, the traditional conception of objects and subjects as two separate or even opposed entities becomes problematic. Kant's transcendental approach to cognition only allows us to meaningfully speak about the mutually dependent notions of a 'transcendental object', which is "the representation of appearances under the concept of an object in general" (A251), and a 'transcendental subject', understood as a "wholly empty representation [of a] consciousness that accompanies every concept".[12] The transcendental object is, in other words, the "correlate of the unity of apperception for the unity of the manifold in sensible intuition" (A250).

More than a century later, the Marburger Neo-Kantians proclaim the transcendental method as the central idea of Kant's thought.[13] In order to clarify the meaning of this method, they however take it as their task to purify the critical discourse. Thus, in an essay titled 'Kant und die Marburger Schule' (1912), Natorp challenges Kant's distinction between a receptive and a spontaneous faculty because the concept of receptivity implies the existence of an object that exists independently of our perception thereof.[14] This concept, he holds, is a remnant of dogmatic 'metaphysicism' that contradicts the idea behind the transcendental method: from a critical perspective, all content of our consciousness is 'from the very beginning' formatted by us, and the idea of an unknown object is consequently an absurdity.[15]

In this spirit, Natorp attempts to develop a 'critical psychology' that builds on the idea of the primacy of the relation for cognition. Already in his early work *Einleitung in die Psychologie nach kritischer Methode* (1888), he holds that all content of consciousness has a relational character: "If we can only

---

[10] *CPR* A42/B59, A44/B61, A253.   [11] *CPR* A347/B405, A372, A400–402, B406–411.

[12] *CPR* A345–346/B404 – see also A341/B399–400: "This concept is the vehicle of all concepts [that] serves only to introduce all thinking as belonging to consciousness".

[13] The founder of the 'Marburger Schule', Hermann Cohen, treats the transcendental method as the key insight of Kant's thought from *Kants Theorie der Erfahrung* (1871) onwards, and increasingly emphasizes it throughout his oeuvre. Natorp endorses this method in 'Kant und die Marburger Schule', in: *Kant-Studien* 17, 1912, 194–196, and Cassirer repeatedly promotes it as the unifying factor of Marburger Neo-Kantianism (consult, e.g., *KLT* 3; 'Beiträge zu: Hermann Cohen', in: *ECW:17* 290; and 'Was ist 'Subjektivismus'?', in: *ECW:22* 169).

[14] Natorp, 'Kant und die Marburger Schule', 200–205.

[15] Natorp consequently suggests replacing the dualism of sensibility and the understanding by a distinction between 'object thinking' (*volles Gegenstandsdenken*) and 'lawful thinking' (*blosses Gesetzesdenken*; 'Kant und die Marburger Schule', 204).

become conscious of a certain content by apprehending it, and if apprehension can only be grasped psychologically in the relation of contents, it must be this relation that expresses the peculiarity of consciousness".[16] In *Allgemeine Psychologie nach kritische Methode* (1912), Natorp insists that relation is so essential to consciousness that "all consciousness is in fact relation", so that an isolated content must be the result of a process of abstraction that obscures what can only be clear in the correlation that this process dissolved.[17] For Natorp, consciousness is therefore not a subjective entity that we can oppose to its objects, but rather itself consists of a so-called 'subjective' and 'objective' moment.[18] Hence, in his thought

> the relation of opposition becomes one of reciprocity, which simultaneously means necessary correlation. [...] The initially sharp-looking opposition of objectivity and subjectivity completely dissolves in the *lively process* of objectification on the one hand and subjectification on the other, in which there is neither something objective nor something subjective as such, but always only a comparatively objective and subjective moment.[19]

In this way, Natorp contends to have thought through Kant's insight in the intimate correlation between subjectivity and objectivity.

Cassirer in turn endorses Natorp's claim that the relation is the primary element of our cognition in both his early treatise on mathematics and natural science and his mature philosophy of culture. In the introduction to *Substance and Function* (1910), Cassirer aims to draw out the consequences of Kant's 'Copernican revolution' for a truly critical logic: with this 'revolution in the way of thinking', he argues, the concept of substance loses not only its ontological but also its logical priority over relational concepts. Traditional logic, he explains, understood substance as the highest concept because it signifies the independence of all specifying, secondary, relations, and therefore unites the widest range of objects (*SF* 8). On Kant's critical perspective, on the

---

[16] Paul Natorp, *Einleitung in die Psychologie nach kritischer Methode*, Tübingen: Mohr-Siebeck Verlag, 1888, 23 (23–26).

[17] Paul Natorp, *Allgemeine Philosophie nach kritischer Methode*, ed. by Sebastian Luft, Darmstadt: Wissenschaftliche Buchgesellschaft, 2013, 56 – hereafter indicated as '*AP*'. See also *AP* 59.

[18] According to Natorp, consciousness (*Bewusstsein*) actually consists of three intimately related moments: content, or that of which one is conscious; the I, or that which is conscious of something; and 'Bewusstheit', or the mutual relation between these moments, or the fact that something is conscious of something. This relation, he claims, is 'an irreducible *Letztes* that allows for no further explanation or reduction' (*AP* 24–28). Von Wolzogen elaborates on this topic in *Die autonome Relation*.

[19] *AP* 71; see also 22, 202, 210–211. Natorp continues that the same holds for the conceptual pairs of form and matter, determination and undetermined, representation and presence, and being and appearing (72–90). In the end, he suggests dropping the terms 'objectivity' and 'subjectivity' altogether (213–214), although his own texts do not live up to this recommendation.

other hand, the category of substance originates in transcendental subjectivity and expresses one type of objectifying relationship between perceptions. Cassirer favors this view and concludes that "the relation [...] is in each case decisive", whereas "the concept is merely the expression and husk of it".[20] He then calls these logical relations 'functions' because they relate phenomenal objects in the same way that a mathematical function (y) connects a series of variables (x1, x2, ...): serving as "a universal *rule* for the connection of the particulars themselves" (20), a function mediates between 'the particular contents' and 'the specific form of the concept' (15).

In his mature thought, Cassirer confirms that "it is precisely the pure relation that governs the building of consciousness and that stands out in it as a genuine a priori" (*PSF:III* 202–203). Like Natorp, he holds that "there cannot be any such thing as an isolated 'merely sensory' consciousness [of an object] – that is, a consciousness that is not at all determined by theoretical functions of signification and that precedes them as an independent datum".[21] In Cassirer's own distinctive terminology, this means that our cognition of objects is always already determined by our symbolic way of understanding the world: "Human knowledge is by its very nature symbolic knowledge" (*EM* 57). Just as his original function-concept, the concept of a 'symbol' expresses an intimate relation between a subjective and objective, formal and material, or intelligible and sensible moment. In *The Phenomenology of Knowledge*, Cassirer thus claims that "from the standpoint of phenomenological inquiry there is no more a 'matter in itself' than a 'form in itself'; there are only total experiences which can be compared from the standpoint of matter and form and determined and ordered according to this standpoint".[22] Accordingly, he holds that objectivity "lies in the manner and form of *objectification* that each symbolic form accomplishes" (*PSF:II* 14).

Cassirer's rejection of the objective-subjective dichotomy evidently also has consequences for his understanding of subjectivity. For the same reason that we cannot perceive a 'naked object', he claims that we cannot perceive a 'naked subject' either: "However deeply we may penetrate into the formations

---

[20] *SF* 16. In 1914, Cassirer in a more critical fashion holds that "relation [...] does not signify one of the classes of categories, as Kant thought, but is simply 'the' category, of which all particular ways of connecting of which our knowledge is capable – especially the forms of space of time – are nothing but individual subspecies" ('Charles Renouvier, Essais de critique générale', in: *ECW:9* 485).

[21] *PSF:III* 8 – translation modified; see also *PSF:II* 34–35; *PSF:III* 14–15, 32.

[22] *PSF:III* 199. In language that closely resembles Natorp's, Cassirer further holds that "the meaning of cognition is first constituted by means of a twofold 'reference' that it contains: the reference to the unity of knowing and to that of the object – the I-intention and the is-intention [...] are equally necessary and essential to it. [...] When we think of them separately, we have not isolated an element of our cognition, but we have destroyed it entirely" ('Erkenntnistheorie nebst den Grenzfragen der Logik und Denkpsychologie', in: *ECW:17* 72).

of the sensuous-spiritual consciousness, we never find this consciousness absolutely objectless, as something absolutely simple, prior to all sensations and distinctions" (*PSF:III* 93). Hence, when Cassirer posits that "the analysis of consciousness can never lead back to absolute elements" (202), this counts for both its 'objective' and 'subjective' moments. All that we can know about consciousness we must therefore gather from a transcendental investigation of its cultural accomplishments:

The essence of man is to be found nowhere but in his works – in those fundamental activities on which all social life and all cultural life is based. To understand man we have no other way than to inquire into these activities. We have no more reliable access to the knowledge of human nature than by exploring the nature of language, of art, of science, of religion, of morality.[23]

Since we can never grasp the human subject in its so-called naked existence, we must be content with the way it expresses itself in various forms in our cultural life: "In each one of its freely projected signs the human spirit apprehends the object and at the same time apprehends itself and its formative law" (*PSF:I* 92). Does this mean, then, that Cassirer's transcendental method allows us to grasp human consciousness after all, namely through a mediate way of access?

5.3   Cassirer's Functional Conception of the Human Being

Despite his focus on the symbol, Cassirer nevertheless manages to develop a meaningful account of human consciousness. His view that 'objectivity' and 'subjectivity' are but two sides of the same relation after all did not prevent him from investigating the constitution of cultural objectivity. Should it then not be possible, by means of a 'turn around', to also examine the nature of our subjectivity? Once again, Cassirer finds inspiration for this undertaking in Kant and especially Natorp.

Kant defines transcendental philosophy as concerned not with objects but with the universal conditions of possibility of our cognition thereof (*CPR* A11/B25). Since he situates these conditions in the structure of the human mind (*das Gemüt*), it has been suggested that we might also refer to (a part of) Kant's project as 'transcendental psychology'.[24] Of course, this type of psychology must be very different from empirical psychology, which Kant identifies as "a species of physiology of inner sense" that can offer no apodictic cognition and cannot, therefore, belong to philosophy (A347/B405–406).

---

[23] Cassirer, 'Seminar on Symbolism and Philosophy of Language', in: *ECN:6* 244–245. See also *PSF:I* 86, 88; and *EM* 11.
[24] See Patricia Kitcher, *Kant's Transcendental Psychology*, New York/Oxford: Oxford University Press, 1990, 19.

Kant's transcendental psychology is more akin to his critical conception of rational psychology: if the latter is properly understood as a merely hypothetical discipline about the regulative idea of the soul, both center on the 'I think' or transcendental subject as their 'sole text' (A343/B401). However, rational psychology aims to think this subject as a substance, simple, identical, and related to other objects in space, and thereby turns it into a problematic object. Transcendental psychology, on the other hand, merely describes our subjective capacities *qua* subjective capacities – whether they bring about the objects of mathematics and physics or allow us to think ourselves.[25]

If, then, the first *Critique* really offers a transcendental psychology, we must consider it as the mere counterpart of Kant's investigation of the possibility of objectivity in general. His transcendental philosophy and transcendental psychology are, in other words, two sides of the same coin.[26] This is, in any case, the insight that guides Natorp's thinking in the *Allgemeine Psychologie*. Once he has established the boundaries of his critical method, he sets out to investigate the constitution of both objectivity and subjectivity:

> Now that we have determined the strict unity of the correlative relation of objectivity and subjectivity as a certain foundation, we shall investigate [...] first the direction of objectification, and second that of subjectification with regard to the general laws of its method of execution. (*AP* 154)

---

[25] Avery Goldman therefore argues for the circularity of Kant's argumentation in the *Critique of Pure Reason* in *Kant and the subject of critique. On the regulative role of the psychological idea*, Bloomington: Indiana University Press, 2012, 3, 169–177). This circularity, Goldman holds, does not render Kant's project incoherent, but rather expresses his original transcendental method (11, 180).

[26] Kant suggests the *possibility* of a 'transcendental psychology' in the introduction to the A-edition of the first *Critique*. There, he distinguishes between a subjective and an objective moment of the deduction of the categories of the understanding: the 'objective deduction' "refers to the objects of the pure understanding, and is supposed to demonstrate and make comprehensible the objective validity of its concepts a priori", whereas the 'subjective deduction' "deals with the pure understanding itself, concerning its possibility and the powers of cognition on which it itself rests" (*CPR* Axvi). The 'objective deduction' thus establishes the objectivity of our experience, and the 'subjective deduction' grounds this objectivity in the structures of transcendental subjectivity. Kant, however, immediately displays an ambiguous stand with regard to the status of the latter deduction: "Although this exposition is of great importance with regard to my chief end, it does not essentially belong to it" (Axvii). This ambiguity foreshadows Kant's difficulties *executing* a 'subjective deduction' of the categories in the Transcendental Analytic: in the A-edition he tackles this task by "assessing the transcendental constitution of the subjective sources that comprise the a priori foundations for the possibility of experience" (A97), but the result is both extraordinarily complex and dropped entirely in the B-edition, which adopts an approach that is more in line with Kant's conception of the 'objective deduction' instead – and that turns out to be equally problematic. Regarding the specifics of Kant's transcendental psychology here, one should consult Patricia Kitcher, *Kant's Transcendental Psychology* and *Kant's Thinker*, New York: Oxford University Press, 2011, 81–200, and Dieter, Sturma *Kant über Selbstbewußtsein*, Hildesheim: Georg Olms Verlag, 1985.

As it turns out, the latter task is however not at all evident: "While objectivity is generally considered unproblematic, and we only doubt how precisely we can determine it", Natorp holds, "the subjectivity of our appearances is either overlooked or naively derived from objectivity" (194). The process of the 'subjectification of consciousness', which is the theme of Natorp's transcendental psychology, thus poses a serious difficulty. On the one hand, every description and even every look (*jede Blick*), whether scientific or prescientific, entails a fixation and objectification of our appearances (193). All our experience implies a construction of facts. On the other hand, as the transcendental ground of all experience, our consciousness cannot itself be a fixed fact: by "bringing to a halt our stream of sensations, [the process of objectification] kills consciousness, whose immediate and concrete character is actually like perpetually flowing life, never stagnation" (190–191). Earlier on, Natorp already pointed out that when we try to grasp the conscious self, we run the risk of turning it into its own opposite, namely an *object of* consciousness (28–31). The subjective kernel of our consciousness can thus nowhere be met directly as itself (191).

According to Natorp, the only way to establish a critical psychology is consequently by reconstructing the objects that our consciousness has first construed. We can only grasp our subjectivity as subjectivity by undoing the objectifications that destroyed our actual, complete, experiences, by reconnecting what abstraction had separated, or by reviving the flow of conscious life that was brought to a halt by our use of rigid concepts. The reconstructive method of Natorp's transcendental psychology entails, in sum, "a complete and pure reversal of the procedure of objectifying cognition, be it of a scientific or prescientific kind: while the latter constitutes objects out of appearances, psychology reconstructs the appearances out of the objects, as if they are the given" (193).

Natorp does not, in this way, promise access to a 'pure subject' after all: his critical psychology conducts a reversal of consciousness' usual direction (*eine Art Umkehrung*) that remains within the framework established by Kant's Copernican revolution: "The unity of consciousness is itself unthinkable [...]. It constitutes [...] not so much the genuine task of psychology as its final boundary" (199). Like Kant, Natorp thus regards the idea of the subject as a limiting concept. Unlike Kant, however, he fully endorses the project of a transcendental psychology – even though he never executes its ambitious program: Natorp's *Allgemeine Psychologie* argues for the necessity of a transcendental psychology as the systematic counterpart of transcendental philosophy and determines its methodology accordingly.

Cassirer explicitly subscribes to Natorp's project in *The Phenomenology of Knowledge*. Referring to his teacher, he here holds that we can never lay bare the immediate life and being of consciousness as such. But it is a significant task to seek a new aspect and meaning for the perpetual process of objectification by exploring it in a twofold direction: from *terminus a quo* to *terminus ad quem* and back again. (*PSF:III* 53; modified translation)

Not surprisingly, Cassirer further claims that this twofold exploration is not only necessary with regard to scientific objectivity, but must be executed with respect to each cultural domain: "If we are to gain a concrete view of the full objectivity of the spirit on the one hand and of its full subjectivity on the other, we must seek to carry out the methodological correlation, which Natorp set forth in principle, in every field of spiritual endeavor".[27] Cassirer announces that he will therefore approach "the question of the structure of the perceptive, intuitive, and cognitive modes of consciousness [...] by means of a reconstructive analysis", starting from the problems of objective spirit in order to "find our way back to their elementary presuppositions, the conditions of their possibility" (*PSF:III* 57).

The third volume of *The Philosophy of Symbolic Forms* indeed not only investigates the symbolic form of scientific knowledge, but also reflects on its differences with the forms of mythical thinking and language that were discussed in the previous volumes. In a brief but enlightening passage, Cassirer explains that the cultural domains are grounded in different subjective principles of objectification: mythical thinking, language, and science derive their particular character from the 'expressive', 'representational', and 'signifying functions of consciousness'.[28] Conversely, for Cassirer, "consciousness is nothing but pure potentiality for all objective formations" (53). Adopting Natorp's reconstructive approach to consciousness within the framework of a philosophy of culture leads him to identify human subjectivity as the unity of the rational capacities to constitute different symbolic forms: "It is the totality

---

[27] *PSF:III* 57, 88. Cassirer, moreover, holds that Natorp established the basic program for a 'phenomenology of consciousness' (54), a term that he used earlier to describe his own philosophical project (*PSF:II* xv). Later, he adds that we must gain "insight into the methodological relation between phenomenological analysis and a purely objective philosophy of the human spirit" because they "are so closely linked and necessarily interdependent that not only are their positive results closely related but, conversely, every false move in one direction makes itself felt forthwith in the other" (*PSF:III* 74). On this basis, Martina Plümacher claims that the philosophy of symbolic forms executes a plan that was first sketched by Natorp as a psychological philosophy (*Wahrnehmung, Repräsentation und Wissen. Edmund Husserls und Ernst Cassirers Analysen zur Struktur des Bewusstseins*, Berlin: Parerga Verlag, 2004, 243, 412). Sebastian Luft, however, depicts Natorp's general psychology and Cassirer's philosophy of culture as each other's radical opposites (*AP* xxx). These views need not contradict each other if, as I suspect, Plümacher refers to Natorp's attempt in the *Allgemeine Psychologie* to establish the relational nature of consciousness and consequently investigate the processes of objectification *and* subjectification, whereas Luft solely refers to the latter, most original, aspect of Natorp's thought.
[28] *PSF:III* 448–453. I elaborate on these functions in Chapter 7 (Section 7.1).

of these rules that constitutes the true unity of consciousness, as a unity of time, space, objective synthesis, etc." (*PSF:I* 102; *PSF:II* 13). This unity, Cassirer further specifies, does not consist in a substantial identity, but in a functional continuity: "The term 'Geist' is correct; but we must not use it as a name of a substance – a thing [...] We should use it in a functional sense as a comprehensive name for all those functions that constitute and build up the world of human culture".[29]

Over against the variety of cultural meaning, Cassirer thus posits a functional conception of human consciousness. This conception is not distorted, but rather confirmed by the wealth of human culture: "Such a unity does not presuppose a homogeneity of the various elements of which it consists. Not merely does it admit of, it even requires a multiplicity and multiformity of its constituent parts. For this unity is a dialectic unity, a coexistence of contraries" (*EM* 222; *PSF:III* 41). It is, then, precisely because Cassirer's conception of subjectivity has no content of its own that it can structurally relate the variety of our cultural manifestations as elements of the same human culture:

The philosophy of symbolic forms starts from the position that, if there is any definition of the nature or 'essence' of man, this definition can only be understood as a functional, not a substantial one. We cannot define man by an inherent principle that constitutes his metaphysical essence – nor can we define him by an inborn faculty or instinct that may be ascertained by empirical observation. Man's outstanding characteristic, his distinguishing mark, is not his metaphysical or physical nature – but his work. It is this work, it is the system of human activities, which defines and determines the circle of 'humanity'. (*EM* 67–68)

5.4   From 'Animal Rationale' to 'Animal Symbolicum'

I established earlier why Cassirer's thought does not permit a separate account of human subjectivity. Now, we can understand why it does not even require one: Cassirer's conception of human consciousness is already indirectly expressed in the array of empirical and anthropological examples of our symbolic formation of the world that we encounter throughout his writings. We recall that in the opening passage of the first volume of the *Philosophy of Symbolic Forms*, Cassirer pleads for a 'morphology of spirit' that would explain the constitution of the different cultural domains (*PSF:I* 69). In *An Essay of Man*, he furthermore holds that a *philosophy of man* would be "a philosophy that would give us insight into the fundamental structure of each of the human activities [of language, myth, religion, art, science, history],

---

[29] *ECW:24* 313; see also *CPPP* 62: "We must replace with a functional conception the substantive conception of reason". In *The Philosophy of the Enlightenment*, Cassirer praises the eighteenth-century Enlightenment thinkers for achieving this insight for the first time (*PE* 13).

and that at the same time would enable us to understand them as an organic whole" (*EM* 68). This could have been just as well Cassirer's definition of a *philosophy of culture*.[30] By focusing on the symbols, Cassirer can simultaneously offer a philosophy of the human being and a philosophy of culture: while the philosophy of symbolic forms situates the *ratio essendi* of all cultural objectivity in symbolic consciousness, it conversely considers the sphere of cultural meaning as the *ratio cognoscendi* of human subjectivity.[31] As such, despite being an essential, foundational, element of Cassirer's thought, his account of human subjectivity necessarily withdraws in the background of his writings.

This explains why the clearest arguments for Cassirer's view of human subjectivity appear in two atypical passages in Cassirer's oeuvre, namely a biological-psychological discussion in *An Essay on Man* (*EM* 23–41) and the lengthy chapter 'Toward a Pathology of the Symbolic Consciousness' in the *Phenomenology of Knowledge* (*PSF:III* 205–277). In both cases, Cassirer compares 'natural' human consciousness with that of animals and people who display pathological behaviour.

According to Cassirer, all our experience is grounded in the power of symbolic imagination or the awareness of the 'symbolic pregnancy' (202) of our perceptions. This means that our experience always contains a spiritual element that connects our current perceptions to previous, future, or even merely possible ones. We are, in other words, not absorbed in our momentaneous intuitions but are capable of taking a certain distance to them. The difference between the expressive, representational, and signifying functions of consciousness lies in the degree of distance that they install to the sensuous world. However, in the 'pathology chapter' Cassirer nuances that this capacity only characterizes 'healthy experience': the "ability to interchange present and non-present, the real and the possible", distinguishes "a normal individual" from a pathological one (271). Pathological experience means, on this account,

---

[30] Recki points out that Cassirer refers to the symbolic forms as "spiritual forms or 'basic spiritual functions'", or as "the 'form of spirit' that conscious and organized life takes on". She adds that "each cultural construction is founded on an 'original act of spirit', and that it does not surprise in light of his abundant data of historical and systematic presentation of the symbolic forms that Cassirer fundamentally aims at 'a philosophical system of spirit'" (*Kultur als Praxis*, 54–55).

[31] "The determination of the human being, on the basis of which the determination of reality can first take place, here turns out to be the fundamental problem of philosophy" (Orth, *Von der Erkenntnistheorie zur Kulturphilosophie*, 197). Recki (*Kultur als Praxis*, 33–34, 57–62) and Oswald Schwemmer (*Ernst Cassirer: Ein Philosoph der Europäischen Moderne*, Berlin: Akademie Verlag, 1997, 31) also emphasize the close connection between philosophy of culture and philosophical anthropology in Cassirer's thought, but above all Gerald Hartung (*Das Maß des Menschen*, esp. 342–343) splendidly explains how these two currents form the *terminus ad quem* and *terminus a quo* of the philosophy of symbolic forms.

that one is incapable of making spiritual connections between perceptions because one has lost the ability to perceive symbolic meaning:

In pathological cases the close-knit unity is loosened or may threaten to disintegrate entirely. The contents of certain sensory spheres seem somehow to lose their power of functioning as pure means of representation: their existence and facticity no longer bear any representative character or objective pregnancy. (235–236, 208, 277)

Cassirer gives the example of a patient who is perfectly capable of using a spoon or cup during a meal but unable to point out their use when encountering them in a different situation (276). This person lacks the capacity to grasp the abstract meaning of the utensils and make free use of them.

Non-pathological individuals may all be able to relate to this phenomenon of the loss of meaning by bringing to mind the rare and temporary experience of a culture shock, when the coherence of our cultural world seems to dissolve entirely. Cassirer points out that we cannot, however, conceive of a *complete* lack of symbolic understanding of the world:

The disintegration of those 'vortices', those dynamic unities through which normal perception functions [. . .], can never mean total destruction, for that would mean the extinction of sensory consciousness itself. But it is conceivable that this consciousness moves within narrower limits, in smaller and more restricted circles than in the case of normal perception. (222)

If we lost our symbolic grasp of the world entirely, Cassirer further explains in *An Essay on Man*, "man's life would be confined within the limits of his biological needs and his practical interests; it could find no access to the 'ideal world' which is opened to him from different sides by religion, art, philosophy, science" (*EM* 41). The behaviour of animals consists of merely instinctive responses to stimuli and lacks the ability to isolate meaningful relations from a given situation and imagine them in another. Therefore, the world of the animal is confined to the present and the actual (24, 38). Accordingly, in so far as the pathological individual shows certain behaviour that is analogical to that of animals, on Cassirer's account it finds itself on the dividing line between the biological and spiritual spheres (*PSF:III* 276).

Problematic as the failure of symbolic imagination may be for the pathological individual, Cassirer regards the partial breakdown of normal, symbolic, experience as highly instructive for his philosophy of culture: "The pathology of speech and action gives us a standard by which to measure the distance separating the organic world and the world of human culture, the sphere of life and the sphere of objective spirit".[32] Discussing numerous cases of pathological experience and behaviour, Cassirer is led to conclude that our symbolic

---

[32] *PSF:III* 277. Krois accordingly calls Cassirer's theory of the 'pathology of symbolic consciousness' a 'negative proof' of his theory of the symbol ('Problematik, Eigenart und Aktualität der Cassirerschen Philosophie', 25).

understanding is not merely an intellectual accomplishment but occurs at the heart of even our most basic forms of perception: "Now it becomes fully apparent to how great an extent not only our thinking of the world but even the intuitive form in which reality is present for us is subject to the law of *symbolic formation*" (208–209). Hence, in 'Toward a Pathology of Symbolic Consciousness' Cassirer most explicitly argues that the capacity of symbolic imagination is the essential characteristic of human consciousness:

> All knowledge of the world, and all strictly spiritual action upon the world requires that [...] I gain a certain distance from it. Animals do not know this distance: the animal *lives* in his environment; he does not place himself over against it to represent it. The acquisition of the world as idea is, rather, the aim and product of the symbolic forms – the result of language, myth, religion, art, and theoretical knowledge. Each of these builds up its own intelligible realm of intrinsic meaning, which stands out sharply and clearly from any merely purposive behavior within the biological sphere.[33]

For Cassirer, this ultimately means that the traditional definition of the human being as a 'rational animal' can no longer hold: "Reason is a very inadequate term with which to comprehend the forms of man's cultural life in all their richness and variety" (*EM* 26). His philosophy of culture shows that the sphere of objective experience is much broader than that of (scientific) reason narrowly conceived. Moreover, Cassirer occasionally insists on conceiving of human consciousness in terms of action and energy because the term reason suggests a substantial identity (*PSF:III* 274–275; *CIPC* 71). The idea of the symbol, in contrast, refers to the variable and active relationship of the human being with its surroundings. On these grounds, Cassirer substitutes the traditional definition of the human being as *animal rationale* for the title of *animal symbolicum* (*EM* 26). His entire philosophy of symbolic forms should, then, be understood as a morphology of this peculiar animal.

5.5   Cassirer's Metaphysics of Human Subjectivity

Since the publication of Cassirer's *The Metaphysics of Symbolic Forms* (1996), scholars have insisted that his account of human consciousness is primarily, or even solely, found in this unfinished work.[34] By positing his

---

[33] *PSF:III* 275–276; translation modified.
[34] The most extensive commentary on *The Metaphysics of Symbolic Forms* to this date is Thora Ilin Bayer's *Cassirer's Metaphysics of Symbolic Forms. A Philosophical Commentary* (New Haven: Yale University Press, 2001). In the introduction to this work, Bayer states that what was "missing in Cassirer's philosophy of symbolic forms was a treatment of the metaphysical principles that supported it" (2). In this way, she suggests that Cassirer's metaphysics offers a crucial yet previously lacking moment of his philosophy of culture. Bayer does not stand alone with this view: for example, Reto Luzius Fetz also holds that the metaphysics of symbolic forms answers questions that remained open in Cassirer's published writings, especially that of the

own thought with regard to the contemporary movements of phenomenology and Lebensphilosophie, Cassirer here indeed establishes two accounts of the relation between 'life' and 'spirit'. The remaining question is how this 'metaphysical account of the human being' relates to the 'functional account' found in his published writings.

The 'fourth volume of the philosophy of symbolic forms' is a posthumous compilation of an essay called 'On the Metaphysics of Symbolic Forms' (1928) and two collections of notes titled 'On Basis Phenomena' (ca. 1940) and 'Symbolic Forms: For Volume Four' (ca. 1928). John Michael Krois, the late chief editor of the *Cassirer Nachlass*, admits that these texts at first sight serve rather different purposes: while 'On the Metaphysics of Symbolic Forms' and 'Symbolic Forms: For Volume Four' offer an earlier announced criticism of contemporary philosophy[35], 'On Basis Phenomena' presents a

---

final justification of the philosophy of symbolic forms ('Forma formata – forma formans. Zur historischen und systematischen Bedeutung von Cassirers Metaphysik des Symbolischen', in: *Lebendige Form. Zur Metaphysik des Symbolischen in Ernst Cassirers 'Nachgelassenen Manuskripten und Texten'*, Hamburg: Meiner Verlag, 2008, 15). I do not endorse this reading or the reasons that Bayer offers for it. She refers to the 1949 volume on Cassirer in the *Library of Living Philosophers*, in which, she holds, William Curtis Swabey, Felix Kaufmann, Robert S. Hartman, and Wilbur R. Urban already addressed this hiatus in Cassirer's thought. However, Swabey notes that his own comments are "made in the name of metaphysics [understood] as a theory of being in general" and point out difficulties "not so much in Cassirer's writings as such, but in the point of view of idealism itself" (La Salle: Open Court Publishing Company, 1973, 123–124). Kaufmann, in turn, opens his essay by characterizing Cassirer as a typical product of Marburger Neo-Kantianism (185), who "rejects all varieties of trans-empirical metaphysics" and replaces it by an "analysis of experience" (206). Hartman, finally, repeatedly stresses that Cassirer's philosophy was never concerned with metaphics in the sense of 'a discipline of pure Being' (293–296). If, then, these authors regret the absence of a metaphysical, foundational, theory in Cassirer's philosophy, they seem to project their own philosophical interests on Cassirer's thought rather than to judge it on its own merits. The same seems to hold for Bayer, who argues that "the view that Cassirer had a philosophy without a metaphysics reinforced the popular view that his philosophy of symbolic forms was basically an extension of Marburg neo-Kantianism" (*Cassirer's Metaphysics of Symbolic Forms*, 3). Even if we disregard the diminutive phrase 'basically an extension' – it is not evident that we today should still find Cassirer's debt to his Neo-Kantian teachers problematic – once again no argument for the need for a metaphysics of symbolic forms is given on the basis of Cassirer's own writings. Finally, Bayer describes the philosophy of symbolic forms as "a series of analyses of areas of human culture" and wonders: "But what understanding of reality, especially human reality, does it entail?" (3–4). Since one can very well answer this question based on his published writings, we need not pin our faith to a metaphysics of symbolic forms for this.

[35] 'On the Metaphysics of Symbolic Forms' was initially conceived as the final chapter of *The Phenomenology of Knowledge*, and meant to "justify the basic attitudes of the Philosophy of Symbolic Forms toward present-day philosophy as a whole" (*PSF:III* xvi). Like the notes of 'Symbolic Forms: For Volume Four', it deals with the thought of thinkers like Georg Simmel, Ludwig Klages, Max Scheler, Henri Bergson, and Heidegger. Cassirer decided, however, that this addition would render the third volume of the *Philosophy of Symbolic Forms* both too long and incoherent: positioning his thought within the philosophical landscape of the early twentieth century is an entirely different undertaking than analysing the symbolic form of science and comparing it to the forms of language and myth. The former project reflects upon the basic

more thorough investigation (*Vertiefung*) of the foundations of Cassirer's own thought.[36] The first two texts, therefore, seem of no import for our study, since we are not interested here in Cassirer's relation to his contemporaries other than Heidegger. However, as Krois adds, 'On the Metaphysics of Symbolic Forms' clearly transcends its stated goal and also offers an account of human subjectivity in terms of 'life' and 'spirit'.[37] In this way, it relates to the topic of 'On Basis Phenomena' after all, since these notes present yet another view of the human being in terms of the 'basis phenomena' of 'I', 'action', and 'work'. We thus find in Cassirer's *The Metaphysics of Symbolic Forms* two 'metaphysical accounts of human subjectivity'.[38]

Before looking into the specifics of these accounts, we should preclude possible misunderstandings of the idea of a 'metaphysics of symbolic forms'. These writings offer neither a traditional type of ontology nor a kind of rational psychology that would support Cassirer's philosophy of culture.[39] It would be implausible to expect this from Cassirer – especially in texts that were written at the same time as *The Phenomenology of Knowledge* – who even here insists on critical conceptions of objectivity and subjectivity that are intimately connected to each other:

principles of the philosophy of symbolic forms, whereas the latter is instructed by them. In the end, Cassirer's 'justification of the philosophy of symbolic forms' would only be published fifty years after his death.

[36] Cassirer, *Zur Metaphysik der symbolischen Formen*, ECN:1 xi.

[37] In this regard, 'On the Metaphysics of Symbolic Forms' is also much more comprehensive than Cassirer's 1930 essay "'Geist' und 'Leben' in der Philosophie der Gegenwart' (*ECW:17* 185–205), which was based on the lectures that he gave at the 1929 *Davoser Hochschulkurse*.

[38] I have a number of reservations with regard to the usage of the texts that are compiled in *The Metaphysics of Symbolic Forms*. First, Cassirer never authorized the publication of 'On the Metaphysics of Symbolic Forms'. In the next seventeen years of his life, he decided to commence numerous other essay and book projects, which he completed at a tremendous pace, rather than publish this seemingly finished text. This suggests that he was not satisfied with it, and that we should be careful to draw conclusions about his view of human subjectivity from it. Second, to say that Cassirer did not even complete 'On Basis Phenomena' would be an understatement: the German edition of *The Metaphysics of Symbolic Forms* at this point consists of a scattered series of notes which rarely even form full sentences. It is difficult, therefore, to distill a coherent argument from this 'text', let alone determine which position Cassirer takes up here. Third, Bayer points out that although Cassirer's two accounts of "the processes that ground and define the human being [...] are not ultimately at odds with each other", it is not clear how exactly they relate to each other either (*Cassirer's Metaphysics of Symbolic Forms*, 151–152). These matters compromise, in my view, the reliability of the 'fourth volume of the philosophy of symbolic forms' as a source for Cassirer's understanding of the human being.

[39] See Donald Phillip Verene, 'Cassirer's Metaphysics', in: *The Symbolic Construction of Reality: The Legacy of Ernst Cassirer*, ed. by Jeffrey Andrew Barash, Chicago: The University of Chicago Press, 2008, 66: "Cassirer has not presented an ontology; there is no Cassirerian doctrine of being [...] What Cassirer has offered is literally a metaphysics of symbolic forms, that is, a broadly stated analysis of the opposition that is at the basis of the human world, that allows us to place the symbolic forms in a total context".

All objective and subjective truth, all certainty about the outer world as well as all certainty about itself that mankind is able to attain, appears to depend on the function of representation. Man knows the world and himself only through the image that he makes of both. (*PSF:IV* 93, 102)

Accordingly, the *task* of Cassirer's metaphysics of symbolic forms does not seem to differ from that of the philosophy of symbolic forms itself. At the beginning of 'On the Metaphysics of Symbolic Forms', Cassirer claims that the philosophy of symbolic forms should be concerned not only with our cultural domains in their static existence – as his previous writings were – but also "with the dynamics of giving meaning, in and through which the growth and delimitation of specific spheres of being and meaning occur in the first place. It seeks to understand and illuminate the riddle of the becoming of form as such" (4). In 'On Basis Phenomena', he further holds that metaphysics concerns "the question of the functions that disclose and make 'reality' accessible to us at all" (153). However, *The Phenomenology of Knowledge* already analysed the 'dialectics of meaning-giving' as a dialectics between symbolic pregnancy and symbolic imagination, and explained the 'disclosing of reality' in its account of expressive, representational, and signifying functions. *The Metaphysics of Symbolic Forms* does not, therefore, cover a topic that Cassirer's previous investigations had ignored altogether.[40]

It rather seems, then, that Cassirer's metaphysics offers a new *methodology* for approaching the subjective foundation of human culture. Reflecting back upon the three volumes of the philosophy of symbolic forms, he remarks that these writings were only concerned with the content, but never with the origin of the symbolic forms: "Even where the analysis attempted to investigate the makeup of this content, to discriminate between different 'levels' in it, the guiding interest was not genetic-historical, but purely phenomenological" (40–41). Cassirer thus distinguishes between the transcendental or phenomenological approach of the philosophy of symbolic forms, which argues from the existing cultural domains to their subjective conditions of possibilities, and the genetic-historical approach to the metaphysics of symbolic forms, which explains how human consciousness develops in such a way that it gives rise to the symbolic forms of myth, language, and ultimately science: "Our investigation [seeks] to show how the course of human knowledge leads from 'representation' to 'signification', from the schematism of perception to the symbolic grasp of pure relationships and orders of meaning" (111). To this end, Cassirer turns to the origin of the symbols and 'asks about their ground and significance' (54). He thereby emphasizes that this approach pays more

---

[40] In a letter to Husserl from 10 April 1925, Cassirer in fact holds that already the third volume of the *Philosophy of Symbolic Forms* offers "the actual systematic foundation and, in so far as this is possible, a kind of systematic completion of the investigations of the problem of the symbol".

attention to the unity of the (subjective) process than to the diversity of its (objective) results.[41]

Cassirer also holds, however, that the metaphysics of symbolic forms cannot replace the "'discursive' type of conceptualization with immediate vision" (53). Instead, he explains, "we can only make the world of 'immediacy' visible" by 'turning around' that same process of conceptualization:

What cannot be given to us directly through metaphysical intuition or by empirical observation becomes indirectly accessible through a kind of systematic 'reconstruction'. This provides us in general with the method by means of which we are able to expose the unique character of 'subjectivity'.

Cassirer's metaphysics thus proceeds according to the reconstructive method that he already promoted in *The Phenomenology of Knowledge*.[42] Once again, he distinguishes two complementary directions of investigation: "The critical analysis of consciousness remains incomplete and one-sided insofar as it is directed exclusively to the world of the 'object' or to that of the 'subject', instead of recognizing that both are related and correlatively connected to each other" (56).

The Metaphysics of Symbolic Forms does, therefore, primarily *translate* the philosophy of symbolic forms into the terminology of 'life' and 'spirit' that dominated nineteenth and twentieth century metaphysics (8). First, Cassirer only vaguely describes life as "an 'undifferentiated unity', the unity of the 'natural world-picture'" and as "a uniform and simple beam of light, which has not yet been refracted and dispersed by different mediums of meaning" (5). A more detailed account of life seems impossible, since he also claims that

the hypothesis of 'pure' form (as well as the hypothesis of 'pure' life) already contains a contradiction within itself. No matter how deeply we enter into the realm of organic processes or how high we go into the sphere of intellectual creativity, we never find these two subjects [...]. We meet up with completely formless life as seldom as we meet up with a completely lifeless form. (15, 38)

Hence, just like Cassirer rejected the distinction between objectivity and subjectivity or matter and form, he now holds that we can never perceive either life or spirit separately, but only the becoming of spirit, or form, out of life in our cultural world. Life, he holds, "'comes to itself' in the medium of the

---

[41] Ernst Cassirer, 'Seminar on Symbolism and Philosophy of Language', Yale 1941/1942, Box 51, Folder 1024, Bl. 54: "We must try to follow up, step by step, the gradual evolution that leads from the first dawnings of symbolic thought to its achievement, to its most perfect and refined forms. By slowly and patiently pursuing this way we may hope to reach our aim: to come to a philosophical concept of man that comprises the whole of its fundamental faculties and his most characteristic activities."

[42] *PSF:IV* 53. Cassirer also endorses the reconstructive approach to subjectivity in 'On Basis Phenomena', 150.

symbolic forms. It possesses and grasps itself in the imprint of form as the infinite possibility of formation, as the will to form and power to form".[43]

Second, Cassirer presents this becoming as identical to the evolution of mythical thought into language, art, religion, and ultimately scientific thought.[44] While *The Metaphysics of Symbolic Forms* offers no definition of spirit, Cassirer in this way suggests that it can be understood as 'cultural life' (230–231). He calls myth the "original 'form of life'" and holds that in this symbolic form, the distance between life and spirit is almost non-existent; the latter is here "entered into" and "interwoven with" the former (19). The 'stability and consolidation' that is later introduced by language indicates an increased distance between life and spirit (74), whereas our theoretical worldview displays "a rigid balance", an "unconditioned constancy and identity" that seems to break entirely with the undifferentiated nature of life (20). Thora Ilin Bayer claims that for Cassirer "life requires spirit because no shared or fixed experience is possible in it; all is becoming", but also that spirit in turn "requires life because it structures and preserves the differences it forms from life".[45] While spirit establishes the constitutive principles of the symbolic forms, the restlessness of life continuously pressures them to evolve and eventually causes new forms to develop out of the existing ones.

We find a similar account of the evolution of human culture in the conclusion of *An Essay on Man*. There, Cassirer holds that all symbolic forms are marked by a "tension between stabilization and evolution, between a tendency that leads to fixed and stable forms of life and another tendency to break up this rigid scheme [. . .], a ceaseless struggle between tradition and innovation, between reproductive and creative forces" (*EM* 224). He further identifies the dominance of one of these tendencies over the other as the factor that determines the 'particular physiognomy' of the symbolic forms of mythical thinking, language, and scientific thought. We can now understand the tension within these forms as a struggle between the metaphysical forces of life and spirit. Unlike in *The Metaphysics of Symbolic Forms*, in *An Essay on Man*, Cassirer, however, considers this struggle from the point of view of spirit. Here, he after all ascribes stability foremost to mythical thought, which sticks closely to what is empirically given, whereas science is said to be more fluid because it takes the most distance from what is given (224–228).

---

[43] *PSF:IV* 19; see also 113–114. Accordingly, Fetz holds that "the sole principle that unifies life and spirit is therefore the form, more precisely the strive for form that is inherent in life, that transcends the organic shapes and by means of the symbolic forms constitutes the spiritual sphere" ('Forma formata – forma formans', 24). This form, the symbol, was of course already the central topic of the philosophy of symbolic forms.

[44] *PSF:IV* 5–6, 19–23, 67–102.   [45] Bayer, *Cassirer's Metaphysics of Symbolic Forms*, 64.

Third, in order to explain the development of life into spirit, Cassirer once again opposes human consciousness to that of animals[46] and to the borderline case of pathological behaviour (*PSF:IV* 74, 77). As was the case in his published writings, this comparison serves the equation of spirit (cultural life) with freedom.[47] In 'On Basis Phenomena', Cassirer replaces the twofold distinction between life and spirit by a threefold, originally Goethean, distinction between 'I', 'action', and 'work'. He describes the concept of 'I' (*Ich*) as 'life itself' or that which "cannot be inferred from something else, but instead lies at the basis of everything else" (138). The novelty of Cassirer's second metaphysical account with regard to the first one must, therefore, lies in the distinction between action (*Wirkung*) and work (*Werk*). While Cassirer's notes seem to suggest that 'action' corresponds to the 'will' or 'blind drive' of animal consciousness (157), they present 'work' as the exclusively human product of culture: it is the "persisting remainder of activity [that] gives rise to that kind of being which we call culture" (158). Cassirer then lists 'the works of art, science, politics, the history of religion, and mathematical sciences' as examples of this remainder (164–165). "In contrast to the level of 'action'", he writes, a work is something fixed and enduring, and as such "opens up to mankind the 'objective' sphere, the sphere of 'things'" (141–142).

Hence, the ambiguity pointed out by Krois remains: it is unclear from Cassirer's notes whether the metaphysics of symbolic forms is meant to deepen what he had established in the philosophy of symbolic forms or merely reiterates his view in then popular terminology. While the term 'metaphysics' suggests the former, Cassirer never really breaches the boundaries of transcendental philosophy, and even repeats his functional definition of human subjectivity: "The unity of Geist is to be found only in the plurality of symbolic forms, not as a substantial unity, but as a functional unity. Geist becomes one through it conscious awareness of its identity (as action in general) in the plurality of various activities".[48] *The Metaphysics of Symbolic Forms* thus confirms Cassirer's original account of human consciousness as the foundation of culture that plays a crucial role in his thought from the very beginning. It therefore remains to be seen if its use of the language of his contemporaries manages to bring this account any closer to Heidegger's view of the human condition.

---

[46] *PSF:IV* 39–40, 62–64, 76–77.   [47] *PSF:IV* 19, 111, 228.
[48] *PSF:IV* 225. Conversely, Cassirer reaffirms that "the philosophy of symbolic forms finds that it meets with Geist everywhere [...] as the 'Will to Formation'" (28).

6   Heidegger's Existential Analytic of Dasein

While Cassirer's account of human consciousness mostly remains hidden in the background of his writings, Heidegger's analysis of the human condition famously takes front and center in *Being and Time*, as the primary task in the retrieval of the meaning of being. This 'existential analytic of Dasein' consists of five main steps, which gradually reveal the fundamental meaning of our existence. Starting from our everyday comportment, in Division One Heidegger argues that we have a pre-ontological understanding of being, that the conditions of possibility of this understanding are found in the structural moments of Dasein's being-in-the-world, and that the unity of these moments is grounded in care. Division Two subsequently distinguishes between an average and an – arguably more fundamental – authentic mode of care, and ultimately rephrases all previous steps in more original terms of Dasein's ecstatic temporality.

Before considering Dasein's authentic and temporal ways of being, it pays off to first gain a more systematic view of its basic existential constitution. Due to Heidegger's phenomenological method, which is descriptive rather than argumentative, *Being and Time* does not always follow a clear explanatory thread. Further, because of his hermeneutic style, which constantly moves back and forth between the constitutive elements and the whole of Dasein's being, Heidegger often seems to presuppose what he aims to demonstrate. By reading Division One first forwards and then also backwards, it however becomes clear that on Heidegger's view Dasein *itself* has a fundamentally ontological, phenomenological, and hermeneutic disposition. As such, his interpretation of the human condition prefigures his reading of Kant's transcendental philosophy a few years later.

6.1   Dasein's Pre-Ontological Understanding of Being

In the introduction to *Being and Time*, Heidegger presents his 'ontological', 'fundamental', or 'existential analytic of Dasein' as a necessary preliminary step in his attempt to retrieve the meaning of being. Since long, he holds, both our everyday and our philosophical understanding have exclusively focused on being*s*, and forgotten about being altogether. While Heidegger's writings on Kant tackle the philosophical tradition in light of this forgetfulness, *Being and Time* focuses on the human being's common understanding of the being of beings. Heidegger points out that, even though we are unable to define being or pinpoint its meaning, we use this word all the time and seem to have an implicit understanding of it: "We do not know what 'being' means. But already when we ask, 'What is being?', we stand in an understanding of the 'is' without being able to determine conceptually what the 'is' means. [. . .] *This average and vague understanding of being is a fact*" (*BT* 5). Heidegger even holds that this everyday understanding of being fundamentally distinguishes Dasein from all other beings: "Understanding of being is itself a definite characteristic of Dasein's being. Dasein is ontically distinctive in that it *is* ontological".[1] The goal of his phenomenology of Dasein will therefore be to rethink the human being in such a way that both our natural understanding and our natural forgetfulness of being are elucidated. Heidegger is confident that such an elucidation of our own existential constitution will provide "the soil from which we may reap the meaning of being in general" (17).

The first step in Heidegger's existential phenomenology consists, then, in demonstrating that Dasein indeed has a natural and continuous ontological understanding of the being of beings, since this is the assumption on which the entire undertaking rests. This assumption may, however, not seem all that evident at first. Is our everyday engagement in the world not always focused on beings rather than being? When assembling a piece of furniture, am I not practically engaging with my hammer, nails, and the different parts of the chair-to-be without ever reflecting on their essence or being? Is 'the being of beings' therefore not a specifically scientific, philosophical, or even mystical interest rather than something that concerns our everyday existence?[2] Heidegger answers these questions negatively, arguing that we in fact always understand beings on the basis of their being – and only in a derivative, theoretical, manner also the other way around (§14–18).

First, Heidegger holds that our initial and predominant (*zunächst und zumeist*) engagement with other beings is of a pragmatic rather than an observational nature:

The primary kind of dealing [with beings] is not mere perceptual cognition, but rather a handling, using, and taking care [. . .] What shows itself in taking care in the

---

[1] *BT* 12, 16. In *Phenomenological Interpretation*, Heidegger even holds that "understanding of being as such [. . .] is the most original and necessary condition for the possibility of human existence" (*PIK* 38).

[2] On the unwarranted mystification of Heidegger's conception of being in *Being and Time*, see William Blattner, *Heidegger's 'Being and Time'*, London/New York: Bloomsbury Publishing, 2006, 14, 16.

surrounding world [...] is not the object of a theoretical 'world'-cognition; it is what is used, produced, and so on. (67)

Our everyday comportment indeed shows that we have a certain understanding of beings that does not entail theoretical insight: we do not need to know out of which materials our hammer is made of in order to 'know' how to use it and whether it will be suited for a given task. In fact, not only does such under- standing not rely on a theoretical account – we acquire most of our skills solely through practice – but it even resists one. On the one hand, the finesses of our practical understanding often cannot even retroactively be formalized: most skills remain far too complex to be captured by a set of rules.[3] On the other hand, theoretical insight tends to disturb our usual engagement with other beings, rendering otherwise easily performed activities into unexpected riddles. Once we reflect on how to unlock our front door or how to insert our USB-stick, we only get confused over a simple task that usually poses no difficulties. Likewise, once we overthink our throwing skills, we are more likely to miss the target – as long as we need to think through our movements, we will never be a good athlete. Such instances show that a theoretical, observational, attitude not only differs from, but even conflicts with a practical one.

Over against "just looking at things theoretically" (*der nur 'theoretisch' hinsehende Blick*), Heidegger thus places "a dealing that makes use of things" (*der gebrauchend-hantierende Umgang*) as our primary way of understanding beings (69). Accordingly, he rejects the common idea that material objects are the basic elements of our world and the primary entities that we encounter in it. In Heidegger's terminology, beings first appear to us as 'ready-to-hand' (*zuhanden*) or as useful 'tool' (*Zeug*) that we employ, and only in a derivative way as 'present-at-hand' (*vorhanden*) objects that we contemplate: "The less we just stare at the thing called hammer, the more we take hold of it and use it, the more original our relationship to it becomes and the more undisguisedly it is encountered as what it is, as a useful thing". A hammer is not primarily an object of a certain material and weight, but foremost a handy piece of equipment.

Second, Heidegger contends that in this pragmatic perspective we are not even primarily focused on the beings that are involved, but rather immersed in the tasks for which they are useful. When hammering, the object of my intentional act is *not* the hammer itself. Instead, my attention is directed towards assembling a chair. According to Heidegger, beings thus initially appear to us as related to each other within a specific, useful, context:

---

[3] Blattner calls our 'skills and capacities' "too refined, too submerged in immediate action, and too fluid to be captured in a theory" (*Heidegger's 'Being and Time'*, 97).

"The structure of being of what is ready-to-hand as a useful thing is determined by references" (74). He even holds that

there 'is' no such thing as *a* useful thing. There always belongs to the being of a useful thing a totality of useful things in which this useful thing can be what it is. A useful thing is essentially 'something in-order-to . . .'. [It] contains a reference of something to something. (68)

This of course does not mean that Heidegger denies the material individuality of things. A chair does not depend on a table or Dasein for its existence (at least not after it has been manufactured). However, what *we* initially and predominantly *encounter* are relations between beings rather than individual objects. In this – ontological rather than ontic – sense, the practical context within which we engage with beings precedes and makes possible our understanding of beings: "A totality of useful things is always already discovered *before* the individual useful thing" (69, 84). Heidegger designates this totality – which encompasses the relations between my hammer, nail, and wooden planks – as 'work': "What every-day dealings are initially busy with is not tools themselves, but the work. [. . .] The work bears the totality of references in which useful things are encountered" (69–70). Our work is, then, that in function of which we encounter other beings: the chair is the 'what-for' (*Wozu*) of our equipment.

On this basis, Heidegger holds that our practical comportment "has its own way of seeing which guides our operations and gives them their specific certainty" (69, 67). This comportment is after all not aimless, but envisages the possible uses of beings in light of our work. Whereas the theoretical viewpoint is set on analysing the material components and characteristics of an object, our everyday understanding of beings thus maintains a synthetic perspective that focuses on the context in which we encounter beings. Heidegger calls this attentiveness to references and context 'circumspection' (*Umsicht*; 69).

Third, Heidegger adds that we also understand other beings as ultimately referring to ourselves. My assembling a chair serves a further purpose, namely my wish to eat dinner in a comfortable manner, to host a dinner party, or to sell enough chairs in order to make a living. Heidegger here uses the example of fixing a roof:

The thing at hand that we call a hammer has to do with hammering, the hammering has to do with fastening something; fastening something has to do with protection against bad weather. This protection 'is' for the sake of providing shelter for *Dasein*, that is, for the sake of a possibility of its being. (84)

Our everyday understanding of beings is thus an engaged understanding not only in the sense that it is grounded in practical activities, but also because things appear as 'relevant' (*bewandt*; 84), 'significant' (*bedeutsam*; 87), and 'familiar' (*vertraut*; 86) to us through our work. Conversely, we initially and predominantly understand ourselves as that for-the-sake-of-which (*Worum-willen*) other beings meaningfully relate to each other: I am a being for which the hammer is of use. This implies yet another contrast with the theoretical perspective, from which other entities have no intrinsic relation to us and hence no immediate meaning for us.

Heidegger calls the encompassing whole in light of which (*Woraufhin*; 86) equipment and work refer to us and in which we relate to beings in a meaningful manner our 'world': "World is always already 'there' in all things at hand. [It] is already discovered beforehand with everything encountered, although not thematically. [...] World is that in terms of which things at hand are at hand for us" (83). Accordingly, Heidegger calls the beings that we understand as equipment 'innerworldly beings' (66), and describes our own mode of being as 'being-in-the-world': "Being-in-the-world signifies the unthematic, circumspect absorption in the references constitutive for the handiness of the totality of useful things" (76).

Heidegger most clearly – and beautifully – illustrates these three points in *Ontology – The Hermeneutics of Facticity*, the 1923 lecture course in which he first developed many of the key ideas of his existential phenomenology. Heidegger here contrasts two ways to describe an ordinary being such as a table: one that views it as a thing (*HF* §19) and one that grasps its being (§20). On the one hand, we can conceive of a table in our living room as a material object that has a certain mass, colour, shape, and surface, that could be broken or burned, and towards which we can take a spatial position and distance that allows us to perceive it from a certain angle and under a certain light. In addition, we can of course also attribute some value to this table, and charac-terize it as beautiful or usable. Heidegger points out that such a description is not altogether fictitious (*erfunden*), enforced (*erkünstelt*), or false (*falsch*), since it is grounded in theoretical observations, but that it nevertheless fails to describe (*eine Fehldeskription*) the 'phenomenal coherence' (*phänomenalen Zusammenhang*) of the table. On the other hand, we can then also perceive the same table as our specific, familiar living room table that we use for writing and eating, that nicely matches the rest of the room, that is well positioned for late night reading, that enabled a dinner party that we fondly remember, and whose spot marks take us back to our children's youth. Heidegger holds that it is in this manner that we actually become acquainted with the table "in the concrete ways in which we pass the time" (*im konkret verweilenden Umgang*):

What is there in *the* room there at home is *the* table (not 'a' table among many other tables in other rooms and houses) at which one sits in order to write, have a meal, sew, play. Everyone sees this right away, e.g., during a visit: it is a writing table, a dining table, a sewing table – such is the primary way in which it is being encountered in itself. (69)

In a clear and succinct manner, Heidegger here illustrates the practical, contextual, and meaningful characteristics of our pre-ontological understanding. Furthermore, this example shows that the difference between theoretical and pre-ontological understanding should not be equated to that between 'knowing that' and 'knowing how'. While the equipment examples from *Being and Time* suggest that our everyday understanding of beings relies on skillfulness, if even of the simplest kind, the example from *The Hermeneutics of Facticity* shows that it constitutes the much broader context of our lived experience as a whole.

In sum, Heidegger opposes the theoretical understanding that isolates individual objects to a practical understanding whereby the beings encountered are nested in a familiar, meaningful, context. While it is clear now why the latter mode of understanding is more original, we have yet to explain why Heidegger calls this a 'pre-ontological understanding of being' (*BT* 12). That is, how is this an understanding of *being* (and not just an alternative, non-theoretical, understanding of being*s*) and it what sense is it *pre*-ontological?

As it turns out, we should take Heidegger's provisional definition of being as "that in terms of which beings have always been understood" (6) at face value. This definition does not merely suggest our capacity to understand or retrieve the meaning of being, but it formally indicates what being *is*. According to Heidegger, the being of beings *is* that as which beings are 'encountered in themselves' in our initial and predominant comportment. Being is, in other words, Heidegger's notion for the meaningfulness or intelligibility of beings.[4] Hence, the being of other beings lies in their 'ready-to-hand', referential, or innerworldly structure, and our own being in our 'for-the-sake-of-which' or our 'being-in-the-world'.

Yet, our initial and predominant understanding of being as intelligibility is inevitably *pre*-ontological by virtue of its implicit or unthematic nature (*PIK* 23). The reason for this is that the two constitutive factors of our natural ontological understanding of being must withdraw in the background in order

---

[4] See John Haugeland, 'Truth and Finitude: Heidegger's Transcendental Existentialism', in: *Heidegger, Authenticity, and Modernity. Essays in Honor of Hubert L. Dreyfus, Volume I*, ed. by Mark Wrathall and Jeff Malpas, Cambridge: The MIT Press, 2000, 47–48: "It is all too easy to get baffled or intimidated—not to say exasperated—by the way Heidegger talks about being. But that's not necessary; the basic idea is in fact fairly straightforward. The *being* of entities is that in terms of which they are *intelligible as entities*. [...] Understanding an entity *as an entity* —and there is no other way of *understanding* it—means understanding it in its *that*-it-is and its *what*-it-is. Disclosing the being of entities amounts to letting them become accessible in this twofold intelligibility—that is, as phenomena that are *understood*. When taken with sufficient generality, a pretty good colloquial paraphrase for 'disclosing the being of' is *making sense of.* " See also Taylor Carman, *Heidegger's Analytic. Interpretation, Discourse, and Authenticity in 'Being and Time'*, Cambridge: Cambridge University Press, 2003, 15; Steven Crowell, *Normativity and Phenomenology in Husserl and Heidegger*, Cambridge: Cambridge University Press, 2013, 27; or Thomas Sheehan, 'Facticity and *Ereignis*', 42.

for this understanding to take place, that is, for beings to become intelligible. I indicated earlier that our usual, circumspective, understanding of being does not focus on particular beings but rather on the referential context within which they are 'ready-to-hand'. In fact, our practical comportment is successful *precisely in so far as* our equipment remains unthematic:

That which is handy is not grasped theoretically at all, nor is it itself initially a circumspective theme for circumspection. What is peculiar to what is initially at hand is that it withdraws, so to speak, in its character of handiness in order to be really handy. (*BT* 69)

We pay no attention to the hammer or the tennis racket when using them; they rather function by becoming an extension of our own body.

At the same time, the encompassing context within which beings refer to each other in a meaningful manner – our world – also remains in the background of our everyday understanding of beings. Again, it is *precisely* the unthematic character of our world that enables it to structure our meaningful relations to other beings: "The condition for the possibility of what is at hand not emerging from its inconspicuousness is that the world does *not announce itself*" (75, 86). Something can only appear to us as intelligible if the preconditions of intelligibility as such do not themselves come into view. Hence, our initial and predominant understanding of the being of beings happens thanks to its non-conceptual nature. By calling it '*pre*'-ontological, Heidegger however also suggests that a conceptualization of intelligibility is nevertheless somehow possible.

6.2   Dasein's 'Being-in-the-World'

In the early sections of *Being and Time*, Heidegger thus shows that we indeed have a pre-ontological understanding of being, but also that this understanding tends to veil itself. This seems to pose a problem for his existential phenomenology, which aims to turn our pre-ontological understanding of being into a thematic, ontological, understanding. Yet, in a way this problem suggests its own solution. If our understanding is successful precisely in so far as it remains unthematic, it follows that our understanding can become thematic when it fails. Hence, Heidegger proceeds by investigating instances in which intelligibility is momentarily lacking, that is, when for some reason the beings that surround us no longer appear to us as useful equipment. The second challenge of *Being and Time* is, then, to capture this intelligibility in a theoretical manner without distorting its original, pre-theoretical structure.[5]

---

[5] Katherine Ward discusses at length how Heidegger relies on experiences of breakdown in order to overcome the phenomenological problem of "observation distortion", in 'Breaking Down Experience – Heidegger's Methodological Use of Breakdown in *Being and Time*', in: *European Journal of Philosophy*, 2020; 1–19 (https://doi.org/10.1111/ejop.12600).

This challenge prompts Heidegger to analyse the conditions of possibility of our factual, everyday understanding of being (§19–38).

Being and Time famously discusses three ways in which our attention is drawn to beings rather than their being because they strike us as out of place, namely when an otherwise useful tool such as the hammer breaks (it is 'not handy'), is missing (it is 'not at hand at all'), or hinders our usual engagement (it 'gets in the way'; 73–74). No longer referring to other beings in a meaningful way, these beings – either absent or somehow 'too present' – gain a respective conspicuous (*auffällig*), obtrusive (*aufdringlich*), or obstinate (*aufsässig*) character. In each case, the hammer becomes a thematic object:

> When we discovers its unusability, the thing becomes conspicuous. *Conspicuousness* presents the thing at hand in a certain unhandiness. But this implies that what is unusable just lies there; it shows itself as a thing of use which has this or that appearance and which is always also objectively present with this or that outward appearance in its handiness. (73)

Heidegger points out that the conspicuous, obtrusive, or obstinate appearance of a being does not, however, automatically turn it into a mere material object. In these modes, the hammer still appears as a tool, albeit one that no longer fulfills its function: "This objective presence of what is unusable still does not lack all handiness whatsoever; the useful thing *thus* objectively present is still not a thing which just occurs somewhere" (73, *PIK* 25). Therefore, the disturbance of our work allows us to respond in different ways: a practical, a theoretical-scientific, and a philosophical response.

Our most common response to the deficiency of our equipment is to maintain the practical attitude and simply shift our attention to a new activity that will allow the continuation of our work. We then attempt to fix the hammer, go out to buy a new one, or figure out how to remove that annoying hard plastic foil in which it was packaged by the manufacturer. Even if the breaking, missing, or obstructing of the hammer thus forces us to reflect on our next act, we in each case remain circumspective: by employing another tool – glue, a car, or a pair of scissors – we engage in a new practical endeavour that still refers to the original work and to ourselves as its 'for-the-sake-of-which'. In this case, we remain on the pre-ontological level: while making no effort to spell out the ontological status of our tools, we nevertheless continue to understand them as such.

We can, however, also exchange our practical attitude altogether for a theoretical one, thus considering our previous work and the tools we used for it from a detached perspective. We then try to figure out why the hammer broke or why manufacturers use these foils despite their obstinacy. In this case, the useful context within which we initially perceived the hammer becomes irrelevant, and the individual, material, thing stands out as both distinct from other beings and indifferent to my existence. This theoretical perspective is further developed in the scientific approach to understanding beings, which deliberately omits "all those purposes of comportment [that] aim at employment of what is uncovered and known" because it is "solely aimed at beings themselves" (26). Because of its exclusive attention to beings, Heidegger calls this an 'ontic' perspective, and any attempt to render it philosophical 'epistemology'. Although this perspective has come to dominate both our general and our philosophical way of thinking, according to Heidegger it relies on a derivative way of understanding beings that precludes a profound insight into their meaningful relations to both each other and ourselves, that is, into their being.

Heidegger, therefore, offers a third alternative, namely a perspective that also reflects on our practical engagement with beings, but that does not break with its circumspective view. This ontological perspective aims to articulate what we previously already understood exactly in the way that we understood it. Instead of examining the particular thing that is broken, absent, or obstructing, we then try to make sense of the event of the breaking, missing, or obstruction. In other words, we consider what the deficiency of our equipment in retrospect reveals about our usual, unreflective, engagement with beings. For one, it allows us to consider the ontological nature of the previously understood beings, or their *Zuhandenheit*: Heidegger describes conspicuousness, obtrusiveness, and obstinacy as three "modes that let the beings taken care of be encountered in such a way that the worldly character of innerworldly beings appears" (*BT* 73). Further, the meaningful context in which we understood these beings, that is, our world, becomes apparent as something that was always already there, even though we were not thematically aware of it: "The context of equipment is lit up, not as something never seen before, but as a totality constantly sighted beforehand in circumspection. With this totality, the world announces itself" (75). Finally, the deficiency of our equipment is also a philosophically fruitful event because it reveals something about our own being that allowed for this understanding, namely our 'being-in-the-world'. Each of these insights renders our pre-ontological understanding of either other beings or ourselves into an ontological one. As such, they provide the basis for what Heidegger considers to be true philosophy: he may not show much interest in the being of innerworldly beings, but *Being and Time* proceeds by examining the 'worldliness of the world' (§19–24) and the structure of our own 'being-in as such' (§28–38).

For our purposes here, we need not expand on the idea of world beyond what we have already explained in the previous section. Instead, we now turn to Heidegger's elaborate analysis of our own existential constitution: "The preparatory stage of the existential analytic of *Dasein* has as its leading theme this being's basic constitution, being-in-the-world" (130). From here on,

Heidegger full-on addresses our 'Da-sein' or our 'being-there (in the world among other beings)': "The being which is essentially constituted by 'being-in-the-world' *is* itself always its 'there'" (132). 'Being-in' and 'Da-sein' are thus synonyms for what Heidegger calls our 'disclosedness' (*Erschlossenheit*) to being: "This being bears in its ownmost being the character of not being closed. The expression 'there' means this essential disclosedness. [. . .] *Dasein is its disclosure*".[6] Heidegger's investigation into our 'being-in' thus focuses on the "existential constitution of the there", thereby distinguishing between three "equiprimordially constitutive ways to be the there": attunement (*Befindlichkeit*; §29–30), understanding (*Verstehen*; §31–33), and discourse (*Rede*; §34).

It has already become clear that Heidegger's notion of Dasein's understanding does not refer to an epistemological capacity that we can willingly apply or not, but rather to the primordial way in which we always already perceive beings as significant and as for-the-sake-of ourselves. In his analysis of 'being-in', Heidegger further characterizes this understanding as a mode of 'projection' (*Entwurf*; 145). In understanding, we after all foresee possible configurations amongst beings, by casting a certain light onto our surroundings that allows them to be perceived as something intelligible at all. Our pre-ontological understanding of the hammer as a tool that is useful for assembling a comfortable chair thus projects a possible world in which I enjoy a dinner party with friends. Such projection must of course take into account the material limitations of beings: we cannot use an egg in order to build our chair. Yet, it looks beyond any material conditions in so far as it is capable of seeing their potential: thanks to our understanding, "innerworldly beings are freed for *their own* possibilities. What is at hand is discovered as such in its service*ability*, us*ability*, detriment*ality*" (144). In hammering, that is, in projecting the chair, the dining room, and the idea of a dinner party, I disclose a possible, meaningful world that would otherwise not be. As such, Dasein's understanding is a condition of possibility for something to appear as something intelligible.

Since our pre-ontological understanding of other beings is accompanied by an understanding of our own being as their for-the-sake-of-which, we also always project our own possible ways of being into our world: "As long as it is, Dasein has always understood itself and will understand itself in terms of possibilities" (145). When assembling the chair, we picture ourselves as the

---

[6] *BT* 132–133. As Samuel IJsseling puts it, "as the *'there' of Being*, the *Da des seins*, *Dasein* is the place where being takes place" ('Heidegger and the Destruction of Ontology', in: Joseph J. Kockelmans (ed.), *A Companion to Martin Heidegger's 'Being and Time'*, Washington DC: The Center for Advanced Research in Phenomenology and University Press of America, 1986, 134).

host of a dinner party, or perhaps someone who could make a career as a cobbler. Our 'being-in-the-world' then not only constitutes a condition of possibility for making sense of other beings, but also for making sense of ourselves: in our attempt to fix a squeaking chair, the screwdriver is understood as a useful tool, and our own actions are understood as that of a perfect dinner host. Dasein thus also understands itself as a project, or projects its own being.

Our capacity to render things intelligible, however, requires yet another constitutive factor of being-in-the-world that Heidegger calls our 'attunement' to being. If the existential of understanding constitutes the ontological condition for our everyday, factual, understanding of being(s), then the existential of attunement likewise forms the ontological condition for something that "ontically [. . .] is most familiar and an everyday kind of thing", namely our 'moods' (*Stimmungen*; 134). For Heidegger, this notion does not indicate a psychological state but a fundamental structure of *Dasein*. Being attuned to the world in a happy, fearful, or depressed mood is a state of being that enables us to feel gay, threatened, or indifferent about a particular thing or event.[7] Phrased differently, being attuned in these manners enables us to understand a particular being as pleasant, threatening, or uninteresting. According to Heidegger, our moods thus 'set the tone' or set up a context for any possible understanding of being: "Mood has always already disclosed being-in-the-world as a whole and first makes possible directing oneself toward something" (137). If through understanding "the world already disclosed lets innerworldly things be encountered", then our attunement first enables the "prior disclosedness of the world" and "the primary discovery of the world".[8] Another way to put this, is that in order for beings to become intelligible to us, they must, in an ontological sense, matter to us:

Being affected by the unserviceable, resistant, and threatening character of things at hand is ontologically possible only because being-in as such is existentially determined beforehand in such a way that what it encounters in the world can *matter* to it in this way. This mattering to it is grounded in attunement, and as attunement it has disclosed the world, for example, as something by which it can be threatened. Only something

---

[7] As Sharin N. Elkholy eloquently puts it: "Mood does not rise in response to a particular situation. Rather, mood is the way in which a certain situation initially arises as mattering to Da-sein" (*Heidegger and a Metaphysics of Feeling. Angst and the Finitude of Being*, in: *Continuum Studies in Continental Philosophy*, London/New York, 2008, 27).

[8] *BT* 137, 138. In *The Fundamental Concepts of Metaphysics*, which discusses *Dasein*'s attunement at length, Heidegger likewise holds that "attunements are the fundamental ways in which we *find* ourselves *disposed* in such and such a way" and "the fundamental way in which *Dasein* is as *Dasein*" (*FCM* 101). He also offers an insightful assessment of this existential in his 1934–1935 lectures *Hölderlin's Hymns: 'Germania' and 'The "Rhine"'* (tr. by William McNeill and Julia Ireland, in: *Studies in Continental Thought*, Bloomington: Indiana UP, 2014, esp. 80–81).

which is the attunement of fearing, or fearlessness, can discover things at hand in the surrounding world as being threatening. [...] In attunement lies existentially a disclosive submission to world out of which things that matter to us can be encountered.[9]

This existential openness too applies both to other beings and to our own being. When we are fearfully attuned to the world, we are led to understand a hammer in the hands of stranger as something threatening, whereas a hopeful mood allows us to perceive it as a possible solution to a problem. Likewise, the way we are attuned to being also conditions how we can understand ourselves. When we are fearful, we project much fewer possibilities for ourselves than when we are fundamentally optimistic: only in the latter case can we conceive of ourselves as a perfect host, which in turn allows us to disclose other beings as useful for that purpose. Through attunement, Dasein thus discloses not only the world, but also itself.

That our understanding of being is prefigured by our moods poses another limit for our projected possibilities, one that is existential rather than material. Heidegger points out that this is all the more the case because, even though we can shift between moods, we always already find ourselves 'in' one: "The fact that moods can be spoiled or change only means that Dasein is always already in a mood" (134; FCM 102). Whereas understanding establishes Dasein's projective nature, attunement attests for "the 'thrownness' (*Geworfenheit*) of this being into its there" or the "facticity (*Faktizität*) of its being delivered over" to being (135). Thrownness constitutes our original 'being-there' (*da-sein*), the brute reality that we are and have to be. Through its moods, Dasein thus always finds itself in a certain openness towards other beings and their being, that is, towards a meaningful world (137).

We can now also understand why Heidegger introduces attunement and understanding as equiprimordial (*gleichurspünglich*) existentials of Dasein (133). Because moods make beings matter to us, these beings appear to us as intelligible, they solicit us to be understood as somehow significant: "Significance is that for which world is disclosed as such" (143). This significance of other beings and ourselves can, however, only be understood in so far as a mood has already disclosed the world as such. Hence, these existentials cannot be meaningfully thought of separately: "Attunement always has its understanding [...] Understanding is always attuned" (142). Heidegger concludes that Dasein's 'being-in-the-world' – the attuned understanding which allows us to grasp the being of both other beings and ourselves – is "thrown possibility throughout" (144) or a "thrown project" (148).

---

[9] *BT* 137–138. Sheehan accordingly distinguishes between "first, the emergence of meaning as such, i.e., the disclosure (opening up) of the meaning-giving world in correlation with one's a priori engagement with it; and second, [...] the intelligibility – the normal everyday significance – of this or that thing within the meaning-giving world." ('*Facticity and Ereignis*', 50–51).

The structural unity of Dasein's attuned understanding is further cemented in 'discourse' (*Rede* §34), which Heidegger defines as "the articulation of the intelligibility of the there" (161). Although it seems to take a less prominent place in the analysis of being-in-the-world, Heidegger holds that "discourse is existentially equiprimordial with attunement and understanding", and hence is "constitutive for the existence of Dasein" as a being that discloses being. Our everyday comportment in the world after all consists not only in a pragmatic, but also a discursive understanding. We naturally convey the intelligibility of other beings as well as ourselves through various kinds of non-theoretical communication, that is, when I tell my apprentice to hit the nail in this or that way, or when my body language expresses my comfort as a dinner host: "Dasein as discoursing being-in has already expressed itself" (165). Whereas attunement grounded moods and understanding knowledge, the existential of discourse then constitutes the ontological foundation for the ontic phenomenon of language. On an existential-ontological, pre-theoretical and pre-linguistic, level, "the attuned intelligibility of being-in-the-world expresses itself as discourse". This expression lends structure (*Gliederung*) to our holistic attuned understanding of the world (*das Bedeutungsganze*, 161–162) and on that basis ties us back to innerworldly beings and other Dasein.[10]

6.3   Dasein as Care

We have seen that, early on in *Being and Time*, Heidegger faced the double challenge of how we can actually be aware of our implicit, pre-ontological understanding of being and how one can subsequently turn this into a thematic, ontological understanding without corrupting its original structure. Heidegger answered these questions through his accounts of the deficiency of our equipment and the structural moments of Dasein's 'being-in-the-world'. A similar twofold challenge now surges with regard to Dasein's attunement. First, how can we be aware of our original 'being-there' if we are always already in a particular mood and this always already leads to a certain understanding of the world? In other words, how can we grasp the structure of the world as such, if we are always already thrown into it? Second, how can we understand the unity of Dasein's attunement and understanding, or our 'thrown projection', without compromising their structural difference, or vice versa? Heidegger's answers to these questions are found in his accounts of the 'fundamental

---

[10] As Blattner explains, discourse does not primarily have the function of conveying information, but foremost of setting a meaningful tone or mood for a conversation (*Heidegger's Being and Time*, 102–103). Furthermore, such conversations need not be limited to the realm of natural language; discourse can also take the form of "body-language, 'the language of art', dance, gardening, and much more" (101).

mood' (*Grundbefindlichkeit*) of anxiety (*Angst;* §39–40) and the "primordially unified phenomenon" of care (*Sorge;* §41–42).[11]

Heidegger famously distinguishes anxiety from fear. As existential moods rather than psychological states, neither is directly concerned about a particular object. However, a 'regular' mood enables objects to appear to us in a meaningful way – when in fear, we understand the knife in the hands of a stranger as threatening us. It also relates to the feasibility of our concrete projects – our party getting cancelled – and to the attainability of the particular roles that we project for ourselves – our career as a cobbler being uncertain. Heidegger thus holds that "that *of which* (*Wovor*) we are afraid, the 'fearsome', is always something encountered within the world", and that "that *about which* (*Worum*) fear is afraid is the fearful being itself, *Dasein*" (140–141). In fearing an object, another person, or an event, we fear for our plans to fall through, for our self-understanding to be shattered, or ultimately for our life: "Fear [...] always equiprimordially discloses [...] innerwordly beings in their possibility of being threatening and being-in with regard to its being threatened" (141).

The fundamental mood of anxiety, on the other hand, is completely without object: its occurrence precisely means that we no longer understand any surrounding beings as significant. Hence, whereas a regular mood opens up the world to our understanding, allowing beings to become intelligible and familiar to us, anxiety blocks our access to it and makes us feel 'uncanny' (*unheimlich*) or not at home in the world. This is comparable to the mood that befalls us when we experience a culture shock: while the world is still there and beings still seem to *somehow* relate to each other – part of the disorienting experience is that things still do make sense to other people – we no longer understand them as for-our-sake. In anxiety, the world is likewise not absent, but precisely present in its insignificance: "The world has the character of complete insignificance".[12] In this rare (190) and uncanny state of existence we are still attuned to being, but we are unable to understand being*s* in one or other way: the world is in a sense muted, things are merely present in an

---

[11] While *Being and Time* famously discusses the basic attunement of anxiety in *The Fundamental Concepts of Metaphysics* Heidegger for similar purposes analyses that of boredom (*Langeweile*, esp. *FCM* §20) and that of awe or wonder in *Basic Questions of Philosophy: Selected 'Problems' of 'Logic'* (tr. by Richard Rojcewicz and André Schuwer, Bloomington: Indiana University Press, 1994). Klaus Held has argued that lending more weight to the mood of awe can enrich the existential analytic of Dasein and counter the political stance that Heidegger drew from this analysis ('Fundamental Moods and Heidegger's Critique of Contemporary Culture', trans. Anthony J. Steinbock, in: *Reading Heidegger: Commemorations*, ed. by John Sallis, Bloomington: Indiana University Press, 1993, 286–303).

[12] *BT* 186. See Blattner, *Heidegger's 'Being and Time'*, 141: "Anxiety discloses life's possibilities as well, but without the imports that normally move one to action. In anxiety, we cannot press forward into possibilities, because we cannot understand ourselves in terms of the world. Anxiety discloses possibilities as irrelevant or insignificant".

unsettling way. Moreover, faced with the insignificance of other beings, we can no longer project meaningful possibilities for ourselves and thus also lose the everyday basis for our self-understanding: "The 'world' can offer nothing more. [...] Thus anxiety takes away from Dasein the possibility of understanding itself [...] in terms of the 'world'" (187, 184). In anxiety, we are acutely aware of ourselves and yet – or precisely because – we lack any sense of a tangible self. In sum, anxiety puts us in the ambiguous situation in which both the world and ourselves still matter to us but are no longer intelligible.

Out of touch with all beings, what then could we be anxious of and about? With regard to fear, this distinction between what is threatening and what is threatened was a clear-cut distinction between two beings: we fear certain objects or circumstances because we fear for particular projects to fall through or a certain self-image to be shattered. With regard to anxiety, the distinction is less clear. When Heidegger first discusses this ground mood, he states that "that about which we have anxiety is thrown being-in-the-world; that for which [or 'of which'] we have anxiety is our potentiality-for-being-in-the-world" (191). This means that we are frightened by our (in)capacity to project meaningful possibilities *at all* and frightened about our factical being-there *as such*. Failing to render anything intelligible is then an unsettling experience that confronts us with our profound need for things to matter to us. However, it makes at least as much sense to say that what is unsettling is the realization that we are thrown into the world, and that we are subsequently worried about us completely failing to understand beings – what Heidegger later calls the 'possibility of impossibility' (266) or 'death' (§49–53). In Division Two of *Being and Time*, he indeed holds that "in anxiety, Dasein finds itself faced with the nothingness of the possible impossibility of its existence. Anxiety is anxious about the potentiality-of-being" (266). On this view, what frightens us is the fact that we have to be (in the world), and what we are frightened about is the possibility that we are unable to do so in a meaningful manner.

This ambiguity about what frightens us and why we are frightened, that is, about the cause and the concern of anxiety is not an inconsistency in Heidegger's writing but rather reflects the existential condition of Dasein. We have seen earlier that the existentials of attunement and understanding are equiprimordial and codependent constituents of our being-in-the-world. Hence, when one of them is disclosed, so is the other. Heidegger's alternative analyses of anxiety therefore do not really contradict each other. Either way we look at it, what is at stake in anxiety is our own being-in-the-world: "Being-in-the-world is both what anxiety is anxious in the face of and what it is anxious about" (343, 186). Heidegger thus considers "that about which and that for which one has anxiety" an "existential sameness" (188). Anxiety at the same time discloses that we are both without a stable ground and without a guaranteed purpose. Each of these revelations is frightening, and each will make us deeply worry about ourselves and our existential well-being, causing Dasein to swirl around itself without any firm footing in sight. We can now fully understand why anxiety does not have an object: it concerns our way of being *and* it shows that this being does not have a fixed essence, nor can be granted one.

In sum, the experience of anxiety makes us aware of the unity as well as the complexity of our being-in-the-world. As such, anxiety is structurally similar to the experience of the malfunctioning tool and it can play the same methodological role in Heidegger's existential analysis. In both experiences, a breakdown of meaning occurs that allows everyday Dasein to shift between different existential attitudes, and the phenomenological philosopher to gain a more profound insight into our own being.

Both when equipment fails us and when anxiety assails us, a relation that we usually take for granted is disturbed: the broken hammer no longer refers to certain other tools in a meaningful way, while anxious Dasein no longer seems connected to any other being. In other words, the world's internal referential structure is disturbed in the former case, whereas our relation to world as a whole is challenged in the latter. As pointed out before, these "disruptions of reference" (74) are never absolute: we still recognize what the unhandy tool used to be, and we still recognize the world as world, albeit one in which we no longer feel at home. This makes it possible for us to easily resume our circumspective understanding of beings and to feel at home again once our anxious mood passes.

More interestingly, however, these disruptive experiences also invite us to adopt a different attitude to beings and their being than the one we maintain in everydayness. As explained earlier, following the breaking of the hammer, we can come to see it in a derivative, theoretical manner as an independent entity with certain objective qualities that can be scientifically examined, or in a philosophical manner that reflects on the conditions of possibility of everyday experience. Likewise, because anxious Dasein is not absorbed by any of its worldly projects, it has an opportunity to modify its overall relation to the world. We can now adopt a theoretical, objectifying attitude that turns our felt separation from our surroundings into a psychological, neurological, or metaphysical theory that places an isolated – and self-sufficient – subject over against a world of objects. For Heidegger, this view is however once again derivative, if not fundamentally mistaken. Even in an anxious mood we are still open to the world, as Dasein *is* and remains being-in-the world. This means, alternatively, that we can now also orient ourselves towards the world as a whole: "Being anxious discloses, primordially and directly, the world as world" (187). Anxiety thus allows us to switch from our everyday being-absorbed-in-the-world, which Heidegger describes as Dasein's 'fallenness' (*das Verfallen*; §35–38), into an authentic mode of existence that acknowledges its own lack of ground.

Thanks to their transformative impact on Dasein's self-understanding, the disruptive experiences of malfunctioning equipment and anxiety also provide phenomenological insights that propel Heidegger's analytic of Dasein. The first experience reveals that Dasein stands out among all beings: prior to ontic characterizations of beings as material, psychological, or otherwise, there appears to be an ontological difference between innerworldly beings as ready-to-hand and Dasein as being-in-the-world. Heidegger concludes from this that the conditions of possibility for understanding the being of beings ought to be found in Dasein's 'being-in'. The second experience shows that, underlying these conditions, Dasein is ultimately a being that cares about intelligibility, about making sense of things. Understanding and attunement can seem like opposing ontological structures given that the former marks Dasein's potentiality whereas the latter signals its facticity. Anxiety puts this distinction into sharp relief, but thereby paradoxically demonstrates what holds the usual unity of attuned understanding together. On a deeper ontological level, both existentials are grounded in Dasein's existential need to lend significance to beings: "Anxiety provides the phenomenal basis for explicitly grasping the primordial totality of being of Dasein. Its being reveals itself as care *(Sorge)*".[13]

Heidegger emphasizes that care must be understood as the original unity of Dasein's being and not as a 'sum' of its existentials (181). Understanding and attunement should not be thought of as separate structures that can subsequently be combined, but intrinsically relate to each other (191). 'Care' thus simultaneously designates the unity *(Einheit)* as well as the "structural breakdown" *(strukturale Gliederung)* of Dasein's being (200, 192). Further, in the same way that understanding and mood needed to be understood in an ontological, and not an epistemological or psychological manner, Heidegger's conception of care precedes and grounds the distinction between theoretical and practical behaviour (193, 300). He likewise holds that human "drives, such as willing and wishing or urge and predilection [. . .] are necessarily rooted ontologically in Dasein as care" (194). In this way, Heidegger casts the traditional philosophical characterizations of the human condition in terms of reason, politics, will power, or lust as derivative of his more original definition of Dasein as concern for being.

---

[13] *BT* 182. See Robert B. Pippin, 'Necessary Conditions for the Possibility of What Isn't. Heidegger on Failed Meaning', in: *Transcendental Heidegger*, 207: "A collapse of significance [. . .] allows us to see that what had 'kept up' such a structure of significance was 'nothing' but our caring to keep it up in place, a care originating and failing in utter contingency." Crowell puts it even stronger when holding that "what looks like a collapse of everything that matters instead reveals the condition for the possibility that anything can matter at all" (*Normativity and Phenomenology in Husserl and Heidegger*, 190).

6.4   Dasein's Ontological, Phenomenological, and Hermeneutic Being

Heidegger describes the project of *Being and Time* as an 'ontological' (15), 'fundamental' (41), or 'existential analytic of Dasein' (50). As we have seen, Division One of this book indeed analyses our everyday existence in order to reveal the basic ontological character of the 'human condition': "In the foregoing interpretations, which finally led to exposing care as the being of Dasein, the most important thing was to arrive at the appropriate ontological foundations of the being which we ourselves actually are and which we call 'human being'"(196–197). Heidegger first argued that Dasein's usual and predominant comportment relies on a 'pre-ontological understanding' of both other beings and itself, then laid out the different structural moments of 'being-in-the-world' as the conditions of possibility of this understanding, and finally presented Dasein's 'care' as the foundational unity of these conditions, or "the primordial totality of the structural whole of Dasein".[14] These three steps explained *that* we have ontological understanding, *how* we can have this understanding, and *why* we have it.[15]

More specifically, the nature of Heidegger's argumentation is indeed analytical in the sense that its conclusion – 'Dasein's existential meaning is care' (41) – while offering profound new insights, does not provide any novel information. In retrospect, each earlier discussed characteristic of Dasein already expresses this fundamental reality about Dasein that it cares about being. When discussing our pre-ontological understanding of being, Heidegger holds that our "nearest kind of association is not mere perceptual cognition, but, rather, a handling, using, and taking care of things which has its own kind

---

[14] *BT* 180. Division Two of *Being and Time* adds three more steps to this existential phenomenology. The first two of these steps expand on Heidegger's account of anxiety and could have been part of Division One. As we have seen, attunement, understanding, and discourse are equiprimordial moments of Dasein's being-in-the-world. As a consequence, there must correspond to the fundamental mood of anxiety a fundamental mode of understanding and of discourse. On the one hand, anxiety enables an ontological understanding of death, which then allows Heidegger to grasp Dasein's finite nature (§46–53). On the other hand, anxiety and death also evoke the discourse of conscience, which in turn allows Heidegger to distinguish between an inauthentic mode of Dasein that characterizes our everyday falling into the 'they' and an authentic mode of Dasein as a resolute self (§54–60). I will discuss these conceptions of death and authenticity in Chapters 7.2 and 10.2, respectively. In the third and final step, Heidegger unearths a final layer to his existential phenomenology, namely Dasein's temporality (§61–83).

[15] Engelland nicely sums up how Heidegger's accounts of attunement, understanding, and care represent three stages of Dasein's ontological concern: "At the heart of Heidegger's thought is the quest to experience the dynamic movement of experience [...] His concern for the movement of experience is threefold: concern for the going beyond that enables us to encounter things, concern for the opening up of the domain in which the encountering takes place, and concern for how experiencing the going beyond and opening up might be motivated." (*Heidegger's Shadow. Kant, Husserl, and the Transcendental Turn*, 2).

of 'knowledge'" (67, 57). When it comes to other Dasein, he specifies that "this being is not taken care of [*Besorgen*], but is a matter of concern [*Fürsorge*]" (121, 122–123). But most of all, Heidegger emphasizes time and again, Dasein is fundamentally concerned about its own being: "*Dasein is a being that does not simply occur among other beings*. Rather it is ontically distinguished by the fact that in its being this being is concerned about its very being" (12, 141, 191). This is why the experience of anxiety is philosophically insightful: by depriving Dasein from any connection to objects, anxiety confirms this ongoing assumption that "Dasein is a being that is concerned in its being about that being" (191). Finally, we may also understand in this sense Heidegger's description of care as "a primordially unified phenomenon which already lies in the whole in such a way that it is the basis for every structural moment in its structural possibility" (181). The so far final stage of Heidegger's analytic of Dasein merely thematizes what was implicitly assumed from the beginning.

This means that, once we have identified care as the being of Dasein, we can retrace our steps and recast all previous steps of the existential analytic in a more original manner as explaining our concern for being. By rereading Division One of *Being and Time* backwards, we can now see that to be Dasein means to be an ontological, phenomenological, and hermeneutic being. On this reading, Heidegger's account of care first establishes *that* Dasein is at its ultimate core an ontological being, that is, a being that is *fundamentally* concerned with the being of beings. The analysis of 'being-in' as a thrown project or attuned understanding further explains *how* Dasein enacts this concern in a phenomenological manner. Finally, Heidegger *further specified how* this phenomenological understanding of being is both enabled and complicated by a hermeneutic situation that is inherent to Dasein's everydayness.

We figured out earlier that, in *Being and Time*, Heidegger understands the being of beings as their intelligibility, or their potential for having meaning or making sense. We further saw that he ultimately defines Dasein as a way of being that is characterized as caring for meaning. It follows that Heidegger considers Dasein to be foremost an ontological being – not just initially and predominantly, but throughout all of its being and even in its rarest states: "An understanding of being belongs to the kind of being of the being that we call *Dasein*" (200). Once again, Heidegger's account of care hereby only confirms the assumption that he already put forward in the introduction to *Being and Time*, namely that "understanding of being is itself a determination of being of Dasein. The ontic distinction of Dasein lies in the fact that it *is* ontological" (12). Heidegger usually refers to Dasein's understanding of being as 'pre-ontological', and "reserve[s] the term ontology for the explicit, theoretical question of the being of beings", because he wants to avoid the misconception that our default way of being is theoretical or 'rational'. However, this "being in the manner of an understanding of being" could as well be called the original, existential meaning of ontology, upon which any ontological theory is grounded. Heidegger further points out that this (pre-)ontological way of being concerns Dasein's understanding of both its own being and that of other beings, and that Dasein therefore is "the ontic-ontological condition of possibility of all ontologies" (13). Hence, our care for being is the condition of possibility and the *raison d'être* of ontology.

Later on in the introduction to *Being and Time*, Heidegger holds that ontology designates the object of philosophy (being), while phenomenology characterizes its procedure or methodology – namely to examine the things themselves (beings) in the way they show themselves (34). *In se*, ontology and phenomenology are however (about) the same thing. Likewise, there is no substantial difference between Dasein's care and its being-in-the-world; when fully and originally understood, both terms describe the complex unity of "being-ahead-of-itself-in-already-being-in-a-world" (192). Yet, while the former term merely affirms *that* Dasein is a being that makes sense of beings, the latter specifies *how* Dasein does so. If care marks Dasein as an ontological being, it should therefore follow that the existentials of understanding and attunement mark it as a phenomenological being – or a pre-phenomenological one if we reserve the term 'phenomenology' for a philosophically developed methodology.

Dasein's fundamentally ontological nature, its care, does not mean that it is at heart a rational being that is capable of theorizing about 'being as such' or aims to understand universal essences. Instead, it is concerned about how being shows itself as itself, that is, prior to any conceptualization, not in its abstract nature but as the being of particular beings: "Being is always the being of beings, [and] we must first of all bring beings themselves forward in the right way if we are to have any prospect of exposing being" (37). What makes Dasein a (pre-) phenomenological being, then, is that its concern for being extends to, or rather even begins at, being*s* as they appear to us in a meaningful way. Dasein's being-in-the-world, its attuned understanding, enables precisely this: while a mood "first makes possible directing oneself toward something", through understanding "the world already disclosed lets innerworldly things be encountered" (137). Attunement and understanding are thus ontological structures of Dasein that enable the disclosure of being by letting *beings* matter and make sense to us. Our moods open up a horizon within which beings can first appear, and our projects cast them as this or that particular (ready-to-hand) being.

In his writings on Kant, Heidegger equates this view of how Dasein comes to understand beings with Kant's theory of the transcendental constitution of objectivity. He rephrases the notion 'being-in-the-world' in more traditional philosophical terms as the 'transcendence' of human reason, and the 'thrown project' of being-in as the 'ecstatic-horizonal structure of transcendental subjectivity'. Heidegger then reads Kant's accounts of transcendental imagination and the transcendental deduction of the categories as precursors of his own views of attunement and understanding: they respectively explain how transcendental subjectivity/Dasein opens up a general horizon of object-ivity/the world as a whole and how this horizon enables the experience of objects/intelligible beings.

It is important to further note that understanding and attunement are not capacities that Dasein *has at its disposal*, in the sense that we apply them at our own volition, but are innate to what Dasein *is*: "The analysis of the character-istics of the being of Dasein is an existential one. This means that the characteristics are not properties of something objectively present, but essen-tially existential ways to be" (133, 42). This is clearly the case for Dasein's attunement, which discloses "the facticity of its being delivered over" or its being-there – we are and have to be attuned to our surroundings. But Heidegger also emphasizes that Dasein does not just have projects or possibilities, but that it *is* a (thrown) project – it is always attempting to make sense of itself – and that it *is* its possibilities – it can never arrive at a fixed identity. He thus holds that "in understanding lies existentially *Dasein*'s manner of being as being-possible. *Dasein* is not something objectively pre-sent which then has [in] addition the ability to do something, but is rather primarily being-possible (*Sein-können*)" (143, 42). Being-phenomenological is then not an optional way of being for Dasein, but the unavoidable way in which it enacts its existence.

Finally, we should nevertheless recall that in our everyday comportment we actually are not usually focused on beings. Due to the circumspective nature of our pre-ontological understanding, Dasein is first and foremost oriented towards the context (work) and the purpose (for-the-sake-of-Dasein) that render these beings meaningful. Heidegger therefore argues that all under-standing has a "fore-structure" (*Vorstruktur*) that is shaped by a "fore-concep-tion" (*Vorgriff*), "fore-having" (*Vorhabe*), and "fore-sight" (*Vorsicht*). Simply put, this means that beings are always immediately conceived as intelligible in view of a relevant context and of its significance for us (151). Because this fore-structure remains in (or rather: is) the background of understanding, Dasein can project the possibility of hammering onto a particular being or of cooking onto itself, without needing to explicitly identify these particular beings as a hammer or a dinner host.

This changes in 'interpretation' (*Auslegung*, §32). In Heidegger's view, interpretation is "the development of possibilities projected in understanding" (148). This means, on the one hand, that interpretation is "existentially based in understanding" and that, rather than reviewing or expanding the intelligi-bility of beings, it merely thematizes what was already vaguely understood: "In interpretation understanding does not become something different, but rather itself". On the other hand, interpretation thus 'makes explicit' (*ausdrücken*) or 'elaborates on' (*ausarbeiten*) what understanding has projected, by casting *something as something* (148–149). Through interpretation, we understand the hammer *as* a hammer and ourselves *as* a host. And since the 'as-structure' of interpretation echoes the fore-structure of understanding (151), we also understand the hammer *as* useful for our work and *as* significant for our own way of being. It is, then, in interpreting that Dasein renders the being of beings, or their intelligibility, meaningful:

> When innerworldly beings are discovered along with the being of Dasein, that is, when they become intelligible, we say that they have *meaning (Sinn)*. But strictly speaking, what is understood is not the meaning, but beings (*Seiende*) or being (*Sein*). Meaning is that wherein the intelligibility of something maintains itself. What can be articulated of that which understanding discloses, we call meaning. [...] *Meaning is the upon-which of projecting, is as such structured by fore-having, fore-sight, and fore-conception, and is that in terms of which something becomes intelligible a something.*[16]

While attunement makes beings matter to us and understanding renders them intelligible, in interpretation they are ultimately assigned a certain meaning.

Once again, this affirmation of meaning through interpretation is not just an optional feature of being-there. Although Heidegger does not present interpretation as equiprimordial to understanding and attunement, it is part of "the existential constitution of the being of the there" and "meaning is an existential of Dasein". In other words, Dasein *is* a being that interprets other beings and its own existence. Heidegger accordingly does not consider hermeneutics, which is the study of interpretation, as an alternative to phenomenology but rather as an existential modification thereof: "The methodological meaning of phenomenological description is *interpretation*" (37). This intrinsic relationship between phenomenology and hermeneutics echoes the one between attuned understanding and interpretation that is constitutive of Dasein's being-in-the-world and that guides our everyday comportment. Hence, Dasein *is* finally also a hermeneutic being – or a pre-hermeneutical one if we reserve the term 'hermeneutics' for a developed philosophical methodology.[17] In sum, Heidegger's existential analytic presents the human being as an ontological, phenomenological, and hermeneutic being.

---

[16] *BT* 151; translation modified. See also 153: "What is articulated as such in interpretation and is prefigured as articulable in understanding in general is meaning."

[17] See Holger Zaborowksi, 'Heidegger's hermeneutics: towards a new practice of understanding', in: *Interpreting Heidegger*, 30: "Because Dasein is always already hermeneutical, philosophy as a hermeneutics is possible. [...] Far from simply indicating a method of research, it indicates a mode of Dasein in which Dasein interprets itself as the being that always already understands being so as to be able to answer the fundamental ontological question."

7   Infinity or Finitude

The Quest for Existential Orientation

An account of the human condition constitutes the beating heart of both Cassirer's overall philosophy of culture and Heidegger's early thought – even if their ultimate interests lie elsewhere. *Being and Time* is entirely dedicated to an existential analysis of Dasein that ought to prepare a retrieval of the meaning of being as such. Cassirer's functional account of symbolic consciousness forms the 'subjective' foundation and intrinsic counter part of the philosophy of the symbolic forms, which aims to comprehend the 'objective' domains of human culture. In view of this, it is no surprise that the question 'What is the human being?' took a central role in the Davos debate. My reading of the transcript of this debate indeed showed that Cassirer and Heidegger quickly shifted from discussing the proper meaning of Kant's thought to a debate about the human condition. Concretely, Cassirer and Heidegger's disagreement about the fundamentally spontaneous or receptive character of theoretical and practical reason gave way to a dispute about the infinite or finite nature of human existence.

In order to grasp the meaning of the latter dispute, it is useful to first consider the common philosophical ground between Cassirer and Heidegger. In their own ways, both thinkers present the human being as driven by an innate capacity to orient itself in the world. These views of the human quest for orientation complement each other, in so far as Cassirer gives a richer account of how we can orient ourselves in thinking and acting, while Heidegger is most invested in the deeper question of why we have to do so. On the basis of these different angles, we can account for the second part of the Cassirer–Heidegger dispute, concerning the infinite or finite nature of human being.

7.1   Cassirer's General Plan of Ideal Orientation

In 1785, Kant wrote a short but very rich essay called 'What does it mean to orient oneself in thinking'?[1] This essay first discusses the conditions of

---

[1] Immanuel Kant, 'What Does It Mean to Orient Oneself in Thinking?', in: *Religion and Rational Theology*, ed. by Allen W. Wood and George Di Giovanni, Cambridge: Cambridge University Press, 1996, 8:133–146 – hereafter indicated as '*WDO*'.

possibility of geographical orientation and then extrapolates the same conditions to the increasingly abstract situations of mathematical orientation and orienting oneself in pure thinking. Kant's overall argument is that all orientation is guided by a subjective principle. He explains that we can only orient ourselves in an unknown area (geographically) or a completely dark room (mathematically) based on the feeling of the difference between our left and right side: even when we have spotted the polar star or detected a piece of furniture, we can still only locate the cardinal directions or other furniture if we also have a sense of left and right (*WDO* 134–135). Kant emphasizes the 'felt' nature of this difference, which cannot be empirically perceived. If orientation only requires a subjective principle, he can after all conclude that it must also be possible to orient oneself in the sphere of pure reason, which by its very nature can take no directions from the empirical world: "Thus to *orient* oneself in thinking in general means: when objective principles of reason are insufficient for holding something true, to determine the matter according to a subjective principle" (136). In fact, whereas the polar star and furniture piece were still objective orientation points, both the compass (*Wegweiser*) and the orientation point of pure thinking will have to be subjective matters. For those familiar with Kant's *Critiques*, it comes as no surprise that he subsequently posits the idea of God as the orientation point, and the reasonable faith in God's existence as the compass of pure reason. But while the first *Critique* describes theoretical reason as 'interested' in the coherent unity of all cognition, Kant's orientation essay posits a "need of reason" (*Bedürfniss der Vernunft*; 139) that coordinates all our objective cognition and speculative thinking by means of the subjective idea of an all-encompassing being.

Cassirer refers to Kant's orientation essay as "an article which despite its brevity is highly characteristic of his manner of thinking" (*PSF:II* 93), yet he never really engages with its content.[2] Inspired by Kant's distinction between three kinds of orientation, he however describes mythical, artistic, and mathematical space as distinct "stages of orientation" (*Stufengang der Orientierung*). We could take this as a suggestion that the philosophy of symbolic forms offers a theory of the diverse domains of cultural orientation, that is, of how we can orient ourselves in mythical, linguistic, artistic, religious, scientific, or political 'thinking'. On such a reading of Cassirer's thought, the symbols are our cultural orientation points, and our subjective principles of orientation are located in what Cassirer calls the 'functions of consciousness'.

When we first discussed Cassirer's concept of a symbol, we distinguished two main characteristics. First, Cassirer does not conceive of the symbols as

---

[2] Cassirer also only quickly and partially summarizes Kant's account of orientation in *KLT* 42–43.

purely intellectual forms that we impose upon raw sensible material. Rejecting the classic oppositions between matter and form, and sensibility and understanding, he instead holds that our perceptions are always already 'pregnant' or 'saturated' with meaning: "It is perception itself which by virtue of its own immanent organization takes on a kind of spiritual articulation" (*PSF:III* 202). The symbols that express this organization thus have inseparable empirical and conceptual components. Second, Cassirer also rejects the idea of one-on-one relations between certain symbols and particular symbolic forms. Instead, he demonstrates that the same symbols recur in a different 'modality' or 'tonality' in each cultural domain:

Certain concepts – such as those of number, time, and space – represent original forms of synthesis that are indispensable wherever a 'multiplicity' is to be taken together into a 'unity', wherever a manifold is to be broken down and articulated according to determinate forms. But [...] this articulation is not effected in the same way in all fields: rather, its mode depends essentially on the specific structural principle that is operative and dominant in each particular sphere. Thus, in particular, language and myth each reveal a 'modality' that is specific to it and in a sense lends a common tonality to all its individual structures. (13)

This implies that the symbols receive their actual, concrete meaning from a certain "direction of vision and from the ideal goal toward which the vision aims" (*PSF:II* 48), or that their meaning is relative to the symbolic form in which we employ them. Hence, even though the symbol of space is a constitutive component of all symbolic forms, each form is characterized by a particular conception thereof: the mythical space of a sacred area, the artistic space of a canvas, the scientific notion of a three-dimensional space, or the political space of a state are delimited by distinctive logics and seem to have little in common. The canvas or state then function as an orientation point for a meaningful artistic or political worldview.

Cassirer weds the dual and versatile character of the symbols through his account of the 'functions of symbolic formation', which we find in the 1927 essay 'Das Symbolproblem und seine Stellung im System der Philosophie' and again in the final chapter of *The Phenomenology of Knowledge*. Here, Cassirer distinguishes between the 'expressive', 'representational', and 'signifying functions' that determine the particular outlook of the symbolic forms of myth, language, and natural science, respectively.[3] These

---

[3] See Cassirer, 'Das Symbolproblem und seine Stellung im System der Philosophie', in: *ECW:17* 260–271; and *PSF:III* 448–453. For extensive discussions of the functions of consciousness that constitute the different symbolic forms, consult Heinz Paetzold, *Die Realität der symbolischen Formen. Die Kulturphilosophie Ernst Cassirers im Kontext*, Darmstadt: Wissenschaftliche Buchgesellschaft, 1994, XII-51; Plümacher, *Wahrnehmung, Repräsentation und Wissen*, 463–484; and Catia Rotolo, *Der Symbolbegriff im Denken Ernst Cassirer*, tr. by Leonie Schröder, Frankfurt am Main: Peter Lang Gmbh, 2013, 93–140.

functions alter the meaning of the symbols by establishing different kinds of relationships between their sensible and intelligible moment.

In Cassirer's view, mythical thought understands empirical phenomena as immediate expressions of a divine presence in our world: the gods are considered to be truly present in the priest or ritual, or to speak to us directly through a natural object like a 'holy tree'. This means that there is no distinction between the signifier and the signified of these phenomena,[4] or between a natural and divine order (*PSF:II* 35–40). The 'expressive function' (*Ausdrucksfunktion*) of mythical thought does, then, not differentiate between the content and form of our perceptions at all, but allows us to consider the world as an inherently meaningful whole: "The mythical world [...] is concrete because in it the two factors, thing and signification, are undifferentiated, because they merge in an immediate unity" (24). In this context, "anything can come from anything", because causality is perceived in "every simultaneity, every spatial coexistence and contact".[5]

Cassirer discerns a more flexible relationship between the matter and form of our symbols in natural language. In this symbolic form, the symbols "possess not a merely 'presentative' but rather 'representative' character: they do not simply 'stand there' – they stand for one another" (*PSF:III* 119). The *word* 'God', for example, can *refer to* a manifold of godly beings, and is thus not inhabited by a particular divine entity in the way that a tree is in the mythical worldview. Hence, while language can surely express individual phenomena, it can also transcend them and establish certain recurring, general, structures of meaning: "The pure *function* of representation (*Darstellungsfunktion*) is not attached to any concrete sensuous *material*" (113). The term 'causality' can thus establish patterns in our sensible world that are not bound to what is concretely, presently, given.

The bond between the sensible content and intelligible form of our perceptions is even more flexible in the formal or 'pure' language of the natural sciences (330–334). According to Cassirer, the 'signifying function' (*Bedeutungsfunktion*) that shapes this symbolic form manages to establish truly systematic meaning with universal applicability by installing "a conscious detachment from the world of expression" (451). Deliberately breaking with our life-world, science denounces all similarity to our concrete, individual, sensations: it is not concerned with a particular tree or individual human being, but only with the universal laws that explain their existence and

---

[4] See *ECW:17* 260; and *LM* 58.

[5] *PSF:II* 45–46. Cassirer likens the mythological conception of causality to Hume's conception thereof, since both require only a succession and contiguity of phenomenal events: "[We] come to the astonishing conclusion that Hume, in attempting to analyze the causal judgment of science, rather revealed a source of all mythical explanation of the world".

behaviour as a member of a certain natural kind: "Science is content if it succeeds in apprehending the individual event in space and time as a special instance of a general law but asks no further 'why' regarding the individual-ization as such, regarding the here and now" (*PSF:II* 48). This tendency reaches its clearest, and most extreme, form in the highly abstract symbols used by geometry:

The function of pure *signification* is separated from the sphere of representation because it breaks away from the basis of concrete shapes in which representation is rooted and from which it time and again takes its force [...] The purely signifying sign does not express or represent anything – it is a sign in the sense of a merely abstract *assignment*. [...] What matters in each geometrical proposition is after all only the constitutive law of meaning, and not the concrete determination of its elements. (*ECW:17* 261)

Nevertheless, for Cassirer even the scientific use of the symbols can only be meaningful in so far as they still relate, in an a priori manner, to our particular sensations: "But though the world of ideas, of meanings, relinquishes all similarity to the empirical, sensuous world, it cannot dispense with all *relation* to it" (*PSF:III* 452). In the scientific worldview, causality requires the "specific limiting formal conditions" of constant elements, "an unequivocal causal order", and universal lawfulness (*PSF:II* 47–49).

Additionally, in *The Logic of the Cultural Sciences* Cassirer introduces a fourth type of function that is constitutive of the human or cultural sciences.[6] Like the signifying function, this type expresses a relationship between universal concepts and particular phenomena. Unlike them, however, it acknowledges the "characteristic indeterminateness" of such concepts: here, the particular is "*classified* by the universal, but it is never subordinated to it" (*LCS* 70). Drawing on Kant's distinction between determining and reflective judgements, Cassirer states that whereas the exact sciences determine their objects, the cultural sciences "characterize" them (73). I therefore suggest calling this type of relations between intelligible meaning and phenomenal instances the 'characterizing function' of the cultural sciences. The idea of historical causality, for example, invokes a kind of lawfulness that nevertheless cannot predict the sequence of particular events: it can only in hindsight characterize these events as causes and effects.

Even though Cassirer does not provide similar accounts for other symbolic forms, such as politics, we may assume that their worldviews are formed by particular functions of consciousness as well. Each time, these 'functions of symbolic formation' explain the inner coherence of a cultural domain:

---

[6] Cassirer, 'Concepts of Nature and Concepts of Culture', in: *LCS* 69–73. Cassirer considers history, art, religion, and our social and political life as the objects of the cultural sciences (*LCS* 78). Although he does not elaborate on this, we may expect that these sciences are constituted by different 'sub-modalities' of the characterizing function.

"For each of these contexts, language as well as scientific cognition, art as well as myth, possesses its own constitutive principle that sets its stamp, as it were, on all the particular forms within it" (*PSF:1* 97). In other words, they allow the animal symbolicum to orient itself in a mythological, linguistic, scientific, or historical way. In 'Das Symbolproblem und seine Stellung im System der Philosophie', Cassirer thus concludes that his distinction between the three basic functions of consciousness offers a guideline for "a general plan of ideal orientation, upon which we can so to speak indicate the place of each symbolic form" (*ECW:17* 262).

What is entirely lacking in Cassirer's writings, however, is a principle that explains how human consciousness can (re)orient itself from one cultural domain to another – he merely affirms that we can do so:

The depth of human experience in the same sense depends on the fact that we are able to vary our modes of seeing, that we can alternate our views of reality. [...] It is characteristic of the nature of man that he is not limited to one specific and single approach to reality but can choose his point of view and so pass from one aspect of things to another. (*EM* 170)

The functional account of human consciousness guarantees an underlying unity of the entire cultural world but does not explain our capacity to coordinate our different cultural interests. Hence, a desideratum for any philosophy of culture on Cassirer's own standards seems to be missing in his thought.[7]

7.2   Heidegger on Orientation within and towards the World

While Cassirer expresses his appreciation for Kant's essay 'What does it mean to orient oneself in thinking?', but provides no reasons for this, Heidegger by contrast critically engages with this essay in his discussion of 'the worldliness of the world' in *Being and Time* (*BT* §23). At the beginning of the 'orientation essay', Kant argues that we can orient ourselves in a geographical and mathematical space, thus determining the cardinal directions and navigating within a dark room, by relying on the subjective feeling of a difference between our left and right side. On this basis, he claims that all orientation, including that in thinking, must rely on a subjective principle that functions as our compass. Heidegger fully endorses the idea that the capacity for orientation is a basic

---

[7] I have made a case elsewhere that Kant's often overlooked account of transcendental reflection at the end of the first *Critique*'s 'Transcendental Analytic' harbours the seeds for such an inter-worldly principle of orientation (Simon Truwant, 'Kant's Transcendental Reflection: An Indispensable Element of Philosophy of Culture', in: *Critical Studies in German Idealism, vol. 15: The Marriage between Aesthetics and Ethics:*, ed. by Stéphane Symons, Brill Academic Publishing, 2015, 169–184.

characteristic of human being, but regrets the almost exclusive focus of Kant's essay on this 'subjective feeling'.

Heidegger points out that Kant in fact mentions two conditions for orientation in a dark room: in order to apply this subjective principle, we also must be able to locate at least one known object ("one single object whose position I remember"; *WDO* 135). Indeed, orientation requires not only a compass but also an initial orientation point: our subjective capacity for orientation remains useless as long as we do not have a concrete point of reference such as the polar star, a piece of furniture, or a natural idea of reason. What is important about this orientation point is however not the object 'in itself', but that the presence of this object tells me that I am in a "room that is familiar to me". For Heidegger, this familiar room symbolizes our being-in-the-world:

[W]henever *Dasein* has this 'mere feeling', it is always already in a world *and must be* in order to be able to orient itself at all. [. . .] If I am to get oriented, the 'mere feeling of the difference' between my two sides does not help at all as long as I do not apprehend some particular object 'whose position', as Kant casually remarks, 'I have in mind'. But what else does this mean except that I necessarily orient myself in and from already being in a 'familiar' world. The context of useful things must already be given to Dasein. The fact that I am always already in a world is no less constitutive for the possibility of orientation than the feeling of left and right. (*BT* 109)

Heidegger concludes that Kant "failed to understand the full context of the constitution of a possible orientation" because of his 'psychological interpretation of the ego' as a subject that 'has something in mind' and that is guided by a 'subjective feeling'. These ontic characterizations fail to acknowledge, or even conceal, that the condition for orientation does not lie 'within' us, but in our openness to the world. If Dasein was not already in-the-world, the difference between left and right would have no significance: "The a priori of the directionality in terms of left and right [. . .] is grounded in the 'subjective' a priori of being-in-the-world" (110).

Hence, for Heidegger the fact that we orient ourselves in the world is the most evident characteristic of our being, and can therefore serve as the starting point of his existential analytic. Dasein's initial and predominant comportment is marked by 'circumspection': we understand both other beings and ourselves on the basis of their mutual references, and these references are grounded in the a priori horizon of our world. In a few passages in *Being and Time*, Heidegger indeed describes this circumspective nature of our pre-ontological understanding in terms of orientation: "Circumspect overseeing does not comprehend what is at hand; instead, it acquires an orientation within the surrounding world" (79, 80, 103). As the constitutive moments of our 'being-in-the-world', attunement, understanding, and discourse are then also preconditions of orientation. Attunement opens up the horizon within which meaningful beings can appear (it enables 'subjective feelings'), and understanding assigns their position in the world (it allows us 'to have something in mind'). Interpretation highlights the orientational nature of this projecting by articulating how we always understand beings on the basis of a fore-having (a meaningful world), a fore-concept (an orientation point), and a fore-sight (a principle of orientation). Discourse then communicates this understanding to other Dasein. Together, these existentials enable Dasein to pragmatically and discursively locate the hammer, the nail, the soon-to-arrive guests of the dinner party, and itself as the dinner host with regard to each other. To be-in a familiar world is to be-oriented. Or, to say that Dasein naturally orients itself in the world is just another way of saying that it is a hermeneutic-phenomenological being.

The mode of being-in, or of orientation, that I have described so far is that of 'everydayness' (*Alltäglichkeit*) and 'averageness' (*Durchschnittlichkeit*, 127): it guides our initial and predominant ways of understanding beings. Heidegger also discusses two other modes of being-in in *Being and Time*: the existential attitudes of 'inauthenticity' or 'disownedness' (*Uneigentlichkeit*) and 'authenticity' or 'ownedness' (*Eigentlichkeit*). In the disowned mode of existence, Dasein's comportment is dictated by 'the they' (*das Man*). This mode closely aligns with Dasein's everyday mode of being-in, because both are common ways in which Dasein orients itself *within* the world.[8] One could designate their interplay as the topic of Division One of *Being and Time*. In contrast to both, the mode of ownedness that is evoked by anxiety is a much rarer way of being in which Dasein orients itself *towards* the world.[9] This mode is announced in Division One but truly explained in the first two

---

[8] As multiple commentators have pointed out, Heidegger fails to properly distinguish the modes of everydayness and disownedness, at times differentiating them while in other passages conflating them. Consult in this regard, for example, Michael E. Zimmerman, *Eclipse of the Self. The Development of Heidegger's Concept of Authenticity*, Athens: Ohio University Press, 1981, 44–46; Jo-Jo Koo, 'Heidegger's Underdeveloped Conception of the Undistinguishedness (*Indifferenz*) of Everyday Human Existence', in: *From Conventionalism to Social Authenticity. Heidegger's Anyone and Contemporary Social Theory*, ed. by Hans Bernhard Schmid and Gerhard Thonhauser, Springer, 2017, 53–78; or Blattner, *Heidegger's Being and Time*, 127–131. Each one of these commentators uses different terms for the three modes of being-in: 'authenticity', 'everydayness', and 'inauthenticity' (Zimmerman); 'ownedness' and two forms of 'unownedness': 'undistinguished-ness' and 'disownedness' (Koo); or 'owned', 'unowned', and 'disowned' (Blattner). I will use yet another combination and talk about disowned, average or everyday, and owned modes of being-in. I do so because whether one 'owns' oneself is a much clearer description than whether one is 'authentic', because I find that the term 'undistinguishedness' (*BT* 43, 232) could also aptly describe the disowned mode that is governed by the indifferent 'they', and because 'average' or 'everyday' is a more affirmative (phenomenologically positive) expression than 'unowned'.

[9] Charles Guignon likewise holds that "Heidegger describes this distinction between inauthentic and authentic understanding as resulting from different orientations or directions of focus" ('Heidegger's concept of freedom, 1927–1930', in: *Interpreting Heidegger*, 87).

chapters of Division Two. As different modalities of being-in, disownedness and ownedness are constituted by distinct modes of attunement, understanding, and discourse (166–167).

The general description of being-in-the-world as attuned understanding indicated that Dasein's capacity to project meaningful possibilities of being into the world is conditioned by its prior being thrown into this world. This means that we always find ourselves in a pre-arranged context of significance in which other beings, other Dasein, and we ourselves already refer to each other in particular meaningful ways. In our everyday lives, that is, in the way we initially and for the most part find ourselves, these references are however often prescribed by what Heidegger calls 'the they': "The they, which is nothing definite and which we all are, though not as a sum, prescribes the kind of being of everydayness" (127). This ontological mode of Dasein grounds the ontic, sociological, phenomenon of the public opinion, in which we all to some extent partake but which not one of us can ever control. Instead, 'the they' steers us, since it erases any sharp distinction between me and other Dasein: "Everyone is the other, and no-one is himself. The they [. . .] is the nobody to whom every Dasein has always surrendered itself, in its being-among-one-another" (128). The public opinion thus shapes my opinion and that of my peers in a uniform manner: we say what 'they say', we expect what 'one expects to happen', or we reject what 'is considered wrong'. Ontologically speaking, I disclose beings by adopting the way 'they' disclose beings. Heidegger calls this common tendency inherent in our everyday way of being 'disownedness', since Dasein no longer owns its comportment, it is no longer 'its own'.

Succumbed to 'the they', Dasein's attunement is marked by 'ambiguity' (*Zweideutigkeit*; §37), its understanding by 'curiosity' (*Neugier*; §36), and its discourse turns into 'idle talk' (*Gerede*; §35). Heidegger's presentation of these disowned modes of being-in-the-world is, even more than other sections in *Being and Time*, confused. For one, his explanations of these modes each refer to all three ontological structures of Dasein – or all four, if we also count interpretation. Heidegger does admit that these modes "were set forth in such a way as to indicate that they are already interconnected in their being" (168), a view that squares with the interrelatedness of the existentials of attunement, understanding, interpretation, and discourse as such. Further, the order in which Heidegger discusses the disowned modes of being-in – idle talk, curiosity, ambiguity – reverses the order in which way he previously introduced these existentials – first the attuned openness to the world as such, then the understanding projection of particular beings, and finally the discursive communication of this understanding. While Heidegger offers no explanation for this, one could suspect that in disownedness, in so far as it is ruled by 'the they', discourse about beings comes to shape our understanding of them, which in turn influences our mood.

Through discourse, Dasein discloses the intelligibility of beings to other Dasein. Given Dasein's concern for being, this supposedly happens by articulating how beings show themselves as themselves. However, Heidegger points out, discourse "has the possibility of becoming idle talk, and as such of not really keeping being-in-the-world open in an articulated understanding, but of closing it off and covering over innerworldly beings" (169). In this mode, discourse turns into gossip, talking points, or bullshit, whereby we do not consider the ontological potential of beings but "things are so because one says so" (168). Put differently, in idle talk we only (small)talk *about* beings without letting them speak to us: "Idle talk is the possibility of understanding everything without any previous appropriation of the matter." The value of such talk does not lie in disclosing meaning – be it profound or even just pragmatic – but in the talking itself, the superficial nature of which easily lends itself to endless and careless repetition. Heidegger thus describes idle talk as "the mode of being of the uprooted understanding of Dasein" (170). Indeed, in many social interactions we simply repeat arguments without actually considering what they reveal about the world or about ourselves.

This disowned mode of discourse deeply affects Dasein's ability to understand beings: "Idle talk [. . .] not only divests us of the task of genuine understanding, but develops an indifferent intelligibility, for which nothing is closed off any longer" (169). Idle talk after all dictates what is worthy of understanding and what is not, or which beings or states of affairs ought to be considered meaningful in which way. This leads to a disowned mode of understanding that Heidegger calls 'curiosity'. In the same way that idle talk is only interested in talking and not in what is talked about, curiosity "takes care to see not in order to understand what it sees, [. . .] but *only* in order to see [.] It makes sure of knowing, but just in order to have known" (172, 346). In other words, curious Dasein becomes solely directed to being*s* and how they appear right now, and no longer to their being. Instead of dwelling on the intelligibility of beings, we then just assume their potential and immediately move on to other projects that seem new and exciting: "Curiosity [. . .] seeks restlessness and excitement from continual novelty and changing encounters. In not-staying, curiosity makes sure of the constant possibility of *distraction*".[10] Hence, when Heidegger holds that for curiosity "there is nothing that is not understood" (173), this only means that Dasein has a superficial, disengaged understanding of every thing, but no true insight into their meaning:

---

[10] *BT* 172; see also 117: "Curiosity discloses each and every thing, but in such a way that being-in is everywhere and nowhere".

The care of averageness reveals [...] an essential tendency of Dasein, which we call the leveling down all possibilities of being [...] Publicness initially controls every way in which the world and Dasein are interpreted, and it is always right, [...] because it does not get to 'the heart of the matter', because it is insensitive to every difference of level and genuineness. (127)

Because disowned understanding is aimed at joining *any* conversation, it rests content with gathering as much factual knowledge as possible. This entails that our self-understanding is also reduced to an ontic apprehension of certain possibilities. When discussing our disowned everydayness, Heidegger thus clarifies that we often understand our own being not by projecting a meaningful path for ourselves, but by following the ways in which 'the they' has already decided on who or what we are, for instance the one who always happily hosts dinner parties for others.

Idle (superficial) talk and curious (restless) understanding also affect Dasein's attunement to the world, meaning that Dasein's moods too become prescribed by 'the they':

The domination of the public way in which things have been interpreted has already decided upon even the possibilities of being attuned, that is, about the basic way in which Dasein lets itself be affected by the world. The they prescribes that attunement, it determines what and how one 'sees'. (169–170)

Following Heidegger's account of disowned existence, this mode of attunement is supposed to be explained by the phenomenon of 'ambiguity'. Yet, his discussion of this phenomenon offers no insight into how these ways of existence are connected,[11] and we can only derive its meaning from Heidegger's general notion of attunement. The way in which Dasein is attuned to being, and which makes beings matter to us in a certain manner, sets the context and tone – the mood – for any possible understanding of and discourse about being. An 'ambiguous context' or 'ambiguous tone' would then be set by a state of existence in which Dasein constantly shifts between moods. A person who is under the spell of the public opinion will indeed not only be pulled back and forth between different takes on particular issues, but also between overall happy, fearful, or depressed ways of disclosing the world as a whole.

The state of ambiguous attunement is not only provoked by idle talk and curiosity, but also in turn reinforces these modes of understanding and discourse: "Ambiguity is tossing to curiosity what it seeks, and it gives to idle talk the illusion of having everything decided in it" (174). Constantly shifting

---

[11] For this reason, Blattner proposes to read §35–37 of *Being and Time* as a mere 'confused presentation', rather than "a systematic account of the fallen modes of each of the three facets of disclosedness" (*Heidegger's Being and Time*, 131).

between moods enables us to understand beings in virtually any possible way, but also causes these understandings to quickly lose their bearing again: "Ambiguity has already seen to it that the interest for what has been realized will immediately die away" (173–174). Likewise, the restless character of curiosity enables the "groundless floating" of idle talk (177). Idle talk, curiosity, and ambiguity thus reciprocally stimulate each other.

In sum, Heidegger's analysis of Dasein's disowned way of being-in depicts the human being as orienting itself within the world by following the ways in which 'the they' has already established the meaning of other beings, other Dasein, and ourselves. In so far as the public opinion has already figured out the proper uses of tools, our social relations, and our own career and life paths, it makes our lives rather easy. The task of orienting ourselves in the world is delegated to 'the they', which takes over our ontological compass and provides us with a surveyable map on which all worldly beings are already located with regard to each other. Surely this map is constantly being redrawn, given the ambiguous and restless way in which 'the they' discloses the world. Yet, as long as 'the they' rules, individual, disowned Dasein never needs to worry about how it can orient itself in thinking or acting.

The "disburdening" (127) inclination of Dasein to go along with 'the they' – that is, to disclose the world through ambiguous attunement, restless curiosity, and repetition of hearsay – is abruptly halted in anxiety. In this experience, Heidegger explains, Dasein is incapable of relating to other beings or Dasein in a meaningful way. As our usual way of understanding things no longer makes sense, 'the they' can no longer hold sway over Dasein, the world loses its familiar character, and we feel uncanny or no-longer-at-home (*Un-zuhause*; 189). The experience of anxiety in this way confirms Heidegger's reading of Kant's 'orientation essay', which emphasizes that orientation requires both a 'subjective' compass (attuned understanding) and an 'objective' orientation point (a familiar phenomenal being). When the latter is lacking for anxious Dasein, its usual capacity to orient itself in the world is shaken. However, for Heidegger anxiety does not entail the impossibility of Dasein's orientation *altogether*, but only of a particular mode thereof. Even in an anxious mood, Dasein remains open to the world – after all, Da-sein *is* being-in-the world. In fact, Dasein now becomes aware of the world *as a whole*: "Being anxious discloses, primordially and directly, the world as world" (187, 188). Hence, anxiety not only makes it temporarily impossible for us to orient ourselves *in* the world, but it also positively opens up a new mode of existence, as it enables us to orient ourselves *towards* this world.

This alternative way of orienting oneself constitutes our owned mode of being-in and is also structured by Dasein's three interrelated existentials. The fundamental attunement of anxiety goes hand-in-hand with the fundamental understanding of being-towards-death (*Sein zum Tode*; §47–53), and these ontological structures enable the fundamental discourse of conscience (*Gewissen*; §54–60).[12]

I explained earlier that, whereas a regular mood such as fear opens up a world for us, the fundamental mood of anxiety opens us up to our being-in-the-world. In other words, anxiety does not throw us into the world, but reveals to us our thrownness. Anxiety thus attunes us to ourselves in a profound way. Rather than as a being that is part of a meaningful world, be it as a dinner host or a cobbler, in anxiety I disclose myself *as Dasein*, that is, as a mode of existence that is its 'there', or as a way of being that has no stable ground or clear purpose and hence no fixed identity. Hence, anxiety does not so much enable us to make sense of things, as it reveals to us that we are a being that *has to* make sense of the world and ourselves over and over again. In disownedness this task is taken over by 'the they', which has already ascribed a particular meaning to my being. In a state of anxiety, in contrast, it can only be taken up by me: I can and have to 'own' my being. Heidegger therefore insists that anxiety individuates Dasein, pulling it out of the anonymity of 'the they': "Anxiety fetches Dasein back out of its entangled absorption in the 'world'. Everyday familiarity collapses. Dasein is individualized but *as* being-in-the-world" (189, 187, 190). The question that remains is how such individuated Dasein, which is existentially cut off from all other beings as well as from its own innerworldly appearance, can still make sense of things? What kind of understanding and discourse are still available for anxious Dasein?

This distinctive mode of attunement enables an owned mode of understanding ourselves, namely the existential understanding of death. Heidegger first clarifies that this understanding concerns Dasein's own death, and not anyone else's. There is a qualitative and important difference here. 'The they' allows us to think of the death of other people, but also of my future self, in a general and anonymous way as 'someone's' passing and as 'a case of death' (252). In owned understanding I cannot delegate my own death in this way, since I now realize that no-one can die for me: "No one can relieve another from their dying. [. . .] Every Dasein itself must take dying upon itself in every instance. [. . .] Death is always essentially my own".[13] Heidegger further specifies that this understanding of death does not concern our biological demise, but the ultimate existential limitation of Dasein's being-in-the-world (234). If understanding is Dasein's capacity to project meaningful possibilities onto beings, then its 'death' is the failure to project any meaning. Of course Dasein cannot experience this failure itself, since it would entail that there is no more Dasein (237). As a mode of understanding, existential death is therefore more

---

[12] I owe this insight to Steve Crowell, *Normativity and Phenomenology in Husserl and Heidegger*, 204.
[13] *BT* 240; my translation, 250.

precisely the projected *potential* failure of care, or "the possibility of the impossibility of existence in general" (262, 250, 266). Heidegger calls this an "eminent possibility" because it is both the most extreme and an enduring possibility of Dasein's existence. As soon and as long as it is, Da-sein is 'being-towards-death' (234).

Whereas in disowned understanding Dasein reduces everything to phenomenal beings, in owned being-towards-death it understands that it is not itself a thing but a way of existence. More specifically, while curious Dasein understands itself in light of *a certain* possibility, such as being a cobbler, in being-towards-death it understands itself *as* possibility (248–249), or as having no prescribed purpose (despite what 'they' may say) (266). In the same way, anxiety does not just throw Dasein into the world according to a certain mood, but confronts it with its thrownness, or with its lack of stable ground.[14] In owned attuned understanding, Dasein – as "thrownness into death" (250) – is thus a being that is acutely aware of its own lack of essence.

The mode of discourse that articulates this peculiar mode of attuned understanding, this anxious-being-towards-death, Heidegger calls 'conscience' (269). Since meaningful communication with other Dasein is not possible in anxiety, the call (*Ruf*) of conscience can only be directed from Dasein towards itself. As explained earlier, what anxiety is motivated by (anxious of) and concerned about (anxious for) are fundamentally the same, namely Dasein's own being-in-the-world. Likewise, being-towards-death is a 'pure' form of Dasein's self-understanding that is not mediated by any particular worldly possibility, and a fortiori not by 'the they'. Accordingly, Heidegger holds that "Dasein calls itself in conscience" (275), whereby this call is directed *from* owned Dasein ("Dasein in its uncanniness") *to* disowned Dasein ("the everyday they-self", 276–277). Inevitably, conscience is then also *about* oneself. But since no meaningful projects present themselves in anxiety, owned discourse is characterized by silence. The call of conscience gives us no direct message, in the sense that it does not tell us how to use a hammer or how to live up to the standards of a good dinner host: "The call does not say anything, does not give any information about events in the world, has nothing to tell" (273, 294). And yet, Heidegger adds, the meaning of the call is clear: disowned Dasein is called forth to 'become itself': "Nothing is called to the self which is summoned, but it is summoned to itself, that is, to its ownmost potentiality-of-being (*Selbstseinkönnen*)".

We can conclude that, in individuated-anxious-being-towards-death-through-conscience, Dasein is solely oriented towards itself. Of course, this does not mean that our existence revolves around a certain clear

---

[14] Withy explains this in the most lucid manner in *Heidegger on being uncanny*, Cambridge: Harvard University Press, 2015, 69–77.

identity – Heidegger ultimately characterizes Dasein as a nullity (*Nichtigkeit*, 285). Rather, in anxiety, death, and conscience our 'self' is, more profoundly than before, disclosed, understood, and articulated as a thrown project. Instead of losing oneself in a particular worldly role that was dictated by 'the they', owned Dasein thus on its own accord confronts and embraces its very own being-in-the-world. In the existential attitude of ownedness we care about how to orient ourselves towards the world at all, prior to figuring out how inner-worldly beings refer to each other.

7.3   Cassirer and Heidegger's Notions of Selfhood

On the foregoing readings of Cassirer's functional account of the animal symbolicum and Heidegger's existential analytic of Dasein, both thinkers present the human condition as a quest for orientation. If orientation is the capacity to determine one's own location in a certain area based on a given reference point, then existential orientation is the capacity to establish for oneself a meaningful position and attitude with regard to other worldly beings and events on the basis of some significant experiences. According to Cassirer, we can orient ourselves in this way because we immediately grasp, through the symbols, the objective meaning of sensible experiences, and because we understand them, by means of the functions of consciousness, as constitutive moments of a cultural domain, such as religion or science. This understanding entails meaningfully relating a symbol like a crucifix with regard to other religious symbols (sacramental bread, a priest) as well as meaningfully distinguishing it from other symbolic conceptions of the same sensations (a mathematical plus sign, an artistic composition). It also includes that we situate ourselves in meaningful cultural domains, by identifying and expressing ourselves as a member of a religious or a scientific community. According to Heidegger, we can likewise existentially orient ourselves because in our everyday comportment we grasp the being of beings and, thanks to our attuned, circumspective understanding, situate these beings in a meaningful world. On this understanding, other beings usually and predominantly appear as tools that refer to each other (the hammer is useful and intelligible in view of the table) and as for-our-sake in the context of work (the table becomes meaningful in view of my dinner party or my career). At the same time, this understanding also always projects a meaningful worldly role for ourselves, for instance as a dinner host or a cobbler.

Both accounts of existential orientation install a transcendental distinction between a self that orients itself and a self that is oriented within the world, or between a world-constituting and a – resulting – worldly self. For Cassirer, the former self is a symbolic consciousness that unites a number of functions which constitute the coherent worldviews of the symbolic forms. However, he also posits 'self' as one of the symbols that make up these cultural worldviews. In the same way that Cassirer distinguishes between a religious, artistic, scientific, or political notion of causality, he discerns a generically different conception of the self in each cultural context: the same individual can be a religious devotee, an artistic persona, a member of the human species, and a citizen, but in each cases it means something different to be a 'self'. The same duality is present in Heidegger's existential analytic. Dasein is the ontological being that opens up a world through attunement, and through circumspective understanding it therein relates other beings to itself and vice versa in intelligible ways. But in projecting possible ways of being for itself, Dasein's understanding also establishes a worldly persona for itself. The cobbler, like Cassirer's citizen, must of course still navigate its professional life or political community, but it is a situated self for whom the world makes sense in general.

A superficial reading of Cassirer's writings may suggest that he is only really interested in the many manifestations of the worldly self, given the (comparatively) sparse comments about the symbolic consciousness that grounds and mutually connects them. Such a reading, however, misses Cassirer's systematic ambition: even though his functional conception of human consciousness remains in the background of his writings, it forms an essential, foundational element of his thought. Conversely, Heidegger's focus in *Being and Time* seems to be entirely on Dasein's capacity to constitute a meaningful world, whereas its worldly self-understanding is portrayed as corrupted by 'the they'. Here we should keep in mind that Heidegger nevertheless considers 'the they' as an existential of Dasein, and that our factual self-understanding, be it in our everyday comportment, through the they, or in anxiety, propels his existential phenomenology. While Cassirer and Heidegger's respective focus on the worldly or the world-constituting self clearly betrays their different views of the human condition, it may therefore not be absolutized. We must rather, carefully consider their views on both notions of the self, to examine how their disagreement about the infinite or finite character of the human condition plays out on both fronts.

(1) Cassirer and Heidegger's conceptions of the world-constituting self do not merely assert our capacity to orient ourselves in the world, but furthermore identify this capacity as a defining trait of the human condition. Orientation requires both recognizing empirical appearances as a meaningful reference point (apprehending a symbol or an intelligible being) and connecting this point to all other appearances (constituting a cultural domain or world). Both thinkers consider this twofold ability to see more than what is given – which they also recognized in Kant's account of transcendental imagination – to be what uniquely characterizes the animal symbolicum or Dasein.

Cassirer calls our capacity to perceive objective meaning in the empirical sphere and thereby constitute a variety of cultural expressions and domains 'symbolic imagination', and designates it as the 'differentia specifica' that distinguishes us from all other animals: "The animal possesses a practical imagination and intelligence whereas man alone has developed a new form: a symbolic imagination and intelligence" (*EM* 33, 24). Because other animals perceive the world 'merely as it is', they can only respond to it in certain repetitive ways. While animal behaviour can thus be explained according to a stimulus–response model, specifically human behaviour is marked by the capacity to pause and reflect upon anticipated acts:

Between the receptor system and the effector system, which are to be found in all animal species, we find in man a third link which we may describe as the *symbolic system*. This new acquisition transforms the whole of human life. As compared with the other animals man lives not merely in a broader reality; he lives, so to speak, in a new *dimension* of reality. There is an unmistakable difference between organic reactions and human responses. In the first case a direct and immediate answer is given to an outward stimulus; in the second case the answer is delayed. It is interrupted and retarded by a slow and complicated process of thought. (*EM* 24; *ECW:17* 200–201)

This interruption or delay enables us to ascribe symbolic meaning to our intuitions, that is, to perceive the possible in the real, the there in the here, the future in the now, or the universal in the particular. In Davos, Cassirer holds that this ability leads the human "from the immediacy of its existence into the region of pure form" (*DD* 286). As such, symbolic imagination opens up the cultural world for us and renders us cultural beings: "The principle of symbolism, with its universality, validity, and general applicability [gives] access to the specifically human world, to the world of human culture" (*EM* 35, 62). Cassirer's discussion of pathological consciousness in *The Phenomenology of Knowledge* is meant to provide a negative proof of this view of the human being: by diagnosing pathologies such as aphasia as inabilities to perceive objective meaning, he demonstrates that 'healthy' or 'normal' human consciousness is grounded in the capacity of symbolic imagination (*PSF:III* 277). For Cassirer, then, "consciousness is nothing but pure potentiality for all objective formations" (53).

Heidegger too defines Dasein in terms of possibility: "Dasein is not something objectively present which then has in addition the ability to do something, rather it is primarily possibility. [P]ossibility as an existential is the most primordial and the ultimate positive ontological determination of Dasein" (*BT* 143–144). Dasein does not have a fixed identity: it can neither fall back upon a stable ground, nor aspire towards an existential telos. This means that who or what we are, is the sole result of how we project our own possibilities into the world, but also that we are always more than any of these possibilities. Either way, for Heidegger Dasein can only be pinpointed as a way of being: "The essence of this being lies in its to be. The whatness (*essentia*) of this being must be understood in terms of its being (*existentia*) insofar as one can speak of it at all. [...] The essence of Dasein lies in its existence" (42, 117). The term 'existence' ('ek-sistence') should thereby be understood as 'standing-out', that is, as being opened up to other beings, to the world, and to one's own potential. In *The Fundamental Concepts of Metaphysics* (1929/1930), Heidegger accordingly explains that Dasein fundamentally distinguishes itself from all other beings because it exists. While material objects are 'worldless' (*weltlos*) and animals are 'poor in world' (*weltarm*), only Dasein itself is truly 'amidst' its surroundings (*FCM* 403): it alone understands beings '*as* something' or '*as* such and such' (397). This capacity to disclose more than what is literally given (417) renders Dasein 'world constituting' (*weltbildend*; 414). Heidegger's account of anxiety in *Being and Time* serves as a negative proof of this capacity: in the breakdown of all meaning, that is, when we face the possibility of impossibility, we are indirectly confronted with our fundamental existential need to make sense of things. Thus, for Heidegger, "Dasein *is* always its possibility" (*BT* 42).

Of course, neither Cassirer nor Heidegger holds that the human potential to constitute a meaningful world and a meaningful self is unlimited. Dasein faces such limitations due to the recalcitrant character of ontic beings but also, more interestingly, because of its own ontological constitution. On the one hand, the material nature of beings restricts our range of possible interpretations of their being: we cannot use an egg to assemble a piece of furniture, and in the same way our own body may hinder us from pursuing certain projects (183). On the other hand, our understanding is enabled, but thereby also limited, by our thrownness: we always find ourselves in the world in such a way that some interpretations make sense to us while others are being closed off. The point here is not that our attunement impedes our possibilities – it actually opens up the world in the first place – but more originally that we do not control how we are attuned: as Heidegger puts it, "mood assails us" (136). Similarly, we often succumb to 'the they', which further, and drastically so, prescribes certain possible ways of interpreting and being while dismissing others.

More explicitly than Heidegger, Cassirer admits that, in so far as we are a symbolic *animal*, we are still subjected to biological urges (*ECN:6* 634). He however rejects the idea of stubborn matter that resists our conscious formation of objectivity: there is, for Cassirer, no meaningful way to talk about a 'thing in itself' or a 'pure given'. On the contrary, he points out the tragic feature of human existence that symbolic consciousness is in a way caught in the cultural world that it has brought forth itself:

The human being cannot escape from its own achievement. It cannot but adopt the conditions of his own life. No longer in a merely physical universe, the human being lives in a symbolic universe. [...] No longer can the human being confront reality immediately; it cannot see it, as it were, face to face. [...] Instead of dealing with the things themselves, the human being is in a sense always conversing with itself. It has so enveloped itself in linguistic forms, in artistic images, in mythical symbols or religious rites that it cannot see or know anything except by the interposition of this artificial medium. (*EM* 25; *ECN:6* 260)

Since all human consciousness is founded in symbolic imagination, we cannot get beyond the "spiritual horizon" (*ECW:17* 200) that we ourselves have constituted. In other words, our unlimited capacity to bring forth meaning goes hand-in-hand with our lack of access to anything that would transcend the realm of human culture.

This limitation holds for our knowledge of objectivity as much as it does for subjectivity. Due to his understanding of the transcendental method, Cassirer maintains that the only way we can gain insight into the nature of the human subject is through the symbolic meaning that it constitutes in the form of cultural objects: since we have no access to a 'subject in itself', all we can know about the human being is the way in which it expresses its spontaneous powers: "For the consolidation that life undergoes in the various forms of culture – in language, religion, and art – constitutes [...] a *prerequisite* for it to find and understand itself in its own essence" (*LCS* 107–108). As a consequence, Cassirer conceives of the human being as the functional unity of the functions of symbolic consciousness, which means that it *is nothing but* the sum of these formative principles: "The term 'Geist' is [...] a comprehensive name for all those functions that constitute and build up the world of human culture" (*ECW:24* 313; *EM* 67–68). For Cassirer, his account of the formative principles of consciousness is, then, the whole story of the human condition: any attempt to further ground this pure potentiality in a substantial, metaphysical substrate is futile. As a result, Cassirer's conception of the human condition remains formal and impersonal. The most profound description of human being that he can attain is that of a functional 'totality of rules' (*PSF:I* 102). In his review of *Kant and the Problem of Metaphysics*, Cassirer thus makes it clear that he is not interested in "the *Dasein* of the human being, but [in] its 'intelligible substrate of humanity' (*KPMR* 240). In *An Essay on Man*, he confirms that "it is the system of human activities" which defines and determines the circle of 'humanity'' (*EM* 68). What is at stake for Cassirer is, then, not the concrete individual self, but the possibility of humanity.

Heidegger likewise rejects the idea of a substantial ground for Dasein, yet the analysis of our being-in-the-world as thrown projection is not the end point of his existential analytic. The true nature of our being-there is only revealed when we further inquire about the unitary ground of our attuned understanding, which Heidegger finds in care. After all, Dasein's capacity to orient itself in its surroundings only explains *how* it exists – that is, its hermeneutic-phenomenological way of being – while its care for being establishes *what* it fundamentally is – its ontological being. Preceding our possibility to project meaning, there's an interest and a need to make sense of things, and most of all of ourselves: precisely because we do not have a fixed ground or purpose, our existence is an endless quest for orientation. What would be a domain of speculation for Cassirer thus constitutes the core of Heidegger's view of the human condition – what it means to be Dasein is not only captured by how we express ourselves, but most profoundly by why we (have to) do so. Accordingly, Heidegger describes Dasein's being as existentially and person-ally motivated. Throughout *Being and Time*, he emphasizes that our relation to being, in general as well as our own, is marked by 'mineness' or "always-being-my-own" (*Jemeinigkeit*): "The being which this being is *concerned about* in its being is always my own. Thus, Dasein is never to be understood ontologically as a case and instance of a genus of beings objectively present. [. . .] When we speak of Dasein, we must always use the *personal* pronoun" (*BT* 42).

(2) This fundamental disagreement about the orienting, world-constituting self echoes through Cassirer and Heidegger's accounts of the worldly self. Both thinkers assert that the latter self can appear in multiple ways: while Cassirer distinguishes between a mythical, scientific, or political self, Heidegger opposes the pragmatic self to the isolated subject. Interestingly, in his 1928 review of the second volume of *The Philosophy of Symbolic Forms* Heidegger expresses his appreciation for Cassirer's notion of the mythical self, whose pre-rational and holistic understanding of its surroundings resembles "the elementary Dasein-relations of the human to its world" (*KPM:II* 262). Cassirer and Heidegger indeed agree on the significance of this unreflected manner of navigating the world, in so far as they both consider it the most original way in which the human being finds itself in a human world. Yet, they value this originality in different ways.

Cassirer views mythical thought as the beginning of all human culture because it constituted the first breakthrough from the confined sphere in which the animal lives to the symbolic (intersubjective) sphere. He however also considers it a primitive human worldview that was bound to be overcome by the more formal symbolic forms of language and eventually scientific thought. The mythical worldview after all remains limited because it is unaware of its breakthrough to the 'mundus intelligibilis': even though the mythical self is a symbolic construct, it still takes on a substantial identity – in mythical thinking we coincide with our magical role of priest, woman, or elderly. For Cassirer, the evolution of human culture consists, then, in the gradual overcoming of this pre-critical self-understanding.[15] In the terminology that he used in Davos, myth is the defining starting point ('terminus a quo') of human culture, but by no means its goal ('terminus ad quem'). Accordingly, his lectures at Davos

---

[15] I expand on this claim in Chapter 10.1.2: 'Cassirer's critical perspective on human culture'.

acknowledge Heidegger's pragmatic conceptions of space (as "the sphere of what is ready-to-hand"; *ECN:17* 15) and language (as idle talk; 37) and existential notion of death as legitimate cultural expressions, but challenge their significance for a philosophical anthropology: for Cassirer, the focus should rather be on the transition towards the present-at-hand (29) and "true spiritual behavior" (37).

Heidegger has of course a completely different take on the hierarchy between the pragmatic and the theoretically oriented self: his existential analytic aims to show that our everyday comportment discloses the being of beings, whereas understanding ourselves as isolated, reflective, subjects closes us off from any ontological insights. The challenge for Heidegger is that the latter understanding had become the dominant philosophical and common sense conception of the human being. Counter to this conception, the goal of his existential phenomenology is "that the Dasein in man is first made visible" (*KPM* 234). To accomplish this, Heidegger turns to the existential, lived experience of anxiety and death, in which we become individuated or confronted with the fact that I alone can take up my own being as potentiality.[16] Hence, during the Davos debate, Heidegger rejects Cassirer's claim that the human being finds its highest expression in its cultural, intersubjectively shared, life. Not only is the human essence not found in its rational capacity, he holds, but it is also revealed in uncanny, unintelligible moments of existential solitude.

In sum, both with regard to the world-constituting and the worldly self, Cassirer and Heidegger's views are sufficiently similar to arouse each other's interests, yet their viewpoints are very different, if not conflicting. Both thinkers define the world-constituting self – symbolic consciousness or being-in-the-world – as the possibility for existential orientation, and both consider the pre-reflective worldly self – the mythical self or pragmatic Dasein – as the original manifestation of this possibility. However, they have different understandings of the purpose of this orientation, and as a consequence characterize the human condition in opposite ways.

On both accounts of the self, Cassirer is ultimately only interested in our potential to bring forth objective meaning – his explicit aim is to develop a "definition of the human being in terms of human culture" (*EM* 63). In view of this goal, he consistently emphasizes the formative, spontaneous, or – in the terminology used at Davos – infinite character of symbolic imagination: "The human being's symbolic power ventures beyond all the limits of its finite existence" (55). This breakthrough constitutes the realm of human culture, and the subsequent cultural development from mythical to scientific thought

---

[16] As Withy sums it up, "angst reveals that this being is *mine to be it*" (*Heidegger on being uncanny*, 67).

follows from our gradual living up to the full potential of this typically human capacity. Regarding the world-constituting self, he holds that "the true spiritual realm is just the spiritual world created from itself. That the human being could create it is the seal of its infinitude" (*DD* 286). About the evolving worldly self, he specifies that "the human being is that being which does not just, like all others, *has* limits, but that arrives at an *awareness* of these limits" (*ECN:17* 21), and that it is "the finite being that *knows* about its finitude and that, through this knowing, overcomes its finitude and becomes aware of its infinity" (73). Cassirer adopts a Kantian view about finitude here: while we evidently do not possess the absolute infinitude of a divine being, our unique ability to recognize our own limitations and to not allow ourselves to be defined by them, nevertheless allows for an "immanent infinitude" (*DD* 286).

Heidegger, on the other hand, analyses both the world-constituting self and the worldly self in view of its interest in disclosing being. As a fundamentally ontological being, Dasein is not defined by what it ought to become but by what motivates its existence, namely its care. This motivation becomes apparent in the limit experience of anxiety – that is, of our bare throwness in the world – and the accompanying understanding of oneself as being-towards-death – that is, as a possibly impossible project. Here we realize that our capacity to make sense of ourselves is actually a need that we cannot escape, but at the same time poses a task that we can never definitively fulfill; it is, in other words an existential burden as well as responsibility. This means that Dasein is neither its own ground nor its own purpose, both of which must remain unknown to us (*BT* 136). Hence, for Heidegger the human condition is at its core marked by a double finitude.[17]

This ontological finitude echoes through the phenomenological manner in which Dasein discloses being as the being of beings. On the one hand, Dasein's attunement entails that we always find ourselves situated in the world through an existential mood that we barely control but that limits our possible ways of understanding particular beings:

> With the factical existence of Dasein, innerworldly beings are also already encountered. That such beings are discovered in the there of its own existence is not under the control of Dasein. Only *what*, in *which* direction, *to what extent, and how* it actually discovers and discloses is a matter of freedom, although always within the limits of its throwness. (366)

On the other hand, Dasein's projective understanding – its potentiality or freedom – is also itself inherently limited. Disclosing the meaning of certain

---

[17] Among all the literature about Dasein's finite nature, I have found Katherine Withy's *Heidegger on Being Uncanny*, in particular its analysis of throwness and uncanniness, the most enlightening (70–76, 92–101).

beings after all always implies that one leaves undisclosed, or even covers up, other beings as well as other possible meanings of those very beings. Put more simply, enabling a being to appear in some way always means that it does not appear in another way and that some other beings do not appear at all. Hence, even though Heidegger at one point defines Dasein *as* being-possible, our world and self-disclosure are at any time limited projections of what beings could possibly be. The hermeneutical preconditions for such projecting further constrains our everyday way of understanding being, which we de facto derive from 'the they's pre-established and reductive understanding of being*s*. As existentials of Dasein, attunement, understanding, and 'the they' thus all pose ineradicable limitations to our openness to being. Although the language of finitude is mostly absent from *Being and Time*, Heidegger here clearly portrays Dasein as a fundamentally finite condition.[18] The worldly self, that is, Dasein in its everyday comportment, not only inherits these shortcomings but initially and predominantly falls prey to them, even and especially when it pretends to escape them.

On this basis, we can now confirm that Cassirer and Heidegger's views of the human condition as a quest for worldly orientation motivate their shared interest in Kant's account of transcendental imagination. It is also clear that their conflicting readings of Kant's transcendental philosophy as an exercise in either epistemology or ontology is grounded in their respective interests in our spontaneous formation of culture or our openness and being-delivered to being. At the same time, it appears that Cassirer and Heidegger's conceptions of the human being are in turn motivated by diametrically opposed conceptions of the task of philosophy. While for Cassirer philosophy is the caretaker of our self-liberation through culture, for Heidegger it ought to help us reconcile with our ineradicable shortcomings.

---

[18] This picture of finite Dasein is of course cemented by Heidegger's analysis of Dasein's originary temporality in Division Two of *Being and Time*.

Part III

The Task of Philosophy

8   Cassirer's Functional Conception of Philosophy

We saw earlier that the two structural poles of Cassirer's thought, the realm of culture and the *animal symbolicum*, stand in a functional relation with regard to each other. According to Cassirer, the human being is nothing but the functional unity of its various cultural products, such that neither can be understood independently from the other. This idea of a function is actually a recurring theme throughout Cassirer's oeuvre and a crucial one for understanding his conception of culture and philosophy.

8.1   From Substance to Function

Inspired by contemporary developments in the fields of logic and mathematics, Cassirer argues in *Substance and Function* that traditional, substance-based, logic must be replaced by a critical, functional, one. He most explicitly criticizes Aristotle for initiating 'substance-thinking' and Berkeley for bringing it into psychology, but he actually considers this type of thinking to characterize Western thought as a whole, "in spite of all the manifold transformations it has undergone" (*SF* 8).

Cassirer holds that traditional logic orders concepts according to their degree of abstraction and therefore regards substance as the highest concept: this idea is said to unite the widest range of objects because it is independent of all specifying relations, be it with its own properties or with other entities:

The category of relation especially is forced into a dependent and subordinate position by this fundamental metaphysical doctrine of Aristotle. Relation is not independent of the concept or real being; it can only add supplementary and external modifications to the latter, such as do not affect its real 'nature'.

Cassirer sees two problems with this theory of concept formation. First, it implies that when the extension of our concepts increases, their intension decreases, and thus that a concept that is very limited in content represents the whole of reality. In Cassirer's words, the problem with substance-based logic is that if "all construction of concepts consists in selecting from a plurality of objects before us only the similar properties, while we neglect the rest, [...] a *part* has taken the place of the original sensuous *whole*" and "claims to characterize and explain" it (6). Moreover, he later adds, this logical theory only allows for inductive inferences, but not for deduction (19). Once all particularities – relations, properties, and modifications – are lost in the process of abstraction, there seems to be no way back to the variety of concrete objects. Hence, Cassirer concludes that rather than providing a grasp on reality, traditional logic estranges us from the empirical world:

> We reach the strange result that all the logical labor that we apply to a given sensuous intuition serves only to separate us more and more from it. Instead of reaching a deeper comprehension of its import and structure, we reach only a superficial schema from which all peculiar traits of the particular case have vanished. (19)

Second, according to Cassirer, the process of abstraction is 'one-sided' or biased because it relies on only one of many possible principles of selection, namely the idea of similarity. Once more, the process of concept formation as it is understood by 'substance-thinking' leads to an impoverished view of the world. "In truth", Cassirer counters, "a series of contents in its conceptual ordering may be arranged according to the most diverging points of view", including "equality or inequality, number and magnitude, spatial and temporal relations, or causal dependence" (16). This variety of possible viewpoints implies that we should not merely represent a univocally given order of being, but must actively select the most appropriate rational criterion for relating the content of our perceptions. In sum, Cassirer criticizes the rigidity of both the procedure and the outcome of the traditional way of concept formation.

His solution to these problems consists in a reversal of the order between substance and relation in favour of the latter. We can distinguish three steps in this argumentation. First, he argues that a logic that takes substance as the highest concept only makes sense when it is supported, as it initially was for Aristotle, by a similarly substance-based *metaphysics* (8). Such metaphysics considers substances as the highest ontological entities, the fundamental layer of all being. As a transcendental philosopher, Cassirer evidently does not endorse this view. It no longer makes sense for him to talk about substance as the substratum of the 'things in themselves', and to regard our logical concepts as representations thereof. Instead, we should understand substance as itself a logical concept that originates in the faculty of the understanding and allows us to structure the rhapsody of our intuitions prior to experience. In other words, the concept of substance represents a function of our knowledge rather than a metaphysical entity.

Second, Cassirer stresses that in order to avoid Berkeleyan psychology and draw out the full consequences of Kant's 'Copernican revolution', the shift from traditional metaphysics to transcendental philosophy must be complemented with the introduction of a new *logic*.[1] In contrast to Aristotelian logic, Kant's transcendental logic regards the concept of substance as only one of the twelve categories by means of which we order the manifold of perceptions and make truth claims. This concept has neither ontological nor logical priority over the other categories, but is one of many possible 'points of view' for relating and comparing phenomena. Hence, rather than indicating that which is independent of all relations, the concept of substance expresses a particular type of objective relationship between perceptions.[2] Cassirer concludes from this? the logical priority of relations over concepts: "It is the identity of this generating relation, maintained through changes in the particular contents, which constitutes the specific form of the concept" (*SF* 15). He later adds that "the relation of necessity [...] is in each case decisive", while "the concept is merely the expression and husk of it" (16).

Finally, Cassirer understands these logical relations as 'functions' in the *mathematical* meaning of the term. He holds that they relate to phenomenal objects in the same way that a universal mathematical 'law of arrangement' (y) relates to a series of variables ($x1$, $x2$, ...), namely as a pure relation that indicates a specific 'direction of objective reference' but has no fixed meaning of its own. Understood as such, the concept of function is much better suited for representing the empirical world than an abstract concept such as 'substance'. Because the mathematical function is nothing but "a universal *rule* for the connection of the particulars themselves" (20), it "does not disregard the peculiarities and particularities which it holds under it, but seeks to show the *necessity* of the occurrence and connection of just these particulars" (19, 23). We can, in this case, also 'return' from the function to its variables: "When a mathematician makes his formula more general, this means not only that he is able *to retain* all the more special cases, but also *to deduce* them from the universal formula" (19). Cassirer's concept of function thus eradicates the two problems that he has with the traditional theory of concept formation: its attention to logical relations that validate the particulars overcomes the problem of the poor meaning of the concept of substance, and the consequent relativity of the rational point of view overcomes the one-sidedness of the selection procedure on the basis of similarity alone.

8.2 Cassirer's Historical Writings (1906–1919): A Functional Account of the History of Thought

In 'The Concept of Philosophy as a Philosophical Problem' (1935), Cassirer holds that despite the many forms that philosophy has taken through the

[1] *SF* 11. See Peter Eli Gordon, 'Myth and Modernity: Cassirer's Critique of Heidegger', in: *New German Critique*, 94: *Secularization and Disenchantment*, 2005, 134; and Luft, 'Between Reason and Relativism, a Critical Appraisal', 29.
[2] See Cassirer, 'Charles Renouvier, Essais de critique générale', in: *ECW:9*, 485.

ages – ranging from pure idealism to hardcore realism – its task has always been the same, namely to understand the unities of being and knowing:

> Philosophy claims to be the real, the true unified science; the whole of its striving and its conceptual longing appears to be aimed at absolute unity, at the unity of being as well as the unity of knowledge. But this unity in no way corresponds to an immediate unity of itself, its intellectual structure. (*CPPP* 51)

Cassirer here reiterates the main thesis of some of his earliest writings, the first three volumes of *The Problem of Knowledge* (1906, 1907, 1919), namely that the fundamental problem of both philosophy and science has always been that of the relation between 'the one and the many'.[3] He alternately understands this as the problem of subjectivity and objectivity or form and matter. Throughout the ages we have, however, understood this issue differently. According to Cassirer, then, paradigm shifts between two epochs in the history of thought do not result from a novel answer to the same problem, but rather from an original reinterpretation of this problem itself:

> This is one of the first and most characteristic philosophical accomplishments of each epoch, that it reformulates the *problem* of the correlation between being and thinking [. . .] In this delineation of the *task* consists, even more than in their particular solutions, the originality of each productive era.[4]

First, Cassirer holds that the basic concepts of our worldview – matter, form, object, and subject – have repeatedly been redefined, and did not always mean the same thing: "The concepts of "subject" and "object" are no given and evident possession of thought; each truly creative epoch must first acquire them and actively coin their meaning" (*EP:I* 7). Kant, for example, according to Cassirer no longer understood matter and form as "original determinations of being" but as "structures of signification" (*PSF:III* 9–10). Second, our redefining of these concepts also alters their mutual relation:

> Not only the *content* changes, so that, what previously belonged to the objective sphere is transferred to the subjective one, but the meaning and *function* of both basic elements simultaneously also shifts. The great scientific epochs do not inherit the ready-made schema of opposition to realize it with various, interchanging, contents, but first conceptually construct both opposing terms.

---

[3] At least in recent times, these 'historical writings' have gained much less attention than Cassirer's 'systematic writings', the three volumes of *The Philosophy of Symbolic Forms* in particular. For an extensive account of Cassirer's view of history and philosophy's relation to it, see, nevertheless, Rainer A. Bast, *Problem, Geschichte, Form. Das Verhältnis von Philosophie und Geschichte bei Ernst Cassirer im historischen Kontext*, Berlin: Dunker & Humblot, 2000; and Plümacher, *Wahrnehmung, Repräsentation und Wissen*, 250–263.

[4] *EP:I* 7; see also *CIPC* 68–69.

After Kant's 'revolution in the way of thinking' (*Revolution der Denkart*; *CPR* B XI) – to stick with this example – the unity of our knowledge constitutes rather than copies the unity of being. The relation of dependence between knowing and being has thus turned upside down, but is also rendered much more intimate. With Kant, Cassirer claims, it becomes clear that "all disagreement about the problem of being in the end always originates from a different or conflicting understanding of the problem of truth, its actual source" (*EP:III* viii). Third, it is possible that concepts that are problematic in one era become central to the next: "We thus notice that a concept, which appears in one epoch as a source of contradictions, becomes a tool and necessary condition of all knowledge in the next".[5]

On these grounds, the problem of the relation between the one and the many takes on radically different forms in the subsequent philosophical and scientific epochs, as each of them is established by "a new intellectual orientation".[6] It consequently seems impossible to perceive any real progress in the history of thought: "In the actual crucial epochs of knowledge, the many basic intuitions do not relate to each other according to a steady, quantitative, development, but in the most sharp dialectic contradictions" (*EP:I* 4). Cassirer wonders, however, if it might not be possible

to discern in this continuous [historical] transformation, if not a consistent, permanent, *content*, then at least a unified *goal*, towards which the ideal development strives? Is there in this process, if there are *no persistent elements* of knowledge, *nevertheless a universal law* that prescribes meaning and direction to this evolution?[7]

In 1906, Cassirer has not yet developed the conceptual distinction between a substantial and functional unity. Nevertheless, the idea behind it is clearly already present in the introduction to the first volume of *The Problem of Knowledge*. The flaw of any metaphysical understanding of the history of thought, he there answers his own question, is that it assumes a substantial substratum that remains the same throughout the different epochs and allows for a cumulative progress in our understanding of the world. A critical approach, on the other hand, searches for a merely ideal continuity, "which is all we need in order to talk about a unity of its process" and which is "the real a priori of history" (13). Only the latter approach can account for true, not merely gradual, differences between the historical epochs.[8]

---

[5] *EP:I* 4. With regard to the Enlightenment, for example, see *PE* xiii.

[6] *PE* 33. Cassirer specifically elaborates on the intellectual orientation of the Enlightenment in *The Philosophy of the Enlightenment* (1932), and on that of the Renaissance in Cassirer's *The Individual and the Cosmos in Renaissance Philosophy* (1927) and *The Platonic Renaissance in England* (1932).

[7] *EP:I* 5; my emphasis.

[8] Cassirer's functional account of the history of thought informed Hans Blumenberg's view on the transition from the pre-modern to the modern age in *The Legitimacy of the Modern Age*.

What Cassirer suggests here is, further, clearly a transcendental move: rather than to focus on what the different epochs pose as facts, the philosopher should take an interest in their subjective conditions of possibility. The goal of critical philosophy, he later proclaims, is to achieve the 'self-understanding of reason' (*EP:III* 1). Progress in our philosophical knowledge should not be measured quantitatively but methodologically: what the philosopher must strive for is, according to Cassirer, not a continuous growth of our knowledge, but a better delineation of what we can possibly know.[9]

For Cassirer, then, Kant's transcendental method marks a crucial contribution to the history of philosophy that informed all post-Kantian thinkers. In the third volume of *The Problem of Knowledge*, he discusses the thought of Jacobi, Reinhold, Aenesidem, Beck, Maimon, Fichte, Schelling, Hegel, Herbert, Schopenhauer, and Fries, and holds that, despite *prima facie* severe differences, they are all deeply indebted to this method. On the one hand, Cassirer even admits that the many disagreements between the different Neo-Kantian schools have become so profound by the beginning of the twentieth century that Kant's legacy seems to have dissolved in a number of dispersed and even contradictory ideas (1). At the same time, however, he regards the dispersion of Kant's thought not as a sign of its decline, but as an indication of its success; it confirms his belief that the heart of transcendental philosophy lies not in a specific doctrine to which it adheres but in its multi-applicable method: "The result of the critique of reason cannot, as a finished product, be brought down to a number of dogma's. It is what it is only by means of the manner in which it was accomplished, and by means of the method upon which it is grounded" (2). Cassirer thus views the evident diversity among post-Kantian thinkers as a surface phenomenon of a single underlying method. In fact, he holds, this diversity should be applauded: "Despite their mutual conflicts, the many attempts to revive Kant's thought stand in a relation of ideal continuity with regard to each other. Together, they accomplish a task that none of them separately could entirely grasp" (Id.). The transcendental method, which consists in a 'direction of question-posing', allows for a

According to Blumenberg, we cannot understand the secularized worldview of the latter as a translation of the Christian worldview of the former, as Karl Löwith holds in *Meaning in History*, but their incommensurability does not preclude a common task either. This task, Blumenberg argues in Cassirer's spirit, originates in the perennial metaphysical questions that the human being has asked throughout the different ages. The constant, ideal factor in the history of human thought lies, then, in the questions we pose and not in the progress among the answers that the different epochs have formulated in response to them. Consequently, these answers stand in a functional, rather than a substantial relation to each other (Hans Blumenberg, *Die Legitimität der Neuzeit*, Frankfurt am Main: Suhrkamp, 1996, 35–38, 74–75, 79).

[9] See Cassirer, 'Formen und Formwandlungen des philosophischen Wahrheitsbegriffs', *ECW, 17*, 342; and *CPPP* 54. In *Einstein's Theory of Relativity* (1921), Cassirer defends a similar view of the history and task of science (*SF* 322).

manifold of applications, each of which confirms its validity and increases its value.

This functional definition of Kantianism serves Cassirer well in a number of ways. First, it allows him to regard (Neo-)Kantian philosophy an ongoing rather than a dead movement. Very different thinkers can, according to Cassirer, legitimately consider themselves to respect the spirit of Kant's writings, as long as they adhere to the transcendental method. As he puts it in the Davos debate, "the term "neo-Kantianism" must be determined functionally rather than substantially. It is not a matter of the kind of philosophy as dogmatic doctrinal system; rather, it is a matter of a direction taken in question-posing".[10]

Second, Cassirer's formal characterization of transcendental philosophy can accommodate the fact that there have been, and still are, both realist *and* idealist continuations of Kant's thought; that there are inspiring epistemological *and* ontological readings of his work; and that, for example, both continental phenomenology *and* certain tendencies in analytic political philosophy are born from his insights. It also explains why the paradigm shifts in natural science, psychology, and neurobiology, may pose new challenges to the Neo-Kantian thinker but do not designate the end of transcendental philosophy.[11] Kant's methodology transcends the domains and doctrines to which Kant or his successors have applied it, so that its value remains unimpaired by scientific revolutions.

Third, Cassirer's focus on the methodological novelty of Kant's philosophy allows him to extend its field of application to all human interests and their corresponding cultural domains:

The problem of Kant is not bound to an inquiry into the special forms of logical, scientific, ethical, or aesthetical thought. Without varying its nature we may apply it to all other forms of thinking, judging, knowing, understanding, and even of feeling by which the human mind attempts to conceive the universe as a whole. (*CIPC* 70–71; *KLT* 286)

Cassirer's philosophy of symbolic forms sets out to transcendentally ground the truth claims of such diverse meaning systems as language, myth, science, etc., while making use of the same, transcendental, method.

---

[10] *DD* 274; Cassirer, 'Beiträge für die Encyclopedia Britannica', *ECW:17* 308. In a funeral oration for Cohen, Cassirer further holds that his former teacher also always considered the 'Marburger Schule' as "held together not by connected results, but by a shared ideal direction of inquiring and questioning" ('Beiträge zu: Hermann Cohen', *ECW:17* 290).

[11] In the first volume of *The Problem of Knowledge* (*EP:1* 12) and in 'Goethe und die mathematische Physik' (*ECW:9* 302), Cassirer opposes the at that time increasingly popular interpretation of Kant's philosophy that reduces it to a mere defence of Newtonian science. Moreover, in *Einstein's Theory of Relativity*, he defends the validity of the theory of relativity from a transcendental perspective.

In sum, Cassirer aims to transcend the ongoing disputes about Kant's philosophy by emphasizing its task and method. In light of its task, Cassirer holds, this philosophy subscribes to the perennial quest for an accurate understanding of the relation between matter and form that constitutes the ideal continuity or functional unity of the entire history of thought. In light of its method, he later adds, it introduces a novel, transcendental, approach to this problem that in turn constitutes a functional unity between a variety of seemingly incommensurable Neo-Kantian positions. For the sake of contemporary philosophy, Cassirer finally suggests that we adapt this approach to a systematic investigation of the different domains of culture (*EP:I* 11). This is indeed the task that Cassirer takes up in his mature thought.

8.3   Cassirer's Systematic Writings (1923–1942): A Functional Definition of Human Culture

In the opening lines of *The Phenomenology of Knowledge* (1929), Cassirer announces a "return to the investigations with which I began my work in systematic philosophy two decades ago", but also immediately adds that "both in content and in method, the Philosophy of Symbolic Forms has gone beyond this initial formulation of the problem" (*PSF:III* xiii). Indeed, Cassirer's mature philosophy draws out the consequences of the functional logic he established in *Substance and Function* within the framework of a philosophy of culture. The logical theory that was initially meant to found scientific knowledge ("mathematical-physical objectivity") now serves the understanding of our scientific as well as our natural and mythical worldviews, and eventually our cultural world as a whole.

First, the symbols around which Cassirer's mature philosophy centres – space, time, number, causality, and self – correspond for the most part to the functional concepts that he lists in *Substance and Function*: "We can conceive members of series ordered according to equality or inequality, number and magnitude, spatial and temporal relations, or causal dependence" (*SF* 16). Second, Cassirer repeats that it should be "the pure relation which governs the building of consciousness and which stands out in it as a genuine a priori, an essentially first factor" (*PSF:III* 203). Like the concept of function, the symbol expresses nothing but a rational relation between our sensations:

Consciousness cannot devote itself in every moment with equal intensity to all the various sense impressions that fill it; it cannot represent them all with equal sharpness, concretion, and individuality. Thus it creates schemata, total images into which enter a number of particular contents, and in which they flow together without distinction. But these schemata can be no more than abbreviations, compendious condensations of the impressions. Where we wish to see sharply and exactly, these abbreviations must be thrust aside; the symbolic values must be replaced by 'real' values – that is, by actual sensations. (192–193)

Third, the meaning of both the functional relations and the symbols are consequently dependent on a certain intellectual perspective. In *Substance and Function*, Cassirer already stated that

> the similarity of certain elements can only be spoken of significantly when a certain 'point of view' has been established from which the elements can be designated as like or unlike [and which is] something distinctive and new as regards the compared contents themselves. (*SF* 25)

In his mature philosophy, the idea of a 'point of view' and the varieties thereof becomes even more important. Cassirer now distinguishes the symbolic spheres of myth, language, art, religion, natural science, history, law, economics, technology, and politics, arguing that each of them sheds a particular light on the symbols that structure our perception of the world. While our sensations are always loaded with conceptual meaning, a specific "direction of vision" (*PSF:III* 138) in turn always determines this meaning prior to experience:

> If we designate the various kinds of relation – such as relation of space, time, causality, etc. – as R_1, R_2, R_3, we must assign to each one a special 'index of modality,' u_1, u_2, u_3, denoting the context of function and meaning in which it is to be taken. For each of these contexts, language as well as scientific cognition, art as well as myth, possesses its own constitutive principle that sets its stamp, as it were, on all the particular forms within it. (*PSF:I* 97)

Within a specific symbolic form, our understanding of the world is "guided by one and the same fundamental spiritual function" (*PSF:III* 41), but each form has its own function and thus ascribes a different meaning or 'modality' to the same symbols. There consequently is no one-on-one relationship between the functional relations among our perceptions and the point of view from which they are understood: all the symbols that Cassirer mentions occur within each symbolic form – myth, language, science, art, religion, etc. We can perceive a line, which is itself already a spatial construct (symbol), in very different and yet equally meaningful ways, depending on the cultural context (symbolic form): as a geometrical figure, a geographical border, an aesthetic ornament, a mythical dividing line between the profane and divine, or a religious symbol.[12] Likewise, causal relationships are constitutive of both the scientific and mythological worldview, even though these views promote a respective genetic and teleological conception of causality (*PSF:II* 20), and even though they express universal laws in the former and magical inferences in the latter case (48). "Here again", Cassirer holds, "it is not

---

[12] *PSF:III* 202–204. Krois offers a similar overview of the different conceptions of time that we use in our daily lives: lived time ("as we normally conceived it", with changing rhythms), mythic thought time (in which "the ages of life – youth, maturity, and old age – are occupied like spaces"), scientific clock time (which "progresses constantly without any reference to human feelings"), calendar time ("which, unlike clock time, has a distinct beginning"), and the action time of technology ("in which things that would otherwise be inaccessible to us are made present"; *Symbolic Forms and History*, 204–205).

the concept of causality as such but the specific form of causal explanation which underlies the difference and contrast between the two spiritual worlds". These examples show that the decisive interpretative mark of the symbols stems from the cultural point of view in light of which we employ them at a given time:

All cultural objectivity must be defined not thing-wise but functionally: this objectivity lies neither in a metaphysical nor an empirical-psychological 'reality' which stands behind it, but in what [each symbolic form] itself is and achieves, in the manner and form of *objectification* which it accomplishes.[13]

The Phenomenology of Knowledge offers further insight in the relation between these points of view and the modalities of the symbols, when distinguishing between expressive, representational, and signifying functions that correspond to the forms of mythical thought, language, and science (*PSF:III* 448–453; *ECW:17* 260–261), and *The Logic of the Cultural Sciences* contributes to this by introducing the 'characterizing functions' that are constitutive of the human or cultural sciences (*LCS* 70–73).

On the basis of these different types of functions, the different symbolic forms shed "a light of their own" on the symbols and ascribe a particular "grammar" to the human world (*CIPC* 71, 76). As a result, the worlds of myth, art, science, etc., have little in common with each other. In fact, if each type of function "presupposes and applies entirely different standards and criteria" (*PSF:I* 91), their claims can only be measured on the basis of their own standards, but not assessed from another viewpoint: "None of these forms can simply be reduced to, or derived from, the others; each of them designates a particular approach, in which and through which they constitute their own aspect of 'reality'" (78, 177; *EM* 170). Moreover, Cassirer holds that each symbolic form lays an absolute claim to the world:

In the course of its development every basic cultural form tends to represent itself not as a part but as the whole, laying claim to an absolute and not merely relative validity, not contenting itself with its special sphere, but seeking to imprint its own characteristic stamp on the whole realm of being and the whole life of the spirit. From this striving toward the absolute inherent in each special sphere arise the conflicts of culture and the antinomies within the concept of culture.[14]

The same questions that Cassirer raised earlier in a logical (*Substance and Function*) and a historical context (*The Problem of Knowledge*), now recur in the cultural context that interests him the most: how can we, given the

---

[13] *PSF:II* 14; translation modified.
[14] *PSF:I* 81, 82; *PSF:IV* 224. In 'The Concept of Philosophy as a Philosophical Problem', Cassirer even adds that "without the claim to an independent, objective, and autonomous truth, not only philosophy, but also each particular field of knowledge, natural science as well as the humanities, would lose their stability and their sense" (*CPPP* 61).

irreducible manifold of our cultural domains, conceive of the unity of culture as a whole? How can we, a fortiori, reconcile the existence of this manifold with the absolute claims of the symbolic forms? We could assume that Cassirer's answer will once again follow the same, functional, logic. From the point of view of an encompassing philosophy of culture, the viewpoints of the symbolic forms after all appear as variables themselves, for which we must find a higher functional unity and interpretative point of view.

point of view'				?					
function'				?					
point of view	myth	language	art	religion		science		politics	
function	space	time		number		causality		self	
variables	x	x	x	x	x	x	x	x	x	x

Figure 1 Cassirer's functional conception of human culture

The obvious candidate for the role of 'über-function' in Cassirer's thought is his idea of culture. For Cassirer, our cultural world has no substantial identity, no fixed content of its own, but only exists in the interplay between the heterogeneous symbolic forms that, each in their own way, attempt to explain the unity of our world:

Upon closer scrutiny the fundamental postulate of unity [of being] is not discredited by this irreducible diversity of the methods and objects of knowledge [. . .] Instead, a new task arises: to gather the various branches of science with their diverse methodologies – with all their recognized specificity and independence – into one system, whose separate parts precisely through their necessary diversity will complement and further one another. This postulate of *a purely functional unity* replaces the postulate of a unity of substance and origin, which lay at the core of the ancient concept of being. [. . .] Instead of dogmatic metaphysics, which seeks absolute unity in a substance to which all the particulars of existence are reducible, such a philosophical critique seeks after a rule governing the concrete diversity of the functions of cognition, a rule which, without negating and destroying them, will gather them into *a unity of deed*, the unity of a self-contained human endeavor.[15]

This unity of deed – or unity of 'work', as Cassirer calls it in *The Metaphysics of Symbolic Forms* (ca. 1940) – is that of human culture as a whole. The ideal continuity between the different symbolic forms lies, then, like the continuity between the different philosophical epochs, in the shared task of all cultural domains to grasp the relation between the universal and particular in a meaningful

---

[15] *PSF:I* 77; my emphasis; see also *EM* 228.

way: "The various forms of human culture are not held together by an identity in their nature but by a conformity in their fundamental task" (*EM* 223).

However, Cassirer's talk of 'human deed', 'endeavor', or 'task' suggests a second candidate for the role of functional unity between the different symbolic forms, namely human consciousness:

With all their inner diversity, the various products of culture – language, scientific knowledge, myth, art, religion – [are] multiple efforts, all directed toward the one goal of transforming the passive world of *impressions*, in which the spirit seems at first imprisoned, into a world that is pure *expression* of the human spirit. (*PSF:I* 80–81)

Although Cassirer's writings often refer to human consciousness as the seat of all symbolic formation, he almost never thematizes it. Even *An Essay on Man* (1945) mainly engages in an overview of the different symbolic forms and rather briefly addresses the issue of human subjectivity explicitly. The reason for this is that, for Cassirer, just as we cannot perceive an 'object in itself', we cannot perceive a 'subject in itself' either: "However deeply we may penetrate into the formations of the sensuous-spiritual consciousness, we never find this consciousness absolutely objectless, as something absolutely simple, prior to all sensations and distinctions" (*PSF:III* 93). Instead, Cassirer holds, we must approach "the question of the structure of the perceptive, intuitive, and cognitive modes of consciousness [. . .] by means of reconstructive analysis" starting from the problems of cultural life "to find our way back to their elementary presuppositions, the conditions of their possibility" (57). In other words, all that we can know about human consciousness we must gather from a transcendental investigation of our cultural accomplishments: "The content of the spirit is disclosed only in its manifestations; the ideal form is known only by and in the aggregate of the sensible signs which it uses for its expression".

Accordingly, for Cassirer, human subjectivity can only be understood as the unity of the rational capacities that constitute different worldviews: "We take subjectivity as a totality of functions, out of which the phenomenon of a world and its determinate order of meaning is actually built up for us" (*PSF:IV* 50). This unity, he specifies in *An Essay on Man*, is not grounded in an identical substance, but must be understood as a functional continuity:

The philosophy of symbolic forms starts from the position that, if there is any definition of the nature or 'essence' of man, this definition can only be understood as a functional, not a substantial one. We cannot define man by an inherent principle that constitutes his metaphysical essence – nor can we define him by an inborn faculty or instinct that may be ascertained by empirical observation. Man's outstanding characteristic, his distinguishing mark, is not his metaphysical or physical nature – but his work. It is this work, it is the system of human activities, which defines and determines the circle of 'humanity'.[16]

---

[16] *EM* 67–68, 222; see also Ernst Cassirer, 'Structuralism in Modern Linguistics', in: *ECW, 24,* 313: "The term 'Geist' is correct; but we must not use it as a name of a substance – a thing [. . .]"

On this ground, Cassirer also substitutes the traditional definition of the human being as *animal rationale* for the original title of *animal symbolicum* (*EM* 26). He holds that "reason is a very inadequate term with which to comprehend the forms of man's cultural life in all their richness and variety": it does no justice to the diversity of our experience, and it may suggest a substantial substratum as the essence of human being. Cassirer's idea of the symbol, in contrast, refers to the variable and essentially interactive and co-constitutive relationship of the human being with its surroundings.

Whether one locates the functional unity of the symbolic forms in our cultural world ('objectivity') or in the *animal symbolicum* ('subjectivity'), depends on one's (current) philosophical interest and perspective. This viewpoint, Cassirer holds in *The Metaphysics of the Symbolic Forms* (ca. 1928), is generically different from that of the symbolic forms: "Philosophical knowledge [. . .] does not create a principally new symbol form, it does not found in this sense a new creative modality – but it grasps the earlier modalities as that which they are: as characteristic symbolic forms" (*PSF:IV* 226; *PE* xiii). More specifically, the nature and task of philosophy is, according to Cassirer, to enhance "the self-knowledge of reason" through "both criticism and fulfillment of the symbolic forms".[17]

Philosophy can criticize the symbolic forms by countering their absolutizing tendencies: "it grasps these forms as the active intellectual construction of reality, not as directed toward some external "Absolute"". On this basis, it can point out the one-sidedness of our cultural domains: "We must strive to comprehend every symbol in its place and recognize how it is limited and conditioned by every other symbol."[18] In the first volume of *The Philosophy of Symbolic Forms*, Cassirer calls this a 'highly significant insight' of critical philosophy:

With this critical insight, science renounces its aspiration and its claim to an 'immediate' grasp and communication of reality. It realizes that the only objectification of which it is capable is, and must remain, mediation. And in this insight, another highly significant idealistic consequence is implicit. [. . .] We are forced to conclude that a variety of media will correspond to various structures of the object, to various meanings for 'objective' relations. (*PSF:I* 76)

Hence, Cassirer holds that "the fundamental principle of critical thinking is the principle of the "primacy" of the function over the object" (*PSF:I* 79).

We should use it in a functional sense as a comprehensive name for all those functions which constitute and build up the world of human culture".

[17] *PSF:IV* 226. One should recall at this point that Cassirer in the first volume of *The Problem of Knowledge* also already called the 'self-understanding of reason' the goal of critical philosophy (*EP:III* 1).

[18] *PSF:IV* 227. See also *Einstein's Theory of Relativity, SF* 447: "Each particular form [must] be 'relativized' with regard to the others, but [. . .] this 'relativization' is throughout reciprocal and [. . .] no single form but only the systematic totality can serve as the expression of 'truth' and 'reality'".

Further, once we acknowledge the relative character of the cultural domains, we can attempt to establish their mutual harmony. In this way, philosophy can also 'fulfill' the symbolic forms by placing them in the larger context of a cultural world that is much richer than the one they could account for on their own. From the internal, limited, perspective of science or religion, the cultural domains necessarily compete with each other for the title of most accurate explanation of the world. From the detached perspective of Cassirer's transcendental philosophy of culture, on the other hand, they offer equally valid human world*views* that together constitute our culture as a whole:

In the boundless multiplicity and variety of mythical images, of religious dogmas, of linguistic forms, of works of art, philosophic thought reveals the unity of a general function by which all these creations are held together. Myth, religion, art, language, even science, are now looked upon as so many variations on a common theme – and it is the task of philosophy to make this theme audible and understandable.[19]

For Cassirer, then, philosophy is the ultimate or 'highest' human viewpoint, in so far as it seeks for a unity between the symbolic forms that does not compromise their mutual differences (*PSF:I* 82). This means that the philosophy of symbolic forms does not aspire to be a philosophical system that synthesizes all expressions of human culture but merely to offer a "systematic overview" (*PSF:IV* 227) of the different a priori perspectives that ground our cultural domains.

point of view'				philosophy					
function'				culture / symbolic consciousness					
point of view	myth	language		art	religion		science		politics
function	space		time		number		causality		self
variables	x	x	x	x	x	x	x	x	x	x

Figure 2 Philosophy as highest viewpoint

---

[19] *EM* 71. About the 'Sonderstatus' of philosophical reflection, see also Kreis, *Cassirer und die Formen des Geistes*, 459–475; Plümacher, *Wahrnehmung, Repräsentation und Wissen*, 354–372; and Sebastian Ulrich, 'Der Status der "philosophischen Erkenntnis" in Ernst Cassirers "Metaphysik des Symbolischen"', in: Birgit Recki (hrsg.), *Philosophie der Kultur – Kultur des Philosophierens: Ernst Cassirer im 20. und 21. Jahrhundert*. Hamburg: Meiner Verlag, 2012, 297–319.

8.4   Cassirer's Ethical Writings (1935–1946): The Normative Task of Philosophy

In his late writings, Cassirer increasingly emphasizes the importance of maintaining harmony between the symbolic forms: to neglect either the diversity or unity of our cultural life, he argues, can have severe ethical or existential consequences.

On the one hand, an exaggerated dominance of one of the symbolic forms over the others would not only lead to a one-sided but possibly also to an inhumane worldview. In *Form und Technik* (1930), Cassirer warns that a culture that reduces all meaning to what is considered meaningful from a technological viewpoint would inevitably violate certain human rights.[20] A similar but subtler problem arises when the difference between certain symbolic forms becomes blurred. Cassirer's famous example of the merging of two cultural domains is that of the Nazi ideology that he discusses in *The Myth of the State* (1946). This ideology, he explains, efficiently but illegitimately merged mythological and political discourses, the tragic results of which are well known.[21] In today's Western society, we can discern the same phenomenon in the emergence of technocracies, which tend to erase the distinction between economics and politics. Such 'antinomies of culture' (*PSF:I* 81), Cassirer emphasizes more and more toward the end of his life, are not just a philosophical, but also an ethical issue: "Without intellectual and moral courage, philosophy could not fulfill its task in man's cultural and social life".[22]

On the other hand, exclusive attention to the differences between the symbolic forms would lead to an equally undesirable situation. In fact,

---

[20] See Cassirer, 'Form und Technik', in: *ECW: 17* 139–183.

[21] I examined this discourse, which violates two key principles of Cassirer's thought, in more detail in Simon Truwant, 'Political Myth and the Problem of Orientation: Reading Cassirer in Times of Cultural Crisis', in: *Interpreting Cassirer*, 130–148.

[22] *MS* 296. The fact that Cassirer never acknowledges a symbolic form of ethics suggests, moreover, that this ethical character is not a late addition, but actually an intrinsic feature of his conception of philosophy. In *Cassirer und die Formen des Geistes*, Kreis explains that there is no place for ethics as a distinct symbolic form in Cassirer's philosophy of culture since the role that it would have is already taken up by, on the one hand, the symbolic form of law (cf. Cassirer, 'Axel Hägerström') and, on the other hand, philosophy, in so far as it secures the development and self-image of each form and the subject as whole (361–364). Gideon Freudenthal, 'The Hero of Enlightenment', in: *The Symbolic Construction of Reality. The Legacy of Ernst Cassirer*, ed. by Jeffrey Andrew Barash, Chicago: The University Press of Chicago, 2008, 190), and Birgit Recki, 'Kultur ohne Moral? Warum Ernst Cassirer trotz der Einsicht in den Primat der praktsichen Vernunft keine Ethik schreiben konnte', in: *Kultur und Philosophie: Ernst Cassirers Werk und Wirkung*, Dorothea Frede und Reinold Schmücker (hrsg.), Darmstadt: Wissenschaftliche Buchgesellschaft, 1997, 67, 72–78), confirm the ethical character of Cassirer's philosophy as a whole, thus countering Krois' less convincing argumentation for ethics as a separate symbolic form (*Symbolic Forms and History*, 142–171).

Cassirer identifies the neglect of their ideal connection with each other through the *animal symbolicum* as the cause of the general crisis of culture that haunted Europe at the beginning of the twentieth century. In *An Essay on Man*, he holds that previous ages have always been marked by "a general orientation, a frame of reference, to which all individual differences might be referred" (*EM* 21). The symbolic forms of myth, religion, and science have consecutively dominated our culture, taking up the role of the highest viewpoint on the human world.[23] In the twentieth century, however, such dominant perspective has disappeared:

An established authority to which one might appeal no longer existed. Theologians, scientists, politicians, sociologists, biologists, psychologists, ethnologists, economists all approached the problem from their own viewpoints. To combine or unify all these particular aspects and perspectives was impossible.

Paradoxically, Cassirer explains, as the various cultural domains became more and more advanced, we lost sight of their original, shared, task. As a consequence, the human being became lost amidst what seems to be a mere manifold of conflicting viewpoints, facing a "crisis in man's knowledge of himself":

No former age was ever in such a favorable position with regard to the sources of knowledge of human nature. Psychology, ethnology, anthropology, and history have amassed an astoundingly rich and constantly increasing body of facts. Our technical instruments for observation and experimentation have been immensely improved, and our analyses have become sharper and more penetrating. We appear, nevertheless, not yet to have found a method for mastery and organization of this material. When compared with our own abundance the past may seem very poor. But our wealth of facts is not necessarily a wealth of thoughts. Unless we succeed in finding a clue of Ariadne to lead us out of this labyrinth, we can have no real insight into the general character of human culture; we shall remain lost in a mass of disconnected and disintegrated data that seem to lack all conceptual unity. (22)

We already know from his systematic writings that, according to Cassirer, this conceptual or ideal unity is rooted in the human being conceived as 'animal symbolicum'. Furthermore, we know that it requires critical philosophy to grasp this unity: only the detached perspective of philosophy allows us to recognize not just the substantially incommensurable claims of the symbolic forms but also their shared function and, on that basis, their potential harmonious coexistence. In his late works, Cassirer ascribes an existential weight to this insight: "In our time, it is not only a general methodological demand, but a general cultural fate that couples philosophy with the special disciplines of knowledge, and which binds them closely to each other" (*CPPP* 61). As

---

[23] See Orth, *Von der Erkenntnistheorie zur Kulturphilosophie*, 71.

Cassirer sees it, in order for us to once again be able to orient ourselves amidst the variety of symbolic forms, we need the encompassing perspective of a critical philosophy that offers us a coherent account of both ourselves and our cultural world as a whole.

In conclusion, Cassirer's philosophy of culture has an ethical task in so far as it is capable of deconstructing ideologies like Nazism. It has existential import, further, because it can establish the human being's central place in its diversified world, lending us a sense of orientation and our world a sense of unity. Cassirer's 'clue of Ariadne' for holding these matters together is usually taken to be his symbol concept, but this concept in turn relies on the idea of a functional unity. The latter idea structures and connects each phase of Cassirer's thought, and ultimately gives way to his ethically charged conception of philosophy.

point of view'				ethics					
function'				culture / symbolic consciousness					
point of view	myth	language		art	religion		science		politics
function	space		time		number		causality		self
variables	x	x	x	x	x	x	x	x	x	x

Figure 3 Ethics as highest viewpoint

9 Heidegger's Hermeneutic Conception of Philosophy

In previous chapters I have demonstrated a structural parallel between Heidegger's interpretation of Kant's philosophy and his view of the human condition: in Heidegger's view, Kant is best understood as a (semi-) ontological, phenomenological, and hermeneutical thinker and human Dasein is a fundamentally (proto-)ontological, phenomenological, and hermeneutical being. In order to further explain how and why Heidegger's early interest in Kant and Dasein relate to each other, we need to consider how they relate to the primary interest of his philosophical project: the retrieval (*Wiederholung*) of the question of being. This relation, as we will see, is grounded in Heidegger's hermeneutic conception of philosophy.

9.1   The Three Interrelated Projects of Heidegger's Early Thought

9.1.1   *The Interdependence of the Retrieval of Being, the Destruction of History, and the Analytic of Dasein*

Heidegger's philosophy fundamentally rests on the assumption that there is a crucial difference between beings and their being, and that the meaning of the latter cannot be simply deduced from the former. While being*s* are the entities with which we are ordinarily acquainted, the term 'being' refers to their so-called essence, or 'that which determines beings as beings' (*BT* 6). Heidegger however holds that both the Western history of metaphysics and our everyday discourse mostly fail to adequately acknowledge this difference. He distinguishes between a pre-Socratic era that possessed a sensitivity for the meaning of being, on the one hand, and the majority of the philosophical tradition that is characterized by a 'forgetfulness of being' (*Seinsvergessenheit*), on the other hand. While Plato and Aristotle were at least still 'perplexed' (*verlegen*) about our poor grasp of the meaning of being, later philosophers focused exclusively on being*s* and remained 'mute' (*stumm*) with regard to the problem of being (1–2). Heidegger further notices that this philosophical forgetfulness of being has also affected our everyday understanding of the word 'being'. Rather than considering it as a most intriguing concept, we generally take its universal applicability and seemingly indefinable character as a sign of its empty meaning. All significant meaning resides, then, in the realm of particular beings (3–4). *Being and Time* therefore commences with the claim that the question of being "has today been forgotten – although our time considers itself progressive in again affirming 'metaphysics'" (2). Accordingly, Heidegger's thought aims to retrieve not just a genuine understanding of the meaning of being, but first of all the proper way to even just ask about it (4, 38–39). This is the reason why Heidegger denounces many key traditional concepts (e.g. subjectivity) and replaces them with neologisms (e.g. being-in-the-world), and why he proposes a novel philosophical methodology in the form of existential and hermeneutic phenomenology.

In response to the forgetfulness of being in both our ordinary and our philosophical thinking, Heidegger suggests two ways to retrieve the question of being. The first way, which is the topic of *Being and Time*, consists in developing an 'existential analytic of Dasein' that reaffirms the human being's fundamental openness towards being through an analysis of its worldly, caring, and ultimately temporal character. The second way consists in undertaking "a phenomenological destruction of the history of ontology" (39), a task that Heidegger takes up in his subsequent lectures and writings. However, in the introduction to *Being and Time* he already sketches the general outline of both endeavours, asserting the motivation for and the contours of his analysis of Dasein and reading of Kant. Here we can distinguish three ways in which Heidegger's three projects – the recovery of the *Seinsfrage*, the analysis of Dasein, and the reinterpretation of Kant's thought – relate to each other.

First, Heidegger's interest in the meaning of being, on the one hand, and his concern about the history of ontology and constitution of Dasein, on the other hand, are mutually dependent. He clearly states that his interest in Dasein's existential constitution, for which he is probably most famous, is in fact *subordinate* to his quest to retrieve the meaning of being as such. In *Being and Time*, he holds that "the analytic of Dasein is wholly oriented towards the guiding task of working out the question of being", such that "its limits are thereby determined".[1] During the 1929 Davos debate, Heidegger further identifies the question 'What in general is called being?' as the ultimate goal

---

[1] *BT* 17, 183, 436. In *Being and Time*, Heidegger however keeps to his 'preliminary investigation' of Dasein's constitution and must conclude in the end that he has not even begun to pose the ultimate question of the meaning of being (436–437). Moreover, he wonders whether his existential approach (the 'one way') to this question has not proven inadequate for its ultimate task, as it offers no way to ultimately get around Dasein's understanding of being to being itself. This will lead Heidegger to make a 'turn' (*die Kehre*) in his thought: from the 1930s on, he approaches the question of being from new angles that are less conditioned by its interrogator, namely through art and poetry (e.g. in *The Origin of the Work of Art*, 1935–1936) and the idea of a 'history of being' (see Heidegger's texts on *Seynsgeschichte* from 1937 until 1941).

of his philosophy, and reminds the audience that "it was from this question that the problematic of a metaphysics of Dasein arose" (*DD* 288). As such, the 'analytic' (1927) or 'metaphysics of Dasein' (1929) nevertheless occupies an important role in Heidegger's thought. As he sees it, an investigation of this being will *enable* us to once again formulate the question of being as such: "Dasein reveals itself to be that being which must first be elaborated in a sufficiently ontological manner if the inquiry [into being as such] is to become a lucid one" (*BT* 14). On this basis, Heidegger concludes that "the first concern in the question of being must be an analysis of Dasein" (16, 41).

Likewise, Heidegger on the one hand states that the 'phenomenological destruction' performs a *preliminary* task in light of his ultimate interest in regaining a thematic understanding of the meaning of being: "The destruction of the traditional content of ancient ontology [...] is to be carried out along the *guidelines of the question of being*. This destruction is based upon the original experiences in which the first and subsequently guiding determinations were gained" (22, 23). Heidegger's investigation into the history of philosophy thus derives its orientation entirely from the question of the meaning of being, which he, after all, considers "the fundamental question of philosophy in general".[2] On the other hand, the revision of the philosophical tradition is nevertheless an essential component of Heidegger's thought. In order to return from our current state of ignorance about the meaning of being to at least the state of perplexity, we *must* revisit the tradition that has obscured our original understanding of being: "The question of being attains true concreteness only when we carry out the destruction of the ontological tradition. By so doing we can prove the inescapability of the question of the meaning of being and thus demonstrate what it means to talk about a 'revival' of this question." (26). Heidegger therefore plans to revert through the crucial stages of the 'history of *Seinsvergessenheit*', which he finds in the thought of Kant, Descartes, and Aristotle, in order to regain our sensitivity for the meaning of being.[3]

Second, both Heidegger's existential analytic and destruction of the history of ontology ultimately have "a positive intent" (23). Besides positively aiming to retrieve the meaning of being, these 'preliminary tasks' also have a constructive purpose in their own regard. *Being and Time* of course challenges the common understanding of the human being as a rational subject, of other beings as 'present-at-hand' objects, of truth as correctness, of our world as a

---

[2] *BT* 27, 5; *PIK* 37; *WT* 64.

[3] After the publication of *Being and Time*, Heidegger first focused on Kant (1927–1930), and then recuperated his reading of Aristotle from the early 1920s in the framework of his phenomenological destruction (1931, 1939). He, however, never carried out his planned destruction of Descartes' thought, apart from the brief comments on *BT* 24–25. I will focus on Heidegger's Kant interpretation and consider it as representative for his destruction of the history of philosophy as such.

sum total of beings, and of time as the chronological succession of events. Furthermore, this critique addresses not just our natural lack of insight in the true ontological status of both ourselves and other beings but also our limited capacity to overcome this flawed understanding: according to Heidegger, Dasein's awareness of its prevalent disownedness does not automatically result in a resolve for ownedness. Yet, limited as these chances may be, Heidegger's phenomenological analysis of Dasein still has the positive aim to free us for our utmost possibility, our bare *Sein-können*. While preparing the retrieval of the meaning of being as such, *Being and Time* thus also positively reveals the fundamental nature of the human condition.

In a similar fashion, Heidegger does not believe that the recovery of our access to being is accomplished by merely thrusting aside all traditional ontology. His 'phenomenological destruction' rather tries to highlight those moments in the history of philosophy at which the question of being resurfaced: "The destruction has just as little the negative sense of disburdening ourselves of the ontological tradition. On the contrary, it should stake out the positive possibilities in that tradition".[4] Heidegger identifies Kant's doctrines of the schematism and time, Descartes' ontological foundation of the *res cogitans*, and Aristotle's conception of time as such pivotal moments in the history of philosophy (23–26, 40). Since he never elaborated on Descartes' thought in later works, it remains unclear how the latter positively contributes to the quest for the meaning of being. Heidegger's interest in Kant and Aristotle's accounts of time, on the other hand, is rather evident if we keep in mind the central claim of *Being and Time*, namely that time constitutes the 'horizon' that first allows us to properly ask about the meaning of being.[5] The 'positive possibilities' of Aristotle and Kant's thought lie, then, in the insight

---

[4] *BT* 22; see also Martin Heidegger, *What is Philosophy?*, tr. by William Kluback, and Jean T. Wilde, New York: Twayne Publishers, 1958, 33–34/71–73. Michael Gelven therefore holds that "far from having no respect for the history of philosophy, [Heidegger] honors it as few thinkers have ever done". Rather than approaching thinkers such as Aristotle and Kant as a historian of philosophy, threating their thought like "a dead display of obsolete opinions", Heidegger engages with them for the sake of a genuine philosophical interest and even inscribes them into a profound philosophical investigation (*A Commentary on Heidegger's 'Being and Time'*, Dekalb: Northern Illinois University Press, 1989, 36–37). Stephen Mulhall concludes that for Heidegger "there can be no fundamental ontology without the history of fundamental ontology, [and] no philosophy without the history of philosophy" (*Heidegger and 'Being and Time'*, New York: Routledge, 2005, 22). Heidegger confirms this when he explains that "the history of philosophy is not an arbitrary appendage to the business of teaching philosophy, which provides an occasion for picking up some convenient and easy theme for passing an examination or even for just looking around to see how things were in earlier times. Rather, historical-philosophical knowledge is one and the same thing" (*BPP* 31–32).

[5] *BT* 1, 19. 'Part one' of *Being and Time*, which in fact constitutes the entire published book, is accordingly titled 'The Interpretation of Dasein in Terms of Temporality and the Explication of Time as the Transcendental Horizon of the Question of Being'. The destruction of the history of ontology is also most directly guided by and directed towards the problem of temporality (39).

of these thinkers into the original meaning of time.[6] Accordingly, the positive task of the phenomenological destruction of Aristotle and Kant's writings lies in wresting their insight into this issue from the traditional discourse that prevented its ontological significance from being noticed, not only by their interpreters but often also by themselves.[7]

Third, Heidegger's two ways to retrieve the question of being also mutually rely on each other. On the one hand, Heidegger's destruction of the history of ontology seems to depend on the findings of his existential analytic of Dasein. As I just explained, each of these preliminary tasks consists in discrediting a then widespread rationalistic view. The phenomenological analysis of *Being and Time* repudiates the traditional definition of the human being as an *animal rationale* in favour of an account of Dasein as fundamentally characterized by care and temporality. The destruction of the history of ontology in turn replaces the belief in a progressive development of thought by the idea of a gradual fall into forgetfulness of its original concern. The resources for these revisionary ideas are however quite different: while the existential analytic relies on phenomenological insights into the structure of our daily life experiences, Heidegger's destruction consists of a meticulous reading of philosophical texts that not only challenges the canonical understanding of Aristotle and Kant's thought, but also their own self-understanding. As such, this destruction would have little convincing power if it were not supported by Heidegger's original accounts of Dasein and time from 1927. It is no coincidence, therefore, that the existential analytic precedes the phenomenological destruction of the history of ontology in the outline and execution of Heidegger's project.

On the other hand, Heidegger states that his analytic of Dasein remains incomplete if we do not take into account the historical ways in which Dasein has understood itself in the past:

If the answer to the question of being thus becomes the guiding directive for research, then it is sufficiently given only if the specific mode of being of previous ontology – the fate of its questioning, its findings, and its failures – becomes visible as necessarily belonging to the very character of Dasein. (19)

---

[6] Before arguing for the essentially temporal character of Kant's conception of transcendental apperception in *Phenomenological Interpretation*, Heidegger holds that "the following discussion [serves] the general and broader purpose of demonstrating to you the exemplary character of Kant's philosophizing, which – disregarding its content – is contrary to today's increasingly widespread barbarism" (*PIK* 387).

[7] With regard to Kant, as we have seen, Heidegger thus rejects both the idealist and – especially – the Neo-Kantian interpretation of the *Critique of Pure Reason*, and to a certain extent also Kant's own understanding of his transcendental project: "We are for Kant against Kantianism. And we are for Kant only in order to give him the possibility to live with us anew in a lively debate" (*PIK* 279).

In Division One of *Being and Time*, Heidegger presents Dasein as a being that always already understands itself in a particular way, and in Division Two he argues that it is a fundamentally temporal and thus historical being. Hence, historical self-understanding is constitutive of Dasein's very being: "This being is in itself 'historical', so that its most proper ontological illumination necessarily becomes a 'historical' interpretation" (39). In this sense, the complete execution of the analytic of Dasein also relies on the results of the destruction of the history of ontology.[8]

9.1.2   Ontology, Phenomenology, and Hermeneutics

Heidegger's early thought thus entertains three key questions – concerning being as such, the human being, and the history of ontology – that are essentially and mutually related. Heidegger formally confirms this interconnection in § 7 of *Being and Time*, where he describes his philosophical enterprise as a phenomenological ontology that requires hermeneutics for its execution:

Philosophy is universal phenomenological ontology, taking its departure from the hermeneutics of Dasein, which, as an analysis of *existence*, has fastened the end of the guideline of all philosophical inquiry at the point from which it *arises* and to which it *returns*. (*BT* 38, 436)

In an analogous way, Heidegger's 1927 seminar *The Basic Problems of Phenomenology* discerns three inseparable moments of the phenomenological method: phenomenological reduction, phenomenological construction, and phenomenological destruction (*BPP* 27–32). These passages are worth discussing here because they explain how the relations between the three tasks of Heidegger's early thought are methodologically grounded in his threefold conception of philosophy.

First, Heidegger establishes a relation of mutual dependence between ontology and phenomenology. As mentioned earlier, he sharply distinguishes between being and beings, and declares his prime interest in the meaning of the former: "The task of ontology is to set in relief the being of beings and to explicate being itself" (*BT* 27, 38). *Being and Time* thus opens with a chapter on 'the necessity, structure, and priority of the question of being'. Yet, Heidegger also holds that "being is always the being of a particular being" (9). For this reason, the retrieval of being *calls for* a phenomenological

---

[8] *BT* 20–21, 6. See Gelven, *A Commentary on Heidegger's 'Being and Time'*, 37: "The *ways* in which past philosophers have implicitly dealt with the question of being have affected our own understanding of it, and are hence a legitimate part of the inquiry as to how Dasein understands its own being. Part of Dasein's being is its history (i.e., part of what it means for Dasein to be is to be in history), and this history affects Dasein's understanding of itself".

investigation of certain being*s*. Heidegger explains that phenomenology differs from disciplines like theology or biology because it indicates a methodology (*Methodenbegriff*; 34–35; *BPP* 27). As the term 'phenomenology' indicates, *what* this method considers are phenomena broadly conceived: anything that 'shows itself' or is 'manifest' (*BT* 28). The *how* of this consideration is a purely descriptive approach: "Science 'of' the phenomena means that it grasps its objects in such a way that everything about them to be discussed must be directly indicated and directly demonstrated" (35). Hence, in Heidegger's view the task of phenomenology is "to let what shows itself be seen from itself, just as it shows itself from itself" (34).

According to this formal task, which Heidegger takes from Husserl, phenomenology is useful with regard to all phenomena that are, for various reasons, "initially and for the most part not given" (36). However, Heidegger also considers phenomenology a necessary approach, indicating *its profound philosophical task*, with regard to a certain type of phenomena in particular: "The necessary theme of an explicit determination is something that is concealed but at the same time essentially belongs to what initially and for the most part shows itself, indeed in such a way that it constitutes its meaning and ground."[9] If Heidegger in this way intensifies the focus of phenomenology after all, his criterion is still not the content, but the *way* that certain phenomena appear: the "phenomenon in a distinctive sense" is not, for example, the mathematical or theological object, but it is the constitutive and yet naturally and predominantly elusive moment of all our appearances.

What is at stake here becomes clear when Heidegger subsequently equates the 'essential relation between that which initially and for the most part shows itself and that which does not' with the ontological difference:

What remains *concealed* in an exceptional sense, or what falls back and is *covered up* again, or shows itself only in a '*disguised*' way, is not this or that being but rather [. . .] the being of beings. It can be covered up to such a degree that it is forgotten and the question about it and its meaning altogether omitted. [. . .] The phenomenological concept of phenomenon, as self-showing, means the *being* of beings – its meanings, modifications, and derivatives. (35)

In *The Basic Problems of Phenomenology*, Heidegger reinterprets Husserl's crucial idea of a 'phenomenological reduction' in a similar way: on his account, this reduction "leads phenomenological vision back from the apprehension of a being, whatever may be the character of that apprehension, to the understanding of the being of this being" (*BPP* 29). Heidegger here affirms that we require this 'guidance of vision' because "being does not become

---

[9] *BT* 35; my translation.

accessible to us like a being. We do not simply find it in front of us [...] but it must always be brought to view" (29; *BT* 36).

On this basis, Heidegger concludes that, "as far as content goes, phenomenology is the science of the being of beings – ontology" (37). Conversely, "phenomenology is the way of access to [...] that which is to become the theme of ontology. *Ontology is possible only as phenomenology*" (35). Taken as the titles for the respective object and procedure of philosophy, ontology and phenomenology are thus for Heidegger essentially bound up with each other (38; *BPP* 28). In this way, he methodologically justifies his strategy to approach the question of the meaning of being through a phenomenological analysis of Dasein and a phenomenological destruction of the history of philosophy.

Second, in *The Basic Problems of Phenomenology*, Heidegger describes his phenomenological ontology as a "reductive construction" (31). The central component of the phenomenological method, he here holds, is the phenomenological construction through which "we positively approach being" (29): this positive aim alone lends the phenomenological reduction guidance and meaning. Heidegger's 'phenomenological ontology' shares in the positive intent of "indicating being*s* as they show themselves in themselves" (*BT* 35). In *Being and Time*, he expresses this intention by adopting Husserl's famous adagio 'To the things themselves!' (27, 34) as the slogan of ontology.

Third, Heidegger explains that his phenomenological ontology is to be executed in a hermeneutical fashion: he holds that "the methodological meaning of phenomenological description is *interpretation (Auslegung)*", and that "hermeneutics in the original signification of that word [...] designates the work of interpretation" (37). But how, one may wonder, can Heidegger's method for approaching the being of beings be both descriptive and interpretive? How, in other words, can his philosophical enterprise combine phenomenology and hermeneutics?

The answer to this question can be found in Heidegger's original conception of interpretation. In § 32 of *Being and Time*, he defines interpreting as 'making explicit' (*ausdrücken*) or 'elaborate' (*ausarbeiten*) what we already implicitly and vaguely understand. Rather than adding meaning to an initially meaningless phenomenon, interpretation articulates "something that is understood but still veiled" (150, 152). The attempt to interpret a philosophical text, for example, only makes sense if we assume that this text itself contains a certain meaning *and* that we already understand it to some extent – it would be impossible for anyone to interpret a text written in a language that they do not recognize at all, or for someone without any philosophical training to interpret *Being and Time*. There is, then, for Heidegger no contradiction between phenomenologically describing beings and hermeneutically interpreting them: both approaches aim to bring out the inherent meaning of things; they articulate what shows itself implicitly.

The title 'hermeneutics' does, however, specify the way in which phenomenology can uncover the being of beings: while phenomenology avoids "all non-demonstrative determinations" (35) and focuses on that which needs to be unconcealed, namely being, hermeneutics thematizes the context within which this can be done, namely our current understanding of being and beings. According to Heidegger, "interpretation is never a presuppositionless apprehending of something presented to us" (150). Instead, it relies on a 'fore-having' (*Vorhabe*) or a pre-given understanding of a "totality of relevance", a 'fore-sight' (*Vorsicht*) or an anticipatory direction of inquiry, and a 'fore-conception' (*Vorgriff*) or a preliminary conception of what is to be interpreted. As a whole, this 'fore-structure' (*Vorstruktur*) or 'hermeneutical situation' (232) constitutes the horizon within which we can first approach the object of our inquiry. We can indeed only interpret a philosophical text if we already have a sense of the context and purpose for which it was written – for example, whether *Being and Time* was meant as an anthropological, ethical, or onto-logical treatise. We further always approach this text with a certain interest that will guide our interpretation – academics scientists narrow down this interest to a research question or hypothesis. Finally, in order to interpret our text we must already be familiar with at least some of the philosophical concepts that are used in it – Heidegger's novel notions of 'world', 'mood', 'care', 'death', etc., become intelligible by contrasting *and relating* them (as *Being and Time* carefully does) to our common understanding of these terms. The first task of hermeneutics is therefore to attune our 'fore-structure' to the object of our actual investigation – the text – so that we approach it in a manner that can do justice to its being – its message: "The first, constant, and last task [of interpretation] is not to let fore-having, fore-sight, and fore-conception be given to it by chance ideas and popular conceptions, but to secure the scientific theme by developing them in terms of the things themselves."[10] Our interpret-ation may then confirm, enrich, or significantly correct our previous under-standing, but the important point for Heidegger is that we can never produce it out of thin air.

In *The Basic Problems of Phenomenology*, Heidegger confirms that philo-sophical understanding is "always determined by the factual experience of beings and the range of possibilities of experience that at any time are peculiar to a factical Dasein, and hence to the historical situation of a philosophical investigation" (*BPP* 30). Therefore, the 'reductive construction' of the mean-ing of being requires a phenomenological destruction of metaphysics' current and past understanding of beings: "Construction in philosophy is necessarily destruction, that is to say, a de-constructing of traditional concepts carried out

---

[10] *BT* 153, 303; *HF* 80.

in a historical recursion to the tradition" (31). Such destruction stakes out the limits of traditional ontology by setting aside the theories that have covered up our pre-ontological understanding of the meaning of being (*BT* 22, 67). Once again, however, Heidegger emphasizes that this endeavour signifies "a positive appropriation of the tradition" that traces back its concepts "down to the sources from which they were drawn" (*BPP* 31).

9.1.3   The Hermeneutic Set-Up of Heidegger's Philosophy

Heidegger's hermeneutic approach is arguably the most distinct trademark of his early thinking: it sets up his analytic of Dasein and destruction of the history of philosophy for the rediscovery of the question of being, and it productively relates these two preliminary tasks to each other.

In § 2 of *Being and Time*, 'The Formal Structure of the Question of Being', Heidegger claims that every question contains three moments: what is asked (*das Gefragte*), what is interrogated (*das Befragte*), and what is to be ascertained (*das Erfragte*; 5). In the case of Heidegger's own core question, these moments correspond to the difference between being, being*s*, and the meaning of being (6) – or, we can now add, to that between ontology, phenomenology, and hermeneutics. We have indeed seen that, in Heidegger's view, being "is always the being of a particular being" (9) and, more specifically, "essentially belongs to, and constitutes the meaning and ground of [. . .] beings (35). For this reason, he holds that "beings themselves turn out to be what is interrogated in the question of being" (6), and that "we must first of all bring beings themselves forward in the right way if we are to have any prospect of exposing being" (37, 67). Hence, for Heidegger, asking about the meaning of being always involves interrogating being*s*, and the first task of philosophy consists in carefully selecting the right being(s) and assuring "that the right access to beings is gained and secured in advance with regard to what it interrogates" (6).

The first question that *Being and Time* aims to answer is, therefore, the following: "In which being is the meaning of being to be found, from which being is the disclosure of being to get its start? [. . .] What is this exemplary being, and in what sense does it have priority?" (7). Heidegger's answer is, of course, Dasein: "Dasein has proven itself to be that which, before all other beings, is ontologically the primary being to be interrogated" (13, 14, 42). Therefore, "the access to this being becomes the first problem" of his ontological investigation (16, 200). The true task of the analytic of Dasein is, then, to determine this being's everyday fore-conception, fore-having, and fore-sight with regard to being as such. *Being and Time* situates these moments of Dasein's fore-structure in its respective pre-ontological understanding of being, its being-in-the-world, and its care for being.

However, if Dasein's understanding of beings and their being is always handed down to us by tradition, asking about the meaning of being must also involve an interrogation of our traditional understanding thereof (20–21). Accordingly, the true task of Heidegger's writings on Kant and Aristotle is to critically assess the fore-structure of *their* way of questioning the meaning of being. Heidegger finds Kant's philosophical fore-conception, fore-having, and fore-sight of being in his conception of the a priori, his account of transcendental knowledge, and his 'oscillating' between the critical and pre-critical approaches to the problem of metaphysics, respectively.

If Heidegger rightly assumes that Dasein's existential constitution and Kant's philosophical writings harbour a privileged understanding of the meaning of being, then the fore-structure of Kant's philosophical should run parallel to Dasein's everyday understanding of being. Concretely, there should be an affinity between their respective fore-conception of being, namely Dasein's pre-ontological understanding and Kant's conception of the a priori; between their respective fore-having of being: Dasein's being-in-the-world and Kant's critical conception of transcendental knowledge; and between their respective fore-sight towards the meaning of being, that is, between Dasein's care for being and Kant's concern about the fate of metaphysics. In order to confirm this, we must return to the main body of *Being and Time* and to Heidegger's writings on Kant, where Heidegger unfolds his hermeneutic-phenomenological interpretations of Dasein's existence and the first *Critique*.

Fore-structure *Seinsfrage*	Dasein's existence	Kant's critique of pure reason
fore-conception of being	pre-ontological understanding of being (*BT* §15, 16, 18)	the concept of the a priori (introduction *PIK, KPM, WT*)
fore-having of beings	being-in-the-world (§29-31)	the account of transcendental knowledge (body *PIK, KPM, WT*)
fore-sight towards meaning	care for being (§39-42)	the problem of metaphysics (conclusion *KPM*)

Figure 4 Dasein's natural and Kant's philosophical fore-structure to the question of being

9.2   Heidegger's Hermeneutic-Phenomenological Approach to Kant and Dasein

Heidegger thus revisits both the human condition and Kant's thought in function of his own interest in the meaning of being. In his view, it lies in their essential structure that they possess an adequate hermeneutical situation for asking the question of being. However, these interpretations of the *Critique of Pure Reason* and the existential constitution of Dasein, of course, rely on Heidegger's own hermeneutical situation.[11] Hence, his idea of the task and method of philosophy in turn informs his forceful approach to Dasein's existence and his 'violent' interpretation of Kant's thought.

9.2.1 A 'Violent' Interpretation of Kant's Thought

Heidegger's remarks on the 'phenomenological destruction of the history of ontology' in the introduction to *Being and Time* imply that his reading of Kant constitutes an essential and positive element of his own philosophical project. Yet, the full depth of Heidegger's affinity with Kant's thought only becomes clear during the following years, when he executes this destruction in especially *Phenomenological Interpretation of Kant's Critique of Pure Reason* (1927–1928), *Kant and the Problem of Metaphysics* (1929), and *What Is a Thing?* (1935–1936). As I have demonstrated, Heidegger in these works argues that the three moments of his own philosophical project – ontology, phenomenology, hermeneutics – also directed Kant's undertaking in the first *Critique*. First, in the introduction to each of his writings on Kant, Heidegger praises Kant for 'conceiving anew the concept of ontology' in the form of transcendental philosophy. Second, in the main body of these works, he argues that Kant does so by employing the phenomenological method in the form of critical philosophy. Third, in *Kant and the Problem of Metaphysics*, Heidegger calls Kant's overt struggle with his hermeneutical situation the true accomplishment of the *Critique of Pure Reason*.

Because my earlier analysis of Heidegger's Kant interpretation focused on its inner coherence, its most controversial aspect remained undiscussed: the at times 'violent' way in which Heidegger appropriated Kant's thought.[12] I will now address the nature of this 'interpretative violence'. In other words, after considering Heidegger's reading of Kant *as* a hermeneutic-phenomenological

---

[11] Heidegger is well aware that his own interpretations of both our ordinary and Kant and Aristotle's philosophical understanding of being are themselves also coloured by a hermeneutical situation (*BPP* 31). He, thus, rejects the idea of philosophy as a detached reflection on the way that things are: philosophers are as incapable of escaping their historical context as any other interpreter.

[12] Heidegger's interpretation of Kant is commonly labelled as an 'appropriation' of the latter's thought (William Blattner, 'Laying the ground for metaphysics: Heidegger's appropriation of Kant', in: *The Cambridge Companion to Heidegger*, 149–176; Han-Pile, 'Early Heidegger's Appropriation of Kant'; and Elliott, 'Heidegger's appropriation of Kant'). Given the evident inaccuracy of Heidegger's Kant interpretation that has been displayed by these commentators, I deem it more relevant to consider its philosophical motives than to define its precise interpretative limitations.

thinker, I now present this reading as a hermeneutic-phenomenological approach *to* Kant's writings. This means that I will still not assess the accuracy of Heidegger's reading of the first *Critique* from a Kantian point of view. Instead, I continue to stick to the Heideggerean perspective and focus on the way in which this reading is influenced by his overall view of the procedure of philosophy.

It should be clear, first of all, that the designation of Heidegger's Kant interpretation – and of his approach to the history of philosophy at large – as 'violent', was not primarily a critique uttered by his opponents or later commentators, but rather a way for Heidegger himself to describe and defend his own approach. Throughout his writings on Kant, Heidegger not only evaluates Kant's wavering insight into the accomplishments of the *Critique of Pure Reason* (as well as the complete misunderstanding of this work by the Neo-Kantians), but he also repeatedly reflects on the status of his own interpretation. On these occasions, Heidegger discusses the phenomenological and hermeneutic nature of his reading of Kant.

As we have seen, Heidegger describes the *phenomenological* approach as the "explicit determination [of] something that is concealed but at the same time essentially belongs to what initially and for the most part shows itself, in such a way that it constitutes its meaning and ground".[13] In general, phenomenology thus aims to thematize the constitutive but essentially elusive moment of our experiences. Accordingly, a phenomenological reading of a text entails that one aims to retrieve its hidden, essential, 'message': the idea that guides the entire text even though it may never be explicitly expressed. Hence, in *Phenomenological Interpretation* Heidegger distinguishes between a 'factual' (*sachliche*) and an 'essential (*wesentliche*) reading' of the first *Critique* (*PIK* 67). He identifies the epistemological interpretation of this work defended by the Neo-Kantians as an example of the former type of reading: sticking to 'the letter of the text', their reading is neither arbitrary nor false, but nevertheless misses Kant's true philosophical point. Heidegger takes his own ontological interpretation of Kant, on the other hand, to grasp the underlying intention that impels the first *Critique*:

> We must be able to see what Kant saw as he determined the problems, came up with a solution, and put it into the form of the work that we now have before us as the *Critique of Pure Reason*. It is of no use to *repeat* Kantian concepts and statements or to reformulate them. We must get so far that we speak these concepts and statements *with* Kant, from within and out of the same perspective. (5)

Only on this basis, Heidegger adds, can we discern 'the concept and method' of Kant's philosophy (6). He thus insists that "the only way that we could and

---

[13] *BT* 35; my translation.

should approach Kant" is not by dwelling on his words, but "by coming philosophically to terms with him [...] according to his own challenge".[14]

Heidegger, however, not only claims that his reading of the first *Critique* is more insightful than other interpretations of this work, but even questions Kant's own understanding thereof, suggesting that the true 'challenge' of this text was not, or at least not always, clear to the author himself.[15] In this way, the distinction between what Kant literally wrote and what he actually wanted to say, gives way to the distinction between what he wrote and what he, according to Heidegger, *should* have written.[16] In the preface to *Phenomenological Interpretation*, Heidegger openly declares that he will attempt to "understand Kant better than he understood himself [...] by concentrating on what Kant wanted to say, that is, by not stopping at his descriptions but going back to the foundations of what he meant".[17] When discussing the pure synthesis of the imagination, he further holds that "we must relentlessly strive more than ever for what Kant wanted to say – or for what Kant should have said" (*PIK* 338, 359). Heidegger's phenomenological reading is, then, ultimately not interested in Kant per se, but rather in the philosophical insights that allegedly propelled his thought. The philosopher Kant is, in other words, approached as the vehicle for a philosophical problem: "It is important that in coming to terms with Kant, we strive to bring *things themselves* to light – or at least to put into a new ambiguity *the problems* that Kant has elucidated".[18] This preconceived interest permits Heidegger to consider the A-edition of the first *Critique* as "more genuine and more radical" (216) and "remaining closer to the innermost thrust of the problematic of laying the ground for metaphysics" (*KPM* 197) than the B-edition, thus countering the intuitive idea that a revised edition of a text better reflects the author's intentions. It also allows Heidegger to positively evaluate Kant's alleged wavering with regard to the foundation of metaphysics, thus rejecting the common appreciation of consistency and systematicity in a philosophical text (*PIK* 68, 216–217).

In addition to following the phenomenological method, Heidegger's reading of the first *Critique* is also a *hermeneutic* one. As explained earlier, according to Heidegger any interpretation necessarily relies on a number of constructive presuppositions: a particular interest that guides the interpretation (fore-sight), a preliminary conception of the object or topic at stake (fore-conception), and a

---

[14] *PIK* 74, 2; Heidegger, *The Essence of Human Freedom*, tr. by Ted Sadler, London/New York: Continuum, 2002, 200.

[15] In his 'Preliminary Considerations' to *Phenomenological Interpretation*, Heidegger argues that such an unearthing reading finds support in two passages from the *Critique of Pure Reason* (*PIK* 2–3), a reference to Plato in the Transcendental Analytic (*CPR* A314/B370) and a comment on scientific research in the Transcendental Method (A834/B862).

[16] Consult Heidegger's 1938 *Contributions to Philosophy (of the Event)*, tr. by Richard Rojcewicz and Daniela Vallega-Neu, in: *Studies in Continental Thought*, Bloomington: Indiana University Press, 2012, 253; and *Logic* 335–336.

[17] *PIK* 3; translation modified.   [18] *PIK* 75; my emphasis.

sense of the context within which the interpretation occurs (fore-having). Heidegger's own interpretation of Kant forms no exception to this: it self-consciously relies on the parameters that were set out by his conception of philosophy in *Being and Time*. In fact, we must even distinguish between two hermeneutical situations that inform Heidegger's reading of the first *Critique*: the fore-structure that he developed in the introduction to *Being and Time*, namely the search for the meaning of being, and the one that he develops in the core of this work, that is, the phenomenological analysis of Dasein.

As we have established, Heidegger revisits the *Critique of Pure Reason* in order to retrieve our lost sense of the meaning of being, which he deems the essential task of philosophy. As a consequence, his reading of Kant is based on his own interest in the meaning of being (fore-sight), his conception of philosophy as 'phenomenological ontology' (fore-conception), and his view of the history of metaphysics as one of *Seinsvergessenheit* (fore-having). In a 1973 preface to *Kant and the Problem of Metaphysics*, Heidegger admits that "the manner of questioning from *Being and Time* came into play as an anticipation of my attempted interpretation of Kant. Kant's text became a refuge, as I sought in Kant an advocate for the question of being that I posed" (*KPM* xvii–xviii). This is confirmed by the opening statement of this work, which establishes that the Kant book is "devoted to the task of interpreting Kant's *Critique of Pure Reason* as laying the ground for metaphysics and thus of placing the problem of metaphysics before us as a fundamental ontology".[19] The way in which Heidegger seeks to achieve this task is, then, by wresting Kant's true understanding of the concept and method of philosophy from the traditional way in which he presents this insight in the first *Critique*.

To make matters even more complex, Heidegger's approach to the first *Critique* is also informed by the account of Dasein that he developed in *Being and Time*. Heidegger's existential analytic thus forms an additional 'fore-structure' for his reading of Kant, namely one that considers Dasein's pre-ontological understanding of being (fore-conception), being-in-the-world (fore-having)[20], and care (fore-sight) to constitute the most appropriate hermeneutical situation for interpreting the meaning of being (). In *Phenomenological Interpretation*, Heidegger prefaces his actual analysis of the Transcendental Aesthetic and Analytic by a reflection on 'the horizon of inquiry' (*Fragehorizont*) of the *Critique of Pure Reason* (*PIK* § 4). In this paragraph, he holds that "*the general horizon of the problematic of the Critique* is, according to our interpretation, *human Dasein with respect to its understanding of being*".[21] Towards the end of this work, Heidegger again asserts that

---

[19] *KPM* 1; translation modified.   [20] See *HF* 80.
[21] *PIK* 69–70; see also *KPM* 205, 208, 213, 218.

it was only on the basis of [*Being and Time*] that the possibility arose for me to understand what Kant is actually seeking, respectively must seek. Only from out of that investigation can we grasp the unity of receptivity and spontaneity, of time and the transcendental apperception, as a possible problem.[22]

In sum, Heidegger's reading of Kant deliberately takes directions from his own thought in order to 'understand Kant better than he understood himself'. Heidegger admits that this approach entails a certain interpretative violence:

> Certainly, in order to wring from words what it is they want to say, every interpretation must necessarily use violence. Such violence, however, cannot be roving arbitrariness. The power of an idea that shines forth must drive and guide the laying-out. Only in the power of this idea can an interpretation risk what is always audacious, namely, entrusting itself to the concealed inner passion of a work in order to be able, through this, to place itself within the unsaid and force it into speech. That is one way, however, by which the guiding idea, in its power to illuminate, comes to light. (*KPM* 202)

For Heidegger, such violence is not a flaw, but rather the essence of any true philosophical reading of a text: "'Understanding better' expresses the necessity of the philosophical struggle that goes on with every real interpretation" (*PIK* 4). Heidegger's interpretative violence is the immediate result of the historical destruction that he considers necessary for the retrieval of the meaning of being, and thus follows directly from his conception of philosophy. We must keep in mind, moreover, that the goal of this violence is not to thrust aside Kant's philosophy altogether. On the contrary: Heidegger's "progressive interpretation" (*KPM* xix) positively aims to reveal Kant's contribution to the retrieval of the problem of metaphysics. Finally, as Heidegger clearly indicates, such a revelation is only possible when there is indeed something that can and must be retrieved, when there is indeed an idea that shines forth from itself yet requires guidance in order to come to light (*PIK* 4). This, however, means that Heidegger's phenomenological interpretation of Kant's thought ultimately relies on his assumption that, despite the flaws in Kant's execution, his intentions were indeed similar to Heidegger's own.

9.2.2   A Forceful Analysis of Dasein's Existential Constitution

Compared to his interpretation of the *Critique of Pure Reason*, Heidegger's analysis of Dasein is usually considered much less problematic. This assessment is, however, questionable in two regards. On the one hand, Heidegger's conception of the human being has been criticized by other thinkers who examined the human condition – his phenomenological disciples

---

[22] *PIK* 394. In *Kant and the Problem of Metaphysics*, Heidegger further holds that his interpretation of the *Critique of Pure Reason* "serves as a 'historical' introduction of sorts to clarify the problematic treated in the first half of *Being and* Time" (*KPM* xi) and that it "is oriented to fundamental ontology (245).

Merleau-Ponty and Levinas, close challengers like Scheler and Cassirer, and more analytic adversaries such as Carnap alike – at least as often and as rigorous as his reading of the first *Critique* has been dismissed by other Kant interpreters. On the other hand, if we stick to the internal coherence of Heidegger's early thought, his existential analytic is no less than his Kant interpretation coloured by his conception of philosophy, which serves as the hermeneutical situation for both 'preliminary tasks'. Hence, Heidegger also analyzes the existential constitution of Dasein in a phenomenological and hermeneutic way, relying on certain philosophical presuppositions in order to understand the human being better than it understands itself. As such, his existential analytic also "has the character of *doing violence*, whether for the claims of the everyday interpretation or for its complacency and its tranquilized obviousness" (*BT* 311).

As we have seen earlier, according to Heidegger Dasein stands apart from all other beings because it takes a natural interest in its own being. For this reason, he considers Dasein as "the ontologically primary being to be interrogated" (13), and takes its understanding of being as the basis for ontology. However, Dasein's ontological nature does not entail that we constantly or inevitably engage in theoretical reflections on the being of beings. In fact, our understanding of being remains mostly implicit and confused, and is therefore better termed a 'pre-ontological understanding of being' (12). In order to retrieve the meaning of being, the philosopher must therefore 'radicalize' Dasein's pre-ontological understanding, or render it into a thematic or ontological understanding of being.

Heidegger maintains that this radicalization must be enforced in a *phenomenological* manner for two reasons, namely because "an interpretation of [Dasein] is confronted with peculiar difficulties rooted in the mode of being of the thematic object *and* in the manner of thematization itself".[23] First, Heidegger dismisses the traditional 'manner of thematizing' the human being because it overlooks the fundamental difference between the being of this being and that of all other beings. Therefore, it can only display certain superficial characteristics (e.g. reason) but never penetrate into that which constitutes the true nature of Dasein (care). According to Heidegger, Dasein can after all not be understood as a thing, but only as a way of being: "The 'essence' of this being lies in its to be. The whatness (*essentia*) of this being must be understood in terms of its being (*existentia*) in so far as one can speak of it at all" (42). In order to uncover the true being of the human being, we must therefore show it in its actual comportment

---

[23] *BT* 16; my translation and emphasis. Heidegger therefore holds that "the correct presentation of [Dasein] is so little evident that its determination itself constitutes an essential part of the ontological analytic of this being" (43).

as it is *initially and for the most part – in its average everydayness*. Not arbitrary and accidental structures but essential ones are to be demonstrated in this everydayness, structures that remain determinative in every mode of being of factual Dasein. By looking at the fundamental constitution of the everydayness of Dasein we shall bring out [. . .] the being of this being. (16–17)

The "manner of access and interpretation" that in this way allows Dasein to "show itself to itself on its own terms" (16) is that of (existential) phenomenology. This approach thrusts aside all theoretical constructs and uncovers the everydayness of Dasein, or "the indifferent way in which it is initially and for the most part" (43).

Second, the task of a phenomenological thematization of the being of Dasein, however, proves even harder once Heidegger further explains the nature of its everyday 'mode of being'. Heidegger after all holds that, "as a being, Dasein always defines itself in terms of a possibility that it is" (43), and that Dasein "has the inclination to be entangled in the world in which it is and to interpret itself in terms of that world" (21, 15). The true nature of Dasein is, in other words, such that it tends to understand itself on the basis of its projects, thus facilitating a superficial characterization of itself in terms of ontic characteristics such as our social roles. This means that our everyday ontological understanding consists of an unthematic insight into being as such that harbours a continuously flawed – 'disowned' – understanding of our own being. As Heidegger famously holds, "Dasein is ontically 'nearest' to itself, yet ontologically farthest away" (16). Not only can Dasein's mode of being not be accurately captured by a traditional ontic characterization, *its own* ontological nature also actively resists a phenomenological thematization. The interrogation of Dasein's existential constitution for the sake of retrieving the meaning of being therefore cannot simply adopt "the most readily available pre-ontological interpretation of its being [. . .] as an adequate guideline" (15). Instead, we must wrest Dasein's 'true being' from the prevailing views on the human condition: the existential analytic needs to counter not only the traditional philosophical misconceptions of the human being, but most importantly the misguided *self*-understanding of Dasein that enables them. It must, in sum, find a way to 'understand Dasein better than it understands itself'.

In order to accomplish *this* task, Heidegger once again invokes the *hermeneutical* method:

The logos of the phenomenology of *Dasein* has the character of a *hermeneuein*, through which the proper meaning of being and the basic structures of the very being of Dasein are *made known* to the understanding of being that belongs to Dasein itself. Phenomenology of Dasein is *hermeneutics* in the original signification of that word, which designates the work of interpretation. (37–38)

A phenomenological interpretation of Dasein must, then, rely on a predetermined 'fore-structure', or an initial understanding of the thematic object that guides our actual interrogation. This is of course the case for Heidegger's analytic of Dasein, which is motivated by his interest in the meaning of being (fore-sight). Heidegger holds that "the possibility of carrying out the analysis of Dasein depends upon the prior elaboration of the question of the meaning of being in general" (13). Further, when he anticipates interpretative difficulties due to the common 'manner of thematization' and initial 'mode of being' of Dasein, his view on the human condition clearly also relies on his own 'phenomenological conception of the phenomenon' (fore-conception) and starts from his conviction that our age is marked by *Seinsvergessenheit* (fore-having). With regard to his preconception of being, early in *Being and Time* Heidegger claims that "the interpretation of the average understanding of being attains its necessary guideline only with the developed concept of being" (6). In the concluding paragraph, he reaffirms that "our *thematic* analytic of existence needs [...] the light from a previously clarified idea of being in general" (436). Concerning the relevant context of his existential analytic, finally, Heidegger explains that "the fact that we live already in an understanding of being and that the meaning of being is at the same time shrouded in darkness, proves the fundamental necessity of retrieving the question of the meaning of 'being'" (4).

Moreover, Heidegger's existential analytic undoubtedly borrows from the argumentative structure of Kant's *Critique of Pure Reason*. Although he only later explicitly characterizes Kant's thought as a promising attempt to establish the intimate relation between being and time – thus indicating the meaning of being – he had already studied it prior to writing *Being and Time*.[24] We may safely assume, therefore, that the later developed interpretation of Kant's 'transcendental analytic' in fact informed, and not merely followed, Heidegger's 'existential analytic'.[25] First, his account of Dasein's pre-ontological understanding of being (fore-conception) is inspired by Kant's notion of the a priori: as we have seen, Heidegger's magnum opus defines being by referring to Kant's conception of the a priori forms of intuition. Second, Heidegger's understanding of Dasein's being-in-the-world (fore-having) is a phenomenological reformulation of Kant's critical view of transcendental knowledge: his account of mood and understanding as the two moments of Dasein's 'being-in' operates as an existentialist alternative to Kant's dualism of receptivity and spontaneity. Third, Heidegger's

---

[24] Consult, in this regard, Theodore Kisiel's magnificent *The Genesis of Heidegger's 'Being and Time'*, Berkeley: University of California Press, 1995.

[25] Frank Schalow confirms this reciprocal influence when he holds that "Heidegger vacillates between the attempt to develop the implications which transcendental philosophy has for clarifying his own point of departure, and seeking in phenomenology the key to break Kant's thought of its tie to a narrowly epistemic mode" ('Thinking at Cross Purposes with Kant', 202).

understanding of Dasein's care for being (fore-sight) echoes Kant's assumption that there is a metaphysical interest inherent to reason.

On this basis, we can conclude that Heidegger's idea of the task and method of philosophy establishes the hermeneutical situation for his two 'preliminary investigations' *and* that, within this context, these investigations also inform each other. Heidegger's focus on Kant's attention to the a priori, critical conception of transcendental knowledge, and concern about the fate of metaphysics, and parallel to this on Dasein's pre-ontological understanding, being-in-the-world, and care for being, thus reflect his own interest in the meaning of being, conception of 'phenomenological ontology', and attempt to overcome an era of *Seinsvergessenheit*. These three guiding elements of Heidegger's early thought constitute the respective fore-sight, fore-conception, and fore-having of his interpretation of the *Critique of Pure Reason* and existential analytic.

9.3 The 'Seinsfrage' as the Radicalization of Dasein's Hermeneutical Situation

In the first section of this chapter, I explained why exactly Heidegger's analysis of Dasein and interpretation of Kant constitute essential moments in his attempt to retrieve the meaning of being: in his view, this ontological problem can only be approached in a phenomenological and hermeneutic manner. In the second section, I demonstrated how this twofold approach deliberately guides Heidegger's views of the human condition and Kant's thought in a particular direction, via a 'forceful' interpretative scheme that Heidegger considers both necessary and unavoidable. On this basis, we can now conclude that Heidegger's quest for the meaning of being takes the form of a circular investigation: in order to retrieve this meaning, Heidegger investigates Dasein's pre-ontological and Kant's philosophical understanding of being, but in order to grasp these understandings, he relies on a provisional conception of being.

Heidegger admits to this circular procedure on three occasions in *Being and Time*, but each time denies its problematic character.[26] His account of the hermeneutical situation after all explained that any successful interpretation presupposes a preliminary conception of what needs to be interpreted (fore-conception). A good interpreter therefore neither ignores nor denies the 'hermeneutical circle', but makes sure to accurately understand its nature. First, unlike a logical circle, which renders a deductive proof illegitimate, this circle does not begin and end at the same point. Instead, it leads us from a vague –

---

[26] *BT* 7–8, 152–153, 314–316.

pre-ontological – understanding of being to a more articulate – ontological – comprehension thereof that does not merely repeat, but refines or corrects the former:

The interpretation of the average understanding of being attains its necessary guideline only with the developed concept of being. From the clarity of that concept and the appropriate manner of its explicit understanding we shall be able to discern what the obscure or not yet elucidated understanding of being means, what kinds of obfuscation or hindrance of an explicit elucidation of the meaning of being are possible and necessary.[27]

The 'hermeneutical circle' is therefore perhaps more aptly called a 'hermeneutical spiral': it can lead to a more profound understanding of being, thus allowing for the development of ontologies (38), and thereby provide the basis for a better comprehension of Dasein's existential constitution: "Once we have reached the horizon for the most primordial interpretation of being, the preparatory analytic of Dasein requires repetition on a higher, genuinely ontological basis".[28]

Second, Heidegger points out that his 'circular' procedure is not a mere theoretical construct, but in fact springs from Dasein's peculiar mode of being:

The 'circle' in understanding belongs to the structure of meaning, and this phenomenon is rooted in the existential constitution of Dasein, that is, in interpretative understanding. Beings that, as being-in-the-world, are concerned about their being itself have an ontological structure of the circle. (153)

Because we always already understand both being as such and our own being on the basis of our situatedness in the world, any development of our ontological understanding must take the form of a 'circle'. Combining these two points, Heidegger holds that "this circle of understanding (*Zirkel des Verstehens*) is not a loop (*Kreis*) in which any random kind of knowledge operates, but it is the expression of the existential fore-structure of Dasein itself". Properly understood, the 'hermeneutical circle' thus prompts rather than compromises Heidegger's conception of philosophy.

However, this rebuttal of the objection of circularity only points to another problem with the way that Heidegger relates his interest in the meaning of being to the 'preliminary tasks' of the existential analytic and destruction of the

---

[27] *BT* 6, 8. While Heidegger thus admits that "a 'circle' in the proof cannot be 'avoided' in the existential analytic", he also holds that the notion of a deductive proof inaccurately captures the hermeneutic procedure of the existential analytic, "because that analytic is *not* proving anything according to the rules of the logic of consequence *at all*" (315).

[28] *BT* 17; translation modified.

history of ontology. It after all remains unclear on which grounds Heidegger inscribes an ontological, phenomenological, and hermeneutic moment into the heart of Dasein's *own* existential constitution and Kant's *own* philosophical thinking. A hermeneutic-phenomenological approach to a certain subject need not entail that this subject also itself has a hermeneutic-phenomenological nature. Does not Heidegger, even on his own terms, take his 'interpretative violence' a step too far here? The answer to this question depends on whether we take the *Seinsfrage* or Dasein's understanding of being as the starting point of the hermeneutic spiral.

The *Seinsfrage* is the evident starting point for an ontological investigation. *Being and Time* indeed opens by distinguishing the three constitutive moments of this question: in asking about being, it interrogates beings, and aims to ascertain the meaning of being. Next, Heidegger develops these moments into the three moments of his conception of philosophy: ontology fundamentally asks about being, phenomenology interrogates beings in order to retrieve this hidden but constitutive being, and hermeneutics aims to wrest the meaning of being from the misguided way these beings are commonly understood. We have seen that these three moments, further, determine the fore-conception, fore-having, and fore-sight of Heidegger's existential analytic and historical destruction. Heidegger asks about Dasein and Kant's (pre-)ontological understanding of being, in doings so he interrogates the phenomenological nature of Dasein's being-in-the-world and Kant's account of transcendental knowledge, and he thereby aims to ascertain their respective care for the meaning of being or for the possibility of metaphysics. On this basis, it seems that Heidegger's account of the question of being prescribes the *formal* hermeneutical situation for his view of the human condition and interpretation of Kant's thought, while his threefold conception of philosophy forms their *methodological* hermeneutical situation.

However, Heidegger made it clear from the outset that the *Seinsfrage* has been forgotten, and that a – his – philosophical effort is first needed to retrieve and properly formulate this question, before we can begin to answer it. Since this retrieval calls for a hermeneutical investigation into the fore-structure of the question of being, this means that Heidegger's early philosophy is first and foremost an exercise in hermeneutics (whereas doing ontology is his ultimate aim). Accordingly, in § 5 of *Being and Time*, Heidegger holds that the *Seinsfrage* is "nothing other than the radicalization of an essential ontological tendency that belongs to Dasein itself" (15, 200). This suggests that we should actually understand this core philosophical question on the basis of Dasein's existential constitution, instead of the other way around. In other words, Dasein's everyday understanding of being constitutes a *factual* and inescapable hermeneutical situation that informs both Heidegger's account of the *Seinsfrage* and his conception of the aim and task of philosophy: "This guiding look at being grows out of the average understanding of being in which we are always already involved *and which ultimately belongs to the essential constitution of Dasein itself*" (8). A philosophical interpretation cannot create new meaning out of thin air, but 'merely' articulates a certain pre-given, provisional, understanding. As an explicit philosophical question, the *Seinsfrage* can then not operate as the factual point of departure of Heidegger's thought. *In fact*, Dasein's care for being fore-sees the possibility of ontology, its being-in-the-world establishes the fore-having for a phenomenological approach, and its pre-ontological understanding of being delivers the fore-conception that can be destructed by hermeneutics.

On this basis, the problem with Heidegger's violent interpretation of the first *Critique* and Dasein's existential constitution disappears. As it turns out, Heidegger ascribes the moments of his philosophical method to Dasein's existential constitution because he believes that he has first *derived* them from this being's own way of being – we recall that he defines philosophy as "universal phenomenological ontology, taking its departure from the hermeneutics of Dasein, which, as an analysis of *existence*, has fastened the end of the guideline of all philosophical inquiry at the point from which it *arises* and to which it *returns*".[29] Instead of imposing a theoretical framework onto the human condition, his philosophy articulates and develops what Dasein shows itself to be. Similarly, the *Seinsfrage* is an ontological articulation of the ontic fore-structure of our pre-ontological understanding. If the primordial, but implicit, hermeneutical situation for asking the question of being resides in Dasein's existence, Heidegger can coherently claim that the fore-structure of his own thinking and of Dasein's everyday understanding of being are essentially the same – or that only their degree of articulateness or 'radicality' differs. Likewise, Heidegger ascribes his own philosophical method to the procedure of the first *Critique*, because he assumes that Kant also grafted his thinking on Dasein's existential constitution. If he considers all true philosophy to be rooted in Dasein's everyday understanding of being, Heidegger can reasonably maintain that Kant's critical-transcendental philosophy to a certain extent structurally resembles his own hermeneutic-phenomenological

---

[29] *BT* 38, 436. Holger Zaborowksi draws the same conclusion from Heidegger's Freiburg lectures *Hermeneutik der Faktizität*. For Heidegger, Zaborowski holds, "philosophy, then, is not an abstract theoretical discipline [but] needs to be understood as a primordial 'mode' of Dasein's being that is concerned with interpreting its own being. [...] This is to say that the beginning and the end of philosophy *as a hermeneutics* lies in factical life. It is a *self*-interpretation" ('Heidegger's hermeneutics: towards a new practice of understanding', in: *Interpreting Heidegger*, 23–24).

ontology – or that their similarities and differences are grounded in their varying success to articulate or 'radicalize' this pre-ontological understanding. In this way, Heidegger's interpretation of the human condition and appropriation of Kant's philosophical undertaking are warranted by his early hermeneutical conception of philosophy.[30]

factual situation -->	formal radicalization (Heidegger/Kant)	-->	methodological articulation (Heidegger/Kant)
Dasein's everydayness	Seinsfrage 'How are synthetic a priori...?'		phenomenological ontology critical-transcendental philosophy
care for being	being a priori		ontology transcendental philosophy
being-in-the-world	beings transcendental knowledge		phenomenology critical philosophy
pre-ontological, everyday understanding of being	meaning problem of metaphysics		hermeneutics the 'retreat to reason'

Figure 5 The three moments of the hermeneutical circle in Heidegger's thought

---

[30] As noted in Chapter 3, Heidegger would later renounce his appropriation of Kant's thought once he had abandoned his early conception of the hermeneutic method of philosophy.

10 Enlightenment or Therapy

The Cosmopolitan Task of Philosophy

Having established the systematic contours of Cassirer and Heidegger's respective conceptions of philosophy, we can now at last consider their views on philosophy's existential or cosmopolitan task. Building on my earlier argumentations that both Cassirer and Heidegger understand the human condition as a quest for existential orientation, I approach these views as answers to the question how the human being *should* orient itself in and towards the world.

10.1 Cassirer's Enlightened View of the Task of Philosophy

10.1.1 The (Im)possibility of a Hierarchy of the Symbolic Forms

Since most of Cassirer's writings set out to explain the constitution of a particular symbolic form – he successively discusses mythical thought, religion, language, art, natural science, technology, law, the human sciences, and politics – the relation between these forms is rarely a prominent theme in his oeuvre. Moreover, when Cassirer does approach this issue, he seems to offer contradictory statements that obscure not only his overall view of human culture but also the goal of his philosophical project.

On the one hand, Cassirer offers a relativistic account of the worldviews established by the different symbolic forms. The fundamental premise of Cassirer's philosophy of culture is that all human understanding of the world, be if of the mythological, linguistic, or scientific kind, is mediated by symbolic imagination. The symbolic forms do not, therefore, represent a pre-existing world in diverse ways, but instead spontaneously "constitute their own aspect of 'reality'" (*PSF:I* 78). This means that we cannot assess their worldviews in terms of accuracy, measured by a 'world in itself' (188–189). Furthermore, Cassirer holds that "the difference between the spheres of spiritual meaning is specific and not quantitative" (*PSF:III* 54). At various occasions, he insists that each symbolic form applies "entirely different standards and criteria" (*PSF:I* 91) or ascribes its own particular "grammar" to the world (*CIPC* 76), thus "giving rise to a new total meaning of reality" (*PSF:III* 448). As a consequence, our cultural domains offer radically distinct perspectives that cannot be reduced to or derived from each other either.

Cassirer therefore states that the symbolic forms can only be assessed on the basis of their own internal logic: "In defining the distinctive character of any spiritual form, it is essential to measure it by its own standards. The criteria by which we judge it and appraise its achievement, shall not be drawn from outside, but must be taken from its own fundamental law of formation" (*PSF:I* 177). In *An Essay on Man*, he accordingly holds that

two views of truth are in contrast with one another, but not in conflict or contradiction. Since art and science move in entirely different planes they cannot contradict or thwart one another. The conceptual interpretation of science does not preclude the intuitive interpretation of art. Each has its own perspective.[1]

On these grounds, we must conclude that Cassirer is a cultural relativist, as he seems to accept no criterion – neither taken from an outside world, nor found in one of the symbolic forms – by means of which we could establish a hierarchy of our cultural domains: "Instead of being taken as absolute", the validity of their constitutive principles is to be "recognized as specific and relative – as a validity that is not given in the simple *content* of reality but partakes of a certain *interpretation* of reality".[2]

On the other hand, Cassirer nevertheless occasionally holds that certain symbolic forms are more valuable than others. First, he hints at the inferiority of the symbolic form of mythical thought. In the introduction to the second volume of *The Philosophy of Symbolic Forms* (1925), he asserts that the other symbolic forms need to make sure to "free themselves" from this way of thinking, and that we need to "master" or "overcome" the mythological worldview (*PSF:II* xv, xvii). When Cassirer twenty years later discusses the particular case of political myths, he further warns for the imminent threat of a "sudden relapse" into mythical thinking, and seeks for an "antidote to myth".[3]

Second, Cassirer repeatedly claims that the symbolic form of language provides the most important access to the world of spirit. In *The Phenomenology of Knowledge* (1929), he holds that "every conscious, articulated, perception presupposes [...] language" (*PSF:III* 232), and in his 1941/1942 'Seminar on Symbolism and Philosophy of Language' he claims that "language is to be regarded as the focus of all human activities", in such a way that "none of these activities would be possible without its constant help".[4] Cassirer further propagates the special place of language in the whole of human culture during the Davos debate, when calling the shared language that

---

[1] *EM* 170; *PSF:I* 91; *PSF:III* 55.   [2] *PSF:III* 28; *PSF:I* 76; *SF* 447.
[3] *MS* 371–373; and 'The Myth of the State', in: *ECW:24* 264.
[4] Cassirer, 'Seminar on Symbolism and Philosophy of Language', in: *ECN:6* 304.

enables this debate the sharpest indication of the human capacity to partake in the realm of cultural objectivity.[5] Additionally, there is the remarkable fact that Cassirer discusses this symbolic form in the first volume of *The Philosophy of Symbolic Forms*, even though he considers mythical thought – the topic of the second volume – the most original form of human culture.

Third, in *An Essay on Man* (1945) Cassirer holds that "science is the last step in man's mental development and [. . .] may be regarded as the highest and most characteristic attainment of human culture" (*EM* 207). While unrepeated in his oeuvre, this claim had a big impact on the reception of Cassirer's thought, and for many scholars it overrules his extensive interests in mythology, art theory, and linguistics. Often guided by an erroneous conception of the Neo-Kantian tradition, they invoke Cassirer's appraisal of the symbolic form of science to argue that he in the end still in positivistic fashion evaluates human culture by the achievements of the natural sciences.

Contrary to this one-sided view of Cassirer's thought, in what follows I will show that he deliberately maintains both a relativistic and a hierarchical account of the symbolic forms. Before exploring how Cassirer can reconcile these seemingly contradictory views, we must however briefly address two points of tension in his philosophy of culture that are related to but not identical with the one that is at stake here. First, there is the earlier discussed contrast between the relativistic nature of the philosophy of symbolic forms and the absolutist tendencies that instruct the symbolic forms themselves. Cassirer admits that, for the artist, religious person, or scientist, the symbolic form of art, religion, or science may offer a comprehensive and final look on the world:

In the course of its development, every basic cultural form tends to represent itself not as a part but as the whole, laying claim to an absolute and not merely relative validity, not contenting itself with its special sphere, but seeking to imprint its own characteristic stamp on the whole realm of being and the whole life of the spirit. (*PSF:I* 81)

To a certain extent, Cassirer even embraces this dogmatism, since he considers it the motor behind all formation of culture (82; CPP 61). Yet, he insists that the philosopher must maintain a more detached viewpoint that regards each symbolic form as offering one, partial and subject-based, perspective on the world (*PSF:IV* 226; *EM* 71). We can call this a conflict between the (absolutist) 'internal perspective' of the singular symbolic forms and the (relativist) 'external perspective' of transcendental philosophy.[6] In contrast, the conflict

---

[5] *DD* 293. Ironically, earlier in the Davos debate Hendrik Pos had already severally questioned the very idea that Cassirer and Heidegger shared a common language (287).

[6] This conflict has been carefully addressed in Kreis, *Cassirer und die Formen des Geistes*, 147–158; and Sebastian Luft, *The Space of Culture. Towards a Neo-Kantian Philosophy of Culture (Cohen, Natorp, Cassirer)*, Oxford: Oxford University Press, 2015, 176–180.

that occupies us here concerns two 'external viewpoints', or two positions that Cassirer holds in his capacity as a philosopher: his claims for and against a hierarchy of the symbolic forms *both* express a philosophical take on human culture as a whole.

Second, on this philosophical level the conflict between Cassirer's relativistic and hierarchical accounts of the symbolic forms does not simply reflect a clash between Romantic and Enlightened elements of his thinking either. One cannot contest that Cassirer's openly confessed affinity to the Enlightenment motivates his appraisal of the natural sciences. On the other hand, his inclusive stance with regard to the cultural domains of language and mythology as legitimate products of reason is indeed inspired by Romantic thinkers such as Goethe, von Humboldt, and Schelling, to which he refers often and at length. However, Cassirer's subsequent relativistic take on this variety of cultural expressions is rooted in his commitment to Kant's 'Copernican revolution' (*PSF:I* 78–79; *PSF:II* 29). Cassirer considers it the logical outcome of critical idealism that all cultural meaning, and not just scientific objectivity, is grounded in an a priori perspective on the world:

With this critical insight, science renounces its aspiration and its claim to an 'immediate' grasp and communication of reality. It realizes that the only objectification of which it is capable is, and must remain, mediation. And in this insight, another highly significant idealistic consequence is implicit. [...] We are forced to conclude that a variety of media will correspond to various structures of the object, to various meanings for 'objective' relations.[7]

Hence, Cassirer's claims for and against a hierarchy of the symbolic forms are *both* based on the tenets of Enlightenment thinking. In contrast, I will now argue, his relativism originates in a transcendental perspective on human culture, while his hierarchical account of the symbolic forms results from a critical reflection on symbolic consciousness that presupposes, rather than contradicts, this perspective.

10.1.2 Cassirer's Critical Perspective on Human Culture

We have seen earlier that Cassirer's transcendental investigation of cultural meaning delivered two conditions of possibility: the symbols and the functions of symbolic formation (or three, if we also count the symbolic pregnancy of all human impressions). While the symbols of space, time, or number transcend and connect the diverse symbolic forms, the expressive, representational, signifying, and characterizing functions of consciousness set them apart, as

---

[7] *PSF:I* 76; see also Cassirer's 1936 essay 'Critical Idealism as a Philosophy of Culture', especially *CIPC* 70–71.

they account for the specificity of mythical, linguistic, scientific, or historical meaning. On the basis of these different types of functions, Cassirer holds that the symbolic forms "move in different paths and express different trends of spiritual formation" (*PSF:III* 56). This leads to the unsurpassable "'poly-dimensionality' of the cultural world" (13): while the mediating symbols of consciousness preclude any access to a unified 'world in itself' beyond our perceptions, the generically different functions of consciousness rule out the possibility of a synthetic account of human culture as a whole. Hence, the philosophy of symbolic forms does not aspire to be a philosophical system, but merely to offer a "systematic overview" (*PSF:IV* 227) of the different a priori perspectives that ground our cultural domains.

Cassirer's relativistic account of human culture thus results from his tran-scendental investigation of 'the facts of culture': a transcendental perspective after all reveals that our world is currently composed of a series of totally dissimilar worldviews. Cassirer, however, points out that we gain a very different picture when we look at human culture from a genetic perspective.[8] On this view, the symbolic forms appear not at all as radically distinct, but rather as closely interwoven with each other:

[The] moment we consider the genesis of the basic forms of cultural life [we find that] none of these forms started out with an independent existence and clearly defined outlines of its own [...] The question of the origin of language is indissolubly interwoven with that of the origin of myth: the one can be raised only in relation to the other. Similarly, the problem of the beginnings of art, law, or science leads back to a stage in which they all resided in the immediate and undifferentiated unity of the mythical consciousness. Only very gradually do the basic theoretical concepts of knowledge (space, time, and number) or of law and social life (the concept of property, for example) or the various notions of economics, art, and technology free themselves from this involvement. (*PSF:II* xiv–xv)

Cassirer's genetic account of the symbolic forms thus identifies mythical thought as the original form from which all others, and hence human culture as a whole, have sprung: "None of [the symbolic forms] arise initially as separate, independently recognizable forms, but every one of them must first be emancipated from the common matrix of myth" (*LM* 44; *CIPC* 87). Through a gradual process, religion, art, language, and science have each in their own way liberated themselves from this type of understanding until they reached a point at which they offer completely distinct worldviews:

---

[8] Cassirer describes the genetic perspective on human culture in the preface to *The Phenomenology of Knowledge*: instead of focusing on "the relative end that thought has achieved" – the 'facts of culture' – it is concerned with the "necessary intellectual mediations" and "the mode and form of the procedure" of thinking itself (*PSF:III* xiv–xv).

In all spiritual growth we can discern a twofold trend. On the one hand, it is related to natural, purely organic growth insofar as both are subject to the law of continuity. The later phase is not absolutely alien to the earlier one but is only the fulfillment of what was intimated in the preceding phase. On the other hand, this interlocking of phases does not exclude a sharp opposition between them. For each new phase raises its own pregnant demand and sets up a new norm and 'idea' of the spiritual. Continuous as the process may be, the accents of meaning are forever shifting within it – and each of these shifts gives rise to a new total meaning of reality. (*PSF:III* 448)

Cassirer most clearly explains this process of emancipation when he distinguishes between a 'mimetic', 'analogical', and 'symbolic' stage in the development of the symbolic form of language.[9] In its initial, 'mimetic', stage, language remains very much akin to mythical thought in so far as the first words are characterized by a physical – that is, auditory – resemblance to their sensible content, as is still the case with onomatopoeia (*PSF:II* 25; *PSF:III* 450–451). In the 'analogical stage', language comes to its own terms as it breaks with this mimicry: "Language [...] *begins* only where our immediate relation to sensory impression and sensory affectivity *ceases*. The uttered sound is not yet speech as long as it purports to be mere repetition, as long as the specific factor of signification and the will to 'signify' are lacking" (*PSF:I* 189). When language tries to represent more complex states of affairs, our words and phrases inevitably cease to resemble the objects to which they refer. In the 'symbolic stage', finally, grammatical constructions arise that bear no physical resemblance to our sensations whatsoever: there is, for example, no sensible counterpart to the copula 'is'. This mature stage of natural language furthermore prepares the way for the pure language of the natural science (*PSF:I* 313–318).

Cassirer holds that we can also, albeit "with a certain methodological reservation", frame the history of scientific thought from Aristotle over Descartes to Leibniz by means of these 'mimetic', 'analogical', and 'symbolic' stages: throughout this history, he explains, the scientific idea of space evolved from describing a tangible substance into denoting a pure relation of coordinates (*PSF:III* 452–459). We can furthermore perceive the same scheme in the development from mythic to mythological and eventually religious thought (*PSF:II* 237–261), and in the evolution from traditional, representational, towards contemporary, abstract art (*LM* 98).

Hence, considered from the genetic perspective, the range in flexibility between the sensible and intelligible moments of the symbols does not so much explain the differences between the symbolic forms as it shows that each

---

[9] See *PSF:I* 186–197; *PSF:III* 450–451; and *ECW:17* 261–264. For a more extensive discussion of these stages, consult Paetzold, *Die Realität der symbolischen Formen*, 26–32.

of these forms undergoes a similar evolution.[10] While thus reconnecting the symbolic forms, this perspective can however still not justify a *progress* in the development of human culture. To this end, we must reconceive the genetic perspective as a critical perspective that does not focus on the distinct world-views, but – building on the transcendental perspective – on the evolving symbolic consciousness that grounds them:

> This genetic relationship is not understood in its true significance and depth so long as it is regarded as merely genetic. [...] Genetic problems can never be solved solely by themselves but only in thoroughgoing correlation with structural problems. The emergence of the specific cultural forms from the universality and indifference of the mythical consciousness can never be truly understood if this primal source [is not] recognized as an independent mode of spiritual formation. (*PSF:II* xv)

For Cassirer, then, the increasing distance between the content and form of the symbols becomes truly relevant when considered as the gradual differentiating of the object and subject of symbolic formation. Of course, this process of differentiation cannot lead to an actual separation of the transcendental spheres of objectivity and subjectivity, which must remain bound up with each other. Instead, this evolution signals an advanced understanding of the symbolic forms *as symbolic forms* as well as an advanced 'self-understanding' of symbolic consciousness:

> Thus, although myth, language, and art interpenetrate one another in their concrete historical manifestations, the relation between them reveals a definite systematic gradation, an ideal progression towards a point where the spirit not only is and lives in its own creations, its self-created symbols, but also knows them for what they are.[11]

On the basis of *this* critical principle of 'self-awareness', Cassirer regards myth, language, and science as the most important symbolic forms.

Cassirer calls mythical thought "the first attempt at a knowledge of the world" (*PSF:II* 23). As such, it is however marked by an ambiguous stance. On the one hand, the mythical worldview cannot be understood as a pure reflection of the sensible world: grounded in a symbolic form, it is mediated by a function of symbolic consciousness and constituted by the symbols in their original modality. In this capacity, it breaks with the animalistic way of perceiving the world and carries the seeds for the development of the other

---

[10] It thus seems that the three transcendental 'functions of symbolic formation' correspond to the three genetic stages in the evolution of the symbolic forms. Cassirer does not explain this relationship, although in 'Das Symbolproblem und seine Stellung im System der Philosophie' he claims that throughout its development, each symbolic form relates differently to the functions of expression, representation, and signification (*ECW:17* 262).

[11] *PSF:II* 26. In *An Essay on Man*, Cassirer alternatively describes this ideal progression as a gradual evolution from tradition to innovation, reproduction to creation, and collectivism to individualism (*EM* 224–227).

forms. On the other hand, the mythical worldview nevertheless in no way manifests this mediation. Instead, it sticks as closely as possible to the undifferentiated chaos of our sensations:

> From the very start, myth, as an original mode of *configuration*, raises a certain barrier against the world of passive impression; it, too, like art and cognition, arises in a process of separation from immediate reality, i.e. that which is simply given. But though in this sense it signifies one of the first steps beyond the given, its product at once resumes the form of the given. Thus myth rises spiritually above the world of things, but in the figures and images with which it replaces this world it merely substitutes for things another form of materiality and of bondage to things. (24)

In mythical thought, the world is still understood as "acting directly on the emotions and will" (*PSF:III* 113), and the mythological symbols conversely as "a fully objective reality" (*PSF:II* 23). This is the case, Cassirer explains, "because at this stage there is not yet an independent self-conscious I, free in its productions". In other words, in mythical thinking the 'animal symbolicum' seems completely unaware of its own accomplishments, and therefore also of the nature of this symbolic form: "This creation does not yet bear the character of a free spiritual act; it has a character of natural necessity, of psychological 'mechanism'". According to Cassirer, such psychologism can only be overcome when "the spirit places itself in a new relation to the world of images and signs – [when] while still living in them and making use of them it achieves a greater understanding of them and thus rises above them" (25; *PSF:I* 188).

This condition is met for the first time in language, which Cassirer thus considers the first 'self-conscious' symbolic form. He holds that natural language aims at "a lasting intellectual form" and "a certain objective relationship that it strives to describe and arrest".[12] This stability or objectivity, Cassirer adds, "is alien to the purely expressive experience [of mythology] that lives in the moment and spends itself in the moment".[13] In language, however, symbolic consciousness initiates a deliberate manner of structuring the meaningful content of our impressions: here "perception is no longer passive, but active, no longer receptive, but selective. [...] The world of language makes explicit the representative values and meanings that are embedded in perception itself".[14] Through this accomplishment, language attests to symbolic consciousness' increased awareness of its creative powers. As such, natural language also points both forwards and backwards. On the one hand, it forms the precondition for every abstract expression of meaning: "In order to grasp [abstract] meaning, man is no longer dependent upon concrete sense data, upon visual, auditory, tactile, kinesthetic data. [...]

---

[12] *PSF:III* 449–450; *ECW:17* 260–261.   [13] *PSF:III* 115, 113; *PSF:I* 189; *ECW:17* 261.
[14] *PSF:III* 232, 451; *LM* 99.

Without the preliminary step of human language such an achievement would not be possible" (*PSF:III* 232; *EM* 38). On the other hand, the symbolic creativity expressed by language also forms the precondition for us recognizing any symbolic form as a symbolic form, including mythical thought. This could explain why the symbolic form of language is discussed in the first volume of *The Philosophy of Symbolic Forms*: Cassirer first had to explain the nature and constitution of a more evident symbolic form before he could argue that even irrational myths were grounded in one.

With the rise of the exact sciences, the process of awareness reaches its completion: "What is unconsciously done in language is consciously intended and methodologically performed in the scientific process" (*EM* 210). The natural sciences discard all that is concrete and subjective so that the symbols can signify universally and necessarily valid, or 'purely objective', meaning. Especially modern science, characterized by its hypothetical and experimental method as well as its formal language, installs "a conscious detachment from the world of expression" (*PSF:III* 451), thus signalling a highly advanced awareness of the creative powers of symbolic consciousness.[15] It is no coincidence, then, that Cassirer – like Kant – first conceives of the transcendental logic that founds physics and only later realizes that similar logics also characterize the other symbolic forms.[16]

Hence, mythical thought holds a crucial stage in human culture because it installs the first break with the immediacy of impressions, but it also needs to be overcome because its world view does not attest for this accomplishment. Language is, then, in a sense the most important symbolic form because it first introduces meaningful distinctions that do not claim to represent a pre-given reality but instead deliberately aim to constitute a cultural world: "Human speech prepares and makes possible that modifiability of thought that is the very basis of all the other human activities" (*ECN:6* 341). Modern science, finally, is the 'highest attainment of human culture', not because it offers the most accurate view of the world or the purest access to 'reality', but because it

---

[15] Since scientific thought first developed through a 'mimetic' and 'analogical' stage, this insight was a "rather late achievement in man's intellectual and cultural development" (*EM* 36). Cassirer holds that "even for mathematics, it proved to be extremely difficult to discover the new dimension of symbolic thought" (210–221). He sees a first significant breakthrough in the experimental methodology of modern science as it was practised by Galilei or Newton, and a second in the complete prioritizing of relations over entities in Einstein's theory of relativity.

[16] Cassirer already investigated the a priori conditions of possibility of contemporary mathematics and physics in his first systematic monograph *Substance and Function* (1910). In the prefaces to the first and third volumes of *The Philosophy of Symbolic Forms*, he refers to the general findings of this investigation and conveys his subsequent realization that they must apply "everywhere [. . .] where the phenomenal world as a whole is placed under a specific spiritual perspective" (*PSF:I* 69; *PSF:III* xiii).

fully recognizes itself as an a priori framework of interpretation, or a symbolic form:

For what distinguishes science from the other forms of cultural life is not that it requires no mediation of signs and symbols and confronts the unveiled truth of 'things in themselves', but that, differently and more profoundly than is possible for the other forms, it knows that the symbols it employs are *symbols* and comprehends them as such. (*PSF:II* 26)

Cassirer's appraisal of scientific thinking, then, does not betray a positivist stance: instead, his hierarchical account of the different symbolic forms is grounded on the criterion of the self-knowledge of symbolic consciousness.

10.1.3   The Twofold Task of a Philosophy of Culture: Self-awareness and Self-realization

We can now understand on which grounds Cassirer simultaneously maintains a relativistic and a hierarchical account of the symbolic forms. These accounts do not contradict each other because they result from two different perspectives on human culture. Cassirer's transcendental investigation of our cultural domains shows that we cannot reasonably compare our mythological, linguistic, and scientific *understanding of the world* because they are constituted by radically distinct functions of symbolic formation. However, his subsequent critical reflection on these functions, however, shows that they *can* be compared on the basis of the *self-understanding of symbolic consciousness*. As we shall now see, these transcendental and critical perspectives of human culture moreover relate to each other through their shared commitment to the Enlightened program of critical idealism: to reveal and further the autonomy of reason.[17] In 'Critical Idealism as a Philosophy of Culture', Cassirer after all holds that "all the various problems of a philosophy of culture may be summed up and concentrated in the question, in which way and by what means the autonomy of reason is to be reached".[18]

Cassirer's transcendental perspective on human culture reveals the autonomy of symbolic consciousness by showing that *all* cultural domains, and not just (modern) science, are grounded in a symbolic form, meaning that they are constituted by an a priori 'function of symbolic formation'. By subjecting

---

[17] As mentioned in Chapter 8, the third volume of Cassirer's *The Problem of Knowledge* (1919) already called "the self-understanding of reason" the goal of critical philosophy (*EP:III* 1). Explaining the unity and progress among historical epochs, Cassirer there dealt with a problem that resembles the one occupying us now: the unity and hierarchy among our cultural domains. While his functional conceptions of history and culture can account for their unities, Cassirer must invoke the idea of reason's developing 'self-understanding' in order to also explain their inner progress and hierarchy.

[18] *CIPC* 84; translation modified.

human culture in its entirety to the 'Copernican revolution', Cassirer here shows that the domain of reason's autonomy is much broader than Kant allowed for. His transcendental perspective moreover promotes the autonomy of symbolic consciousness in so far as it dismantles what Cassirer calls the 'antinomies of culture' (*PSF:I* 81; *PSF:IV* 224). As pointed out earlier, all cultural domains tend to lay an absolute claim on the world. In doing this, they deny the autonomy of reason twice: by considering one cultural domain as an accurate reflection of a 'world in itself', and by discarding all others as unreasonable or unfounded. The result of such dogmatism is that human culture is dominated by, and eventually narrowed down to, the viewpoint of one symbolic form – for example, scientific or religious thinking. Cassirer's transcendental perspective of the symbolic forms counters such one-sided views: in so far as it explains the radical differences between our cultural domains, it helps secure their mutual balance. In this way, his relativism enables the uninhibited expression of symbolic consciousness in all its forms.

Cassirer's critical perspective on human culture further reveals the autonomy of symbolic consciousness by showing that it forms the impetus behind the evolution of human culture from mythological thought over language to science. His critical reflection on the different functions of consciousness leads Cassirer to the conclusion that

human culture taken as a whole may be described as the process of man's progressive self-liberation. Language, art, religion, science, are various phases in this process. In all of them man discovers and proves a new power – the power to build up a world of his own, an 'ideal' world. (*EM* 228)

This critical perspective moreover promotes the autonomy of symbolic consciousness in so far as it nuances – but not retracts – the relativistic view of the symbolic forms. By valuing more highly those cultural expressions that signal a greater awareness of the symbolic formation of our world, Cassirer's philosophy encourages the further development of the formative powers of our consciousness. An important concern for Cassirer in this regard is the ever-threatening revival of mythical thought, which obscures these powers and which he therefore labels 'the enemy of philosophy'.[19] The hierarchical account of the symbolic forms concretely counters the new, 'intoxicating' political myths that arrest or even overturn the autonomy of symbolic consciousness.[20]

[19] See *ECW:24* 252, 264; and *MS* 348–373.

[20] Krois thus holds that "self-liberation is the struggle for a harmony between the mythic and critical forces in culture [. . .] With the mythic forces in check, man can liberate himself from ignorance and fear – this is the positive content of Cassirer's conception of the function of human culture" (*Symbolic Forms and History*, 186). Cassirer is, of course, aware of the limited practical power of philosophy: he admits that it can only expose, but not actively destroy

What is at stake in Cassirer's philosophy of symbolic forms is, then, first of all the self-*understanding* of symbolic consciousness. In the opening line of *An Essay on Man*, Cassirer states "that self-knowledge is the highest aim of philosophical inquiry appears to be generally acknowledged" (1). In *The Metaphysics of Symbolic Forms*, he likewise defines philosophical knowledge as the "self-knowledge of reason".[21] Ultimately, however, Cassirer's philosophy of culture is invested in the self-*realization* of symbolic consciousness. This self-realization takes places in each cultural domain, and this in a progressive manner throughout the development of human culture. More specifically, philosophy is the means to discern and accommodate this process[22], which Cassirer alternatively defines as the formation of civilization (26), humanity,[23] and, eventually, freedom: "The true and highest aim of every 'symbolic form' consists in its contribution toward this goal; by means of its resources and its own unique way, every symbolic form works toward the transition from the realm of 'nature' to that of 'freedom'" (111).

Hence, despite its relativistic moment, the philosophy of symbolic forms does not present a neutral overview of the cultural domains: it is motivated by the ideal of a 'poly-dimensional' cultural realm in which symbolic consciousness – liberated from 'the bondage to things' – can optimally express itself. Despite its reflective stance, this philosophy is not passive either but imposes a task that may take courage in the face of dogmatism: 'Freedom cannot be acquired but by the work of the mind's self-realization' (*CIPC* 88). Despite its detached perspective, finally, Cassirer's philosophy of culture does not merely entertain a 'philosopher's problem' but is concerned with the fate of all human beings: "In our time, it is not only a general methodological demand, but a general cultural fate that couples philosophy with the special disciplines of knowledge, and which binds them closely to each other".[24]

As such, Cassirer's philosophy of symbolic forms aspires to be a philosophy in the cosmopolitan sense in Kantian tradition. From the outset, it attempts to establish "a general plan of ideal orientation, upon which we can so to speak

---

political myths (*MS* 373, *CPPP* 60; see also Truwant, 'Political Myth and the Problem of Orientation', 135–136).

[21] *PSF:IV* 226. Already in the opening sentence of the third volume of *Das Erkenntnisproblem* (1919), Cassirer had described the task of critical philosophy in this way: "Among the many attempts to summarize the intent of critical philosophy in a brief expression, the declaration that the spirit of criticism consists in the 'self-reconciliation' (*Selbst-verständigung*) of reason' is probably the most succinct and precise" (*EP:III* 1).

[22] In *The Metaphysics of Symbolic Forms*, Cassirer defines philosophy as the "criticism and fulfillment of the symbolic forms" (*PSF:IV* 226). See also Krois, *Symbolic Forms and History*, 214: "The symbolic forms are the means for the process of human self-liberation; the philosophy of these forms provides the theory of their origin and of their phenomenological development".

[23] See *EM* 68, 70, 228. See also Krois, *Symbolic Forms and History*, 214.

[24] *CPPP* 61, 59; *EM* 'Chapter 1: The crisis in the knowledge of man of itself'.

indicate the place of each symbolic form" (*ECW:17* 262). On a theoretical level, this attempt is motivated by the 'antinomies of culture'. In the same way that Kant aimed to overcome the antinomies of reason by turning to its underlying interests, Cassirer's philosophy of culture tries to establish a harmony between the symbolic forms, without dissolving their mutual conflicts, by grounding the variety of cultural worldviews in the functional unity of symbolic consciousness. For Cassirer, philosophy is thus "the guide and caretaker of reason in general" (*CPPP* 60) because it aids us in orienting ourselves in the world of human culture. While the different cultural domains enable different modes of human orientation, philosophy of culture describes and suggests how we can orient ourselves towards these domains.[25]

On a practical level, Cassirer's search for a phenomenology or morphology of symbolic consciousness is motivated by the precarious situation of European culture in the first half of the twentieth century. As we have seen, he holds that previous ages have always been marked by "a general orientation, a frame of reference, to which all individual differences might be referred", whereas in his own time "an established authority to which one might appeal no longer existed" (*EM* 21). In light of this existential problem, Cassirer revisits Kant's "ideal of a concept of philosophy as 'related to the world'" (*CPPP* 58–59). However, whereas Kant considered philosophy in cosmopolitan sense to bring theoretical and practical reason in harmony, Cassirer – who does not conceive of ethics as a separate symbolic form – views this harmonizing itself as an ethical task. The critical philosopher projects the ethical idea of humanity as the point of orientation for the constitution and interpretation of all cultural meaning. Both Cassirer's relativistic and his hierarchical account of the symbolic forms are motivated by this ethical, cosmopolitan view of human culture.

10.2   Heidegger's Therapeutic Conception of Philosophy

Like Cassirer's take on the hierarchy among the different symbolic forms, Heidegger's view on the relation between disowned and owned existence is a

---

[25] Orth splendidly describes this orientational task of philosophy of culture in 'Zugänge zu Ernst Cassirer. Eine Einleitung': "Even though Cassirer combatted the possibility of a philosophical system just as much as the tenability of metaphysics, the systematic perspective nevertheless seems necessary to him for making sense of and developing a basis for the problem of human orientation - be it in the sciences or in the so-called natural life. The theorem of the 'symbolic form' can be downright understood as a basic structure of precisely this human orientation. [. . .] If we reserve the label 'philosophy of culture' for Cassirer's philosophy, we cannot understand philosophy of culture as a philosophy among others: instead, it is rather an intellectual endeavor that encompasses all human understanding of the world. It is orientation with regard to orientation" (*Über Ernst Cassirers Philosophie der symbolischen Formen*, 8–9).

much debated topic among scholars. This debate is fueled by the fact that, again like Cassirer, Heidegger makes a number of contradictory claims about this relation. On the one hand, he repeatedly emphasizes that the term and phenomenon of 'disownedness' (or 'inauthenticity', as *Uneigentlichkeit* is often translated) should not be understood in a pejorative or inferior way, but concern an essential and positive characteristic of Dasein. On the other hand, Heidegger's further explanation of this mode of being is riddled with dismissive-sounding terminology, and there is no denying that his fundamental ontology favours, if not promotes, the mode of ownedness.[26] What are we to make of this?

When Heidegger first introduces the distinction between ownedness and disownedness, he immediately states that "the inauthenticity of Dasein does not signify a 'lesser' being or a 'lower' degree of being" (*BT* 42). A first reason for this is that Heidegger, as a phenomenological thinker, intends to merely describe Dasein's ontological constitution and therefore steers away from normative assessments. In this approach, any constitutive moment or 'existential' of Dasein's being, including 'the they' (129), is considered a 'positive' moment, meaning that it asserts an innate characteristic of our existence:

Inauthenticity does not mean anything like no-longer-being-in-the-world, but rather it constitutes precisely a distinctive kind of being-in-the-world which is completely taken in by the world and the Dasein-with of the others in the they. Not-being-itself functions as a *positive* possibility of beings which are absorbed in a world, essentially taking care of that world. This *non-being* must be conceived as the kind of being of Dasein closest to it and in which it mostly maintains itself.[27]

A disowned way of being, in which we allow 'the they' to prescribe our attuned understanding and interpretation of beings, is still an active mode of caring. In fact, Heidegger posits this mode, which he describes as Dasein's 'entanglement' (*Verfallen*) in the world (175), as a feature of our being that is equiprimordial with our existentiality and facticity: "Falling prey reveals an essential, ontological structure of Dasein itself. Far from determining its nocturnal side, it constitutes all of its days in their everydayness" (179, 181, 316–317).

---

[26] Carman was one of the first scholars to point out and criticize this ambiguity in *Being and Time*: "Heidegger's distinction between authenticity and inauthenticity is systematically ambiguous, and so lends itself to two completely different interpretations. Naturally, authenticity in human understanding and conduct is supposed to be something desirable, while inauthenticity is somehow undesirable. Heidegger regularly insists that such seemingly pejorative terms as 'idle talk', 'falling', and 'inauthenticity' have no evaluative content. But this is utterly unconvincing. No one can come away from the text with the idea that such notions are value-neutral." (*Heidegger's Analytic of Dasein*, 269–270)

[27] *BT* 176. Heidegger makes the same claim regarding the disowned mode of interpretation, idle talk (167), and the general structure of 'the they', 'entanglement' (175).

Furthermore, as the above quotes indicate, disownedness is not just an essential but also our initial and predominant mode of being-in-the-world: "*Initially*, factical Dasein is in the with-world, discovered in an average way. *Initially*, 'I' 'am' not in the sense of my own self, but I am the others in the mode of the they. [. . .] Initially, Dasein is the they and for the most part it remains so' (129). For this reason, Heidegger emphasizes that the disowned mode of being "must not be interpreted as a 'fall' from a purer and higher 'primordial condition'" (176). Our entanglement in the world is not a downfall from a more original way of being, like the biblical fall of mankind from grace into sin, but is itself our primary existential attitude. Heidegger confirms this when stating that owned existence is only possible by overcoming the spell of 'the they', which means that we must pass through disownedness in order to shake it off: "If Dasein [. . .] discloses its authentic being to itself, this discovering of 'world' and disclosing of Dasein always comes about by clearing away coverings and obscurities, by breaking up the disguises with which Dasein cuts itself off from itself" (129). Hence, if there is any hierarchical order between modes of existence on Heidegger's descriptive account of Dasein's ontological constitution, it prioritizes our inauthenticity. Disownedness is not a corrupted mode of authenticity; rather, owned existence is grounded in, and defined by its distance from, disownedness: "Authentic being a self is not based on an exceptional state of the subject, detached from the they, but is an existential modification of the they as an essential existential" (130, 179).

Neverthelesss, most further descriptions of disownedness and entanglement contradict this allegedly neutral or 'positive' picture. Despite his plea to not understand our inauthentic mode of being as a fallen state of existence, Heidegger uses exactly this term to describe our succumbing to 'the they': in this mode, he holds, Dasein has "fallen away from itself and fallen prey to the world" (175) and has taken "a plunge (*Absturz*) into the groundlessness and nothingness of inauthentic everydayness" (178). In line with this, Heidegger also writes that disowned Dasein "*has lost itself* precisely in its everydayness and 'lives' *away from itself* in falling prey" (179), and that "entangled being-in-the-world is [. . .] alienating" (178). Most tellingly, of course, is the very notion of *Uneigentlichkeit* – *dis*ownedness or *in*authenticity – itself, which portrays this phenomenon as the absence of a default mode of ownedness. Each of these expressions reinforces the idea that inauthenticity is a degraded existential attitude.[28]

---

[28] See Blattner, *Heidegger's Being and Time*, 131: "Being-amidst is a structural element of Dasein's being, not a degraded or even merely average mode of disclosedness. Nevertheless, the dominant use of 'falling' and 'fallen' in *Being and Time* is to refer to a degraded mode of disclosedness, rather than to being amidst."

On multiple occasions, Heidegger even refers to disowned existence as an evasion (*ausweichende Abkehr*) and a flight (*Flucht*) of Dasein from itself: "It is true that existentielly the authenticity of being a self is closed off and repressed in entanglement, but this closing off is only the *privation* of a disclosedness which reveals itself phenomenally in the fact that the flight of Dasein is a flight *from* itself".[29] In contrast, the owned self is described as "the self which has explicitly grasped itself" (129). This more active language clearly indicates a hierarchy between a way of existing that lives up to one's own potential and a way in which one decides against being truly oneself. More generally, it confirms the idea that ownedness is Dasein's 'essential' way of being (323). In line with this idea, but completely contrary to his earlier claims, in Division Two of *Being and Time* Heidegger thus holds that "inauthenticity has possible authenticity as its basis" (259).

Heidegger thus wavers, often in the same passages in *Being and Time*, between outrightly rejecting a hierarchy between disowned and owned existence and heavily implying one. In doing so, he alternatively emphasizes the primacy of either mode of being. In order to make sense of this twofold ambiguity, we must refine (1) which modes of existence are being ranked, as well as (2) what kind of hierarchy is thereby established. On that basis, we can determine how, according to Heidegger, Dasein *should* existentially orient itself.

(1) Regarding our possible modes of existence, we should recall that Heidegger's existential analytic discusses not two, but three existential attitudes: in addition to ownedness and disownedness, there is also an 'indifferent' possibility that structurally precedes them: "Mineness belongs to existing Dasein as the condition of the possibility of authenticity and inauthenticity. Dasein exists always in one of these modes, or else in the modal indifference to them" (53). This 'modal indifference' should not be understood as a lack of care for being, but on the contrary as the average mode of our being-in-the-world:

At the beginning of the analysis, Dasein is precisely not to be interpreted in the differentiation of a particular existence; rather, it is to be uncovered in the indifferent way in which it is initially and for the most part. This indifference of the everydayness of Dasein is *not nothing*; but rather, a positive phenomenal characteristic. All existing is how it is out of this mode of being and back into it. We call this everyday indifference of Dasein *averageness*.[30]

Dasein's averageness corresponds to the general structure of our pre-ontological understanding of being. To exist as being-in-the-world means that we always find ourselves in a meaningful environment that serves a horizon

---

[29] *BT* 184; see also 136, 139, 254, 390, 424.   [30] *BT* 43, 53; *Logic* 192.

against or within which beings can make sense to us. As Heidegger explains, our ontological understanding of other beings (as tools) presupposes a familiar world in which they relate to each other in a meaningful manner. Likewise, we initially and predominantly understand and interpret ourselves on the basis of worldly projections, namely as a potential dinner host or cobbler: "As something factical, the understanding self-projection of *Dasein* is always already together with a discovered world. From this world it takes its possibilities." (194) As we have seen, this potential for circumspective self-understanding is grounded in a need for existential orientation: as caring beings who lack a fixed identity, we have to stand out (ek-sist) to the world in order to make sense of ourselves. Hence, because of the kind of being that we are, we cannot but understand ourselves *through* our worldly engagement with other beings or *based upon* our worldly projects. Heidegger thus repeatedly holds that, "initially and for the most part, Dasein *is* in terms of *what* it takes care of" (141, 43, 146).

As our basic way of being-in-the-world, this average mode of being can however be modified through two movements (*Bewegtheit*): Heidegger calls our movement towards disownedness 'falling prey' (134, 177) and that towards ownedness 'resoluteness' (*Entschlossenheit*, 270). Put differently, entanglement and resoluteness are the respective inauthentic and authentic modifications of circumspective understanding. In disowned existence, we completely hand over our existential compass to 'the they', meaning that our attuned understanding of beings becomes entirely *derived from* the public opinion. In this way, being-circumspective dwindles down to being-entangled or being-absorbed-in: "Falling prey to the 'world' means being absorbed in being-with-one-another as it is guided by idle talk, curiosity, and ambiguity. What we called inauthenticity may now be defined more precisely through [this phenomenon]" (175). Instead of orienting ourselves in the world, we are now being oriented by the public opinion towards certain pre-established uses of other beings and projects for ourselves. Since 'the they' only allows for superficial interpretations, this means that we no longer understand ourselves in light of a certain projection but *as* that project: we do not just find meaning in our parenthood or our career as cobbler, but understand ourselves as if we coincide with these particular possibilities. We are, in sum, absorbed by the world or entangled in our current relations to other beings.

Heidegger often seems to conflate the neutral mode of averageness with our alienating tendency to succumb to this disowned existence. He holds, for instance, that "the self of everyday Dasein is the they-self, which we distinguish from the authentic self".[31] Other passages in *Being and Time*, however,

---

[31] *BT* 129, 139, 179, 299; *BPP* 228. As Carman explains, "the problem is that terms like 'idle talk' and 'falling' do double duty both as descriptions of the indifferent ontological structures

point to a subtle nuance: not the influence of 'the they' as such, but the Dasein's succumbing to it marks the difference between average and disowned understanding. Heidegger considers 'the they' as an existential, that is, as a structural component of Dasein's ontological constitution (130). The fact that by being attuned we always already find ourselves in a potentially meaningful world entails that Dasein does not project meaning in a vacuum but that this projection always happens within 'the they': "The they prescribes the nearest interpretation of the world and of being-in-the-world" (129). While our everyday understanding of beings is thus also already affected by 'the they', disowned existence distinguishes itself by fully embracing this pre-established interpretation.

Heidegger yet further complicates matters when he adds that disownedness is a natural tendency of Dasein: "*Dasein* has the inclination to be entangled in the world in which it is and to interpret itself in terms of that world" (21, 15). The dictate of 'the they' is then not only initially present in our everyday circumspection, but also presents inauthenticity as an attractive mode of being. This attraction follows from its disburdening (*entlastend*) and tranquillizing (*beruhigend*) character: "Dasein prepares for itself the constant temptation of falling prey. Being-in-the-world is in itself tempting (*versucherisch*)" (177). As a result, we *de facto* initially and predominantly exist in an inauthentic manner: "Dasein [. . .] *can* be inauthentic and factically it is this initially and for the most part" (193, 136). Nevertheless, the distinction between the average and disowned mode of existence remains valuable because it indicates that the latter still requires a choice that Dasein has to make.[32] Our casually going along with the public opinion may be inevitable given our throwness into the world, but our endorsement thereof is not. We do not necessarily succumb to 'the they', even though we are inclined to do so. There remains an important ontological distinction between Dasein's average and disowned modes of existence, even though they are practically or existentially akin.

Both of these manners of being oriented within the world entail that we are practically engaged with other beings in a way that effectively renders both these beings and our own worldly self meaningful. To be oriented *towards* the world, on the other hand, means to focus on our overall relation with the world as a whole, or on the very possibility that this world provides a meaningful

---

underlying the invidious distinctions Heidegger does draw between authentic and inauthentic modes of existence, and as names for the specifically negative instances or manifestations of those structures. Consequently, Heidegger's language inclines in a pejorative direction and systematically blurs the distinction between indifferent ontological conditions and the specifically undesirable ontic syndromes they condition" (*Heidegger's Analytic of Dasein*, 270).

[32] See Zimmerman, *Eclipse of the Self*, 44, 46: "I am convinced that we can make sense of *Being and Time* only if we see that inauthenticity involves a deliberate choice to conceal the truth, while everydayness is to a large extent unavoidable and necessary".

home. This is a difference between being praxis-oriented and being norm-oriented: in the first case one simply goes along with or succumbs to the pre-established rules for human behaviour, whereas in the latter case Dasein endorses certain norms (and disavows others). The owned mode of orientation is thus a self-reflective one in which Dasein reflects on its own reasons for adopting these rules and takes ownership of its comportment.[33] Whereas disowned Dasein hands over its existential compass to 'the they', owned Dasein seizes control over it – authentic orientation "originat[es] from its own self as such" (146). Heidegger will call this existential choice, which is much less inviting than the choice for entanglement and therefore requires a lot more decisiveness, 'resoluteness'.

(2) In view of the hierarchical order of Dasein's existential modes, we must distinguish the above, hermeneutical, perspective from an ethical and an ontological one. Although there is little use in denying that Heidegger does in fact consider authentic existing more valuable than succumbing to 'the they', we shall maintain that this valuation is not of a normative or ethical kind, neither in the narrow sense of ethics as concerning good versus bad behaviour, nor in the broader sense of a worthy versus an unworthy life. There is nothing inherently deplorable or evil about simply adopting the ways in which 'the they' has interpreted other beings or us, nor will an owned attitude guarantee that we live a morally upright life. These modes of Dasein are general manners of existential orientation, not rules for ethical conduct. Such existential orientation may not be understood as providing a guideline for 'the good life' either, which is the sense in which authenticity is usually understood today. Heidegger's existential analytic is not concerned with existential questions about how to lead a fulfilling life: even if it may provide some answers to these questions, this does not constitute the goal of Heidegger's thought and is thus not the criterion for his evaluation of (dis)owned existence. Instead, he only examines the human being in view of his attempt to develop a

---

[33] Charles Guignon likewise holds that "becoming authentic involves a second-order stance with respect to one's choices. Authenticity involves a 'choosing to choose' in which one stands behind one's choices, owning them and owning up to them. It is this higher-order stance that is called 'resoluteness'" ('Heidegger's concept of freedom, 1927–1930', 90). Denis McManus describes this 'choosing to choose' (*BT* 270) as a "willingness to make decisions oneself" and as "taking responsibility oneself for one's actions" ('Anxiety, Choice and Responsibility in Heidegger's Account of Authenticity', in: *Heidegger, Authenticity and the Self. Themes From Division Two of 'Being and Time'*, ed. by Denis McManus, New York: Routledge, 2015, 179). For an elaborate discussion of Dasein's capacity to give reasons and to be answerable for its behaviour, see Crowell, *Normativity and Phenomenology in Husserl and Heidegger*, Chapters 8–10.

fundamental ontology that retrieves the question of being: "Our interpretation has a purely ontological intention and is far removed from any moralizing critique of everyday Dasein and from the aspirations of a philosophy of culture" (167). As a consequence, the tension between Heidegger's neutral and hierarchical views regarding (dis)ownedness is not a conflict between an ontological and an ethical viewpoint but must reside entirely within the ontological sphere.

As we have seen, the ontological being of Dasein can, however, be coherently understood from two angles: from its concrete interpretations of beings or from its fundamental concern about the meaning of being. On this basis, we have further distinguished between Dasein's hermeneutical character and its ontological nature per se. These moments of Dasein's being are of course intrinsically related to each other: our hermeneutical approach to beings is aimed at revealing their being, while our fundamental ontological interest relies on gaining proper access to beings. Yet, depending on whether one adopts the phenomenological-hermeneutical or the ontological viewpoint, we gain different takes on the hierarchy between disowned, average, and owned existence. As a hermeneutic thinker, Heidegger describes a neutral interplay between being oriented in and towards the world, whereby the difference between average and disowned existence is not that relevant. As an ontological thinker, he defends an asymmetric opposition between ownedness and disownedness specifically.

From the phenomenological-hermeneutic perspective, there can be no hierarchical order between orienting oneself in the world or towards the world. Factually, our existential orientation starts within the world, where we try to make sense of the beings near us and our own concrete situation. We are initially not concerned about the orienting norms of our comportment – that is, about the existential question whether being a good dinner host would really make our life significant – but with the proper, meaningful use of certain tools – that is, with the pragmatic question how to become such a host. Although we could imagine other triggers as well, according to Heidegger in *Being and Time* the former question is first stirred in the experience of anxiety, when our usual comportment is disturbed and we are thrown back upon ourselves. Nevertheless, once we have somehow oriented ourselves towards the world, it becomes a precondition for our pragmatic orientation within the world. Finding it somehow meaningful to be a social and welcoming person is a transcendental condition for investing in the many practical preparations for a dinner party. To adopt the owned, reflective perspective – 'Do I really want to be this kind of sociable person?' – entails putting on hold the average, engaged perspective – 'How does one make a desert that my guests will like?' – but this pause happens in order to then return to a practical engagement with beings. Our average and owned modes of being are, therefore, also in line with each other. In authentic disclosedness "the world at hand does not become different as far as 'content'" (297–298), but the same world is understood in a different, encompassing, light.[34]

There is even a close connection between ownedness and disownedness. This is the case because even owned existence, as a modification of our average being-in-the-world that itself is marked by thrownness and 'the they', inevitably remains informed by the way we were previously oriented within the world: "As authentic being a self, resoluteness does not detach Dasein from its world, nor does it isolate it as free floating ego. How could it, if resoluteness as authentic disclosedness is, after all, nothing other than authentically being-in-the-world?" (298, 305). Our existential decision to give meaning to our life by identifying as a dinner host or a cobbler still always happens against the background of our everydayness. It must be noted, further, that the owned mode of existence is not a mode in which we can hold ourselves for a very long time: not only do practical matters quickly call us back into the world, but we also cannot endure the uncanniness of anxiety.

Dasein's relation to the modes of everydayness and ownedness thus takes the form of a hermeneutic circle, since these ways of interpreting the world mutually inform each other. This circle is expressed in Heidegger's account of conscience, the owned mode of discourse, according to which an individuated self calls upon a worldly self to become itself.[35] While both selves are of course but two moments of the same Dasein, the worldly self is dispersed throughout its many projects, whereas the owned or world-constituting self is a 'whole' (§46–48) and 'constant' (322–323) self: "The sameness of the authentically existing self is separated ontologically by a gap from the identity of the I maintaining itself in the multiplicity of its experiences" (130). These conceptions of ourselves complement each other: both positively express what and how Dasein is. In fact, insight into their hermeneutic dynamic is a crucial aspect of Heidegger's notion of resoluteness:

Resoluteness means letting oneself be summoned out of one's lostness in the they. The irresoluteness of the they nevertheless remains dominant, but it cannot challenge resolute existence. [...] Even resolutions are dependent upon the they and its world. Understanding this is one of the things that resolution discloses, insofar as resoluteness first gives to Dasein its authentic transparency. In resoluteness, Dasein is concerned with its ownmost potentiality-of-being that, as thrown, can project itself only upon definite, factical possibilities. Resolution does not escape from 'reality', but first

---

[34] Guignon accurately decribes these "two 'modes' or core possibilities-of-being for humans [as] an orientation directed primarily toward productive activity, in which the 'for-the-sake of-itself' is 'forgotten' or 'covered up' as one is absorbed in the work at hand, and an orientation in which the primary focus is the activity of self-making in one's productive activity" ('Heidegger's concept of freedom, 1927–1930', 83–84).

[35] *BT* 287. See also John D. Caputo, *Hermeneutics. Facts and Interpretation in the Age of Information*, Penguin Books, 2018, 49.

discovers what is factically possible in such a way that it grasps it as it is possible as one's ownmost potentiality-of-being in the they. (299)

If, however, we adopt an ontological perspective, we get a very different view of Dasein's existential orientation. If our aim is not just to describe how we come to understand beings in the ways that we do, but to consider *why* we do so, ownedness appears as a truthful mode of existence, whereas disownedness appears as a diametrically opposed flight from this. As we have just seen, authenticity is only a 'detached' attitude in the sense that it takes a momentary, reflective distance to our everyday engagement, but not in the sense that it discards the meaning of this practical comportment. On the contrary, as an orientation *towards* the world, it is indirectly still very much an invested attitude and not a merely speculative one. Inauthenticity, on the other hand, "*closes off* to Dasein its authenticity and possibility" (178). The – ontological – problem with a disowned mode of existence lies not, then in the fragmentation of our orientation towards various projects or multiple worldly identities, nor in the fact that, even if we overlook the sum of all these projections, Dasein is still not grasped *as Dasein*. At issue, rather, is the constitutive tendency of disowned existence to willfully obscure Dasein's peculiar being, and to deny the difference between the worldly self and the world-constituting self.

Because the public opinion only superficially looks at and talks about beings without aiming to disclose their being, it cannot grasp our ontological constitution. The they exclusively acknowledges our worldly manifestations as a dinner host or cobbler, and ignores our being-in-the-world: 'Thus, by its very nature, idle talk is a closing off since it *omits* going back to the foundation of what is being talked about' (169). In order to not have to understand anything profound, 'the they' even holds that there is no such thing as profundity: disowned understanding "will never be able to decide what has been drawn from primordial sources with a struggle, and how much is just gossip. Moreover, [it] will not even want such a distinction, will not have of it, since, after all, it understands everything". Hence, 'the they' outright denies the potentiality that is characteristic of human Dasein.[36] Heidegger's case against disownedness is then not merely that it is one-sided, but that it is a truly reductive mode of existence: "The self-certainty and decisiveness of the they increasingly propagate the sense that there is no need of authentic, attuned understanding" (177). Over against the transparent self-understanding of

---

[36] This sets the active movement of dis-ownedness apart from the neutral mode of average un-ownedness. As Blattner puts it, "disowned Dasein flees in the face of death and anxiety and tries to return to everyday life. Having been awakened to the existential challenges, however, one cannot return 'naïvely' to everyday life. One must, rather, cover up or bury the existential challenges, and that involves disowning the sorts of entity we are" (*Heidegger's Being and Time*, 130).

ownedness, an inclusive understanding that also acknowledges our initial and predominant falling prey to 'the they', in disownedness Dasein forfeits any (ontological) insight into its own self.

This contrast between Dasein's owned and disowned attitudes, and hence the possibility and need to adopt either one of them, is first disclosed in anxiety:

> In anxiety there lies the possibility of a distinctive disclosure, since anxiety individual-izes. This individuality fetches Dasein back from its falling prey and reveals to it authenticity and inauthenticity as possibilities of its being. The fundamental possibil-ities of Dasein, which are always my own, show themselves in anxiety as they are, undisguised by innerworldly beings to which Dasein, initially and for the most part, clings. (190–191)

When we previously discussed the mood of anxiety, we were following Heidegger's hermeneutic-phenomenological procedure in *Being and Time*. We then saw that, by radically disrupting the familiar bond between Dasein and its world, anxiety reveals two essential characteristics of Dasein. On the one hand, the complete meaninglessness that we experience in this mood shows us that the only way to make sense of ourselves is through our relation to the world, that is, by projecting a possible worldly self. On the other hand, by exposing our lack of a stable ground or purpose, anxiety also shows that any such projection is contingent and fleeting. Taken together, anxious Dasein becomes aware that we have to be our own potentiality, or that we *are* care.

Once Heidegger has established the fundamental ontological nature of Dasein, the mood of anxiety can serve a second, existential role: it brings us before the choice between an authentic or an inauthentic way of being, that is, it enables us to be resolute.[37] As long as we are not confronted with our own finitude, there is nothing that counters the temptation of 'the they', which offers us a clearly defined identity. It takes a disruptive, uncanny mood such as anxiety for the limiting nature of this identity and the reductive power of the public opinion to become visible: "Anxiety takes away from *Dasein* the possibility of understanding itself, falling prey, in terms of the 'world' and the public way of being interpreted. It throws Dasein back upon that for which it is anxious, its authentic potentiality-for-being-in-the-world" (187). Positively expressed, anxiety thus allows the possibility of a different

---

[37] I here follow Withy, who distinguishes between the ontological-methodological and the existential-ethical role of Heidegger's account of anxiety ('The Methodological Role of Angst in *Being and Time*, in: *Journal of the British Society for Phenomenology*, 43/2, 2012, 195–211). In Division One of *Being and Time*, anxiety is crucial for phenomenologically revealing the unitary ground of Dasein's being as care (see Chapter 6). Division Two discusses the existential significance of anxiety as an experience that enables a choice between a disowned and an owned way of existing.

existential attitude to arise: "Anxiety reveals in *Dasein* its *being towards* its ownmost potentiality of being, that is, *being free for* the freedom of choosing and grasping itself. Anxiety brings *Dasein* before the authenticity of its being as possibility which it always already is" (188). Given that 'the they' is an existential of Dasein with a tempting and tranquillizing character, the choice that is at stake here cannot be a distinct or definitive one. Instead, the choice for owned existence is one that must be made over and over again. Resoluteness needs to be a continuous effort in "clearing away coverings and obscurities" imposed by 'the they' and "breaking up the disguises with which Dasein cuts itself off from itself" (129). As such, ownedness is an active way of being (300), and thus better described as 'choosing' than as 'a choice'.

While resoluteness is enabled by anxiety, it does not so much result from but rather lives through this mood. To choose an owned mode of existence is to be 'ready for anxiety' (296), to 'anticipate death' (262), and to 'want to have a conscience' (234, 288, 296). In other words, resolute Dasein accepts the possibility that the world in which we find ourselves does not guarantee a meaningful existence for us and that we cannot secure a stable existential purpose for ourselves either. More specifically, it acknowledges that this possibility springs from our very own being. What is at stake in the choice between owned and disowned existence is, then, our self-understanding. According to Heidegger, "the who of everyday Dasein is precisely *not* I myself" (115, 125), whereas "Dasein becomes 'essential' in authentic existence that is constituted as anticipatory resoluteness" (323). The fundamental mood of anxiety reveals to us that we are more than just a worldly self when it "brings the self back from the loud idle chatter of the they's common sense" (296, 290). The owned understanding of this mood, that is, our being-towards death, positively asserts that the world-constituting self which hereby appears "must be understood *as possibility*, cultivated *as possibility*, and *endured as possibility* in our relation to it" (261, 263–267, 305–307). This understanding is then expressed through the discourse of conscience, wherein owned self summons disowned self to live up to its own potential: "Dasein listens to its ownmost possibility of existence. It has chosen itself" (287).

In *Being and Time*, Heidegger does not explicitly connect Dasein's capacity for resoluteness to his own philosophical undertaking. However, since only owned existence asserts itself as a way of being that can and must itself make sense of beings, whereas disowned Dasein flees into an ontic understanding of things, it is the only mode of being that can provide renewed access to the question of the meaning of being. The reason why Heidegger considers the owned mode of existence more valuable than the disowned mode is that it entails an understanding of itself as an ontological being, which is a precondition for properly doing ontology. In *The Fundamental Concepts of Metaphysics*, Heidegger indeed identifies the task of his philosophy as the 'awakening (*Weckung*) of a fundamental mood' (FCM 91), and explains that such awakening is "a manner and means of grasping Dasein with respect to the specific way in which it is, of grasping Dasein as Dasein, or better: of letting Dasein be as it is, or can be, as Dasein" (103). He later adds that "the task which is given over to philosophizing [is] *not to describe the consciousness of man but to evoke the Dasein in man*" (258).

At this point, there is no longer any substantial agreement between Heidegger and Cassirer's philosophical views. We can conclude that they both perceive the task of philosophy as a matter of enabling and promoting self-understanding, and that they both conceive of this understanding as a comprehensive way of orienting oneself in and towards the world. Yet, the message that they promote is very different. For Cassirer, critical self-understanding allows us to overcome the limitation of our human condition. Accordingly, the task of philosophy consists in promoting progressive self-realization through participation in the formation of culture. For Heidegger, on the contrary, this self-understanding means an acceptance of our finitude: the possibility of disownedness not only can never be definitively overcome, but must be given a proper, positive place in the ontological understanding of our Dasein. Furthermore, resoluteness consists in an endorsement of our ontological restlessness and individuality. Hence, "this demand has nothing to do with some human ideal in one or the other domain of possible action. It is the *liberation of the Dasein in man* that is at issue here" (255). If we recall that, for Cassirer, the "true goal is not the Dasein of the human being, but its 'intelligible substrate of humanity'" (KMPR 18), it is clear that his and Heidegger's concrete ideas of the *task* of philosophy are radically opposed to each other. Looking backwards, we can see how this conflict prefigures their disagreements about the human condition and the most insightful reading of Kant's philosophy. It seems that any further deepening of this conflict, on the other hand, would lead us to a series of extra-philosophical motives on the part of both thinkers. Hence, at this point our journey through Cassirer and Heidegger's philosophical engagement with each other comes to an end.

Conclusion

The Terminus a Quo *and* Terminus ad Quem *of the Davos Debate*

This book has attempted to counter two prevalent but mistaken views about the Davos debate: that Heidegger easily won this debate because Cassirer could not match the profundity of his thought, or that no real debate took place between these thinkers because their philosophies share no common ground at all. I have argued, instead, that there is both a coherent structure to their overall dispute and sufficient initial agreement on its key topics to consider this a proper philosophical *Auseinandersetzung*. On this basis, one could even conclude that Cassirer and early Heidegger's thought actually present two moments of an encompassing philosophical project, namely to account for the human need and capacity for existential orientation.

When analysing the Davos debate and the larger Cassirer–Heidegger dispute in Chapter 1, I claimed that Cassirer and Heidegger's interactions hinge on three main issues: the lasting meaning of Kant's thought, the human condition, and the task of philosophy. More specifically, I argued that Cassirer and Heidegger's disagreements about these topics are mutually related in a hierarchical manner: while their debate on the proper reading of the first *Critique* is motivated by their diverging views on the human condition, these views are in turn informed by their radically different conceptions of the task of philosophy. In this way, I tried to demonstrate the philosophical coherence of the Davos debate, and by extension the overall dispute between Cassirer and Heidegger. Throughout the following chapters, I showed how this coherence is further grounded in Cassirer and Heidegger's independently developed philosophy of symbolic forms and fundamental ontology, in which the same three topics play pivotal, structurally related roles. In a nutshell, both thinkers build on Kant's account of transcendental and critical philosophy, and in particular his account of transcendental imagination, in order to develop highly original philosophical theories of cultural and worldly orientation that serve either the emancipation or the self-reconciliation of the human being.

My analysis of Cassirer and Heidegger's philosophical encounters also showed that an initial kinship gradually gave way to a seemingly unsurpassable disagreement. As the stakes got higher, less and less common ground remained between these thinkers. However, if their final difference regarding the task of philosophy informed Cassirer and Heidegger's views on the human condition and Kant's thought from the outset, one may in retrospect still conclude that even their initial closeness was merely superficial, meaning that their philosophies at no point truly touched each other. In other words, we must then confirm that no real debate took place between Cassirer and Heidegger, not because the former was no match for the latter but because they were from beginning to end occupied with two radically different philosophical projects.[1] This conclusion seems to be affirmed by the way in which Heidegger in Davos presents the overall difference between his and Cassirer's thought:

> For Cassirer the *terminus ad quem* is the whole of a philosophy of culture in the sense of an elucidation of the wholeness of the forms of the shaping consciousness. For Cassirer, *the terminus a quo* is utterly problematical. My position is the reverse: The *terminus a quo* is my central problematic, the one I develop. The question is: is the *terminus ad quem* as clear for me? For me, this occurs not in the whole of a philosophy of culture, but rather in the question: what in general is called being? (*DD* 288)

On this picture, the starting point (*terminus a quo*) of Cassirer's philosophy is his conception of the human being as an 'animal symbolicum', and its goal (*terminus ad quem*) is the objective, liberating, realm of cultural meaning. Heidegger takes issue with both of these termini. On the one hand, in *Being and Time* he emphatically dismisses having any interest in developing a philosophy of culture (*BT* 167); his attempt to revive the ontological question of being steers him in a completely different direction. On the other hand, although Heidegger's philosophical trajectory also starts from the human condition, he denies any affinity to Cassirer's conception thereof, which he calls 'utterly problematic'. For Heidegger, the idea of symbolic consciousness in no way touches upon the true essence of human Dasein. Thus, on Heidegger's assessment, their thinking not only diverges in completely opposite directions, but does not even share a common starting point.

One cannot deny these significant differences between the termini of Cassirer and Heidegger's thought. Cassirer's philosophy of symbolic forms

---

[1] Luft holds that the nature and extent of this difference is the most important question that Gordon's *Continental Divide* left unanswered – because he approached the Davos debate from the viewpoint of a historian of philosophy rather than "the philosopher who wants to push aside historical context and focus on the arguments" ('Peter E. Gordon, *Continental Divide: Heidegger, Cassirer, Davos*' (book review), in: *Journal of the History of Philosophy*, 49/4, 2011, 509).

leaves no room for the question 'what in general is called being', while Heidegger deems human culture an at best secondary, and at worst obstructive, topic of philosophical inquiry. Further, despite the broad agreement on understanding the human condition in terms of orientation, their views on this topic are also clearly distinct. Nevertheless, the above picture of Cassirer and Heidegger's diverging philosophical projects is misleading for two reasons: its use of the concept 'terminus' is ambiguous, and its focus on the termini distracts from the philosophical process that is actually central to the thought of both thinkers, and that as such connects them.

Heidegger's identification of his and Cassirer's *terminus a quo* and *ad quem* is misleading because it equivocates between two meanings of this distinction, which can either refer to the substantial foundation and outcome of their philosophical projects, or to their methodological starting point and end point. With regard to Cassirer, he relies on the former meaning. The philosophy of symbolic forms indeed aims to establish the unity of symbolic consciousness as the transcendental foundation of the variety of cultural meaning. However, in order to accomplish this, Cassirer starts from the 'fact of culture' in order to end up at the functions of consciousness. As we have seen, he even holds that this is the only – transcendental – way to proceed, given that our consciousness can only be disclosed via its cultural expressions. When it comes to his own thinking, Heidegger adopts the second meaning: his account of our existential constitution is the methodological starting point of a renewed inquiry into the meaning of being. However, the actual basis of his thought lies in his conception of the *Seinsfrage*, which results in his conception of Dasein. Hence, the human condition does not *in the same sense* function as the *terminus a quo* of Cassirer and Heidegger's thought: understood as a 'starting point', this terminus is either the facts of culture or Dasein's pre-ontological understanding of being, whereas conceived as a 'foundation', it is either symbolic consciousness or the question of being.

At first sight, this more nuanced picture seems to drive a further wedge between Cassirer and Heidegger's thought: while on Heidegger's view they both started from the human condition, albeit differently understood, and then took off in diverse direction, it now turns out that they share neither a *terminus a quo* nor a *terminus ad quem*. As my ultimate argument for the coherence of their philosophical encounter, I however hold that this disentanglement actually reveals a more fundamental resemblance between Cassirer and Heidegger's philosophical procedures. During the Davos debate, Heidegger wonders if it "lies in the essence of philosophy itself that [. . .] it has a *terminus ad quem* that correlates to the *terminus a quo*?" (*DD* 289). Throughout this book, I have demonstrated that Heidegger as well as Cassirer indeed consider such a correlation to be essential to philosophy. As we have seen, Cassirer's idea of a functional relation installs a circular procedure between the transcendental *explanandum* and *explanans* of human culture.[2] Likewise, Heidegger's idea of a fore-structure leads to a hermeneutic circle in which his final and preliminary interests mutually presuppose each other. Hence, both Cassirer and Heidegger's philosophical trajectories display an essentially circular structure. Methodologically speaking, this structure is prior to their two *termini*, which can therefore only be really understood in relation to each other. Moreover, to consider this relation as a matter of foundation and outcome or starting and end point is to see only one moment of a philosophical exercise.

On this basis, I finally contend that Cassirer and Heidegger's philosophies can be perceived as two moments of a shared, encompassing project after all. I have argued that both thinkers are fundamentally concerned with the problem of orientation. In addition, as I just explained, they tackle this problem in the same manner in two regards. First, Cassirer as well as Heidegger's thinking starts at what they take to be the human being's factual orientation point, namely its symbolic and pre-ontological understanding of beings respectively. Second, they invoke a circular methodology that goes back and forth between this understanding and its subjective preconditions. Once again, I do not intend to deny that their substantial positions are radically different on certain decisive points. I however hold that these positions result from a shared interest in and a similar approach to the problem of orientation. In so far as Cassirer and Heidegger are interested in the respective possibilities to orient ourselves *in* and *to* the meaningful world that we inhabit, or in our capacity and need for existential orientation, their philosophical projects can be taken as two complementary variations on the same philosophical theme.

---

[2] See Paul Crowe, 'Between termini: Heidegger, Cassirer, and the two terms of transcendental method', in: *Philosophy Today*, 47, 2003, 100; and Bernet, 'The Hermeneutics of Perception in Cassirer, Heidegger, and Husserl', 43: "The correlation between, on the one hand, the different types of symbolic comportment of the subject, and on the other, the different symbolic forms which form the realm of objective spirit, has the effect of setting the hermeneutic analysis of the *Philosophy of Symbolic Forms* on a circular path. Journeying indefinitely between the terminus a quo and terminus ad quem of the symbolic life of the spirit, Cassirer's hermeneutic forbids all immediate access to the subjective origin of objective culture".

Bibliography

The Davos Debate

DD   'Davos Disputation between Ernst Cassirer and Martin Heidegger', in: Martin Heidegger, *Kant and the Problem of Metaphysics*, Appendix IV, tr. by Richard Taft, Bloomington: Indiana University Press, 1997, 193–207.

'Davoser Disputation zwischen Ernst Cassirer und Martin Heidegger', zgs. von Joachim Ritter und Otto Friedrich Bollnow, in: Martin Heidegger, *Kant und das Problem der Metaphysik*, Anhang IV, Frankfurt: Vittorio Klostermann, 1998, 274–296.

Ernst Cassirer

EP:I   (1906), *Das Erkenntnisproblem in der Philosophie und Wissenschaft der neueren Zeit*, Erster Band, in: *Ernst Cassirer Gesammelte Werke*, Band 2, Hamburg: Meiner Verlag, 1999.

EP:II   (1907), *Das Erkenntnisproblem in der Philosophie und Wissenschaft der neueren Zeit*, Zweiter Band, in: *Ernst Cassirer Gesammelte Werke*, Band 3, Hamburg: Meiner Verlag, 1999.

ECW:9   (1907), 'Kant und die moderne Mathematik', in: *Ernst Cassirer Gesammelte Werke*, Band 9: *Aufsätze und Kleine Schriften 1902–1921*, Hamburg: Meiner Verlag, 2001, 37–82.

SF   (1910), *Substance and Function & Einstein's Theory of Relativity Considered from the Epistemological Standpoint*, tr. by William Curtis Swabey and Marie Collins Swabey, Chicago: The Open Court Publishing Company, 1923.

(1912), 'Hermann Cohen und die Erneuerung der Kantischen Philosophie', in: *ECW:9* 119–138.

(1914), 'Charles Renouvier, Essais de critique générale', in: *ECW:9* 484–486.

KLT   (1918), *Kant's Life and Thought*, tr. by James Haden, New Haven: Yale University Press, 1981.

EP:III   (1920), *Das Erkenntnisproblem in der Philosophie und Wissenschaft der neueren Zeit*, Dritter Band: *Die nachkantischen Systeme*, in: *Ernst Cassirer Gesammelte Werke*, Band 4, Hamburg: Meiner Verlag, 2000.

(1921), 'Goethe und die mathematische Physik. Eine erkenntnistheoretische Betrachtung', in: *ECW:9* 268–315.

PSF:I   (1923), *The Philosophy of Symbolic Forms*, Vol. 1: *Language*, tr. by Ralph Manheim, New Haven: Yale University Press, 1955.

ECW:16   (1923), 'Der Begriff der symbolischen Form in der Aufbau der Geisteswissenschaften', in: *Ernst Cassirer Gesammelte Werke*, Band 16: *Aufsätze und Kleine Schriften 1922–1926*, Hamburg: Meiner Verlag, 2003, 75–104.

PSF:II   (1925), *The Philosophy of Symbolic Forms*, Vol. 2: *Mythical Thought*, tr. by Ralph Manheim, New Haven: Yale University Press, 1955.

     (1925), 'Paul Natorp. 24. Januar 1854 – 17. August 1924', in: *ECW:16* 197–226.

LM   (1925), *Language and Myth*, tr. by Susanne K. Langer, Dover Publications, 1946.

     (1925), [Letter to Husserl, April 10, 1925], Leuven Husserl-Archives, Dokument III/5,5.

     (1927), *The Individual and the Cosmos in Renaissance Philosophy*, tr. by Mario Domandi, New York: Dover Publications, 2000.

ECW:17   (1927), 'Erkenntnistheorie nebst den Grenzfragen der Logik und Denkpsychologie', in: *Ernst Cassirer Gesammelte Werke*, Band 17: *Aufsätze und Kleine Schriften 1927–1931*, Hamburg: Meiner Verlag, 2004, 13–81.

     (1927), 'Das Symbolproblem und seine Stellung im System der Philosophie', in: *ECW:17* 253–282.

     (1928), 'Beiträge zu: Hermann Cohen. Schriften zur Philosophie und Zeitgeschichte', in: *ECW:17* 283–290.

PSF:IV   (1928–1940), *The Philosophy of Symbolic Forms*, Vol. 4: *The Metaphysics of Symbolic Forms*, ed. by John Michael Krois and Donald Phillip Verene, New Haven: Yale University Press, 1996.

ECN:1   (1928–1940), *Zur Metaphysik der symbolischen Formen*, in: *Ernst Cassirer, Nachgelassene Manuskripte und Texte*, Band 1, hrsg. von John Michael Krois und Oswald Schwemmer, Hamburg: Meiner Verlag, 1995.

ECN:17   (1929), *Davoser Vorträge. Vorträge über Hermann Cohen*, in: *Nachgelassene Manuskripte und Texte*, Band 17, hrsg. von Jörn Bohr und Klaus Christian Köhnke, Hamburg: Meiner, 2014.

PSF:III   (1929), *The Philosophy of Symbolic Forms*, Vol. 3: *The Phenomenology of Knowledge*, tr. by Ralph Manheim, New Haven: Yale University Press, 1957.

     (1929), 'Beiträge für die Encyclopedia Britannica', in: *ECW:17* 308–341.

     (1929), 'Formen und Formwandlungen des philosophischen Wahrheitsbegriffs', in: *ECW:17* 342–359.

     (1930), 'Form und Technik', in: *ECW:17* 139–183.

     (1930), '"Geist" und "Leben" in der Philosophie der Gegenwart', in: *ECW:17* 185–205.

KPMR   (1931), 'Kant und das Problem der Metaphysik. Bemerkungen zu Martin Heideggers Kant-Interpretation', in: *ECW:17* 221–250.

PE   (1932), *The Philosophy of the Enlightenment*, tr. by Fritz C. A. Koelln and James P. Pettegrove, Princeton and Oxford: Princeton University Press, 2009.

ECW:18   (1932), 'Shaftesbury und die Renaissance des Platonismus in England',
             in: *Ernst Cassirer Gesammelte Werke*, Band 18: *Aufsätze und Kleine*
             Schriften 1932–1935, Hamburg: Meiner Verlag, 2004, 153–175.
             (1932), 'Das Problem Jean-Jacques Rousseau', in: *ECW:18* 3–82.
CPPP   (1935), 'The Concept of Philosophy as a Philosophical Problem', in:
             Symbol, Myth, and Culture. Essays and Lectures of Ernst Cassirer
             (1935–1945), ed. by Donald Phillip Verene, New Haven: Yale University
             Press, 1979, 49–63.
CIPC   (1936), 'Critical Idealism as Philosophy of Culture', in: *Symbol, Myth and*
             Culture, Essays and Lectures of Ernst Cassirer (1935–1945), ed. by
             Donald Phillip Verene, New Haven: Yale University Press, 1979, 64–91.
ECW:19   (1936), *Determinismus and Indeterminismus in der modernen Physik.*
             Historische und systematische Studien zum Kausalproblem, in: *Ernst*
             Cassirer Gesammelte Werke, Band 19, Hamburg: Meiner Verlag, 2005.
ECW:22   (1939), 'Was ist "Subjektivismus"?', in: *Ernst Cassirer Gesammelte*
             Werke, Band 22: *Aufsätze und Kleine Schriften 1936–1940*, Hamburg:
             Meiner Verlag, 2006, 167–192.
             (1939), 'Axel Hägerström: Eine Studie zur Schwedischen Philosophie der
             Gegenwart', in: *Göteborgs Högskolas Arsskrift*, 45, 1–119.
             (1941–1942), Ernst Cassirer, 'Seminar on Symbolism and Philosophy of
             Language', Beinecke Rare Book & Manuscript Library, Yale University
             1941/42, Box 51, Folder 1024.
ECN:6   (1941–1943), 'Seminar on Symbolism and Philosophy of Language' and
             'An Essay on Man. A Philosophical Anthropology', in: *Ernst Cassirer*
             Nachgelassene Manuskripte und Texte, Band 6: *Vorlesungen und Studien*
             zur Philosophischen Anthropologie, hrsg. von Gerald Hartung, Herbert
             Kopp-Obersterbink, und Jutta Faehndrich, Hamburg: Meiner
             Verlag, 2005.
LCS   (1942), *The Logic of the Cultural Sciences*, tr. by S. G. Lofts, New
             Haven: Yale University Press, 2000.
EM   (1944), *An Essay on Man: An Introduction to a Philosophy of Human*
             Culture, New Haven: Yale University Press, 1992.
ECW:24   (1944), 'The Concept of Group and the Theory of Perception', in: *Ernst*
             Cassirer Gesammelte Werke, Band 24, 209–250.
             (1944), 'The Myth of the State', in: *ECW:24* 251–265.
             (1945), 'Structuralism in Modern Linguistics', in: *ECW:24* 299–320.
MS   (1946), *The Myth of the State*, New Haven: Yale University Press, 1979.
EP:IV   (1950), *Das Erkenntnisproblem in der Philosophie und Wissenschaft der*
             neueren Zeit, Vierter Band: *Von Hegels Tod bis zur Gegenwart*
             (1832–1932), in: *Ernst Cassirer Gesammelte Werke*, Band 5, Hamburg:
             Meiner Verlag, 2000.

Martin Heidegger

HF   (1923), *Ontology – The Hermeneutics of Facticity*, tr. by John Edward van
             Buren, Bloomington: Indiana University Press, 1999.
             (1925), [Letter to Karl Löwith, June 30, 1925], Karl Löwith
             Nachlass, unpublished.

Logic   (1925/1926), *Logic: The Question of Truth*, tr. by Thomas Sheehan,
            Bloomington: Indiana University Press, 2010.
BPP   (1927), *The Basic Problems of Phenomenology*, tr. by Albert Hofstadter,
            Bloomington: Indiana University Press, 1988.
BT   (1927), *Being and Time*, tr. by Joan Stambaugh, Albany: SUNY, 2010.
KPM: (1927), 'On the History of the Philosophical Chair since 1866', in: *Kant*
VI   *and the Problem of Metaphysics*, Appendix VI, 213–217 (304–311).
PIK   (1927/1928), *Phenomenological Interpretation of Kant's 'Critique of Pure*
            Reason', tr. by Parvis Emad and Kenneth Maly, Bloomington: Indiana
            University Press, 1997.
KPM: (1928), 'Ernst Cassirer: Philosophy of Symbolic Forms. Part Two:
II   Mythical Thought. Berlin, 1925' (book review), in: *Kant and the Problem*
            of Metaphysics, Appendix II, 180–190 (255–270).
            (1928), *The Metaphysical Foundations of Logic*, tr. by Michael Heim,
            Bloomington: Indiana University Press, 1984.
GA 27   (1928/1929), *Einleitung in die Philosophie*, in: *Martin Heidegger*
            Gesamtausgabe, II. Abteilung: *Vorlesungen 1919–1944*, Band 27,
            Frankfurt: Vittorio Klostermann, 2001.
KPM: (1929), 'Davos Lectures: Kant's Critique of Pure Reason and the Task of a
III   Laying of the Ground for Metaphysics', in: *Kant and the Problem of*
            Metaphysics, Appendix III, 191–192 (271–273).
            (1929), ['Brief zur Elisabeth Blochmann'], in: *Martin Heidegger –*
            Elisabeth Blochmann, Briefwechsel 1919–1969, ed. by Storck,
            Joachim W., Marbarch am Neckar: Deutsche Schillergesellschaft, 1989,
            29–30.
KPM   (1929), *Kant and the Problem of Metaphysics*, tr. by Richard Taft,
            Bloomington: Indiana University Press, 1997.
            (1929), 'On the Essence of Ground', in: *Pathmarks*, tr. William McNeill,
            Cambridge: Cambridge University Press, 1998, 97–136.
FCM   (1929/1930), *The Fundamental Concepts of Metaphysics: World, Finitude,*
            Solitude, tr. by William McNeill and Nicholas Walker, Bloomington/
            Indianapolis: Indiana University Press, 1995.
            (1930), *The Essence of Human Freedom: An Introduction to Philosophy*,
            tr. by Ted Sadler, London/New York: Continuum, 2002.
KPM: (ca. 1931), 'On Odebrecht and Cassirer's Critique of the Kant book', in:
V   *Kant and the Problem of Metaphysics*, Appendix V, 208–212 (297–303).
            (1934–1935), *Hölderlin's Hymns: 'Germania' and 'The 'Rhine'*, tr. by
            William McNeill and Julia Ireland, in: *Studies in Continental Thought*,
            Bloomington: Indiana University Press, 2014.
WT   (1935/1936), *What Is a Thing?*, tr. by W.B. Barton, Jr. and Vera Deutsch,
            South Bend: Gateway Editions, 1967.
            (1935–1937), 'The Origin of the Work of Art', in: *Off the Beaten Track*,
            tr. by Julian Young and Kenneth Haynes, Cambridge: Cambridge
            University Press, 1–56.
            (1937–1938), *Basic Questions of Philosophy: Selected 'Problems' of*
            'Logic', tr. by Richard Rojcewicz and André Schuwer, Bloomington:
            Indiana University Press, 1994.

(1938), *Contributions to Philosophy (of the Event)*, tr. by Richard
Rojcewicz and Daniela Vallega-Neu, in: *Studies in Continental Thought*,
Bloomington: Indiana University Press, 2012.
(1955), *What Is Philosophy?*, tr. by William Kluback and Jean T. Wilde,
New York: Twayne Publishers, 1958.
(1961), 'Kant's Thesis about Being', in: *Pathmarks*, tr. William McNeill,
Cambridge: Cambridge University Press, 1998, 337–364.
(2005), *'Mein liebes Seelchen!'*. *Briefe Martin Heideggers an seine Frau
Elfride (1915–1970)*, hrsg. von Gertrud Heidegger, München: Deutsche
Verlag-Anstalt.

Further Literature

Abela, Paul, *Kant's Empirical Realism*, Oxford: Clarendon Press, 2002.
Allison, Henry, *Kant's Transcendental Idealism, An Interpretation and Defense*, New
    Haven: Yale University Press, 1983.
Aubenque, Pierre, 'Philosophie und Politik: Die Davoser Disputation zwischen Ernst
    Cassirer und Martin Heidegger in der Retrospektive', in: *Internationale Zeitschrift
    für Philosophie* 2, 1992, 290–312.
Barash, Jeffrey Andrew, 'Ernst Cassirer, Martin Heidegger, and the Legacy of Davos',
    in: *History and Theory*, 51, 2012, 436–450.
Bast, Rainer A., *Problem, Geschichte, Form. Das Verhältnis von Philosophie und
    Geschichte bei Ernst Cassirer im historischen Kontext*. Berlin: Dunker &
    Humblot, 2000.
Bayer, Thora Ilin, *Cassirer's Metaphysics of Symbolic Forms. A Philosophical
    Commentary*, New Haven: Yale University Press, 2001.
Beiser, Frederick, 'Weimar Philosophy and the Fate of Neo-Kantianism', in: *Weimar
    Thought: A Contested Legacy*, ed. by Peter Eli Gordon and John P. McCormick,
    Princeton/Oxford: Princeton University Press, 2013, 115–132.
Bermes, Christian, *Philosophie der Bedeutung – Bedeutung als Bestimmung und
    Bestimmbarkeit. Eine Studie zu Frege, Husserl, Cassirer und Hönigswald*,
    Würzburg: Königshausen & Neumann, 1997.
Bernet, Rudolf, 'Perception et herméneutique (Husserl, Cassirer et Heidegger)', in: *La
    vie du sujet*, Paris: PUF, 1994, 139–161.
'The Hermeneutics of Perception in Cassirer, Heidegger, and Husserl', in: *Neo-
    Kantianism in Contemporary Philosophy*, ed. by Rudolf A. Makkreel and
    Sebastian Luft, Bloomington: Indiana University Press, 2010, 41–58.
Blattner, William, *Heidegger's 'Being and Time'*, London/New York: Bloomsbury, 2006.
'Laying the Ground for Metaphysics: Heidegger's Appropriation of Kant', in: *The
    Cambridge Companion to Heidegger*, ed. by Charles B. Guignon, Cambridge:
    Cambridge University Press, 2006, 149–176.
Blumenberg, Hans, *Die Legitimität der Neuzeit*, Frankfurt am Main: Suhrkamp, 1996.
Theorie der Lebenswelt, Frankfurt am Main: Suhrkamp, 2010.
Bollnow, Otto Friedrich, 'Gespräche in Davos', in: *Erinnerung an Martin Heidegger*,
    hrsg. von Günther Neske, Pfullingen, 1977, 25–29.
Brecht, Franz Josef, 'Die Situation der gegenwärtigen Philosophie', in: *Neue
    Jahrbücher für Wissenschaft und Jugendbildung*, 6/1, 1930, 42–58.

Brown, Gary Ronald, *The 1929 Davos Disputation Revisited*, Ann Arbor: UMI Dissertation Publishing, 2010.

Caputo John D., *Hermeneutics. Facts and Interpretaton in the Age of Information.* Penguin Books, 2018.

Carman, Taylor, *Heidegger's Analytic. Interpretation, Discourse, and Authenticity in 'Being and Time'*, Cambridge: Cambridge University Press, 2003.

'Things Fall Apart: Heidegger on the Constancy and Finality of Death', in: *Heidegger, Authenticity and the Self: Themes from Division Two of Being and Time*, ed. by Denis McManus, New York: Routledge, 2015, 135–145.

Carnap, Rudolf, *Archives for Scientific Philosophy*, University of Pittsburgh Libraries, ASP RC 025-73-03, 30 March 1929.

Carr, David, 'Heidegger on Kant on Transcendence', in: *Transcendental Heidegger*, ed. by Steven Crowell and Jeff Malpas, Stanford: Stanford University Press, 2007, 28–42.

Cassirer, Toni, *Mein Leben mit Ernst Cassirer*. Hamburg: Meiner Verlag, 2003.

Cohen, Hermann, *Kants Theorie der Erfahrung*, Berlin: Ferd. Dümmler Verlagsbuchhandlung, 1871.

Das Prinzip der Infinitesimal-Methode und seine Geschichte: Ein Kaptiel zur Grundlegung der Erkenntniskritik, Frankfurt: Suhrkamp, 1883.

System der Philosophie. Erster Teil: Logik der reinen Erkenntnis, Berlin: Bruno Cassirer, 1902.

Crowe, Paul, 'Between Termini: Heidegger, Cassirer, and the Two Terms of Transcendental Method', in: *Philosophy Today*, 47, 2003, 100–106.

Crowell, Steven, *Normativity and Phenomenology in Husserl and Heidegger*, Cambridge: Cambridge University Press, 2013.

Dahlstrom, Daniel, 'Heidegger's Kantian Turn: Notes to His Commentary on the 'Kritik der reinen Vernunft', *The Review of Metaphysics*, 45/2, 1991, 329–361.

'The *Critique of Pure Reason* and Continental Philosophy: Heidegger's Interpretation of Transcendental Imagination', in: *The Cambridge Companion to Heidegger*, 380–400.

De Boer, Karin, 'Heidegger's Ontological Reading of Kant', in: *The Bloomsbury Companion to Kant*, ed. by Gary Banham, Dennis Schulting, and Nigel Hems, London: Bloomsbury, 2012, 324–329.

'Kant's Multi-Layered Conception of Things in Themselves, Transcendental Objects, and Monads', in: *Kant-Studien*, 105/2, 2014, 221–260.

De Warren, Nicolas, 'Reise um die Welt. Cassirer's Cosmological Phenomenology', in: *New Approaches to Neo-Kantianism*, ed. by Nicolas de Warren and Andrea Staiti, Cambridge: Cambridge University Press, 2015, 82–107.

Dufour, Éric, *Paul Natorp, de la Psychologie générale à la Systématique philosophique*, Paris: Vrin, 2010.

Elkholy, Sharin N., *Heidegger and a Metaphysics of Feeling. Angst and the Finitude of Being*, in: *Continuum Studies in Continental Philosophy*, London/New York: Continuum, 2008.

Elliott, Brian, *Phenomenology and Imagination in Heidegger and Husserl*, London/New York: Routledge, 2015, 84–98.

Engelland, Chad, 'The Phenomenological Kant: Heidegger's Interest in Transcendental Philosophy', in: *Journal of the British Society for Phenomenology*, 41, 2010, 150–169.

Heidegger's Shadow. Kant, Husserl, and the Transcendental Turn. New York: Routledge, 2017.

Englert, Ludwig, 'Als Student bei den zweiten Davoser Hochschulkursen', in: *Nachlese zu Heidegger: Dokumente zu seinem Leben und Denken*, hrsg. von Guido Schneeberger, Bern: Private Edition, 1962, 1–6.

Farias, Victor, *Heidegger and Nazism*, Philadelphia: Temple University Press, 1987.

Faye, Emmanuel, *Heidegger: L'introduction du nazisme dans la philosophie. Autour des séminaires inédits de 1933–1935*, Paris: Albin Michel, 2005.

Ferrari, Massimo, 'Paul Natorp. 'The Missing Link' in der Davoser Debatte', in: *Cassirer-Heidegger: 70 Jahre Davoser Disputation*, hrsg. von Dominic Kaegi und Enno Rudolph, in: *Cassirer-Forschungen*, Band 9, Hamburg: Meiner Verlag, 2002, 215–233.

Ernst Cassirer. Stationen einer philosophischen Biographie. Von der Marburger Schule zur Kulturtheorie, tr. von Marion Lauschke, in: *Cassirer-Forschungen*, Band 11, Hamburg: Meiner Verlag, 2003.

'Is Cassirer a Neo-Kantian Methodologically Speaking?', in: *Neo-Kantianism in Contemporary Philosophy*, ed. by Rudolf A. Makkreel and Sebastian Luft, Bloomington: Indiana University Press, 2010, 293–314.

Fetz, Reto Luzius, 'Forma formata – forma formans. Zur historischen und systematischen Bedeutung von Cassirers Metaphysik des Symbolischen', in: *Lebendige Form. Zur Metaphysik des Symbolischen in Ernst Cassirers 'Nachgelassenen Manuskripten und Texten'*, hrsg. von Reto Luzius Fetz und Sebastian Ullrich, Hamburg: Meiner Verlag, 2008, 15–33.

Figal, Gunther, and Rudolph, Enno, 'Editorial', in: *Internationale Zeitschrift für Philosophie*. Heft 2, 1992, 163–166.

Flynn, Thomas R., '*Angst* and Care in the Early Heidegger: The Ontic/Ontological Aporia', in: *International Studies in Philosophy*, 12/1, 1980, 61–76.

Freudenthal, Gideon, 'The Hero of Enlightenment', in: *The Symbolic Construction of Reality. The Legacy of Ernst Cassirer*, ed. by Jeffrey Andrew Barash, Chicago: The University Press of Chicago, 2008, 189–213.

Friedman, Michael, *A Parting of the Ways. Cassirer, Heidegger, Carnap*, Chicago and La Salle Open Court, 2000.

Gelven, Michael, *A Commentary on Heidegger's 'Being and Time'*, Dekalb: Northern Illinois University Press, 1989.

Goldman, Avery, *Kant and the Subject of the Critique. On the Regulative Role of the Psychological Idea*, Bloomington: Indiana University Press, 2012.

Gordon, Peter E., 'Myth and Modernity: Cassirer's Critique of Heidegger', in: *New German Critique*, 94: *Secularization and Disenchantment*, 2005, 127–168.

Continental Divide. Heidegger, Cassirer, Davos, Cambridge: Harvard University Press, 2010.

'Heidegger, Neo-Kantianism, and Cassirer', in: *The Bloomsbury Companion to Heidegger*, ed. by Francois Raffoulr and Eric S. Nelson, London: Bloomsbury, 2013, 143–149.

Gorner, Paul, 'Phenomenological Interpretations of Kant in Husserl and Heidegger', in: *A Companion to Kant*, ed. by Graham Bird, Oxford: Blackwell, 2010, 502–512.

Gründer, Karlfried, 'Cassirer und Heidegger in Davos 1929', in: *Über Ernst Cassirers Philosophie der Symbolischen Formen*, hrsg. von Hans-Jürg Braun, Helmut Holzhey, und Ernst Wolfgang Orth, Frankfurt: Suhrkamp, 1988, 290–302.

Guignon, Charles, 'Heidegger's Concept of Freedom, 1927–1930', in: *Interpreting Heidegger: Critical Essays*, ed. by Daniel O. Dahlstrom, Cambridge: Cambridge University Press, 2011, 79–105.

Habermas, Jürgen, 'Der Deutsche Idealismus der Jüdischen Philosophie', in: *Philosophisch-politische Profile*, Frankfurt am Main: Suhrkamp, 1981, 39–64.

Han-Pile, Béatrice, 'Early Heidegger's Appropriation of Kant', in: *A Companion to Heidegger*, ed. by Hubert L. Dreyfus and Mark A. Wrathall, Oxford: Blackwell, 2005, 80–101.

Hartman, Robert S., 'Cassirer's Philosophy of Symbolic Forms', in: *The Philosophy of Ernst Cassirer*, ed. by Paul Arthur Schilpp, La Salle: Open Court, 1949, 289–333.

Hartung, Gerald, *Das Maß des Menschen. Aporien der Philosophischen Anthropologie und ihre Auflösung in der Kulturphilosophie Ernst Cassirers*, Weilerswist: Velbrück Wissenschaft, 2003.

Haugeland, John, 'Truth and Finitude: Heidegger's Transcendental Existentialism', in: *Heidegger, Authenticity, and Modernity. Essays in Honor of Hubert L. Dreyfus, Volume I*, ed. by Mark Wrathall and Jeff Malpas, Cambridge: The MIT Press, 2000.

Hendel, Charles W., 'Foreword' in: *Ernst Cassirer, The Myth of the State*, New Haven: Yale University Press, 1979, v–xii.

Held, Klaus, 'Fundamental Moods and Heidegger's Critique of Contemporary Culture', in: *Reading Heidegger: Commemorations*, ed. by John Sallis, Bloomington: Indiana University Press, 1993, 286–303.

Herrigel, Hermann, 'Denken dieser Zeit: Fakultäten und Nationen treffen sich in Davos', *Frankfurter Zeitung*, April 22, 1929, Hochschulblatt, 4.

Holzhey, Helmuth and Mudroch, Vilem, *Historical Dictionary of Kant and Kantianism*, Lanham: Scarecrow Press, 2005.

Howald, Ernst, 'Betrachtungen zu den Davoser Hochschulkursen', in: *Neue Zürcher Zeitung*, April 10, 1929, Morgenausgabe, 1.

Husserl, Edmund, *Cartesian Meditations: An Introduction to Phenomenology*, tr. by Dorion Cairns, The Hague: Martinus Nijhoff, 1973.

Hutter, Axel, *Geschichtliche Vernunft: die Weiterführung der Kantischen Vernunftkritik in der Spätphilosophie Schellings*, Frankfurt am Main: Suhrkamp, 1996.

    Das Interesse der Vernunft. Kants Ursprüngliche Einsicht und ihre Entfaltung in den Transzendentalphilosophischen Hauptwerken, Hamburg: Meiner Verlag, 2003.

Ijsseling, Samuel, 'Heidegger and the Destruction of Ontology', in: *A Companion to Martin Heidegger's 'Being and Time'*, ed. by Joseph J. Kockelmans, Washington DC: The Center for Advanced Research in Phenomenology and University Press of America, 1986, 127–144.

Jaspers, Karl, 'Letter [to Heidegger] 24, July 21, 1925', in: *Briefwechsel, 1920–1963*, hrsg. von Walter Biemel und Hans Saner, Frankfurt: Vittorio Klostermann, 1990, 51–52.

Jenkins, Iredell, 'The Philosophy of Ernst Cassirer' (book review), in: *The Journal of Philosophy*, 47/2, 1950, 43–55.

Kaegi, Dominic, 'Davos und davor – Zur Auseinandersetzung zwischen Heidegger und Cassirer', in: *Cassirer-Heidegger: 70 Jahre Davoser Disputation*, hrsg. von Dominic Kaegi und Enno Rudolph, in: *Cassirer-Forschungen*, Band 9, Hamburg: Meiner Verlag, 2002, 67–105.

Kaegi, Dominic, und Rudolph, Enno, 'Vorwort', in: *Cassirer-Heidegger: 70 Jahre Davoser Disputation*, hrsg. von Dominic Kaegi und Enno Rudolph, in: *Cassirer-Forschungen*, Band 9, Hamburg: Meiner Verlag, 2002, v–viii.

Kant, Immanuel, 'The Jäsche logic', in: *Lectures on Logic*, ed. by J. Michael Young, in: *The Cambridge Edition of the Works of Immanuel Kant*, Cambridge: Cambridge University Press, 1992, 521–640.

Critique of Practical Reason, in: *Practical Philosophy*, ed. by Mary J. Gregor, in: *The Cambridge Edition of the Works of Immanuel Kant*, Cambridge: Cambridge University Press, 1996, 133–271.

'What Does It Mean to Orient Oneself in Thinking?', in: *Religion and Rational Theology*, ed. by Allen W. Wood and George Di Giovanni, in: *The Cambridge Edition of the Works of Immanuel Kant*, Cambridge: Cambridge University Press, 1996, 1–14.

Critique of Pure Reason, tr. by Paul Guyer and Allen W. Wood, in: *The Cambridge Edition of the Works of Immanuel Kant*, Cambridge: Cambridge University Press, 1998.

Prolegomena to Any Future Metaphysics That Will Be Able to Come Forward as Science, tr. by James W. Ellington, Indianapolis: Hackett, 2001.

Metaphysical Foundations of Natural Science, tr. by Michael Friedman, in: *Cambridge Texts in the History of Philosophy*, Cambridge: Cambridge University Press, 2004.

Reflexionen zur Metaphysik, in: *Notes and Fragments*, ed. by Paul Guyer, in: *The Cambridge Edition of the Works of Immanuel Kant*, Cambridge: Cambridge University Press, 2005.

Anthropology from a Pragmatic Point of View, ed. by Robert Louden, in: *Cambridge Texts in the History of Philosophy*, Cambridge: Cambridge University Press, 2006.

Critique of Judgement, tr. by James Creed Meredith, Oxford/New York: Oxford University Press, 2007.

Kaufmann, Felix, 'Cassirer's Theory of Scientific Knowledge' in: *The Philosophy of Ernst Cassirer*, ed. by Paul Arthur Schilpp, La Salle: Open Court, 1949, 183–213.

Käufer, Stephan, 'Heidegger's Interpretation of Kant', in: *Interpreting Heidegger: Critical Essays*, ed. by Daniel O. Dahlstrom, Cambridge: Cambridge University Press, 2011, 174–196.

Kisiel, Theodore, *The Genesis of Heidegger's 'Being and Time'*, Berkeley: University of California Press, 1995.

Kitcher, Patricia, *Kant's Transcendental Psychology*, Oxford/New York: Oxford University Press, 1990.

Kant's Thinker, Oxford/New York: Oxford University Press, 2011.

Koo, Jo-Jo, 'Heidegger's Underdeveloped Conception of the Undistinguishedness (*Indifferenz*) of Everyday Human Existence', in: *From Conventionalism to Social Authenticity. Heidegger's Anyone and Contemporary Social Theory*, ed. by Hans Bernhard Schmid and Gerhard Thonhauser, Berlin: Springer, 2017, 53–78.

Kreis, Guido, *Cassirer und die Formen des Geistes*, Berlin: Suhrkamp, 2010.

Krois, John Michael, *Cassirer: Symbolic Forms and History*. New Haven: Yale University Press, 1987.

'Problematik, Eigenart und Aktualität der Cassirerschen Philosophie der symbolischen Formen', in: *Über Ernst Cassirers Philosophie der symbolischen*

Formen, hrsg. von Hans-Jürg Braun, Helmut Holzhey, und Ernst Wolfgang Orth, Frankfurt: Suhrkamp, 1988, 15–44.

'Aufklärung und Metaphysik. Zur Philosophie Cassirers und der Davoser Debatte mit Heidegger', in: *Internationale Zeitschrift für Philosophie*. Heft 2, 1992, 273–289.

'Cassirer, Neo-Kantianism and Metaphysics', in: *Revue de métaphysique et de morale*, 97/4, 1992, 437–453.

'Warum fand keine Davoser Debatte zwischen Cassirer und Heidegger statt?', in: *Cassirer-Heidegger: 70 Jahre Davoser Disputation*, hrsg. von Dominic Kaegi und Enno Rudolph, in: *Cassirer-Forschungen*, Band 9, Hamburg: Meiner Verlag, 2002, 234–246.

'Why Did Cassirer and Heidegger Not Debate at Davos?', in: *Symbolic Forms and Cultural Studies. Ernst Cassirer's Theory of Culture*, ed. by Cyrus Hamlin and John Michael Krois, New Haven: Yale University Press, 2004, 244–262.

Lafont, Christina, 'Heidegger and the Synthetic a Priori', in: *Transcendental Heidegger*, ed. by Steven Crowell and Jeff Malpas, Stanford: Stanford University Press, 2007, 104–118.

Langer, Susanne K., *Philosophical Sketches*, Baltimore: Johns Hopkins University Press, 1962.

Levinas, Emmanuel, 'Entretien Avec Roger-Pol', in: *Les Imprévus de l'histoire,* ed. Pierre Hayat, Montpellier: Fata Morgana, 1994, 203–210.

Levinas, Emmanuel, et Poiré François, *Essai et Entretiens*, Paris: Actes Sud, 1996.

Levine, Emily J., *Dreamland of Humanists: Warburg, Cassirer, Panofsky, and the Hamburg School*, Chicago: The University of Chicago Press, 2013.

Lofts, S.G., *Ernst Cassirer: A "Repetition" of Modernity*, Albany: SUNY Press, 2000.

Luft, Sebastian, 'Dominic Kaegi/Enno Rudolph, *Cassirer-Heidegger. 70 Jahre Davoser Disputation'* (book review), in: *Journal Phänomenologie*, 19, 2003, 91–94.

'Cassirer's Philosophy of Symbolic Forms: Between Reason and Relativism; a Critical Appraisal', in: *Idealistic Studies*, 34/1, 2004, 25–47.

'Peter E. Gordon, *Continental Divide: Heidegger, Cassirer, Davos'* (book review), in: *Journal of the History of Philosophy*, 49/4, 2011, 508–509.

The Space of Culture. Towards a Neo-Kantian Philosophy of Culture (Cohen, Natorp, Cassirer), Oxford/New York: Oxford University Press, 2015.

Luft, Sebastian, and Capeillères, Fabien, 'Neo-Kantianism in Germany and France', in: *The History of Continental Philosophy, volume 3: The New Century: Bergsonism, Phenomenology, and Responses to Modern Science*, ed. by Keith-Ansell Pearson and Aland D. Schrift, London/New York: Routledge, 2010, 47–85.

Macann, Christopher, 'Heidegger's Kant Interpretation', in: *Critical Heidegger*, ed. by Christopher Macann, London/New York: Routledge, 1996, 97–120.

Maier-Katkin, Daniel, *Stranger from Abroad: Hannah Arendt, Martin Heidegger, Friendship and, Forgiveness*, New York/London: W.W. Norton & Company, 2010.

Makkreel, Rudolf A., *Imagination and Interpretation in Kant. The Hermeneutical Import of the Critique of Judgment*, Chicago: The University of Chicago Press, 1990.

Makkreel, Rudolf A., and Luft, Sebastian, 'Introduction', in: *Neo-Kantianism in Contemporary Philosophy*, Bloomington: Indiana University Press, 2010, 1–21.

McManus, Denis, 'Anxiety, Choice and Responsibility in Heidegger's Account of Authenticity', in: *Heidegger, Authenticity and the Self. Themes from Division Two of 'Being and Time'*, 163–185.

Merleau-Ponty, Maurice, *Phenomenology of Perception*, tr. by Smith, Colin, London/New York: Routledge, 2002.

Moreiras, Alberto, 'Heidegger, Kant, and the Problem of Transcendence', in: *The Southern Journal of Philosophy*, 34/1, 1986, 81–93.

Mulhall, Stephen, *Heidegger and 'Being and Time'*, London/New York: Routledge, 2005.

Natorp, Paul, *Einleitung in die Psychologie nach kritischer Methode*, Tübingen: Mohr Siebeck, 1888.

'Zur Frage der logischen Methode. Mit Beziehung auf Edmund Husserl's 'Prolegomena' zur reinen Logik', in: *Kant-Studien*, 6, 1901, 270–283.

'Kant und die Marburger Schule', in: *Kant-Studien* 17, 1912, 193–221.

'Husserl's Ideen zu einer Reinen Phänomenologie', in: *Logos*, VII, 1917/1918, 224–246.

Vorlesungen über praktische Philosophie, Erlangen: Verlag der philosophischen Akademie, 1925.

Allgemeine Philosophie nach Kritischer Methode. Erstes Buch *Objekt und Methode der Psychologie* (1912), ed. by Sebastian Luft, Darmstadt: Wissenschaftliche Buchgesellschaft, 2013.

Neiman, Susan, *The Unity of Reason. Rereading Kant*, Oxford/New York: Oxford University Press, 1994.

Nuzzo, Angelica, *Kant and the Unity of Reason*, in: *History of Philosophy Series*, West Lafayette: Purdue University Press, 2005.

Orth, Ernst Wolfgang, 'Zugänge zu Ernst Cassirer. Eine Einleitung', in: *Über Ernst Cassirers Philosophie der Symbolischen Formen*, hrsg. von Hans-Jürg Braun, Helmut Holzhey, und Ernst Wolfgang Orth, Frankfurt: Suhrkamp, 1988, 7–11.

Von der Erkenntnistheorie zur Kulturphilosophie. Studien zu Ernst Cassirers Philosophie der symbolischen Formen, Würzburg: Königshausen & Neumann, 2004.

Paetzold, Heinz, *Die Realität der Symbolischen Formen. Die Kulturphilosophie Ernst Cassirers im Kontext*, Darmstadt: Wissenschaftliche Buchgesellschaft, 1994.

'Die symbolische Ordnung der Kultur. Ernst Cassirers Beitrag zu einer Theorie der Kulturentwicklung', in: *Ernst Cassirers Werk und Wirkung*, hrsg. von Dorothea Frede und Reinold Schmücker, Darmstadt: Wissenschaftliche Buchgesellschaft, 1997, 163–184.

Peone, Dustin, 'Ernst Cassirer's Essential Critique of Heidegger and *Verfallenheit*', in: *Idealistic Studies*, 42/2–3, 2013, 119–130.

Pippin, Robert B., 'Necessary Conditions for the Possibility of What Isn't. Heidegger on Failed Meaning', in: *Transcendental Heidegger*, ed. by Steven Crowell and Jeff Malpas, Stanford: Stanford University Press, 2007, 199–214.

Plümacher, Martina, 'Die Erforschung des Geistes – Cassirers Auseinandersetzung mit der zeitgenössischen Psychologie', in: *Kultur und Symbol. Ein Handbuch zur Philosophie Ernst Cassierers*, hrsg. von Hans Jörg Sandkühler und Detlev Pätzold, Stuttgart: Verlag J.B. Metzler, 2003, 85–110.

Wahrnehmung, Repräsentation und Wissen. Edmund Husserls und Ernst Cassirers Analysen zur Struktur des Bewusstseins, Berlin: Parerga Verlag, 2004.

Poiré, François, *Emmanuel Levinas: Qui êtes-vous?* Lyon: La Manufacture, 1987.

Pos, Hendrik J., 'Recollections of Ernst Cassirer', in: *The Philosophy of Ernst Cassirer*, ed. by Paul Arthur Schilpp, La Salle: Open Court, 1949, 63–72.

Recki, Birgit, 'Kultur ohne Moral? Warum Cassirer trotz der Einsicht in den Primat der praktischen Vernunft keine Ethik schreiben konnte', in: *Ernst Cassirers Werk und Wirkung*, hrsg. von Dorothea Frede und Reinold Schmücker, Darmstadt: Wissenschaftliche Buchgesellschaft, 1997, 58–78.

Kultur als Praxis. Eine Einführung in Ernst Cassirers Philosophie der Symbolischen Formen, in: *Deutsche Zeitschrift für Philosophie*, Sonderband 6, Berlin: Akademie Verlag, 2004.

Cassirer, in: *Grundwissen Philosophie*, Stuttgart: Reclam, 2013.

Rotolo, Catia, *Der Symbolbegriff im Denken Ernst Cassirer*, tr. by Leonie Schröder, in: *Philosophie und Geschichte der Wissenschaften*, Band 76, Frankfurt am Main: Peter Lang Gmbh, 2013.

Roubach, Michael, 'The Limits of Order. Cassirer and Heidegger on Finitude and Infinity', in: *The Symbolic Construction of Reality: The Legacy of Ernst Cassirer*, ed. by Jeffrey Andrew Barash, Chicago: The University of Chicago Press, 2008, 104–113.

Rudolph, Enno, *Ernst Cassirer im Kontext. Kulturphilosphie zwischen Metaphysik und Historismus*. Tübingen: Mohr Siebeck, 2003.

Schalow, Frank, *The Renewal of the Heidegger Kant Dialogue: Action, Thought and, Responsibility*, Albany: SUNY Press, 1992.

'Thinking at Cross Purposes with Kant: Reason, Finitude and Truth in the Cassirer-Heidegger Debate', in: *Kant-Studien*, 87/2, 1996, 198–217.

Schwemmer, Oswald, *Ernst Cassirer: Ein Philosoph der Europäischen Moderne*, Berlin: Akademie Verlag, 1997.

Sebastian Luft, Subjectivity and Lifeworld in Transcendental Phenomenology, Evanston: Northwestern University Press, 2011.

Serck-Hanssen, Camilla, 'Towards Fundamental Ontology: Heidegger's Phenomenological Reading of Kant', in: *Continental Philosophy Review*, 48, 2015, 217–235.

Sheehan, Thomas, 'Facticity and *Ereignis*', in: *Interpreting Heidegger: Critical Essays*, ed. by Daniel O. Dahlstrom, Cambridge: Cambridge University Press, 2011, 42–68.

Skidelsky, Edward, *Ernst Cassirer: The Last Philosopher of Culture*, Princeton/Oxford: Princeton University Press, 2008.

Strauss, Leo, 'Kurt Riezler (1882–1955)', in: *What Is Political Philosophy? And Other Studies*, Chicago: The University of Chicago Press, 1959, 233–260.

Sturma, Dieter, *Kant über Selbstbewußtsein*, New York: Georg Olms Verlag, 1985.

Swabey, William Curtis, 'Cassirer and Metaphysics', in: *The Philosophy of Ernst Cassirer*, ed. by Paul Arthur Schilpp, La Salle: Open Court, 1949, 121–148.

Tate, Adam R., 'On Heidegger's Root and Branch Reformulation of Transcendental Psychology', in *The Journal of the British Society for Phenomenology*, 46/1, 2015, 61–78.

Trawny, Peter, *Heidegger und der Mythos der jüdischen Welverschwörung*, Frankfurt: Vittorio Klostermann, 2014.

Truwant, Simon, 'Kant's Transcendental Reflection: An Indispensable Element of Philosophy of Culture', in: *Critical Studies in German Idealism*, vol. 15: *The*

Marriage between Aesthetics and Ethics:, ed. by Stéphane Symons, Brill Academic Publishing, 2015, 169–184.

'Political Myth and the Problem of Orientation: Reading Cassirer in Times of Cultural Crisis', in: *Interpreting Cassirer: Critical Essays*, Cambridge: Cambridge University Press, 2020, 130–148.

Ulrich, Sebastian, 'Der Status der 'Philosophischen Erkenntnis' in Ernst Cassirers 'Metaphysik des Symbolischen', in: Birgit Recki (hrsg.), *Philosophie der Kultur – Kultur des Philosophierens: Ernst Cassirer im 20. und 21. Jahrhundert*, Hamburg: Meiner Verlag, 2012, 297–319.

Verene, Donald Phillip, 'Kant, Hegel, and Cassirer: The Origins of the Philosophy of Symbolic Forms', in: *Journal of the History of Ideas*, 30/1, 1969, 33–46.

'Cassirer's Metaphysics', in: *The Symbolic Construction of Reality: The Legacy of Ernst Cassirer*, ed. by Jeffrey Andrew Barash, Chicago: The University of Chicago Press, 2008, 93–103.

The Origins of the Philosophy of Symbolic Forms. Kant, Hegel, and Cassirer, Evanston: Northwestern University Press, 2011.

Van Eekert, Geert, ''Synthesis Speciosa' en de Taak van de Filosofie. Cassirer en Heidegger voor het Tribunaal van de *Kritik der Reinen Vernunft'*, in: *Gehelen en Fragmenten: De Vele Gezichten van de Filosofie*, red. door Bart Raymaekers, Leuven: Universitaire Pers, 1993, 230–234.

'Freiheit und Endlichkeit: Cassirer, Heidegger und Kant', in: *Life, Subjectivity & Art. Essays in Honor of Rudolf Bernet*, ed. by Ulrich Melle and Roland Breeur, in: *Phaenomenologica* 201, Berlin: Springer, 2011, 195–216.

Von Wolzogen, Christoph, *Die autonome Relation. Zum Problem der Beziehung im Spätwerk Paul Natorps. Ein Beitrag zur Geschichte der Theorien der Relation*, Würzburg: Königshausen und Neumann, 1984.

Ward, Katherine 'Breaking Down Experience – Heidegger's Methodological Use of Breakdown in *Being and Time'*, in: *European Journal of Philosophy* (forthcoming).

Weatherston, Martin, *Heidegger's Interpretation of Kant*, London: Palgrave Macmillan, 2002.

Withy, Katherine, 'The Methodological Role of Anxiety in Being and Time', in: *Journal of the British Society for Phenomenology*, 43/2, 2012, 195–211.

Heidegger on Being Uncanny, Cambridge: Harvard University Press, 2015.

Zaborowksi, Holger, 'Heidegger's Hermeneutics: Towards a New Practice of Understanding', in: *Interpreting Heidegger: Critical Essays*, ed. by Daniel O. Dahlstrom, Cambridge: Cambridge University Press, 2011, 15–41.

Zimmerman, Michael E., *Eclipse of the Self. The Development of Heidegger's Concept of Authenticity*, Athens: Ohio University Press, 1981.

Index

Aenesidem-Schulze, Heinrich, 184
ambiguity, 100, 118, 130, 145, 161, 163–164,
    209, 226, 233, 235–236
analytic
    existential / of Dasein, 12–13, 27, 32, 34, 36,
        38, 43, 70, 131, 139, 144, 147–149, 152,
        159, 167–168, 171, 173, 197–198, 200,
        205, 210, 212–217, 235, 238
    transcendental, 17, 20, 23–24, 41–42,
        58–60, 63–64, 68–70, 73, 75, 78–79, 86,
        88, 118, 158, 209
animal, 13, 30–31, 122–124, 130, 169–170,
    172, 226
    animal symbolicum, 12, 124, 158, 167–168,
        170, 179, 191, 194, 227, 246
antinomies, 188, 193, 230, 232
anxiety, 9, 32–34, 43, 83, 144–146, 148–149,
    160, 164–168, 170, 173–174, 239–240,
    242–243
Aristotle, 10, 68, 71, 83, 179–181, 196,
    198–200, 206–207, 225
attitude, 4, 10, 32, 43, 79, 125, 133, 138, 146,
    160, 167, 234–235, 238, 241–243
attunement, 33, 39, 140–143, 145, 147–148,
    150, 152, 159, 161, 163–165, 168, 170,
    174–175, *See also* mood
authenticity, 13, 33, 35, 131, 146, 148, 160,
    233–236, 238, 240–243, *See also* ownedness
autonomy, 24–25, 229–230

Beck, Jacob Sigismund, 184
being, 9, 13, 28, 31, 35, 64–69, 72–74, 79, 86,
    88–89, 93, 132, 134, 136–137, 139, 142,
    147–152, 162, 167, 173–174, 201–205,
    212
    a being, 59, 65, 73, 102, 135, 138, 143, 147,
        149–150, 152, 165–166, 175, 201–202,
        213, 243
    being-in, 13, 31, 37, 74, 77, 131, 135–136,
        139, 141, 143–150, 152, 159–162,
        164–167, 171, 173, 197, 205–206, 210,
        214–218, 233–237, 240–242

forgetfulness of being (*Seinsvergessenheit*),
    132, 196–198, 201, 210, 214–215
    meaning of, 14, 34, 70–71, 131–132, 136,
        153, 196–199, 203–206, 210–217, 239,
        243, 247
    understanding of, 13, 27–28, 38, 65, 70,
        131–132, 136–137, 141–143, 148–149,
        164, 197–198, 204–207, 210, 212–218,
        235, 247
Blochmann, Elisabeth, 4
Blumenberg, Hans, 3, 7, 183
Bollnow, Otto Friedrich, 1, 15, 249
Bourdieu, Pierre, 7
breakdown, 123, 137, 146–147, 170
Brunschvicq, Leon, 2

care, 43, 78, 132, 139, 144, 147–150, 162, 167,
    171, 197, 200, 205–206, 210, 214–215,
    217–218, 233, 235–236, 242
Carnap, Rudolf, 2, 6–7, 212
categories, 48–50, 54, 57, 60, 75, 77, 80–81,
    83, 90–92, 105–106, 113, 116, 118, 151,
    181
causality, 49, 55–56, 156–157, 168, 186–187
Cavaillès, Jean, 2
circumspection, 134, 137, 139, 159, 237
Cohen, Hermann, 5, 9–10, 20–22, 40, 47, 54,
    106, 114, 185
conscience, 148, 165–166, 240, 243
consciousness, 12–14, 23, 33, 37–38, 41,
    48–49, 52–53, 66, 74, 89, 91, 99, 105,
    107, 111–117, 119–124, 127–128,
    130–131, 153–155, 157–158, 167–171,
    173, 186, 190, 223–224, 226–232, 244,
    246–247
    functions of, 13, 120, 122, 154–155, 157,
        167, 223–224, 230, 247
    symbolic, 14, 112, 122, 124, 153, 167,
        170–171, 173, 223, 226–232, 246–247
Copernican revolution, 9, 34, 37, 54, 66, 71,
    87, 89, 113, 115, 119, 180, 223, 230
crisis, 1, 194, 231

critical idealism, 223, 229
culture, 2–3, 7–9, 11–14, 17, 20, 25, 32–34, 37,
    39, 44, 48, 53–54, 56, 60–61, 86–88, 97,
    104, 106, 111–112, 115, 120–124,
    126–127, 129–130, 144, 153, 158, 169,
    171–173, 175, 179, 186, 188–195,
    220–224, 226, 228–232, 239, 244, 246–248
  development of, 226, 231
  unity of, 60, 189
curiosity, 161–164, 236

death, 3, 26, 30, 32, 34, 43, 126, 145, 148,
    164–166, 173–174, 204, 241, 243
deduction
  objective, 90–92, 118
  subjective, 90, 92, 118
  transcendental, 69, 75–78, 80, 82, 90–92, 98,
      151
Descartes, René, 198–199, 225
disclosedness, 140–141, 163, 235, 240
discourse, 140, 143, 148, 159–161, 163,
    165–166, 193, 196, 200, 240, 243
disownedness, 160–161, 165, 199, 233–237,
    239–241, 244, See also inauthenticity
diversity, 13, 56, 87, 128, 184, 189–191, 193
dogmatism, 61, 222, 230–231

Enlightenment, 2, 14, 43, 121, 183, 193, 223
entanglement, 233–234, 236, 238
epistemology, 12, 19, 47, 86, 88–90, 92, 139,
    175, See also theory of knowledge
Erdmann, Benno, 21
ethics, 9, 24, 26, 29, 42, 54, 193, 232, 238, See
    also morality
everdayness (everyday)
  everyday understanding, 13, 132, 134,
      136–138, 146, 149, 160–161, 163, 196,
      206, 213, 217–218, 233–235, 237, 240
existentialism, 2
existentials, 142, 145, 147, 150, 160–161, 164,
    175
experience, 23, 28, 30, 34, 41–42, 49, 52–53,
    59–61, 65, 68, 75–76, 86, 90, 97, 116,
    119, 122–125, 136, 146, 167, 180, 187,
    191, 198, 200, 204, 208, 227, 240, 242

facticity, 123, 142, 147, 151, 233
faculty, 12, 22–23, 28, 40–41, 49, 51–52,
    55–56, 58–60, 71, 73, 76–77, 80–82, 85,
    88, 93–98, 100–103, 105, 113–114, 121,
    128, 180, 190
fallenness (falling prey), 83, 146, 234
Fichte, Johann Gottlieb, 184
finitude, 9, 16, 26–31, 33–34, 40–41, 102,
    174–175, 242, 244

fore-structure, 84, 151–152, 204–206, 210,
    213, 216–218, 248, See also hermeneutic
    situation
freedom (free), 9, 24, 28, 30–33, 41–42, 51, 55,
    96, 130, 160, 174, 231, 238, 240, 243
Friedman, Michael, 5–7, 47, 69
function, 13, 21, 101, 127, 134, 137, 179, 181,
    186–190, 195, 224, 229, 247
  functional unity, 13, 130, 171, 179, 183,
      186, 189, 191, 195, 232
  of objectification, 60–61
  of language, 55
  of symbolic formation, 155, 157, 171, 223,
      226, 229
  of the power of imagination, 24, 76
  of the soul, 77, 81, 94, 98, 103
  of the understanding, 81, 95, 98

Goethe, Johann Wolfgang von, 10, 111, 185, 223
Goldstein, Kurt, 10, 52
Gordon, Peter E., 2, 4, 6–7, 9, 18, 25, 47, 181,
    246
ground, 16–17, 23, 32, 67, 71, 77, 80, 82–84,
    88, 92–93, 101, 106–107, 209–210

Habermas, Jürgen, 3, 7
harmony, 50, 61, 192–193, 230, 232
Hegel, Georg Wilhelm Friedrich, 47, 106, 184
hermeneutics, 11, 14, 53, 63, 152, 201,
    203–205, 207, 213, 217–218
  hermeneutic circle, 240, 248
  hermeneutic situation, 13–14, 149
hierarchy, 14, 66, 103, 173, 221, 223, 229, 232,
    235, 239
  hierarchical account, 222–223, 229–230, 232
history, 1, 7, 54, 157, 182–184, 187, 194, 201,
    229
  of being, 2, 10, 197
  of metaphysics, 196, 210
  of ontology, 17, 40, 197–201, 207, 217
  of philosophy, 7, 78, 83, 184, 198–199, 203,
      205, 208
  of the problem of knowledge, 89
  of thought, 2, 13, 182–183, 186
horizon, 30–31, 62, 64, 68, 74–77, 89, 93–95,
    150, 159, 171, 199, 204, 210, 216, 235
human condition, 8, 11–13, 19, 26, 30, 32–33,
    35–36, 38, 40, 44, 107, 130–131, 147,
    153, 167–168, 171–175, 196, 199, 206,
    211, 213–215, 217–218, 220, 244–247
human sciences, 11, 220
Humboldt, Alexander von, 223
Husserl, Edmund, 10, 21, 53, 62–63, 67, 70,
    72, 74, 106, 127, 136, 147–148, 165,
    202–203, 238, 248

idle talk, 26, 161–163, 173, 233, 236, 241
imagination, 22–25, 28, 38, 40–41, 48–53, 55,
     75–77, 81–84, 93–95, 97–98, 103, 169,
     209
  symbolic, 23, 25–26, 31, 50, 61, 97, 105,
     113, 122–124, 127, 169, 171, 173, 220
  transcendental, 9, 12, 16, 19, 22–25, 28, 35,
     38, 41–42, 49, 52, 69, 72, 75, 77, 80–83,
     85, 90, 93–99, 101, 103, 105, 151, 168,
     175, 245
inauthenticity, 43, 160, 233–237, 242, *See also*
     disownedness
indifference, 226, 235
infinity, 9, 26–32, 41, 102, 129, 168, 173
intentionality, 69, 74, 106
interpretation, 10, 12–13, 16, 19, 29, 37–38,
     40, 42, 50, 62–64, 66, 71, 81–87, 89–90,
     93, 95, 97–98, 105, 131, 151–152,
     159, 161, 185, 196, 198, 200–201,
     203–204, 207–218, 221, 229, 232–233,
     237, 239
intuition, 23, 28, 49–53, 59, 64–66, 69, 75–77,
     80, 82, 93–99, 101–106, 113–114, 128,
     180, 214

Jacobi, Friedrich Heinrich, 184

Kant, Immanuel, 3, 7–13, 15–19, 21–29, 32,
     34–42, 44–45, 47–52, 54–60, 62–102,
     104–107, 111–115, 117–119, 131, 148,
     150, 153–154, 157–159, 164, 168, 171,
     175, 180, 182, 184–185, 196–200,
     206–211, 214–215, 217–218, 223, 226,
     228, 230, 232, 244–245, 259
knowledge, 6, 12, 16, 19–23, 25, 27, 29, 31,
     51, 58–61, 66, 68–71, 73–77, 79, 81–82,
     87–89, 92, 94, 97, 102–103, 105–107,
     114, 116–117, 120, 124, 127, 143, 149,
     163, 171, 180, 182–184, 186, 189–191,
     194, 199, 216, 224, 226, 229, 231
Krois, John Michael, 5–6, 47, 52–53, 61, 87,
     123, 125, 130, 187, 193, 230–231

language, 11–12, 23, 26, 30–31, 35, 43, 51, 54,
     92, 100, 106, 111–113, 116–117,
     120–121, 124–125, 127, 129–130, 143,
     155–156, 158, 171–172, 175, 185,
     187–188, 190, 192, 203, 220–221,
     223–228, 230, 235, 237
  natural, 26, 143, 156, 225, 227
law, 24, 28–29, 56, 112, 157, 183, 193, 221, 224
  moral, 25, 28–29, 41
Leibniz, Gottfried Wilhelm, 2, 10, 225
Levinas, Emmanuel, 1–3, 7, 212
limitation, 71, 140, 165, 170–171, 174–175,
     244

logic, 99, 106, 179–180, 186, 216
  traditional, 99, 179–180
  transcendental, 92, 98, 105, 181, 228

Maimon, Salomon, 184
Marcuse, Herbert, 2
meaning, 13, 20, 23, 29, 39, 52–53, 55–56, 60,
     74, 87, 91, 99–100, 104–105, 117, 123,
     127, 131, 135–140, 142–146, 149–152,
     155–157, 160–168, 170–171, 187,
     189–190, 193, 203, 208, 225, 227–228,
     235–237, 239–240, 243, 248
  symbolic, 7, 57, 123, 169, 171
metaphysics, 16–17, 19–20, 23–24, 27, 32–34,
     36, 42, 58, 62–63, 67–69, 71, 75, 79–80,
     82–86, 92–93, 96, 99, 102, 106, 124,
     126–128, 130, 180, 189, 197–198, 204,
     206–207, 209–211, 215, 217, 232
  of symbolic forms, 17, 124–128, 130
method
  critical, 58, 63, 71, 73, 96, 98, 118
  reconstructive, 119, 128
  transcendental, 21, 87, 114, 117–118, 171,
     184, 248
mood, 33, 141–148, 150, 161, 163–166, 170,
     174, 204, 214, 242–244, *See also*
     attunement
morality, 60, 117, *See also* ethics
myth, 11, 30–31, 37–38, 43, 54, 60–61, 92,
     106, 113, 121, 124–125, 127, 129, 155,
     158, 172, 185, 187–188, 190, 194, 221,
     224, 226–228
  mythical thinking, 36–38, 43, 120, 129, 172,
     221, 227
  political, 221, 230

Natorp, Paul, 10, 20–22, 37, 47–48, 54,
     113–120, 222
Nazism, 1, 6, 18, 193, 195
Neo-Kantianism, 2, 5–6, 9, 15, 17–22, 37–38,
     40, 47, 53, 85–86, 88, 113–114, 125,
     184–186, 200, 222, 248
Nietzsche, Friedrich, 10
norm, 225, 238–239
  normative, 233, 238

objectivity, 9, 11–12, 22, 25, 29–31, 35, 41–42,
     57–61, 66–67, 69, 73–75, 89–90, 92–93,
     107, 113, 115–118, 120, 122, 126, 128,
     150, 170–171, 182, 186, 188, 191,
     222–223, 226–227
ontology (ontological), 8–12, 14, 16–17,
     19–20, 28, 38, 42, 63–64, 66–73, 78, 82,
     85–86, 88–90, 92, 126, 140, 149–150,
     175, 198–201, 203, 205, 207, 210–212,
     215, 217–218, 233, 239, 243, 245

general, 11, 20, 42, 62, 67, 69–70, 73,
79–80, 82, 86, 88
ontological difference, 64, 66, 147, 202
vs. ontic, 28, 66–68, 74, 86, 88–90, 92, 101,
134, 139, 143, 147, 149–150, 159, 161,
163, 170, 213, 218, 237, 243
orientation, 13, 38, 56, 82, 112, 153–155,
158–160, 164, 167, 172–173, 175, 183,
194–195, 198, 220, 231–232, 236,
238–241, 245, 247–248
owneness, 160, 167, 199, 233–236, 239–241,
243, *See also* authenticity

pathology, 122–123
perspective, 30, 32, 139, 221–224, 229
critical, 96, 104, 114–115, 172, 226, 230
cultural worldview, 168, 232
ontological, 73, 139, 241
transcendental, 185, 223–224, 226, 230
phenomenology (phenomenological), 147,
149, 196, 200–203, 208, 210
phenomenological analysis, 17, 73, 77, 80,
120, 199–200, 203, 210
phenomenological method, 11, 63, 69–70,
72, 97–98, 101, 131, 201, 203, 207, 209
phenomenological reading, 39, 63, 69, 73,
208–209
phenomenological reduction, 201–203
phenomenological destruction, 78, 197–201,
203–204, 207
phenomenon, 26, 30–31, 33–34, 38, 43, 53,
64–65, 80, 82, 99, 123, 143–144, 149,
161, 163, 184, 190, 193, 202–203, 214,
216, 233–234, 236
basis phenomena, 126
philosophy
conception of, 5, 63, 193, 195–196, 201,
210–212, 216–217, 219
critical, 40, 50, 71, 98, 184, 191, 194–195,
207, 229, 231, 245
of culture, 11–12, 17, 25, 33–34, 39, 87,
122, 229, 232, 246
Lebensphilosophie, 2, 17, 125
task of, 8, 10–11, 13–14, 19, 32–33, 35–36,
38, 43–44, 175, 191–192, 205, 210, 218,
232, 244–246
transcendental, 8, 10–11, 15, 19, 47–48, 54,
56, 63–64, 66, 68–69, 72–73, 78–79,
85–86, 88, 91–92, 95, 99, 101, 104,
106–107, 117–119, 130–131, 175, 180,
184–185, 192, 207, 214, 218, 222
politics, 6, 43, 54, 111–112, 130, 147, 157,
187, 193, 220
Pos, Hendrik, 3, 5, 29, 222
possibility, 11, 13, 16–17, 21, 23–24, 28–29,
32, 34, 37, 42–43, 49–50, 53–54, 60,

62–63, 65, 67–68, 70–79, 81–84, 86,
88–91, 114, 117–118, 120, 127, 129,
131–132, 134, 137–138, 140, 142,
144–151, 154, 159, 161–163, 165–166,
169–171, 173, 184, 190, 199–200, 204,
211, 213–214, 217–218, 223–224, 228,
232–233, 235–237, 240–244, 248
potentiality, 120, 145, 147, 166, 169, 171,
173–174, 240–242
progress, 2, 13, 29, 71, 183, 226, 229
projection, 76, 81, 98, 140, 143, 161, 171, 175,
236–237, 241–242
Przywara, Erich, 7
psychology, 12, 42, 68, 98–100, 105, 117,
119–120, 126, 179–180, 185
critical, 114, 119
psychologism, 23, 227
rational, 118

question
of being (*Seinsfrage*), 1, 14, 36, 62, 78, 84,
196–201, 205, 207, 210, 217–218, 239,
246–247

rationalism, 35, 80, 82, 84, 200
rationality (rational), 57, 98, 120, 150, 173,
180–181, 186, 190, 198
reason, 2, 16, 20, 25, 27, 38, 40–41, 47, 49, 55,
67–68, 70–71, 83, 96, 102, 121, 124, 154,
191, 223, 229–232
critique of, 11, 40, 54, 88, 96, 104, 111, 184
practical, 24, 26, 29, 153
pure, 59, 69–71, 83–85, 88, 154, 214
theoretical, 41, 59, 87, 154
receptivity, 12, 23–24, 26, 28, 41, 58, 93, 95,
97–98, 100–102, 114, 211, 214
reflective judgment, 50, 157
Reinhold, Karl Leonhard, 184
relation, 24, 41, 52, 55–56, 58, 88–89, 106,
114–118, 135, 146, 157, 172, 179–183,
186–187, 202, 214, 224–225, 240, 242
relativism, 35, 61, 220, 222–224, 229–232
religion, 6, 18, 20, 37, 43, 54–56, 87, 111, 113,
117, 121, 123–124, 129–130, 154, 157,
167–168, 171, 187, 190, 192, 194, 220,
222, 224–225, 230
resoluteness, 236, 238, 240, 243–244
Rickert, Heinrich, 21
Riehl, Alois, 21
Ritter, Joachim, 7, 15, 249
root, 22–23, 25, 77, 81–83, 94, 96–98, 106

schema, 11, 36, 50, 58, 96, 180, 182
schematism, 22, 24–25, 28, 41–42, 51–53,
69, 77, 93, 95–96, 100–101, 106–107,
127, 199

Schelling, Friedrich Wilhelm Joseph, 184, 223
Schopenhauer, Arthur, 184
science, 20, 30, 35, 54, 65, 67, 71, 79, 85, 88, 92,
    111, 113, 117, 120–121, 123, 125, 127,
    129–130, 156, 167, 182, 184–185, 187–189,
    191, 194, 203, 221–224, 226, 228–230
  cultural sciences, 20, 112, 157, 188
  natural sciences, 20, 55, 60, 67, 79, 85, 87,
    115, 155, 185, 187–188, 220, 225
self, 14, 80, 83, 166, 168, 173, 191, 229, 231,
    235–236, 243, 245
  self-awareness, 226
  self-conscious, 227
  self-knowledge, 191, 231
  self-liberation, 14, 175, 230–231
  self-realization, 231, 244
  self-understanding, 14, 86, 144–145, 147,
    163, 166, 168, 172, 184, 191, 200–201,
    213, 226, 229, 231, 236, 241, 243–244
sensibility, 22–23, 28–29, 40–41, 49, 51, 56,
    58–59, 76–77, 81, 83, 93–97, 99–100,
    102–104, 106, 113–114, 155
space, 26, 30–31, 39, 49, 55, 59, 65, 94, 96,
    104, 113, 116, 118, 121, 154–155,
    157–158, 173, 186–187, 223–225
spirit, 21–22, 29, 34, 37, 39, 41, 54, 56–57, 88,
    100, 107, 112–114, 117, 120–121, 123,
    125–126, 128–129, 184–185, 188, 190,
    221–222, 226–227, 231, 248
spontaneity, 23–24, 26, 31, 77, 93, 95–98,
    100–101, 104, 107, 211, 214
Strauss, Leo, 3, 5, 7, 260
subjectivity, 12–13, 17, 19–20, 22, 31, 42, 60,
    70, 73, 75, 77–78, 80–83, 90–91, 112,
    115–122, 126, 128, 130, 151, 171, 182,
    190–191, 197, 226
substance, 34, 115, 118, 121, 179–181,
    189–190, 225
symbol, 11, 49, 52, 54–56, 155, 186
  modality of, 55, 187, 191
symbolic form, 2–3, 9, 11–12, 20, 23, 25, 30–31,
    34–35, 38–40, 43, 47–48, 50, 53–57, 60,
    86–87, 89, 105–106, 111–112, 116,
    120–122, 124–130, 153–157, 167, 172,
    185, 187–195, 220–232, 245–246, 248
symbolic pregnancy, 52–53, 56–57, 97, 106,
    122, 127, 223
synthesis, 23, 41, 51, 75, 77, 80, 83, 96,
    103–104, 121, 155, 209

task, 8, 11, 13–14, 19, 32–36, 43, 59, 81, 84,
    91, 106, 127, 162, 175, 182, 186, 192,
    202, 207, 210, 213, 215, 231, 243–246
technology, 43, 54, 111–112, 187, 193, 220, 224
temporality, 32, 39, 42–43, 77–78, 80, 131,
    148, 175, 199–200

the they (das Man), 13, 160–161, 163–168,
    170, 175, 233–234, 236, 238, 240–243
theory of knowledge, 19, 85–87, See also
    epistemology
therapy, 14, 19, 33, 44
thing in itself, 57–60, 64, 66, 89, 102, 104, 170,
    180, 229
thrownness, 142, 165–166, 170, 174, 237,
    240
Tillich, Paul, 7
tradition, 78, 82, 129, 198, 226
transcendence, 27, 29, 31, 33, 69, 73–75,
    77–78, 80–83, 98, 150
transcendental
  knowledge, 65, 75, 90, 92, 95, 206, 214,
    217
  deduction, 69, 75–78, 80, 82, 90–92, 98,
    151
  psychology, 117–119
truth, 9, 29, 31, 37, 40, 54, 61–62, 66, 87–89,
    105, 127, 180–181, 183, 185, 188, 191,
    198, 221, 229, 237

uncanny, 144, 164, 166, 173, 242
understanding, 22–23, 27–28, 39–41, 48–51,
    55–56, 58–60, 66, 68–69, 73, 75, 77, 81,
    90–91, 93–94, 96–99, 101–102, 104–105,
    113–114, 118, 161, 180, 186, 202, 213,
    236
unity, 13, 16, 23–25, 35, 49, 54–57, 59–61,
    75–77, 80–81, 87, 94–96, 99, 112–114,
    116, 118–121, 123, 128, 130–131, 143,
    146–148, 150, 154–156, 158, 182–183,
    189–190, 192, 194–195, 211, 224, 229,
    247

validity, 22, 27, 31, 35, 75, 80–81, 91–92, 96,
    107, 118, 169, 185, 188, 192, 221–222,
    228
viewpoint, 31, 35, 40, 42, 57–61, 95, 104, 134,
    188, 191–194, 222, 230, 239, 246,
    See also perspective
violence, 62, 207, 211–212, 217–218

Windelband, Wilhelm, 21
work, 130, 134–135, 138, 152, 167
world, 1, 8, 13, 23–24, 30–31, 37, 42, 48, 54,
    56–57, 61, 74, 77, 80, 107, 122–124,
    127–128, 131, 133, 135–137, 139–148,
    150, 152, 154, 156–162, 164–175,
    180–181, 186, 188–192, 194–195,
    197–198, 204–206, 210, 213–218,
    220–221, 224, 226–228, 230, 233–237,
    239–243, 248
worldview, 37, 48, 55, 129, 155–157, 172, 182,
    184, 187, 193, 221, 226, 228

For EU product safety concerns, contact us at Calle de José Abascal, 56–1°,
28003 Madrid, Spain or eugpsr@cambridge.org.

www.ingramcontent.com/pod-product-compliance
Ingram Content Group UK Ltd.
Pitfield, Milton Keynes, MK11 3LW, UK
UKHW020334140625
459647UK00018B/2135